ECONOMETRIC ANALYSIS OF MODEL SELECTION AND MODEL TESTING

Econometric Analysis of Model Selection and Model Testing

M. ISHAQ BHATTI
La Trobe University, Melbourne, Australia

HATEM AL-SHANFARI
Sultan Qaboos University, Sultanate of Oman

and

M. ZAKIR HOSSAIN
Sultan Qaboos University, Sultanate of Oman

Routledge
Taylor & Francis Group
LONDON AND NEW YORK

First published 2006 by Ashgate Publishing

Published 2016 by Routledge
2 Park Square, Milton Park, Abingdon, Oxon OX14 4RN
711 Third Avenue, New York, NY 10017, USA

Routledge is an imprint of the Taylor & Francis Group, an informa business

British Library Cataloguing in Publication Data
Bhatti, M. Ishaq
Econometric analysis of model selection and model testing
1.Econometric models
I.Title II.Al-Shanfari, Hatem III.Hossain, M. Zakir
330'.015195

Library of Congress Control Number: 2005933219

ISBN-10: 0-7546-3715-8
ISBN-13: 978-0-7546-3715-8

Transfered to Digital Printing in 2010

ISBN 9780754637158 (hbk)

Contents

List of Figures and Tables

List of Figures

List of Tables

Preface

Developments in econometrics during its early stages were mainly concerned with the problems of estimation and inference from a sample of economic data. The main objective of such estimation and inference was to produce consistent and efficient estimates of the parameters and to construct a good confidence interval. During recent years the attention of the subject has been diverted to the problems of diagnostic checking, specification testing, semiparametric estimation and model selection (see for example, Maddala (1988)). In recent years, theoreticians and practitioners have been heavily involved in discussing whether to use model testing and/or model selection procedures in deciding the models that best fit a particular data set. This book attempts to bring together both viewpoints and applies these to various regression models, including the arbitrage pricing theory (APT) models. In Chapters 2 and 3, our discussion will be focused on the testing issue, whereas the topic of 'model selection' and its application will be explored in the proceeding chapters.

Acknowledgements

Whatever the merits of this book may be, they are in large measure due to our teachers at various institutions around the globe from whom we learnt a great deal about model selection, model testing and its application in linear regression models. We also appreciate the patience and understanding of our families who have experienced many lonesome moments while we have laboured to get the text into print.

Finally, we would like to express our appreciation to Pat for typesetting the manuscript in a camera-ready format. Any errors that exist are solely ours; we trust there will be few.

Chapter 1

Introduction

1.1 Preamble

The non-experimental nature of econometrics is a main feature that helps distinguish econometrics from its parent discipline of statistics. Econometricians have little control over sample size and face uncertainty about model specifications as compared to other scientific disciplines in which experiments can be conducted. Another complication is the additional complexity caused by the fact that factors not directly of interest must be taken into account by econometric models rather than handled by experimental design. Thus, these models typically contain large numbers of unknown parameters whose true relationships and growth pattern need to be estimated. The econometrician's task is often made much harder in complex surveys and cross-sectional and time-series applications, where many of the variables whose relationships need to be untangled and estimated exhibit reasonably similar growth patterns.

Furthermore, econometricians have seen the need for reliable hypothesis tests that allow diagnostic checking of model specification, particularly in the presence of nuisance parameters to detect misspecifications. The data problems mean that these tests need to be as powerful as possible. Fortunately, statistical theory is good at providing answers for simple models. But the problem is these answers become less clear for the more complicated models when the number of nuisance parameters become larger while handling complex data, as one can note in Chapter 3 for the case of two-stage models with additional misspecification of block effects. These problems, along with the theory of point optimal testing, testing for block effects and the power and critical point computations of the various tests, will be addressed in Chapters 2 and 3 of this book.

In econometrics and statistics literature, we often need to make a choice between a number of alternative models. In some cases, econometric theory and/or our understanding of the scientific phenomenon, we are trying to model the phenomenon that can help us to make an appropriate decision. However, there are many situations in which we are forced to ask which model is the best fit for a given set of data. The problem of choosing between a limited range of alternative models using only the available data is known as the model selection problem, which will be handled in Chapters 4, 5 and 6.

In recent years, econometricians and statisticians have been faced with the controversial issue of whether to use model selection procedures or formal hypothesis testing when deciding on model specifications. Often they require non-experimental data sets to be modelled; we, the practitioners, are forced to make a choice of model specification from a range of possibilities to suit the data. One common approach is to apply a series of pair-wise hypothesis tests to help make the best choice, but this approach has a number of pitfalls. For example, in each step one model has to be chosen as the null hypothesis and, if the power of the test is low, this model is unfairly favoured. On the other hand, if there is a lot of data and the power of the test is very high, this could disadvantage the null hypothesis model. Also the problem of pre-test bias means that investigators can lose control over the probability of a type I error in sequential tests. Granger, King and White (1995) explained these difficulties in detail.

An alternative and increasingly popular approach favoured by Granger and his associates is to use a model selection procedure based on an information criterion (IC). Typically this involves choosing the model specification with the largest maximized log-likelihood function minus a penalty, which, among other things, reflects the number of estimated parameters in the model (see Hossain and King (2004)). Using an arbitrage-pricing theory model both approaches, that is, hypothesis testing and model selections, are explored to see which approach suits better in Chapters 7, 8 and 9. A recent literature survey of hypothesis testing, model selection, bootstrapping and the Box-Cox transformation in econometrics reveals that none of the comprehensive research book and/or monograms exists in the area of theoretical and applied econometrics catering for both areas; model testing and model selections. The main objective of the current book is to bring together the issues of testing for the misspecification of block effects in econometrics modelling and to lay down the procedure of recent development in model selections (see Al-Shanfari et al. (2004) with reference to application in arbitrage pricing models).

1.2 Outline of the Book

The book consists of nine chapters covering major topics of recent interest in econometrics. Chapter 2 and 3 relate to the testing of hypotheses; Chapters 4 to 6 are on the topic of model selection, whereas Chapters 7 to 9 are based on arbitrage pricing theory (APT) models and their application in financial econometrics.

In the first two chapters, we provide the motivation and background for the study and present a review of the relevant literature on hypothesis testing, more specifically, model testing in econometrics of complex surveys. We introduce the issues of the theory of point optimal testing to search for the uniformly most powerful (UMP) test, testing for misspecification and provide a theoretical comparison of different tests based on likelihood functions while dealing with nuisance parameters in the linear regression model with non-spherical disturbances. In Chapter 3, we derive locally best invariant (LBI), locally mean most powerful invariant (LMMPI), beta optimal invariant (BOI) and point optimal invariant (POI) tests based on maximal invariant likelihood (MIL) function. We show that the LBI, LMMPI, BOI and POI tests are the most powerful tests in the case of the linear regression model. In this chapter a new type of misspecification in model building that may be called block and/or cluster effects (see Bhatti (2004)) is introduced. A computing-based optimal hypothesis testing procedure has been used to detect these effects. Power comparison of the existing classical tests with those of the optimal tests demonstrates the superiority of the new tests.

In Chapter 4, we review the relevant literature on the topic of model selection using information criteria, bootstrapping and the use of Box-Cox transformations. We present the consequences of model selection through testing and error sum of squares and we discuss the bootstrapping technique and the use of the Box-Cox transformation technique in econometric and statistical sciences. Moreover, the theoretical justification of a new modified Akaike's information criterion (AIC) in the presence of restricted parameters is discussed. A range of simulation experiments enables a comparison of the proposed selection methods to their conventional counterparts for selected design matrices and for different sample sizes. This comparison suggests the superiority of the new modified method.

Chapters 5 and 6 are extensions of Chapter 4 wherein a new idea of attempting to control the probability of correct selection is introduced. The two new methods based on the bootstrapping approach are produced. The Monte Carlo simulation shows the comparison between proposed AIC (PAIC), usual AIC (UAIC), proposed BIC (PBIC) and usual BIC (UBIC), controlled IC-1 (CIC-1) and controlled IC-2 (CIC-2) for selected design matrices and for different sample sizes. The simulation results demonstrate that the performance of CIC-1 is much better than the regular AIC and BIC in almost all situations. The CIC-2 on the other hand, has been found to be sometimes better and sometimes worse in comparison to the usual procedures. Moreover, the effects of the Box-Cox parameters λ_1 and λ_2 on the probabilities of correct selections (PCS) are also discussed in this chapter.

In Chapter 7, in light of the literature review the concept of APT and capital assets pricing (CAPM) models along with its application in efficient market hypothesis and factor analysis is presented. Chapters 8 and 9 contain some tests for the APT model in the global context. Particularly, these chapters test the hypothesis of return to predictability of the efficient market using cointegration and model selection procedures in the light of our discussion in earlier chapters.

Chapter 2

Testing Econometric Models

2.1 Introduction

Early developments in econometrics were mainly concerned with the problems of estimation and inference from a sample of economic data. The main objective of such estimation and inference was to obtain consistent and efficient estimates of the parameters and to construct better confidence intervals and hypothesis testing procedures. In an early stage of econometric development, models were typically formulated considering highly parsimonious relationships (according to the present-day economic theories), then estimated and tested statistically for model adequacy. Additional terms in the models were added to those models found inadequate and the process kept repeating. This procedure is often known as being specific to general methodology. Later, in contrast to this idea, the use of Hendry methodology (called general to specific methodology) became popular. It involves the formulation of a general model and then sequentially testing the model for various parameter restrictions until a desirable model is chosen. Recently, the attention of the subject has been diverted to the problems of diagnostic checking, specification testing, semiparametric estimation and model selection.

In recent years, theoreticians and practitioners have been heavily involved in discussing the controversial issue of whether to use model testing and/or model selection procedures in deciding the model among the choices of model that best fits a particular data set. This book attempts to bring together both viewpoints and apply these to various regression models, including the APT and CAPM models. In chapters 2 and 3, our discussion will be focused on the testing issues whereas the topic of 'model selection' and its application will be explored in the proceeding chapters.

There seem to be two main approaches to the model-testing problem; one is based on local optimization of power through the use of the generalized Neyman-Pearson lemma. A variation of this approach is to construct a test that is most powerful among all the tests at a chosen point in the alternative parameter space. This is called a point optimal test. An alternative is to construct tests by maximizing power locally at the null hypothesis. These tests are called locally most powerful (LMP) or locally best (LB), and more generally locally mean most powerful (LMM) tests. The second approach is to construct one-sided versions of conventional likelihood ratio (LR), Wald and LM tests. We shall call these likelihood-based tests as they involve maximization of the likelihood function with respect to parameters subject to the inequality restrictions. Estimation is then a part of the routine testing procedure.

Hypothesis testing is a fundamental tool for evaluating econometric models. It can be used to test various aspects of the econometrics theory as well as to check the various forms of model specification. It is therefore essential to have reliable testing procedures for the small samples econometricians sometimes have to deal with, particularly, when nuisance parameters are present under both the null and the alternative hypothesis. In statistics and econometrics literature, the thirst for using a uniformly most powerful (UMP) test, which maximizes the power curve and/or power envelop (PE) over the whole parameter space, is always preferred. This preference leads us to make use of the PO test for testing various forms of misspecification in regression models. In many studies it had been proved that the PO test is the best solution for one-sided testing problems of various forms of misspecification in regression.

In this chapter an attempt has been made to test a form of misspecification called 'block effects' that arises from symmetric multivariate normal (SMN), standard SMN (SSMN) and various types of regression models based on complex surveys. The structure of the rest of this chapter is as follows. In the subsequent sections, the review of the theory of optimal testing, invariant technique to the testing problem and the criterion for optimality is presented. In section 2.3 we introduce the problem of block effects, the consequences of ignoring them and a brief review of existing tests on block effects. The section 2.4 develops a unified linear regression (LR) model for various forms that incorporate the problem of block effects and the concluding remarks are made in the final section.

2.2 Optimal Hypothesis Testing[1]

In hypothesis testing, one would always prefer to use a UMP test which maximizes the power curve over the entire parameter space. Unfortunately, the existence of a UMP test does not happen very often in practice, perhaps only in special circumstances. When no UMP test exists, it is difficult to decide which is the preferred test as no single test can dominate in terms of power over the whole parameter space.

Apart from this, scientists are often faced with a high degree of frustration in their respective fields of testing for misspecified models because of the limited amount of data available. Furthermore, the requisite data cannot always be generated or controlled by laboratory experiment. Hence with a small amount of information in hand, when testing for an economic theory (or a hypothesis in any other field), it is important to choose some optimal testing procedure which will provide a powerful test.

Cox and Hinkley (1974, p. 102) consider various techniques for constructing tests of simple null hypothesis, H_0, against a composite alternative hypothesis, H_a, when no UMP test exists. One of the techniques they consider is using the most powerful test against a specific alternative $\theta_a \in H_a$ as the test of H_0 against H_a. King (1987b) has labelled this technique the PO approach. In the literature, this method has been shown to work well in a wide variety of testing problems provided that the specific alternative is chosen carefully. For example, a sequence of papers published by King (1982, 1983, 1985a, 1985b and 1987b) examines the performance of PO tests in testing for first order moving average regression disturbances (MA(1)), first-order autoregressive disturbances (AR(1)) and AR(1) against MA(1) disturbances in the linear regression model with small samples. Further, Evans and King (1985) and King and Skeels (1984) investigate the small sample power properties of PO tests for heteroscedastic disturbances and joint AR(1) and heteroscedastic regression disturbances, respectively. Among others who worked in exploring the power properties of PO tests in different areas are Silvapulle (1991), Rahman (1993), Grose (1998), Bhatti (1995a, 2000), and more recently, Begum (2003) and Bhatti (2004).

These studies, viewed together, lead us to the conclusions that certain point optimal tests have more desirable small sample power properties than their other competitors, including the LB invariant (LBI), LMMP and LMMP invariant (LMMPI) tests. These tests will be defined in more detail at a later stage.

Over the past 20 years, the advanced technology provided by the computer revolution has brought enormous benefits to statisticians, econometricians, biometricians and other researchers working in the quantitative method areas. With the ever-cheapening cost of computing operations and the greater capacity of computer memory, optimal testing is becoming more viable and popular and its value is recognized in research work. No matter whether the hypothesis is simple or composite, one-sided or two-sided, with or without nuisance parameters, advances in computing technology have helped us to solve these problems. However, this chapter is limited to only one-sided hypothesis testing problems because the block/sub-block effects under tests are mostly positive.

2.2.1 Review of the Theory of Point Optimal Testing

This subsection begins by considering a general form of hypothesis testing, that is, testing

$$H_0\text{: } y \text{ has density } f(y,\omega), \quad \omega \in \Omega, \text{ against}$$

$$H_a\text{: } y \text{ has density } g(y,\phi), \quad \phi \in \Phi$$

in which y is an observed $n \times 1$ vector, ω is a $j \times 1$ vector and ϕ is an $i \times 1$ vector. It is assumed that the possible range of parameter values has been determined by all given knowledge in order to keep the parameter spaces, Ω and Φ, as small as possible.

2.2.1.1 Case (1) This is a problem of testing simple null against a simple alternative hypothesis, with ω_1 and ϕ_1 fixed and known as parameter values such that $\Omega = \{\omega_1\}$ and $\Phi = \{\phi_1\}$, i.e.:

$$H_0^1\text{: } y \text{ has density } f(y,\omega_1), \text{ against}$$

$$H_a^1\text{: } y \text{ has density } g(y,\phi_1).$$

Therefore, the Neyman-Pearson lemma (see, Lehmann, 1959, p. 65) implies that rejecting H_0^1 for large values of:

$$r = g(y,\phi_1) \,/\, f(y,\omega_1)$$

is a most powerful (MP) test.

2.2.1.2 Case (2) This is a problem of testing a simple null hypothesis, H_0^1 against the composite alternative, H_a. If r is used as a test statistic, then r is the MP in the neighbourhood of $\phi = \phi_1$. The critical value for this test can be found by solving the probability of the form:

$$\Pr\{r > r' \mid y \text{ has density } f(y,\omega_1)\} = \alpha$$

for r' where α is the desired significance level.

2.2.1.3 Case (3) This is probably the most practical case and involves testing a composite null hypothesis, H_0, against the composite alternative, H_a. In this situation, it may be difficult to construct an MP test in the neighbourhood of $\phi = \phi_1$. This is because the size of the test and the power of the test may depend on some unknown values of the parameters, that is,

$$\begin{aligned}\text{Size of Test} &= \Pr\{y \in W \mid H_0 \text{ is true}\} \\ &= \int_W pdf_0\,(y,\omega)dy \\ &= \alpha(\omega), \text{ say.}\end{aligned} \tag{2.1}$$

Note that $\alpha(\omega)$, in (2.7) may depend on the unspecified part of ω where W is the critical region. Similarly:

$$\begin{aligned}\text{Power of Test} &= \Pr\{y \in W \mid H_a \text{ is true}\} \\ &= \int_W pdf_a\,(y,\phi)dy \\ &= \beta(\phi), \text{ say.}\end{aligned} \tag{2.2}$$

Here also note that $\beta(\phi)$ in (2.8), may depend on ϕ and hence the power of the test may not always be large for some values of ϕ. In equations (2.7) and (2.8), pdf_0 and pdf_a are the probability density functions under the null and alternative hypothesis, respectively.

The standard approach suggested by Lehmann and Stein (1948) is to control the maximum probability of a type I error by the choice of critical value. This is done by solving the following probability of the form:

$$\sup_{\omega \in \Omega} \Pr\{r > r^* \mid y \text{ has density } f(y,\omega)\} = \alpha \tag{2.3}$$

for r^* which is the critical value. In general, the choice r' is greater than r^*. Note that if Ω is a closed set, then:

$$\Pr\{r > r^* \mid y \text{ has density } f(y,\omega)\} = \alpha \tag{2.4}$$

will be true for at least one $\omega \in \Omega$. If there is a value for ω_1 which leads to $r' = r^*$, then the critical regions of the two tests correspond. Thus, it can be said that the test based on r is an MP test in the neighbourhood of $\phi = \phi_1$ of H_0 against H_a.

In the case where the ω_1 value exists and is also known, then constructing a PO test will be much simpler. Therefore, it is important to check for the existence of ω_1 before conducting a PO test, i.e., one has to check whether or not there exists ω_1 value such that (2.4) holds for $\omega = \omega_1$ subject to the constraint that (2.3) also holds. King (1987b, p. 175) has outlined the method in calculating the left hand side of (2.4) with the help of readily available computer subroutine packages.

The iterative procedure he mentioned can be summarised as follows:

1 choose a fixed value of ω_1;
2 solve (2.4) to find r^* and then check to see if (2.3) holds. If it does hold, then the values of ω_1 and r^* have been found. If it does not hold, another choice of the ω_1 value is needed by moving it towards the ω values which caused the violation in (2.3). Then repeat step two.

Unfortunately, in practice it is not always so simple. A ω_1 value sometimes might not exist in a particular testing problem. Lehmann (1959, pp. 90–94) developed an approach for overcoming the non-existence of an ω_1 value, that is, to reduce a composite null hypothesis to a simple one by considering the weighted average of the distribution over the parameter space. Thus, H_0 is replaced by H_λ with the density function of y being given by:

$$h_\lambda(y) = \int_\Omega f_\omega(y) d\lambda(\omega).$$

Lehmann assumes that λ is the degenerate distribution at $\omega = \omega_1$. Under this assumption with the size α, if the most powerful test of a simple null hypothesis, H_λ, against a simple alternative, H_a, has a value of its size less than or equal to α with respect to H_0, then the resultant test is also a PO test of H_0 against H_a. However, if this assumption does not hold, Lehmann's approach is not appropriate. King (1987b, pp. 179–80) and Silvapulle (1991) consider an approximate point optimal (APO) testing approach to solve this problem.

For instance, in case (3) above, a test statistic r with its critical value r^* determined by (2.3) is said to be an APO test if $\Pr\{r > r^* \mid H_0^1\}$ is close to α, say within 5 per cent of α. This is because the distribution of H_0 has been changed such that this probability was equal to α then our test would be a PO test. Therefore, there is a need to look for an ω_1 value which minimizes the difference between α and $\Pr\{r > r^* \mid y \text{ which has density } f(y,\omega_1)\}$, i.e.:

$$\alpha - \Pr\{r > r^* \mid y \text{ has density } f(y,\omega_1)\}. \tag{2.5}$$

In addition, since (2.5) also depends on ϕ_1, it is worthwhile to consider varying ϕ_1 to minimize the measure of approximation in (2.5) further. Recently, King (1989) and Silvapulle and King (1991) have used the APO approach for testing AR(4) regression disturbances in the presence of AR(1) and testing MA(1) against AR(1) disturbances, respectively. Brooks (1993) has used an APO test for testing for a single Hildreth-Houck random coefficient against the alternative that the coefficient follows the return to normalcy model.

2.2.2 *Invariance Approach and Optimal Tests*

Apart from these, one of the most common problems involved in hypothesis testing is the existence of nuisance parameters which may be present under both the null and alternative hypotheses. The construction of a PO or an APO test requires searching for an appropriate ω_1 value in the parameter space Ω. If the parameter space Ω can be restricted to be as small as possible, then it will be helpful in finding such a value for ω_1. Obviously, one should check whether theoretical considerations can indicate some possible restrictions which can be imposed on the range of various parameters under both H_0 and H_a.

In general, there are three different approaches which help to solve this problem. They are the 'similar approach' (Hillier (1987)), 'marginal likelihood' approach (Ara (1995)) and the 'invariance approach' (Bhatti (1991, 1992, 1995a) and Begum (2003)). A rejection region of size α is called a 'similar region' of size α if for all values of the nuisance parameters the probability of rejecting the null hypothesis is exactly equal to α when the null hypothesis is true. Hillier (1987) observed that there is an exact equivalance between similar tests and invariant tests of H_0. The 'invariance approach' has had considerable success in the application of PO tests because invariance arguments can be used to eliminate nuisance parameters. The reasoning behind this approach is that if an hypothesis testing problem is invariant to a class of transformations on the observed sample, it is desirable that the test procedure also have this property.

For example, as can be seen in the next chapter in relation to two-stage LR (2SLR), three-stage LR (3SLR) and multi-stage LR models changing the scale of y and adding a known linear combination of regressors to the rescaled y still preserves the family distributions under both the null and the alternative hypotheses. Thus, the invariance transformation may change the numerical values of the parameters but the functional form of the likelihood function still remains the same. Ara (1995) has shown that the tests based on maximal invariant (that is, invariant tests) and tests based on the marginal likelihood procedures are equivalent.

As is known in hypothesis testing, for the purpose of test construction a sample space can be divided into two regions, namely, a rejection region and an acceptance region. An invariant test is one in which each pair of points in the sample space that can be related by a transformation either falls into or outside the rejection region. Therefore, decisions on the problem of how to partition the sample space can be simplified into choosing which sets of points related by transformations shall be in the rejection region and which sets shall be out of it.

A convenient summary statistic called a maximal invariant tends to solve the problem of deciding which set of points is to be in a certain region. A maximal invariant exhibits the property of invariance and every other invariant statistic can be written as a function of it. Hence, only the problem based on the maximal invariant rather than on the observed sample needs to be dealt with. Hopefully, this way the distributions under the null and the alternative hypotheses will have fewer parameters than in the original testing problem. However, the main disadvantage of the invariance arguments is that it is often difficult to find the distributions of the maximal invariant under null and under the alternative hypotheses. Nevertheless, in the next chapter we have used the invariance principle in deriving the PO and the locally optimal tests.

2.2.3 Optimality Criterion

A remaining question is, how does one choose a point at which the power is optimized? In the situation when no UMP test exists, Cox and Hinkley (1974, p. 102) suggest three different approaches in the choice of points:

1. to pick a 'somewhat arbitrary "typical" point' in the alternative parameter space and use it in the test in order to find a point optimal solution;
2. to remove this arbitrariness, choose a 'point' which is very close to the null hypothesis in order to maximize the power locally near the null hypothesis;
3. to choose a test that maximizes some weighted average of the powers.

Option (1) is known as the 'point optimal' solution discussed earlier in this chapter, and reviewed in some detail by Bhatti and King (1990). In that paper, they noted that a class of PO tests is also called 'beta optimal' if its power function is always a monotonic non-decreasing function of the parameter under test and it reaches a predetermined value of the power, say, p_1, most quickly. The concept of beta-optimality was first introduced by Davies (1969) and then followed by Davies (1980, 1987) and Bhatti (1995a, 2001a), where they suggested optimizing power at a predetermined value of the parameter at 0.8, which seems to give good overall power. Our construction of the BO test in Chapter 3 optimizes power at $p = 0.5$ and $p_1 = 0.8$.

In contrast to PO and BO tests, option (2) leads us to a LMP test often also known as a LB test, a term we preferred to use in this book. The LB test is also optimal in the sense that its power curve has the steepest slope at H_0 of all power curves from tests with the same size.

The LB solution has been proposed by Neyman and Pearson (1936) and followed by Ferguson (1969), Efron (1975), King and Hillier (1985) and SenGupta (1987) among others. Let it be assumed that there is interest in testing $H_0{:}\theta = 0$ based on y which has been defined earlier as an $n\times 1$ random vector whose distribution has probability density function $f(y|\theta)$ where θ is a $p\times 1$ vector of unknown parameters. When $p = 1$, the LB test of $H_0{:}\theta = 0$ against $H_a^+{:}\theta = 0$ is that with critical regions of the form:

$$\left.\frac{\partial \ell nf(y\mid\theta)}{\partial\theta}\right|_{\theta=0} > c_1 \tag{2.6}$$

where c_1 in (2.6) is a suitably chosen constant; see Ferguson (1967, p. 235) and King and Hillier (1985). King and Hillier (1985) noted that this test is equivalent to the LM1 test based on the square-root of the standard LM test statistic. Against the two-sided alternative when $p=1$, Neyman and Pearson (1936) proposed a test which has the critical regions of the form:

$$\left.\frac{\partial^2 f(y\mid\theta)}{\partial\theta^2}\right|_{\theta=0} > c_2 f(y\mid\theta)\Big|_{\theta=0} + c_3\left.\frac{\partial f(y\mid\theta)}{\partial\theta}\right|_{\theta=0} \tag{2.7}$$

and which yield LB unbiased (LBU) tests where the constants c_2 and c_3 are chosen so that the critical region has the required size and is locally unbiased. The critical regions of the form (2.7) were labelled as type A regions by Neyman and Pearson in their (1936) paper. They also proposed type A_1 tests which are known as uniformly most powerful unbiased (UMPU) tests. Neyman (1935) showed how to construct type B and type B_1 tests, namely, LBU and UMPU tests, respectively.

For the higher dimension parameter spaces, i.e., where $p \geq 2$, the LBU critical region of H_0: $\theta = 0$ against H_a: $\theta \neq 0$ is obtained by using Neyman and Pearson (1938) type *C* LBU regions. These regions have constant power on each of a given family of concentric ellipses in the neighbourhood of the null $\theta = 0$ and this constant power is maximized locally. Isaacson (1951) introduced type *D* regions to rectify this objection (also see Lehmann, 1959, p. 342). As Wu (1991) pointed out, the type *D* regions are obtained by maximizing the Gaussian curvature of the power function at $\theta = 0$. Further he added, 'in practice, type *D* critical regions need to be first guessed and then verified'. SenGupta and Vermeire (1986) introduced the class of LMMP unbiased (LMMPU) tests which maximize the mean curvature of the power hypersurface at the null point, i.e. $\theta = 0$ within the class of unbiased tests. Their critical region is of the form:

$$\sum_{i=1}^{p} \frac{\partial^2 f(y \mid \theta)}{\partial \theta_1^2}\bigg|_{\theta=0} > c_0 f(y \mid \theta)\bigg|_{\theta=0} + \sum_{i=1}^{p} c_1 \frac{\partial f(y \mid \theta)}{\partial \theta}\bigg|_{\theta=0}$$

where the constants c_j, $j=1,2,\ldots,p$, are chosen such that the test has the nominated size and is locally unbiased.

King and Wu (1994) suggested a multivariate analogue of the one-sided testing problem, i.e. H_0: $\theta = 0$ against $H_a^+ : \theta_1 \geq 0, \ldots \theta_p \geq 0$ with at least one strict inequality. They showed that a LMMP test of H_0 against H_a^+ has the critical region:

$$s = \sum_{i=1}^{p} \frac{\partial \ell n f(y \mid \theta)}{\partial \theta_i} > c. \tag{2.8}$$

They also noted that there is always the possibility that one may be able to find such a test of the form (2.8), which is LB in all directions from H_0 in the p-dimensional parameter space. Neyman and Scott (1967) call this property 'robustness of optimality' while King and Evans (1988) call such tests uniformly LB (ULB). Like UMP tests, ULB tests may not always exist. In such cases, one may wish to consider a weaker optimality criterion. In the next section we will explore the options of constructing PO, BO, LB and LMMP critical regions in relation to a unified regression model for testing block/sub-block effects. Before proceeding further we have to first understand the problem of block effects discussed in the next section.

2.3 Problem of Block Effects

In the last few years there has been a significant growth of research in mining complex databases which have been generated from pattern, longitudinal, time series, panel and complex sample surveys, and their application in econometrics and other social sciences. Indeed, in the last few years, the tremendous growth in the use of sample surveys methods in statistical sciences has dichotomized the subject due to the nature and problems of the economics data in the presence of continuing innovation in computing technology.

In recent years, there has been an increasing use of regression analysis based on survey data in empirical econometrics, statistics, market research, social, physical and biological sciences. Often the data arising from these areas are naturally in blocks. When regression is applied to data obtained from such blocks, sub-blocks or multiblocks (that is, from multi-stage sample design), the regression errors can be expected to be correlated within ultimate blocks or sub-blocks. As one would expect, ignoring such correlation can result in inefficient estimators, and in seriously misleading confidence intervals and hypothesis tests. Part of the growing literature on the subject is based on the traditional sampling framework such as, for example, the works of Konijn (1962) and Kish and Frankel (1974). Others such as Scott and Holt (1982), Deaton and Irish (1983), King and Evans (1986), Christensen (1986, 1987a, 1987b), Moulton (1986, 1990), Dorfman (1993), Rao et al. (1993), Bhatti and Barry (1997), Chaturvedi et al. (1998), Khan and Bhatti (1998), Khan et al. (1999), Chaturvedi and Bhatti (2000) and, just recently, Bhatti (2004) have focused on the model-based approach.

In the rest of this chapter and in Chapter 3 we will follow a model-based approach in order to deal with the regression analysis problems of sample survey data. The literature survey of the model-based approach work reveals that most of the above mentioned authors have considered only the simplest form of intrablock correlation arising from the two-stage cluster sampling. In the next section, an extension of their work is explored in two directions. Initially, a PO test for testing intrablock correlation in a two-stage model so as to achieve comparability with the other existing tests is developed. Next, having found these testing procedures superior in terms of power performance, it is used in Chapter 3 on 2SLR models with fixed and stochastic regressors.

Sometimes in real life situations, the two-stage models are woefully inadequate. For example, in an investigation of a national population with a basic unit of household, a two-stage model would be well-nigh useless. What is needed is a model that allows for blocking and sub-blocking at the levels of regions, states, wards, postal districts, streets or similar. In other words, a multi-stage model is needed. Hence, we consider the use of a three-stage model in order to demonstrate further viability of our testing procedures and to understand the consequences of such an extension to a general multi-stage model in the next subsection.

2.3.1 Historical Background of Sample Surveys

The idea of sample-surveying was developed by Kiaer (1895) and was adopted by the International Statistical Institute in its first meeting in Berlin in 1903. Next, Bowley (1906) supplied the theory of inference for survey samples. Later, Neyman (1934) was concerned with the choice between alternative sampling procedures for survey data, such as stratified, purposive and cluster sampling. Others who contributed significantly were Cochran (1942) who dealt with ratio and regression estimators; Hansen and Hurwitz (1949) who developed the selection procedures with probability proportion to size; and Madow and Madow (1944) and Cochran (1946), who considered the method of systematic selection.

Due to its wide application in different fields of human endeavor, quite a number of textbooks have been devoted to the subject of sample-surveys. Among the notable texts, Yates (1949) was the first, followed by Deming (1950), Cochran (1953), Hansen, Hurwitz and Madow (1953), Sukhatme (1954) and Kish (1965). Their latest editions are largely refinements and improvements on their original work, although they contain new areas of thought which have generated further research in the area. For example, Godambe (1966), Royall (1968, 1970), Hartley and Rao (1968, 1969), Scott and Smith (1969) and Särndal (1978) have used the idea of finite and superpopulation in relation to the case of multi-stage and other survey designs.

Even more interesting work has been done in the last few decades on the method of data analysis of complex sample surveys. Particularly in the field of regression analysis the study by Kish and Frankel (1974), Pfefferman (1985), Ullah and Breunig (1998), and Bhatti (2001a, 2004) represent a new approach. They investigated the impact of an intrablock or equicorrelation coefficient on the regression analysis by using the standard sample-survey framework. They pointed out that, if the intra-block correlation is ignored, then the estimates of the calculated standard errors of the regression coefficients underestimate the true standard errors.

Through the 1980s, the practitioners and theoreticians have discussed the controversial issue of whether a design-based or a model-based approach should be adopted for regression analysis of sample survey data. The difference between the model-based linear least squares prediction approach and the design-based sampling distribution approach is discussed in the next section.

2.3.2 Model-based Versus Design-Based Approach

It is well known among survey statisticians that the design-based approach in regression implies a relationship between the dependent variable, y and the independent variable, x, where x is obtained from well defined clusters or blocks of a finite population. In this approach, each observation is weighted by the reciprocal of its probability of being included in the sample in order to make an inference about the finite population on the basis of the observed sample. Here unbiased estimators of the intercept and the slope coefficient are obtained by taking the expectation over all possible samples and a consistent estimator is obtained by using Cochran's (1953) definition.[2] In the design-based approach, it is believed that the allocation of weights in the sample selection procedure make the inference about population parameters inefficient and hence it does not lead to best linear unbiased estimators (BLUE).

In contrast to the design-based approach, the model-based approach always assumes that there exists a data generating process for the variables and therefore there is not a finite population. For example, when money demand, GDP or any other macroeconomic variable is observed, there is no finite population. This leads to using a stochastic model to explain the data generating process, as correctly as possible. The simplest stochastic model is:

$$y_i = \alpha + \beta x_i + \varepsilon_i$$

where the ε_is are i.i.d. $(0, \sigma^2)$. If the x_is are exactly known, the OLS estimator is the minimum variance linear unbiased estimator (or BLUE) for β and α. In this model, the word 'unbiased' refers to the expectations of overall possible realizations of the stochastic process while 'consistent' is used in the usual econometric or statistical sense.[3]

An interesting evaluation of the model-based and design-based approaches is given by Royall and Cumberland (1981). The authors compare the variance estimates of both approaches. Their empirical results favour the use of the model-based approach due to its efficiency. A further advantage of the model-based approach is that it can be applied using existing software regression packages. Examples of such computer packages are SURREGR (Holt, 1977), SUPER CARP (Hidiroglou, Fuller and Hickman, 1980) and PC

CARP (Fuller, Kennedy, Schnell, Sullivan and Park, 1986), Ullah and Breunig (1998) and Bhatti (2001a). In Chapter 3 we have adopted the procedure of using the model-based approach for the analysis of complex survey data.

2.3.3 Problems of Blocked Data

Scott and Holt (1982) considered the effects of two-stage design on the OLS estimator, particularly on efficiency and on standard errors. They showed that the OLS estimator is consistent but inefficient and the standard estimator for the variance-covariance matrix is consistent only if $\rho = 0$. Kloek (1981), Greenwald (1983) and Moulton (1986) have analysed the magnitude of the bias. They have shown that the magnitude of the downward bias for the standard errors increases with the increase in the average block size, the intra-block or equicorrelation of the disturbances, and the equicorrelation of the regressors. Just recently, Ullah and Breunig (1998) and Khan et al. (1999) addressed the consequences of ignoring block and/or cluster effects while handling the complex surveys.

Despite these problems, survey data would always be preferred by the researchers due to their availability from secondary sources and to time and cost advantages over the time series cross-sectional and/or panel data sets. Because in high-tech and competitive markets the analysis of survey data is very important, the need for diagnostic tests on the validity of such models is a basic requirement for researchers. Discussion on some existing tests and proposed optimal tests in this area are detailed later in the chapter. Before this, the next section presents a discussion on a unified linear regression model.

2.4 A Unified[4] Regression Model for Survey Data

Here a unified regression model means an equation in which the grouping/blocking of homogeneous characteristics is reflected in the disturbance term, u_{ij}.

2.4.1 Two-stage Linear Regression Model

In this model it is assumed that *n* observations are available from a two-stage sample with m blocks or clusters. Let *m*(*i*) be the number of observations from the ith block so that $n = \sum_{i=1}^{p} m(i)$. Then the simplest linear regression model of this form would be:

$$y_{ij} = \sum_{k=1}^{p} \beta_k x_{ijk} + u_{ij} \; (i = 1, 2,\ldots, m, j = 1, 2,\ldots, m(i)) \tag{2.9}$$

in which i is the block identifier, j is the observation identifier in the given block, β_k are unknown coefficients and x_{ijk} for $k = 1, 2,\ldots, p$ are observations on p independent variables, the first of which is a constant. It is assumed that u_{ij} is independent between blocks but equicorrelated within blocks. Hence:

$$E(u_{ij}) = 0$$

and

$$Cov(u_{ij}u_{st}) = \begin{cases} \sigma^2 & (i = s, j = t) \\ \rho\sigma^2 & (i = s, j \neq t). \\ 0 & (i \neq s) \end{cases} \tag{2.10}$$

Here ρ in (2.10), is the equicorrelation coefficient of the disturbances which is also called the block effect.

Models of these forms have been considered by Fuller and Battese (1973), Fuller (1975), Campbell (1977), Holt and Scott (1981), Scott and Holt (1982), Deaton and Irish (1983), Christensen (1984), King and Evans (1986), Honda (1989), Bhatti (1994, 1995), Ullah and Breunig and, more recently, Bhatti (2001, 2004), among others.

If it is assumed that $x_{ijk} = 0$ or $\beta_k = 0$, then the model (2.9) will become Bhatti's (2000) SMN distribution model. The further assumption of $\sigma^2 = 1$ in (2.9) through (2.10) make this as a SSMN distribution model (see Bhatti and King, 1990). The definitions and examples of these distributions are given in the next section whereas the detail testing procedures have been developed in the next chapter.

2.4.2 *Standard Symmetric Multivariate Normal Distribution*

The purpose of this subsection is to define SSMN and SMN distributions and then investigate some of their applications in the field of statistics and econometrics. It is important to note that these distributions arise naturally in biometrics, education, genetics, psychology and related areas. Examples include the analysis of missing observations in time series (Sampson, 1976, 1978), generalized canonical variable analysis (SenGupta, 1983) and distributional modelling of repeated failure time measures (Crowder, 1985).

These distributions have been applied in econometrics and statistics literature, for example, by SenGupta (1987, 1988), Williams and Yip (1989), Bhatti and King (1990), Zhu et al. (1997), and Bhatti (1995a, 2000, 2001a, 2004). To econometricians and statisticians, the best-known model based on these distributions is a special case of pooled time series and cross-section data, which will be discussed in section 3.2. Another important application is in the regression analysis of data drawn from two (or higher) stage cluster or blocked surveys. For example, when census data are used, a block may be defined as a standard city block or an irregularly shaped area with identifiable political or geographical boundaries or it can be a group of industries or occupations etc. For the latter type of data, observations are correlated within ultimate clusters. This correlation is called the intrablock, intraclass, equi-, uniform or familial correlation coefficient, ρ. Ignoring such correlation leads to seriously misleading confidence intervals and hypothesis tests based on inefficient OLS estimates (for example, see Walsh, 1947 and Halperin, 1951), and it also produces inefficient forecasts. In the next section these distributions are defined.

2.4.3 Definitions and Examples of SSMN Distribution

The SMN distribution is a multivariate normal distribution in which all the components of a *k*-dimensional random vector, *y*, have equal means, equal variances and all covariances between components take the same value (see Rao, 1973, p. 196). These common covariances give rise to a common correlation coefficient, ρ, which is called an equicorrelation coefficient. Thus, if $E(y) = \mu$ then the SMN model can be written as:

$$y \sim N(\mu, \sigma^2 \textstyle\sum(\rho))$$

where:[5]

$$\sum(\rho) = \begin{pmatrix} 1\rho\rho \,\ldots\ldots\ldots\, \rho \\ \rho 1 \rho \,\ldots\ldots\ldots\, \rho \\ \rho\rho 1 \,\ldots\ldots\ldots\, \rho \\ \cdot \quad \cdot \quad \cdot \\ \cdot \qquad \cdot\ \cdot \\ \rho\rho\rho \,\ldots\ldots\, \rho 1 \end{pmatrix}. \tag{2.11}$$

Similarly, a k-dimensional random vector y can be said to follow a SSMN distribution if it follows a SMN distribution and additionally its components, means and variances are zero and unity, respectively, i.e., $E(y) = 0$ and $\sigma^2 = 1$ and hence the SSMN distribution model can be expressed as:

$$y \sim N(0, \sum(\rho))$$

where $\sum(\rho)$ is given by (2.11). Though the literature on SMN distributions is quite extensive, no test for ρ has been proposed for SSMN distributions except SenGupta's (1987) LB test, and Bhatti and King's (1990) BO and BO invariant (BOI) tests. Discussion on this test will occur later in this chapter.

Sampson (1976, 1978) has considered theoretical applications of SSMN distributions and developed the simple best asymptotic normal (BAN) estimation procedure for autoregressive, moving average and intraclass or equicorrelated models. He notes that SSMN distributions arise naturally from multivariate models in which means and variances of individual variables are known, thus allowing these variables to be standardized. Such standardizations are always made and play important roles in the techniques for reduction of dimensionality, e.g., in canonical variables (Anderson, 1984) and generalized canonical variables analysis (SenGupta, 1981, 1983).

This distribution is of interest to both theoreticians and practitioners for several reasons. One practical application of the SSMN distribution occurs when there are many observations on the individual variables but, because of historical, financial or practical reasons, there are comparatively few sets of joint observations. The individual observations can be used to obtain excellent estimates of means and variances, which allow one to proceed as if these estimates are the true values. Such practical examples can be found in time series analysis, analysis of missing observations, psychometrics, generalized canonical variables and in biometrics. For some related results on models, which follow this distribution, one may refer to Wilks (1946), Sirivastva (1965), SenGupta (1987, 1988), Zhu et al. (1997) and Bhatti (2001a). Another example of the use of such a distribution can be found in Crowder (1985) who gives a distributional model for repeated failure time measurements. Further, the SSMN distribution provides a practical example of a curved exponential family[6] and illustrates some associated difficulties and techniques concerned with inference on them, particularly when dealing with the testing of hypotheses.

2.4.4 One-Way Error Component Model

The model (2.9), under (2.10) is similar to that of the random effects model or one-way error component model used by econometricians in the analysis of panel data. A simple (re)-formulation appropriate in this case is:

$$y_{it} = \sum_{k=1}^{p} \beta_k x_{itk} + u_{ij}, \; (i = 1, 2, \ldots, N, t = 1, 2, \ldots, T)$$

where:

$$u_{it} = \mu_i + \nu_{it} \tag{2.12}$$

in which $i = 1, 2, \ldots, N$, where N stands for the number of individuals (e.g. households) in the sample and $t = 1, 2, \ldots, T$, where T stands for the length of the observed time series. Each of the μ_is, ($i=1, \ldots, N$) is called an individual effect and ν_{it} is the usual (white noise) error term. In this reformulation (at this stage) it is assumed that every block has the same number of observations (T).

The basic outline of the model (2.12) has been drafted by the pioneers Balestra and Nerlove (1966), Wallace and Hussain (1969) and Maddala (1971). They assume that:

1. the random variables μ_i and υ_{it} are mutually independent;
2. $E(u_{it}) = 0$. This implies that $E(\mu_i) = 0$ and $E(\upsilon_{it}) = 0$;
3. $Var(\mu_i) = \begin{cases} \sigma_\mu^2, \text{for } i = i' \\ 0, \textit{otherwise} \end{cases}$;
4. $Var(\upsilon_{it}) = \begin{cases} \sigma_\nu^2, \text{ for } i = i', t = t' \\ 0, \textit{otherwise} \end{cases}$.

In comparing (2.9) with (2.12), it is noted that $u_{it} = \mu_i + \nu_{it}$, $\sigma^2 = \sigma_\mu^2 + \sigma_\nu^2$ and $\rho = \sigma_\mu^2/\sigma^2$.

The only difference between (2.9) and (2.12) is that in model (2.12) the ith block consists of the time-series of the ith individual and the number of observations in a 'block' is T, the length of the time series. In the econometrics literature, this model is also called the one-way error component model. Useful references include Hsiao (1986), Honda (1989), Moulton and Randolph (1989), Baltagi and Li (1991) and Körösi, Mátyás and Székely (1992). This model is frequently used to model panel data in the econometrics literature. A PO test for the 2SLR will be considered in Chapter 3.

2.4.5 Three-Stage Linear Regression (3SLR) Model

This subsection extends the 2SLR model of the previous subsection to more general situations where each block is divided into sub-blocks and then one can use the error component to capture these block/sub-block effects to form a three-stage cluster sampling design model. The 3SLR model is expressed as:

$$y_{ijk} = \sum_{\ell=1}^{p} \beta_\ell x_{ijk\ell} + u_{ijk}, \; (i = 1,\ldots,m, j = 1,\ldots,m(i), k = 1,\ldots, m(i,j)) \quad (2.13)$$

in which i is the block identifier, j is the sub-block identifier in the ith block, and k is the observation identifier in the jth sub-block of the ith block such that:

$$n = \sum_{i=1}^{m} \sum_{j=1}^{m(i)} m(i,j)$$

where β_ℓ are unknown coefficients and $x_{ijk\ell}$ for $\ell = 1,\ldots, p$ are observations on p independent variables, the first of which is a constant. It is assumed that u_{ijk} are normally distributed with mean zero and its variance-covariance structure is given by:

$$\mathrm{Cov}(u_{ijk}\, u_{rst}) = \begin{cases} 0, \text{ (for } i \neq r, \text{ and } j, s, k \text{ and } t) \\ \rho_1 \sigma^2, \text{ (for } i = r, j \neq s, \text{ any } k, t) \\ (\rho_1 + \rho_2)\sigma^2, \text{ (for } i = r, j = s\ k \neq t) \\ \sigma^2, \text{ (for } i = r, j = s, k = t) \end{cases} \quad (2.14)$$

where, $k, t = 1, 2, \ldots, m(i,j), j, s = 1, 2, \ldots, m(i)$ and $i, r = 1, 2,\ldots, m$. Here in (2.14), ρ_1 and ρ_2 measure the main block and sub-block effects, respectively. Note that if it is assumed that $\rho_2 = 0$, then the 3SLR model (2.13) will become equivalent to a 2SLR model of the form (2.9). Further note that if it is assumed that each sub-block in a main block has only one observation then at least mathematically one can easily show that (2.14) will become equivalent to the two-way error component model.

2.4.6 Random Coefficients Model

Note that a model of the form (2.9) can also be expressed in terms of a random coefficients model where it is assumed that the regression coefficient, β_k, varies from block to block. A formulation appropriate to the random regression coefficient is given by Bhatti (2004). The formulation of Bhatti (2004) is different from Maddala's (1977, p. 326) variance components model and Swamy's (1970)[7] and Hsiao's (1986)[8] random coefficients models.

In developing uniform regression models of the form (2.9) and (2.13) the most popular approach of error component models has been used to model survey data. The general popularity of this approach among survey statisticians and panel data econometricians (see Mátyás and Sevestre, 1992) can be attributed to the following facts:

1 they treat huge databases as well as modest ones with equal ease;
2 estimation and hypothesis testing methods are derived from the classical well-known procedures;
3 the problems and difficulties presented remain within the traditional framework and hence they are well understood;
4 the theoretical frontiers are much more explored than other possible approaches;
5 the estimation and hypothesis testing results can be interpreted easily;
6 most commonly used econometrics and statistical software packages can be applied to these models with only minor modifications.

The use of error component models in panel data was first suggested by Balestra and Nerlove (1966) and its use in survey data was pointed out by Holt, Smith and Winter (1980). Others proposing its use, include Wallace and Hussain (1969), Amemiya (1971), Swamy and Arora (1972), Fuller (1975), Fuller and Battese (1973, 1974), Campbell (1977), Rao and Kleffe (1980), Baltagi (1981), Scott and Holt (1982) and Dickens (1990). Just recently, Baltagi and Raj (1992), and Mátyás and Sevestre (1992) reviewed the various estimation and testing procedures in the context of panel data. As noted above, modelling panel data is similar to that of survey data. Therefore, one can apply nearly the same estimation procedures to the 2SLR or (in special situations) 3SLR models with those used in panel data modelling, in order to obtain efficient estimates of unknown parameters.

The hypothesis testing problems associated with the error components models of the type SSMN, SMN and 2SLR models are the main concern of the next chapter.

2.5 Concluding Remarks

This chapter reviewed the work of other scholars to understand the issues and problems connected with the use of sample surveys in regression analysis. Most scholars considered the 2SLR model with fixed coefficients, which was sometimes inappropriate in real life situations. Therefore, their work was extended to multi-stage model by incorporating block, sub-block and multiblock effects in the error terms and stochastic regressors. The choice of using a model-based approach in the analysis of survey data was explained and a unified regression model for survey and panel data was developed. While these are the preliminary concepts, a proper understanding of them is necessary before embarking on the task of developing the optimal tests. The theory of PO testing was summarized.

Articles which construct exact tests for testing block effects were reviewed so that the tests used in this book could stand alongside for comparison later on. The literature survey of the PO tests revealed that they performed pretty well in other situations, in terms of their size and power properties, as compared to asymptotic tests. This suggests that it is worthwhile to explore the power properties of optimal tests, such as PO, BO, LB and LMMP, in testing these block/sub-block effects. Therefore, in the subsequent chapters tests on SSMM, SMN and 2SLR models are applied.

Notes

1 Some of the material reported in the rest of this chapter is from Bhatti (2001).

2 An estimator is called consistent in this approach if the estimate becomes exactly equal to the population value when $n = N$, that is, when the sample consists of the whole population.

3 A consistent estimator here is an estimator, which converges in probability, as the sample size increases with a decreasing variance, to the parameters of which it is an estimator.

4 It unifies regression modelling of survey and panel data as can be noted from equation (2.9), (2.12) and (3.26).

5 The structure of the variance-covariance matrix of the observed vector, y, is identical to that of the residuals in panel and survey data, see Balestra and Nerlove (1966) and Bhatti (1994), respectively.

6 Efron (1975) considered arbitrary one-parametric families and attempted to quantify how nearly 'exponential' they are. Since it is well known in the literature that one-parametric exponential families have very nice properties for estimation, testing and other inference problems, statistical curvature is identically zero for exponential families and positive for nonexponential families. Statistical curvature is closely related to Fisher (1925) and Rao's (1962, 1963) theory of second-order efficiency.

7 Swamy's (1970) model ignores the equicorrelation coefficient, ρ, within blocks and considers hetroscedasticity. Whereas in the model used in this study the variance terms of the diagonal elements of the ith block are constant within the block.

8 Hsiao (1986) ignores equicorrelation within blocks.

Chapter 3

Testing for Block Effects

3.1 Introduction

In a world that is increasingly becoming competitive, data- and computing-rich, best practices demand greater use of statistics in decision-making, business, computing applications, economics and government. Two important tools are sample surveys and the linear regression model. Cost considerations often mean that survey data is gathered in blocks and/or sub-blocks of observations that may be influenced or affected by common factors. The best examples concern geographical grouping of regional blocks where one may view blocking and regression as a function of efficient data mining that can lead to making optimal decisions about the parameters of our interests.

Economists and statisticians, who need to gather data before making important decisions or giving much needed advice, are increasingly using regression analysis to model complex survey data. It is common practice for survey data to be collected in blocks and the standard linear regression model to be fitted to such data. To analyse such a body of data the classical linear regression model that assumes fixed regression coefficients and spherical disturbances may not always be appropriate, as has been pointed out by Holt, Smith and Winter (1980), Scott and Holt (1982), King and Evans (1986), Wu and Bhatti (1994), Brooks and King (1994) and Bhatti (2000, 2001). Since there are situations in which economic structures change or socioeconomic and demographic background factors differ, it is possible that the response parameters may vary over blocks, groups or regions. To illustrate, equal amounts of labour and capital in a particular production process may yield different levels of output over different blocks in view of technical progress, labour efficiency and managerial ability that may vary from block to block. Similarly, identical applications of fertilizer to different blocks or sub-blocks may yield different outputs because of variation in average temperature, land fertility, rainfall and agricultural land practices. However, Bhatti and Khan (2000) recommended caution while comparing their estimated results of fixed and random coefficient models.

The main aim of this chapter is to investigate and develop an efficient estimation and optimal testing procedure for the linear regression model with stochastic and fixed coefficients based on blocked survey data. The focus of our investigation is to estimate block effects, ρ, block-wise heteroscedasticity, variances of the random coefficients and then conduct optimal testing procedures to develop BO, BOI, PO, POI, LMMPI tests to see the relative power strength of the various tests.

The structure of the rest of this chapter is as follows. In the sections, the stochastic coefficient regression model with block effects is introduced and an algorithm for the efficient maximum likelihood estimator (EMLE) is presented. Both random and fix coefficient models are applied using EMLE method in estimating the unknown parameters. In section 3.3, we use the theory of optimal hypotheses testing to develop BO, BOI, PO, POI and LMMPI tests for the various models whereas an empirical power comparison is done in section 3.4 to choose among them the most powerful test, to be called UMPI. The final section contains some concluding remarks.

3.2 The Models and the Estimation Procedures[1]

3.2.1 The Fix Coefficient 2SLR Model

Following Bhatti (2001), we assume that n observations are available from a two-stage sample survey data with m blocks. Let m(i) be the number of observations from the ith block so that $n = \sum_{i=1}^{m} m(i)$. For ease of notation, we will use a^i to denote i^{th} quantity 'a' associated with the ith block while $(a)^i$ will denote quantity 'a' raised to the power i. An exception will be σ^2, which has its usual meaning. Let us consider the regression model:[2]

$$y_j^i = \sum_{k=1}^{p} \beta_k x_{jk}^i + u_j^i \tag{3.1}$$

for observations $j = 1,2,\ldots, m(i)$ from blocks $i = 1,2,\ldots, m$, with dependent variables y_j^i and p independent variables x_{jk}^i, which are assumed non stochastic, the first of which is a constant. Baltagi (1996) and Bhatti (1999) followed a similar version but in panel data framework. They assumed that the regression errors u_j^i are independent between blocks but equicorrelated within blocks. Hence for (3.1):

$$E(u_j^i) = 0 \text{ for all i and j;}$$

$$E(u_j^i u_t^s) = \sigma^2 \delta_{is} \{\rho + (1-\rho)\delta_{jt}\} \tag{3.2}$$

where ρ is block effects, such that $0 \leq \rho \leq 1$, $\delta_{ii} = 1$ and $\delta_{ij} = 0$, for $i \neq j$. They also assumed that the regression coefficients, β_k; k = 1,2,..., p are constant.

3.2.2 The Random Coefficient Model

In certain applications based on data with a blocking structure, the assumption of response paramater, β_k, being constant may not be appropriate. For example, Hoque (1991) in a similar study with a different data set used the Langrange multiplier test, (i.e. Rao's, 1973, efficient score test, and Wu and Bhatti, 1994) point optimal (PO) test for testing the null hypothesis of fixed regression coefficients against an alternative that they are stochastic. They rejected the null in favour of the alternative hypothesis. Therefore, in this section it may be reasonable to assume that the slope and variances parameters, β_k and σ^2 in (3.1) and (3.2), respectively, change from block to block (or from sub-block to sub-block). Thus we consider the inter-block random coefficients model,[3] which regards the coefficients as having constant means and constant variance-covariances over different blocks and additionally it allows block-wise heteroscedasticity in the disturbance terms, u_j^i.

When regression coefficients vary from one block to another, then we can write model (3.1) with inter-block random coefficients as:

$$y_j^i = \sum_{k=1}^{p} \beta_k^i x_{jk}^i + u_j^i \tag{3.3}$$

for j = 1, 2,..., m(i), block size and i=1, 2,..., m = c, number of blocks. Further, the inter-block random coefficients, β_k^i can be decomposed into a deterministic component (mean) and a random component (deviation from mean). Thus, for the ith block, the regression coefficients can be written as:[4]

$$\beta_k^i = \beta_k + \varepsilon_k^i;\ k = 2,\ldots, p \tag{3.4}$$

where the random component ε_k^i follows the following assumptions,

$$\left.\begin{array}{l}
(i)\ \mathrm{E}(\varepsilon_k^i) = 0, \textit{for all } i \textit{ and } k \\
(ii)\ \mathrm{Var}(\varepsilon_k^i) = \sigma_k^2,\ k = 2,\ldots, p \\
(iii)\ \mathrm{Cov}(\varepsilon_k^i, \varepsilon_l^j) = 0, \textit{for all } i, j, k \textit{ and } l \\
\qquad \text{such that either } i \neq j \text{ or } k \neq l \\
(iv)\ \mathrm{Cov}(\varepsilon_k^i, u_l^j) = 0, \textit{for all } i, j, k \textit{ and } l \\
(v)\ \mathrm{Cov}(x_{jk}^i, \varepsilon_l^j) = 0, \textit{for all } i, j, k \textit{ and } l \\
(vi)\ \mathrm{Cov}(x_{jk}^i, u_l^j) = 0, \textit{for all } i, j, k \textit{ and } l
\end{array}\right\} \tag{3.5}$$

Also, x^i_{jk} is always independent of ε^i_j and u^i_l. Then the assumptions in (3.4) in view of (3.5) are:

$$\left.\begin{aligned} E(\beta^i_k) &= \beta_k, \text{ for all i and k} \\ Var(\beta^i_k) &= \sigma^2_k, \text{ for all i and k} \end{aligned}\right\}, \tag{3.6}$$

Under (3.4), (3.5) and (3.6); that is, for the ith block, the variance term σ^2 in (3.2) is $(\sigma^1)^2$, the regression model (3.3) may be written as:[5]

$$y^i_j = \sum_{k=1}^{p} \beta_k x^i_{jk} + V^i_j; \; j=1, 2,\dots, m(i) \quad i=1, 2,\dots, c \tag{3.7}$$

where:

$$V^i_j = \sum_{k=2}^{p} \varepsilon^i_k x^i_{jk} + u^i_j. \tag{3.8}$$

Note that (3.5) and (3.6) imply that the mean, variance and covariances of V^i_j are as follows:

$$\begin{aligned} E(V^i_j) &= E\left(\sum_{k=2}^{p} \varepsilon^i_k x^i_{jk} + u^i_j\right) \\ &= E\left(\sum_{k=2}^{p} \varepsilon^i_k x^i_{jk}\right) + E(u^i_j) \\ &= 0 \end{aligned}$$

and:

$$\begin{aligned} E(V^i_j V^s_t) &= E\left[\left(\sum_{k=2}^{p} \varepsilon^i_k x^i_{jk}\right)\left(\sum_{k=2}^{p} \varepsilon^s_k x^s_{tk}\right)\right] + E\left[u^i_j u^s_t\right] \\ &= \delta_{is}\left(\sum_{k=2}^{p} \sigma^2_k x^i_{jk} x^i_{tk}\right) + (\sigma^i)^2\, \delta_{is}\{\rho + (1-\rho)\delta_{jt}\} \\ &= (\sigma^1)^2\, \delta_{is}\left\{\left(\sum_{k=2}^{p}\left(\frac{\sigma^2_k}{(\sigma^1)^2}\right) x^i_{jk} x^i_{tk}\right) + \frac{(\sigma^i)^2}{(\sigma^1)^2}\{\rho + (1-\rho)\delta_{jt}\}\right\} \\ &= (\sigma^1)^2\, \delta_{is}\left\{\left(\sum_{k=2}^{p} \lambda_k x^i_{jk} x^i_{tk}\right) + \mu^i\{\rho + (1-\rho)\delta_{jt}\}\right\} \end{aligned} \tag{3.9}$$

where:[6]

$$\lambda_k = \frac{\sigma_k^2}{(\sigma^1)^2}, \text{ for } k = 2,\ldots p, \text{ and } \mu^i = \frac{(\sigma^i)^2}{(\sigma^1)^2}, i = 1,2,\ldots c.$$

For ease of notation, the term $(\sigma^1)^2$, the disturbance variance for the first block, in the remainder of the section will be denoted by σ^2. Therefore, the model (3.7) can be more compactly written in matrix form as:

$$y = X\beta + v. \tag{3.10}$$

Now, let $var(V^i) = \sigma^2\Omega^i$ for the ith block. Then (3.9) implies that:

$$\Omega^i = D^i + F^i$$

where D^i is the matrix whose $(j,t)^{th}$ element is obtained by:

$$\sum_{k=2}^{p} \lambda_k x_{jk}^i x_{tk}^i \tag{3.11}$$

and F^i is of the form:

$$F^i = \mu^i\left[(1-\rho)I_{m(i)} + \rho E_{m(i)}\right] \tag{3.12}$$

where $I_{m(i)}$ is the m(i) × m(i) identity matrix and is the matrix whose elements are all equal to one.

It follows from (3.11) and (3.12) that $V \sim N(0,\sigma^2\Omega)$ where $\Omega = \bigoplus_{i=1}^{c} \Omega^i$ is block diagonal. For any X matrix in (3.10), the distribution of y is determined by $\beta, \sigma^2, \rho, \lambda = (\lambda_2,\ldots, \lambda_k)'$ and $\mu = (\mu^1, \mu^2,\ldots, \mu^c)'$.

If we assume $\varepsilon_k^i = 0$ then the inter-block random coefficient model reduces to a model with fixed coefficients and heteroscedastic variances. If we further assume $\varepsilon_k^i = 0$, and $(\sigma^i)^2 = \sigma^2$, then it will become a special case of Bhatti's (2000) SSMN and SMN models.

In the next subsection we will develop an algorithm in the spirit of Ansley (1979) and King (1986) for finding the true maximum likelihood estimates of the unknown, under the constraints that λs and μs be strictly positive. This solves the problem of negative estimates of variances of the coefficients. However, this boundary condition of having only non-negative variances means that standard methods of estimating the standard errors of the estimates cannot be used. An obvious solution is to use the bootstrap method to estimate them. An overview of the theory and application of bootstrapping is provided by Efron (1979, 1982) and Efron and Tibshirani (1986), while Raj (1989) and Brooks and King (1994) discuss its application to random coefficient models.

3.2.3 An Algorithm for Full Maximum Likelihood Estimation

As we know from the previous section, $V \sim N(0,\sigma^2\Omega)$ where Ω is a block diagonal matrix. It is important to note that the matrix Ω has the Cholesky decomposition $\Omega = LL'$, such that:

$$L = \begin{pmatrix} T^1 & 0 & . & . & 0 \\ 0 & T^2 & . & . & . \\ . & . & T^3 & 0 & . \\ . & . & 0 & . & . \\ 0 & . & . & . & T^c \end{pmatrix}$$

where T^i is an $m(i) \times m(i)$ lower triangular matrix of the ith block, i.e.:

$$\Omega^i = T^i T^{i\prime}.$$

If w^i_{jk} denotes the $(j,k)^{th}$ element of Ω^i then non-zero elements of T^i can be found by the following recursive scheme:

$$t^i_{11} = (\omega^i_{11})^{1/2} \tag{3.13a}$$

$$t^i_{j1} = \omega^i_{j1} \Big/ t^i_{11}, \text{ where } j = 1,\ldots,m(i). \tag{3.13b}$$

The off-diagonal elements of T^i can be obtained by the formula:

$$t^i_{jk} = \frac{1}{t^i_{kk}}\left(\omega^i_{jk} - \sum_{p-1}^{k-1} t^i_{kp} t^i_{jp}\right), \text{ for } k < j,\ldots \tag{3.13c}$$

whereas, the diagonal elements can be obtained by the formula:

$$t^i_{jj} = \left(\omega^i_{jj} - \sum_{k=1}^{j-1} (t^i_{jk})^2\right)^{1/2}. \tag{3.13d}$$

Now, the model (3.10) can be transformed as:

$$L^{-1}y = L^{-1}X\beta + L^{-1}V$$

and may conveniently be written as:

$$\tilde{y} = \tilde{X}\beta + \tilde{V} \tag{3.14}$$

such that $\tilde{V} \sim N(0,\sigma^2 I_n)$. The transformed vector $\tilde{y}$ can be obtained by the recursive relationship:

$$\tilde{y}^i_l = y^i_l / t^i_{ll} \tag{3.14a}$$

and so on, where the jth value of the ith block of y is:

$$\tilde{y}^i_j = \frac{1}{t^i_{jj}}\left(y^i_j - \sum_{k=1}^{j-1} t^i_{jk}\tilde{y}^i_k\right). \tag{3.14b}$$

Similarly, the matrix X may be transformed recursively as follows:

$$\tilde{X}^i_{lk} = X^i_{lk} / t^i_{ll} \text{ where } k = 1,2,\ldots,p \tag{3.14c}$$

and so on, the (j,k)th element of ith blockof transformed matrix $\tilde{X}$ can be obtained by:

$$\tilde{X}^i_{jk} = \frac{1}{t^i_{jj}}\left(X^i_{jk} - \sum_{l=1}^{j-1} t^i_{jl}\tilde{X}^i_{lk}\right). \tag{3.14d}$$

The log likelihood of the original model (3.10) and the transformed model (3.14) is:

$$\begin{aligned}\ell(\beta,\sigma^2,\rho,\lambda,\mu) &= const - \tfrac{n}{2}\log\sigma^2 - \tfrac{1}{2}\log(\Omega(-\tfrac{1}{2\sigma^2}(y-X\beta)'\Omega^{-1}(y-X\beta) \\ &= const - \tfrac{n}{2}\log\sigma^2 - \log(\mathrm{L}(-\tfrac{1}{2\sigma^2}(\tilde{y}-\tilde{X}\beta)'(\tilde{y}-\tilde{X}\beta)\end{aligned} \tag{3.15}$$

where the determinant of the ith block of L can easily be calculated by:

$$\left.\begin{aligned} |L| &= \prod_{i=1}^{c} (|T^i|) \\ &\text{and} \\ |T^i| &= \prod_{j=1}^{m(i)} t^i_{jj} \end{aligned}\right\} . \tag{3.16}$$

Setting $\partial\ell(\beta,\sigma^2,\rho,\lambda,\mu)/\partial\beta$ and $\partial\ell(\beta,\sigma^2,\rho,\lambda,\mu)/\partial\sigma^2$ to zero and solving, we obtain:

$$\hat{\beta} = (\tilde{X}'\tilde{X})^{-1}\tilde{X}'\tilde{y} \tag{3.17}$$

$$\hat{\sigma}^2 = \hat{\eta}'\hat{\eta} / n \tag{3.18}$$

respectively, where:

$$\hat{\eta} = (\hat{y} - \tilde{X}\hat{\beta}) \tag{3.19}$$

is the OLS residual vector from (3.14). Substituting (3.17) and (3.18) into (3.15) yields the concentrated log likelihood:

$$\begin{aligned} \tilde{\ell} &= c - \frac{n}{2}\log \hat{\eta}'\hat{\eta} - \log|L| \\ &= c - \frac{n}{2}\left[\log\left\{\hat{\eta}(|L|)^{1/n}\right\}'\left\{\hat{\eta}(|L|)^{1/n}\right\}\right] \\ &= c - \frac{n}{2}[\log \hat{e}'\hat{e}] \\ &= c - \frac{n}{2}\log\sum_{j=1}^{n}(\hat{e}_j)^2 \end{aligned}$$

where c is a constant and:

$$\hat{e}_i = \hat{\eta}_i(|L|)^{1/n}. \tag{3.20}$$

Therefore, the estimation problem reduces to minimizing the sum of squares of:

$$\hat{S} = \sum_{i=1}^{n} \hat{e}_i^2$$

with respect to ρ, λ_k; (k = 2,..., p) and μ^i; (i = 2,..., c), given that μ^1=1. This may be obtained by using a standard nonlinear least squares algorithm to minimize $\hat{S}$, where for any given ρ, λ_k and $\mu^1\hat{e}_i$; (i = 1, 2,..., n) are obtained as follows:

(i) transform y and X to $\tilde{y}$ and $\tilde{X}$, respectively, using (3.10), (13a–13d), (3.14), (3.14a–14d) and at the same time progressively calculate |L| via (3.16);
(ii)compute $\hat{\beta}$ and $\hat{\eta}$ using (3.17) and (3.19) and the use of (3.20) to calculate.

When the values of $\hat{\rho}$, $\hat{\lambda}$and $\hat{\mu}$which minimize $\hat{S}$ have been found, the MLE of β is $\hat{\beta}$ from step (ii) of the final iteration, while σ^2 can be evaluated by using the final value of $\hat{\eta}$ in (3.18). This procedure converges to a solution of the first-order conditions for maximizing (3.15) that may or may not correspond to the global maximum; see Oberhofer and Kmenta (1974).

3.2.4 Applications of the Models

In this section we use the Cobb-Douglas type production function to estimate unknown stochastic parameters by using the random coefficients model discussed in the previous subsections. The model is applied to Bangledeshi agricultural data for the year 1996–97, collected from 600 farms of the seven selected districts of Khulna and Rajshahi divisions. For computational ease and brevity, we will consider two independent random samples of size 20 observations (farms) from each district of both divisions. The detailed sampling design and measurement of variables are given in Appendix A for the ready reference of the readers from (Bhatti, 2004 and Ali et al., 2005).

The model (3.7), in the form of unrestricted Cobb-Douglas production functions (linear in the logarithms), under (3.4), (3.5) and (3.6), can generally be written as:

$$y_j^i = \sum_{k=1}^{p} \beta_k x_k^i + V_j^i \tag{3.21}$$

where y_j^i is the log of output for the jth farm in the ith block and x_{jk}^i is the log of a (1xp) vector of functions of values of inputs associated with the jth farm from the ith district, such that the first element of the x_{jk}^i is assumed to be one. Thus, we can write model (3.21) as:

$$\log(y_j^i) = \beta_1 + \beta_2 \log(X_{j2}^i) + \beta_3 \log(X_{j3}^i) + \beta_4 \log(X_{j4}^i) \tag{3.22}$$

where:

- y_j^i Total value of output per acre for j^{th} farm in the ith block, in thousands of Taka;
- X_{j2}^i Labour input per acre in man-days of jth farm in the ith block;
- X_{j3}^i BC (biological-chemical) input per acre in thousands Taka, of jth farm in i^{th} block;
- X_{j4}^i Size of jth farm in i^{th} block(district) in acres

and the random variable y_j^i has the distributional properties as in (3.9), (3.10), and (3.11).

Using the likelihood and the concentrated likelihood functions (3.15) and (3.20), respectively, on the Cobb-Douglas type production function (3.21), generally, and (3.22) particularly, we can obtain the estimates of the unknown parameters by the Levenberg-Marguardt algorithm. Thus, the estimated model (3.22) based on the first set of 140 randomly selected farms is:

$$\log(y_j^i) = -0.272 + 0.675 \log(X_{j2}^i) + 0.0351 \log(X_{j3}^i) + 0.0347 \log(X_{j4}^i). \tag{3.23}$$

Similarly, the estimated model (3.22) based on the second set of 140 selected farms is:

$$\log(y_j^i) = -0.269 + 0.674 \log(x_{j2}^i) + 0.033 \log(x_{j3}^i) + 0.04 \log(x_{j4}^i). \tag{3.24}$$

The estimated values of the parameters $\mu^i = \frac{(\sigma^i)^2}{(\sigma^1)^2}$ for $i = 2,\ldots, 7$ blocks from both the samples are given in Table 3.1.

The estimated results in Table 3.1 demonstrate that there exists a high districtwise heteroscedasticity in all the seven districts of Khulna and Rashahi divisions. This is due to different geographical locations, cultural and economic factors, the farmers' motivations are quite different in the two divisions. The Khulna division is the second largest industrial division of the country. Therefore, one can expect extra farm job openings here, which makes the opportunity cost of labour much higher compared to that of the Rashahi division.

The main reason for poor economic results in all districts of the Rajshahi division is its geographical location and being wholly dependent on agro-based

Table 3.1 Estimated values of the parameters based on models (3.23) and (3.24)

Parameters	$\hat{\sigma}$	$\hat{\rho}$	μ^2	μ^3	μ^4	μ^5	μ^6	μ^7
Sample 1 from model (3.23)	0.051	0.0017	0.381	0.223	0.024	0.049	0.078	0.082
Sample 2 from model (3.24)	0.0472	0.0065	0.363	0.22	0.028	0.043	0.083	0.082

industry which is constantly affected by climate and weather conditions, for example, cyclones, floods and droughts. During the monsoon, it has an excess of water, which affects the Rajshahi division, causing considerable damage to its cultivated lands. This restricts farmers to growing particular crops. Moreover, during the dry season, this division faces a shortage of water (see Hossain, 1990). This creates an irrigation problem and, hence, watering the plants involves huge capital investment in the form of deep tubewells. Therefore, farm activities in the Rajshahi are different from those of Khulna and, hence, are the result of high blockwise heteroscedasticity. The estimates of the parameters λ_ks which are the ratio of the variances of random coefficients to the variance of the error term of the first block, i.e. $\lambda_k = \sigma_k^2/\sigma^2$ for $k = 2, \ldots, 4$, are given in Table 3.2 below (see equation (3.9) for the reparameterisation of the λs and μs in our model).

Table 3.2 Some estimates of the random coefficient model

k	β_k Sample 1	β_k Sample 2	λ_k Sample 1	λ_k Sample 2	σ_k Sample 1	σ_k Sample 2
2	0.683	0.681	0.2194	0.2076	0.0191	0.017
3	0.042	0.042	0.0622	0.0155	0.0112	0.0101
4	0.043	0.048	0.5217	0.4710	0.0233	0.0311

The estimates given in models (3.23), (3.24) and in Tables 3.1 and 3.2 provide a local maximum for the criterion function but they do not necessarily correspond to the global maximum required.

Furthermore, the high elasticity of labour as compared to other variables in models (3.23) and (3.24) can be explained in several different ways. Firstly, Bangladesh is a labour intensive country and hence labour is very cheap as compared to land and or BC inputs, etc. Secondly, the shape and small size of the farms prevent the owners from utilizing new technology in order to reap a high level of output. In such environments labour contributions could of course be more important than capital (that is, land and BC inputs). However, one should not forget that there must be some limit to the number of labourers working for a given size of the farm. On the other hand, the estimated coefficients of BC inputs and of farm size are 0.043 and 0.042 in model (3.23) and 0.042 and 0.048 in model (3.24), respectively. These results support the empirical work reported by Hoque (1991), Wu and Bhatti (1994), Parikh (2000), Parikh and Radhakrishna (2002), Ali (2002) and Ali et al. (2005).

3.2.5 Two-Stage Linear Regression (2SLR)

The model (3.1), under (3.2) is similar to that of the random effects model or one-way error component model used by econometricians and other social scientists in the analysis of panel and/or time-series data.

A simple (re) formulation appropriate in this case is:

$$y_{it} = \sum_{k=1}^{p} \beta_k x_{itk} + u_{it}$$

$$(i = 1,2,\ldots,N,\ t = 1,2,\ldots,T)$$

where:

$$u_{it} = \mu_i + v_{it} \tag{3.25}$$

in which i = 1,2,...,N, where N stands for the number of individuals (e.g. households) in the sample and t = 1,2,...,T, where T stands for the length of the observed time series. Each of the μ_is, (i = 1,...,N) is called an individual effect and v_{it} is the usual (white noise) error term. In this reformulation (at this stage) it is assumed that every block has the same number of observations (T). Note that this structure is similar to that of (2.9) with $T = c$ blocks, under the assumptions (2.10).

The pioneers Balestra and Nerlove (1966), Wallace and Hussain (1969) and Maddala (1971) have drafted the basic outline of the model (3.4). They assume that:

1 the random variables μ_i and υ_{it} are mutually independent;
2 $E(u_{it}) = 0$. This implies that $E(\mu_i) = 0$ and $E(\upsilon_{it}) = 0$;

3 $\text{var}(\mu_i) = \begin{cases} \sigma_\mu^2, \text{ for } i = i'; \\ 0, \text{ otherwise} \end{cases}$

4 $\text{var}(\upsilon_i) = \begin{cases} \sigma_\upsilon^2, \\ \textit{for } i = i', t = t'. \\ 0, \textit{otherwise} \end{cases}$

In comparing (3.1) with (3.25), it is noted that $u_{it} = \mu_i + v_{it}$, $\sigma^2 = \sigma_\mu^2 + \sigma_\upsilon^2$ and $\rho = \sigma_\mu^2/\sigma^2$. The only difference between (2.9), (3.1) and (3.25) is that in model (3.25) the ith block consists of the time-series of the ith individual and the number of observations in a 'block' is T, the length of the time series. In the econometrics literature, this model is also called the one-way error component model. This model is frequently used to model panel data in the econometrics literature. Bhatti (1995) discussed this model in detail and refers to it as the 2SLR model, whereas Wu and Bhatti's (1994) model is said to be 3SLR models. For a recent review of these models, one can refer to Bhatti (2001). Empirical comparison of estimates of fixed (3.25) and random coefficient models (3.23) and (3.24) is made in Table 3.3 below.

Table 3.3 Some estimates of random and fixed coefficient models

k	β_k			Standard Error, σ_k			T
	(3.23)	(3.24)	(3.25)	(3.23)	(3.24)	(3.25)	(3.25)
2	0.683	0.681	0.564	0.021	0.020	0.112	5.0748
3	0.042	0.042	–0.044	0.011	0.005	0.069	–1.0289
4	0.043	0.048	0.0867	0.032	0.030	0.053	1.04778

Surprisingly, fixed coefficient model (3.25) reconfirms our results of the stochastic fitted models (3.23) and (3.24) for the high elasticity of labour contribution. However, a negative relationship between farm size outputs may explain the stochastic pattern in the data structure and labour redundancy theory with an increase in technology and the quality of BC, for example, a typical case in underdeveloped countries like Bangladesh. Recently, Bhatti and Khan (2000) compared the efficiencies of the various forms of these models and concluded that the computational cost and time involved in using random coefficient models is much more than in the fixed coefficients model and hence in their study, random coefficient models were not preferred models over the fixed. Their recommendations were to use non-stochastic models, while testing these models due to complexity in computing MLE in the presence of nuisance parameters under the null and alternative parametric spaces. In the rest of this chapter we will concentrate our model testing investigation on 2SLR and multi-stage models.

3.3 Testing for Block Effects[7]

It is important to note that if we assume the inter-block random coefficient model (3.7) will reduce to our 2SLR model discussed in (3.2) and (3.25). For the sake of simplicity we can express (3.25) in matrix form as follows:

$$y(i) = X(i)\,\beta + u(i) \tag{3.26}$$

for $i = 1, \ldots, c = m$, (number of blocks) where $y(i)$ is an $m(i) \times 1$ vector of y_{ij} values, $X(i)$ is an $m(i) \times p$ matrix whose (j,k)th element is x_{ijk} and $u(i)$ is an $m(i) \times 1$ vector of u_{ij} values. If y and u denote the $n \times 1$ vectors of stacked $y(i)$ and $u(i)$ vectors respectively, and X is the $n{\times}p$ stacked matrix of $X(i)$ matrices, then (3.26) can be written as:

$$y = X\beta + u \tag{3.27}$$

such that:

$$u \sim \mathrm{N}(0, \sigma^2\Delta(\rho))$$

where $\Delta(\rho) = \bigoplus_{i=1}^{m} \Delta_i(\rho)$ is block diagonal, with sub matrices:

$$\Delta_i(\rho) = (1-\rho)I_{m(i)} + \rho E_{m(i)} \tag{3.28}$$

in which $I_{m(i)}$ is an $m(i) \times m(i)$ identity matrix and $E_{m(i)}$ is an $m(i) \times m(i)$ matrix with all elements equal to one. Although we can proceed with unequal block sizes in this model, for the sake of simplicity in exposition, we will consider the case of balanced data (that is, equal block sizes) and hence we assume that $m(i) = k$ and $n = km$ in the subsequent subsections. Moreover, it is worth noting that if we assume in (3.25) or (3.26) that the error term $\varepsilon^i_k = 0$, and the variances for each block is the same, that is, $(\sigma^i)^2 = \sigma^2$ then 2SLR becomes a special case of Bhatti's (2000) SSMN, SMN models as have been briefly reported on in Chapter 2.

3.3.1 *The Optimal Tests for Block Effects in LR Models*

The main purpose of this section is to construct a POI test and to investigate whether the power of this test is better than that of the LBI test, for small and moderate sample sizes. It is found that for testing H_0: $\rho = 0$, against H_a: $\rho > 0$, both the LBI and POI tests are approximately UMPI, for some selected block sizes, and for these cases the critical values of this test can be approximated by critical values from the standard F distribution. The estimated sizes based on these critical values have a tendency to become closer to the nominal size of 0.05, when the sample size and the value of ρ_1 increase.

This section derives a locally mean most powerful invariant (LMMPI) test for testing the hypothesis, $\rho = 0$, against the alternative that ρ varies from block to block, and finds that the LMMPI test is equivalent to that of the one-sided Lagrange Multiplier (LM1) test. Finally, some propositions are advanced to relate point optimal tests to the beta optimal (BO) tests.

The contents of this section are divided into the following subsections. In the subsequent subsections, a procedure for constructing a POI test for testing $\rho = 0$, against a positive value of ρ is outlined. The application of King and Wu's (1990) LMMPI test to more complicated model, in which it is assumed that the equicorrelation coefficients vary from block to block is also demonstrated and shows that it is equivalent to the LM1 test. In the next subsection, the critical values of the POI test are approximated using the standard F distribution for selected block sizes and this subsection presents the five versions of the POI tests which optimize power at $\rho = 0.1, 0.2, 0.3, 0.4$ and 0.5, respectively. It is found that the s(0.3) test, which optimizes power at $\rho = 0.3$, is the best overall test. This subsection also reports an empirical power comparison of the s(0.3), LM1, LM2, Durbin-Watson (DW), and King's (1981) modified DW tests with that of the power envelope (PE).

3.3.1.1 Point optimal invariant test In this subsection we construct the MPI test statistic for testing H_0: $\rho = 0$ against the specific alternative H'_a: $\rho = \rho_1 > 0$, in the context of model (3.26), and under the assumptions (1 to 4). This statistic forms the basis of a point optimal test for the wider testing problem.

Observe that the problem of testing H_0: $\rho = 0$, against H_a: $\rho > 0$ is invariant under the group of transformations:

$$y \rightarrow \gamma_0 y + X\gamma \qquad (3.29)$$

where γ_0 is a positive scalar and γ is a $p \times 1$ vector. Let $M_x = I_n - X(X'X)^{-1}X'$,

$\hat{u} = M_x y = M_x u$ be the OLS residual vector from (3.27) and P be an $(n-p) \times n$ matrix such that $PP' = I_{(n-p)}$ and $P'P = M_x$. The vector:

$$\vartheta = \frac{P\hat{u}}{(\hat{u}'P'P\hat{u})^{1/2}}$$

is a maximal invariant under the group of transformations given by (3.29). Based on ϑ, we choose $\rho = \rho_1$, a known point at which we want to have optimal power in the alternative parameter space. By using King's (1987b), equation (18), we can obtain the POI test, which is to reject the null hypothesis for small values of:

$$s(\rho_1) = \frac{\hat{u}'A\hat{u}}{\hat{u}'\hat{u}}, = \frac{u'Au}{u'M_x u} \tag{3.30}$$

where:

$$A = \Delta_1^{-1} - \Delta_1^{-1}X(X'\Delta_1^{-1}X)^{-1}X'\Delta_1^{-1}, \text{ and } \Delta_1 = \Delta(\rho_1).$$

The last equality of (3.30) is obtained by observing that $\hat{u}'A\hat{u} = u'M_x AM_x u = u'Au$. Note, $s(\rho_1)$ in (3.30) can also be written as:

$$\frac{\sum_{i=1}^{n-p} \lambda_i \xi_i^2}{\sum_{i=1}^{n-p} \xi_i^2} \tag{3.31}$$

where $\lambda_i, \ldots, \lambda_{n-p}$ are the reciprocals of the non-zero eigenvalues of $\Delta_1 M_x$ or, equivalently, the non-zero eigenvalues of A. Thus, for any given value of ρ_1, at the desired level of significance, α, the critical value, c_α, can be found by solving:

$$\Pr\left[\sum_{i=1}^{n-p} (\lambda_i - c_\alpha)\xi_i^2 < 0\right] = \alpha. \tag{3.32}$$

This can be done by using either Koerts and Abrahamse's (1969) FQUAD subroutine or Davies' (1980) versions of Imhof's (1961) algorithm or Farebrother's (1980) version of Pan's (1968) procedure to evaluate the left-hand-side of (3.32). More recently, Shively, Ansley and Kohn (1990) and Palm and Sneek (1984) have suggested alternative procedures to compute (3.32) which do not require the computation of the eigenvalues.

Once the critical values have been found, one may wish to calculate the power of the $s(\rho_1)$ test. To do so, one needs to decompose the error covariance matrix $\Delta(\rho)$, or its diagonal component matrices $\Delta_i(\rho)$, in (3.28). This can be done by noting that the Cholesky decomposition of $\Delta(\rho)$ is:

$$\Delta(\rho) = T(\rho)T'(\rho)$$

where $T(\rho)$ can be obtained in a similar recursive scheme given in (3.13a – d). Observe that the power of the critical region $s(\rho_1) < c_\alpha$, in (3.32) can be found by evaluating the probabilities of the form:

$$\Pr\left(s < c_\alpha\right) = \Pr\left[u'\left(A - c_\alpha M_x\right)u < 0\right] \tag{3.33}$$

where:

$$u \sim N(0, \sigma^2\Delta(\rho)).$$

Let $\xi = T(\rho)^{-1}u \sim \mathrm{N}(0, \sigma^2 I_n)$ so that $u = T(\rho)\xi$. Substituting for u in (3.33), one can obtain the power function of the form:

$$\begin{aligned}
&\Pr\left[\xi' T'(\rho)\left(A - c_\alpha M_x\right)\xi < 0\right] \\
&= \Pr\left[\xi' F \xi < 0\right] \\
&= \Pr\left[\sum_{i=1}^{n} \lambda_i \eta_i^2 < 0\right]
\end{aligned} \tag{3.34}$$

where the λ_is are the eigenvalues of $F = T'(\rho)(A - c_\alpha M_x)T(\rho)$ and the η_i^2s are independent chi-squared random variables each with one degree of freedom. It is worth noting that under H_a the matrix A in (3.30), can be expressed as $A = (T^{-1}(\rho_1))' M^* T^{-1}(\rho_1)$, where $M^* = I - X^*(X^{*\prime}X^*)^{-1}X^{*\prime}$ and $X^* = T^{-1}(\rho_1)X$. The block diagonal lower triangular matrix $T^{-1}(\rho)$ is of the form:[8]

$$T^{-1}(\rho) = \begin{bmatrix} Q_k & 0 & \cdots\cdots & & 0 \\ 0 & Q_k & \cdots & \cdots & 0 \\ \cdot & \cdots\cdots\cdots & & & \\ & & \cdot & & \\ \cdot & & & \cdot & \\ \cdot & & & 0 & 0 \\ 0 & \cdots\cdots & & 0 & Q_k \end{bmatrix}$$

where Q_k is a $k \times k$ lower triangular matrix whose elements are obtained by the formula given below:

$$q_{ii} = \sqrt{\frac{[1+(i-2)\rho]}{(1-\rho)[1+(i-1)\rho]}}$$

and

$$q_{ij} = \frac{-\rho}{\sqrt{(1-\rho)[1+(i-1)\rho][1+(i-2)\rho]}}$$

for $i = 1, 2, \ldots, k$; $j = 2, 3, \ldots, k$ and $j > i$. The last equality of (3.34) can be calculated by using any of the methods outlined above for calculating (3.32). Using similar arguments Wu and Bhatti (1994) derived PO, POI and LMMPI tests for the multi block effects using a three stage linear regression (3SLR) model. In case of SSMN and SMN models, the PO test is called BO and the POI test is called BOI. These tests are summarized at the end of this chapter in Tables 3.7–3.8 in Appendix A4.

3.3.1.2 Locally most mean powerful invariant test In previous subsections a POI test has been constructed for the block effects, ρ, which was based on the error covariance matrix (3.28) of model (3.27), and involves only one parameter, ρ, in all the blocks. The more general situation is considered by Bhatti (1995), where it is assumed that the equicorrelation coefficient varies from block to block or from cluster to cluster. Therefore, in such cases the sub-blocks of the error covariance matrix (3.28) can be expressed in the following form, that is:

$$\Delta_i(\rho_i) = (1-\rho_i)I_k + \rho_i E_k, \text{ for } i = 1, 2, \ldots, m.$$

Our problem of interest is to test:

$$\bar{H}_0 : \rho_1 = \rho_2 = \ldots = \rho_m = 0 \tag{3.35}$$

against:

$$\bar{H}_a : \rho_1 \geq 0, \rho_2 \geq 0, \ldots, \rho_m, \text{(excluding H}_0\text{)}. \tag{3.36}$$

Note that this testing problem is invariant under the group of transformations given by (3.29).

King and Wu (1994) showed that a LMMPI test for $\bar{H}_0$ against $\bar{H}_a$ is to reject $\bar{H}_0$ for small values of:

$$d' = \frac{\hat{u}'A^*\hat{u}}{\hat{u}'\hat{u}} \tag{3.37}$$

where

$$A^* = \sum_{j=1}^{m} A_j ;$$

$$A_j = \frac{-\partial\Delta(\rho)}{\partial\rho_i}\bigg|_{\rho=0}$$

for $i=1,\ldots, m$, and $\hat{u}$ is a vector of OLS residual from (3.27).

For our problem of testing (3.35) against (3.36), the LMMPI test is determined by (3.37) with $A = (I_n - D)$, where $D = I_m \oplus E_k$. Substituting A in (3.37), we can express d' as:

$$d' = \frac{\hat{u}'(I_n - D)\hat{u}}{\hat{u}'\hat{u}}$$

$$= 1 - \frac{\hat{u}'D\hat{u}}{\hat{u}'\hat{u}}$$

$$= 1 - \frac{\sum_{i=1}^{m}\left(\sum_{j=1}^{k}\hat{u}_{ij}\right)^2}{\sum_{i=1}^{m}\sum_{j=1}^{k}\hat{u}_{ij}^2} . \tag{3.38}$$

It is worth noting that d' is the LBI test of $\bar{H}_0$ in the direction of $\rho_1 = \rho_2 = \ldots = \rho_m = 0$ (see King and Wu, 1994, for a property of the LMMPI test) and also note that the d' test is equivalent to the LM1 test of H_0 against H_a. Observe that the form of equation (3.38) is a ratio of quadratic forms in normal variables, and therefore its critical values may be determined by the standard numerical techniques. Under H_0, the LM1 test statistic has a standard normal asymptotic distribution while the LM2 test statistic is asymptotically distributed as $\chi^2_{(1)}$. In the next section we will compare the powers of these tests with those of the PE and the existing tests as well.

3.4 An Empirical Comparison of Sizes and Powers

The aim of this section is to explore the small-sample power properties of the $s(\rho_1)$ test of H_0 against H_a when the intra-block or equicorrelation coefficient is present in the two-stage linear regression model. The power functions of the $s(\rho_1)$ tests were evaluated in the context of model (3.27) and (3.28) and were compared with that of the DW (d), King's (1981) modified DW (d*) and the one-sided and two-sided Lagrange multiplier (LM1 and LM2) tests (as calculated and reported by King and Evans, 1986). Exact 5 per cent critical values of the test and the associated values of the power at $\rho = 0.1, 0.2, 0.3, 0.4$ and 0.5 were computed by using a modified version of the FQUAD subroutine of Koerts and Abrahamse (1969), with maximum integration and truncation errors of 10^{-6}.

The X matrices used are based on cross-sectional Australian census data, classified into 64 demographic groups according to eight categories of sex/marital status and eight categories of age (see Williams and Sams, 1981 for detailed discussion of the data). For these categories the regressors are population, number of households, and headship ratios of households. The first three data sets consisted of a constant dummy and all combinations of two of these three regressors for 1961 and, when extra observations were necessary, 1976. The other two design matrices were composed of a constant and all three regressors for 1961 and 1976, and for 1966 and 1971, respectively. In each case, 32, 64 and 96 observations were used, each with equal block sizes of $k = 2, 4, 8$ and $\frac{n}{2}$ (i.e., the block size equivalent to half of the sample size). It was also assumed that the data used in this analysis were ordered so that observations from the same block were together.

For a block size of $\frac{n}{2}$ our results appear to show that the critical region of the $s(\rho_1)$ test is approximately invariant to the choice of ρ_1 value and hence it is approximately UMPI. To investigate this possibility one can re-examine the $s(\rho_1)$ test.

Using (3.31) the critical region of the $s(\rho_1)$ test can also be written as:

$$\frac{\sum_{i=1}^{n-p} \lambda_i \xi_i^2 < c_\alpha}{\sum_{i=1}^{n-p} \xi_i^2} \tag{3.39}$$

where in this case the λ_is are the eigenvalues of the matrix:

$$A = \Delta_1^{-1} - \Delta_1^{-1} X (X' \Delta_1^{-1} X)^{-1} X' \Delta_1^{-1}$$

or equivalently of:

$$\left[I_n - \left(\Delta_1^{-\frac{1}{2}} \right)' X (X' \Delta_1^{-1} X)^{-1} X' \left(\Delta_1^{-\frac{1}{2}} \right) \right] \Delta_1^{-1}.$$

By using King's (1987a, p. 23) Corollary and a knowledge of the eigenvalues of Δ_1^{-1} from lemma 1 of Appendix 3A, we have the following relationships:

$$\begin{cases} \lambda_i = \dfrac{1}{\{1 + (k-1)\rho_1\}}, \text{ for i = 1,...,m−p} \\ \dfrac{1}{\{1 + (k-1)\rho_1\}} \le \lambda_i \le \dfrac{1}{1 - \rho_1}, \text{ for i = m − p + 1,..., m.} \\ \lambda_i = \dfrac{1}{1 - \rho_1}, \text{ for i = m + 1,..., n − p} \end{cases} \tag{3.40}$$

If $m > p$, then (3.39) can be expressed as:

$$\frac{\left\{ \frac{1}{1 + (k-1)\rho_1} \right\} \sum_{i=1}^{m-p} \xi_i^2 + \sum_{i=m\,p+1}^{m} \lambda_i \xi_i^2 + \frac{1}{1 - \rho_1} \sum_{i=m+1}^{n-p} \xi_i^2}{\sum_{i=1}^{n-p} \xi_i^2} < c_\alpha. \tag{3.41}$$

In this case note that when m is small and n is large, the last term of the numerator of (3.41) dominates and hence, $(1-\rho_1)s(\rho_1)$ approximately does not depend on ρ_1. This implies that the $s(\rho_1)$ test for $m > p$ is approximately UMPI.

If $m \leq p$, then (3.41) becomes:

$$\frac{\sum_{i=1}^{n-p} \lambda_i \xi_i^2 + \frac{1}{1-\rho_1} \sum_{i=m+1}^{n-p} \xi_i^2}{\sum_{i=1}^{n-p} \xi_i^2} < c_\alpha \tag{3.42}$$

where the eigenvalues of the numerator of the first term in (3.42) are given by (3.40), i.e.:

$$\frac{1}{[1+(k-1)\rho_1]} \leq \lambda_i \leq \frac{1}{1-\rho_1}, \text{ for i=1,..., m.}$$

Computationally exact values of these eigenvalues for $m = 2$ were computed by using the numerical algorithm TRED2 from Martin et al. (1968). For each of the data sets under consideration, it was found that all of the eigenvalues are $\frac{1}{1-\rho_1}$, except for one, which is very small and is approximately equal to $\frac{1}{[1+(k-1)\rho_1]}$. If we ignore the smallest eigenvalue, then the critical regions (3.42) become:

$$s^* = \frac{\sum_{i=2}^{n-p} \xi_i^2}{\sum_{i=1}^{n-p} \xi_i^2} < c_\alpha(1-\rho_1). \tag{3.43}$$

From (3.43) it is clear that the test is approximately independent of the values of ρ_1 and hence it is almost invariant to the choice of ρ_1. Therefore the test based on s(ρ_1) for $m \leq p$ is an approximate UMPI. This also includes the case of block size, $k = \frac{n}{2}$, or equivalently, $m = 2$, which makes this approximation stronger. Hence we have the following propositions for the $s(\rho_1)$ test.

3.4.1 Some Theoretical Propositions

3.4.1.1 Proposition 3.1 The s(ρ1) test is approximately UMPI for all values of p and m.

It is worth noting that in (3.43), s^* can be expressed in terms of the standard F distribution as follows:

$$\Pr\left[s^* < c_\alpha(1-\rho_1)\right] = \Pr\left[\frac{1}{s^*} > \frac{1}{c_\alpha^*(1-\rho_1)}\right]$$

$$= \Pr\left[\frac{\xi_1^2}{\sum_{i=2}^{n-p}\xi_i^2} < \left(\frac{1}{c_\alpha^*(1-\rho_1)} - 1\right)\right]$$

$$= \Pr\left[\frac{\chi^2_{(1)}}{\chi^2_{(n-p-1)}/(n-p-1)} > \left(\frac{1}{c_\alpha^*(1-\rho_1)} - 1\right)(n-p-1)\right]$$

$$= \Pr\left[F(\vartheta_1,\vartheta_2) > F_\alpha\right]$$

where:

$$F_\alpha = \left(\frac{1}{c_\alpha^*(1-\rho_1)} - 1\right)(n-p-1);$$

$$\vartheta_1 = 1,\ \vartheta_2 = n-p-1$$

and $F(\vartheta_1,\vartheta_2)$ denotes the F distribution with ϑ_1 and ϑ_2 degrees of freedom. If F_α is the *100*$(1-\alpha)$ percentile of the F distribution (obtainable from standard tables), then the approximate critical value, c_α^*, can be obtained by the following equation:

$$c_\alpha^* = \frac{1}{(1-\rho_1)\left(\frac{F_\alpha}{(n-p-1)} + 1\right)}.$$

3.4.1.2 Proposition 3.2 If Y follows a two-stage SSMN model, that is:

$$Y \sim N(0,\Delta(\rho))$$

where the covariance matrix is given in (3.27), then testing:

$$H_0 : \rho = 0$$

against $H_a : \rho > 0$ will reject null for small values of $r(\rho_1) = Y'(\Delta^{-1}(\rho_1) - I_n)Y < c_\alpha$ which is called the beta optimal (BO) test for the two-stage SSMN model. Recently, Bhatti (2000, p. 349) proved in theorem 2 that the BO test given by $r(\rho_1)$ is locally most powerful (LMP) and is called an LB test for the above testing problem.

3.4.1.3 Proposition 3.3 In the case where the block diagonal elements are different in (3.27) for each block then the testing problem will be one of testing, $H_0 : \rho_1 = \rho_2 = \ldots = \rho_m = 0$, against:

$$H_a : \rho_1 \geq 0, \rho_2 \geq 0, \ldots, \rho_m \geq 0$$

which will reject null for small values of:

$$\mathrm{d} = Y'AY = Y'(I_n - D)Y.$$

This is called the LMMP test and is equivalent to an LB test.

3.4.1.4 Proposition 3.4 If Y follows a two-stage SMN model, that is:

$$Y \sim N(0, \sigma^2 \Delta(\rho))$$

then testing:

$$H_0 : \rho = 0$$

against $H_a : \rho > 0$ is to reject null for small values of:

$$s(\rho_1) = \frac{Y'\Delta^{-1}(\rho_1)Y}{Y'Y} < c_\alpha.$$

The $s(\rho_1)$ test is BOI and the UMPI (Theorem 1, Bhatti, 2000). Similarly multi-stage and multiparametric LMMPI tests are given in Appendix A4 can also be derived. In the next subsection we will concentrate only on the 2SLR model and compute its power and critical values.

3.4.2 Approximation of c^*_α and Sizes using F Distribution

A comparison of the approximate critical values, c^*_α, and the exact critical values, c_α, for different values of n, $k = \frac{n}{2}$ (and/or $m = 2$) at 5 per cent significance level is calculated for the years (1961 and 1976), (1966 and 1971) and artificially generated log-normal variable data, respectively (see, Bhatti, 1995). The last data set has been used as a proxy for cross-sectional data in many empirical studies. Examples include, Goldfeld and Quandt (1965), Harvey and Phillips (1974), Harrison and McCabe (1979), Prakash (1979), Harrison (1980) and Buse (1980), among others. The exact values of the F distribution with ϑ_1, and ϑ_2 degrees of freedom are obtained by using the CDFFC subroutine of the GAUSS system version 2.0. It is worth noting that the results of the exact critical values, c_α and the approximate critical values, c^*_α are almost similar. This is because the same households have been used in the samples with different time periods.

The results reveal that in all cases the estimated sizes of the $s^*(\rho_1)$ test are less than the nominal level and greater than half of the nominal level, 0.05, even in small samples, except for $n = 32$, $\rho_1 = 0.1, 0.2$ and for $n = 64$, $\rho_1 = 0.1$. It can also be seen that there is a tendency for the estimated sizes of the $s^*(\rho_1)$ test to become closer to the nominal sizes when the sample size and the value of ρ_1 increase. This is one of the desirable properties of the POI test, namely that it always has sizes over the null parameter space close to the nominal significance level 0.05. The POI test has this property for large and moderate sample sizes. An advantage of this is that applied econometricians can use the standard F distribution to calculate approximate critical values of the requisite POI test.

In the rest of this section we have selected the most powerful tests among the five versions of the $s(\rho_1)$ tests with $\rho_1 = 0.1, 0.2, 0.3, 0.4$ and 0.5, respectively. After comparing the power performance of these tests, the test whose power is the closest to the power envelope (PE) has been chosen for the purpose of comparison with the existing tests. The next subsection compares the power performance of a selected $s(\rho_1)$ test with that of the LM1, LM2, and d* tests and the PE.

3.4.3 Power Comparisons of $s(\rho_1)$ Tests for the 2SLR Model

In general, under H_a, the power function of all five versions of the tests increases with the increase in sample size, block size and the value of ρ. For a block of size two, all of the $s(\rho_1)$ tests are approximately UMPI tests because they are close to the PE. For a block size of $\frac{n}{2}$, they are almost UMPI tests because their power is the closest to the PE (as far as these design matrices are concerned), since the critical regions for this particular block size are almost invariant to the choice of ρ_1 values. For example, consider all of the s(ρ_1) tests, for $\rho_1 = 0.1$ to 0.5, for n = 32 and block of size two. It is found that the power curves of all tests are approximately identical to the PE for all values of $\rho \leq 0.5$. The maximum power difference is negligible for lower values of ρ and/or large sample sizes.

For the comparison of higher blocks of sizes 4, 8 and 16, the s(0.1), s(0.2), s(0.3), s(0.4) and s(0.5) tests are MPI in the neighbourhood of ρ = 0.1, 0.2, 0.3, 0.4 and 0.5, respectively. The choice between the s(0.1) to s(0.5) tests depends upon the researcher's requirement. If a researcher is interested in detecting larger values of ρ in smaller sample sizes then perhaps the s(0.3), s(0.4) or s(0.5) tests could be favoured. If one is interested in detecting smaller values of ρ, then the s(0.1) or s(0.2) tests could be more suitable. For routine use, it is preferable to utilise the s(0.3) test, since under H_a the value of $\rho_1 = 0.3$ seems to be more practicable, and the calculations of its powers and sizes is the closest to the PE at the nominal size of 0.05, respectively. With the increase in the sample size this maximum difference between the PE and the power of s(0.3) tests reduces and with the higher block sizes it increases slightly.

Another procedure for comparing the powers of such tests is given by Cox and Hinkley (1974, p. 102). Their suggestion is to choose a test that maximizes some weighted average of the powers. The problem with this procedure is how to determine the appropriate weighted average, as the selected weights may vary from one person to another. To overcome this problem, Brooks (1992) suggested taking a simple average of the powers. Following Brooks, we have considered a simple average of the powers over a set of ρ values (that is, ρ = 0.1, 0.2, 0.3, 0.4, 0.5) and then compared these between tests. For extensive alternative approaches the reader may refer to the study conducted by Begum (2003). The average power procedure also favours our selection of the s(0.3) test for moderate sample sizes. Hence in the next part of this investigation, the power of the s(0.3) test will be compared with that of the LM1, LM2, *d* and *d** tests. Here some of the power calculations are reported from Bhatti (1995), so that the second part of our investigation should be self-contained.

3.4.4 Power Comparisons of s(0.3), LM1, LM2, d* and d Tests with PE

The numerical results for the powers of the s(0.3), LM1, LM2, *d** and d tests are tabulated in Tables A3.1 to A3.6, for different sample sizes, i.e. n = 32,

64 and 96, respectively. These results demonstrate that the powers of all tests increase as n, k and ρ increase, while other variables remain the same. As expected, the s(0.3) test is always the most powerful of the four tests for almost all values of ρ, followed by the LM1, LM2, d^* and d tests, respectively. The power difference between the s(0.3) and LM1 tests for smaller block sizes is very small. For example, consider the block size of two in Tables A3.1 to A3.6. It is found that the powers of both the tests are approximately identical; with the increase in the sample sizes both the power curves merge. Hence it is confirmed that the LM1 test is a good approximation to the s(0.3) test for this special case. Therefore, the LM1 test is also an approximate UMPI test, as is the case with the s(0.3) test, at least for these design matrices.

For the higher block sizes, the power of the s(0.3) test is superior to that of the LM1 test for all values of $\rho \geq 0.2$. This can be verified by considering $n = 32$, $k = 4$, where the maximum power difference between the LM1 and s(0.3) tests varies from 0.001 to 0.017, and for $k = 8$ varies from 0.006 to 0.028. As the sample size, block size and the value of ρ increase, this maximum difference between the powers becomes smaller and smaller and also the average powers of the s(0.3) and LM1 tests get closer and closer. For example, consider the case of $n = 96$, $k = 8$. For $0.2 \leq \rho \leq 0.5$, the power difference between the two tests varies from 0.003 to 0.001 and the average power difference is 0.002. Also note that for this particular case the power of the s(0.3) test is exactly identical to that of the PE. On the basis of these facts it may be concluded that the POI test is marginally better than the LM1 test, at least for small and moderate sample sizes.

The Durbin-Watson (d) test is the least powerful among all the tests under comparison, although it still has reasonable power in the larger samples and the smaller block sizes. The advantages of using the d test over all other tests are, firstly, it has reasonably small sample power properties when the block structure is unavailable, and secondly, its computations can easily be done by standard regression packages, within the existing bounds of the econometrics literature.

3.5 Concluding Remarks

In this chapter we have developed and illustrated efficient estimation procedures for the linear regression model with fixed and stochastic coefficients, block-wise heteroscedasticity and intra-block correlation, based on two-stage-blocked survey data. Following Hoque (1991), we applied a two-stage blocked sampling procedure, restricted by computational convenience, to Bangladesh data from the selected districts of Khulna and Rajshahi divisions. This chapter further considered the two-stage linear regression model with equicorrelated disturbances and derived BO. BOI, PO, POI and LMMPI tests for the hypothesis that the equicorrelation coefficient, ρ, has any given value. The power of the POI test was compared with that of the existing tests and the PE. The results as detailed in Appendix A3 suggest that the POI test is marginally better than the LM1 test for small and moderate sample sizes, at least for the data sets used in this experiment. It was found that both the tests are approximately UMPI for some selected block sizes. It also showed that for all values of m and p, the POI test is approximately UMPI. Further, the critical values of the POI test can also be obtainable from the standard F distribution for some selected block sizes. The approximate critical values using the F distribution were calculated. It was found that in 87 per cent of the cases the estimated sizes based on these critical values are greater than half of the nominal sizes. A LMMPI test for testing the hypothesis that ρ has different values for each block was derived and it was found that the LMMPI test is equivalent to the LM1 test. Moreover, it was observed that if the disturbances follow SSMN and SMN distributions then the PO test is called BO and the POI test is called BOI. A further extension in relation to multi-block effects is summarized in Appendix A4.

Notes

1 Some of the findings reported in this section are from Bhatti (2004).

2 If we assume $X^i_{jk} = 0$ and $\sigma^2=1$, then the model (3.1) becomes a standard symmetric multivariate model (see Bhatti and King, 1990 and Bhatti, 2000).

3 Alternatively known as stationary random coefficient models, for example see Hsiao (1986) and Baltagi (1996), which ignore equicorrelation within blocks.

4 Note that there is an identification problem if the intercept term is also assumed to follow (3.4).

5 If we asume $\varepsilon^i_k = 0$ then the inter-block random coefficient model reduces to a model with fixed coefficients and heteroscedastic variances. If we further assume $\varepsilon^i_k = 0$, and $(\sigma^i)^2 = \sigma^2$, then it will become a special case of Bhatti's (2000) SSMN and SMN models.

6 Swamy's (1970) model ignores equicorrelation within block and considers heteroscedasticity i.e. $(\sigma^i_k)^2$; k = 1,...,p. Whereas, in our model the variance terms of the diagonal elements of the ith block are $(\sigma^i_k)^2$, that is, constant within blocks.

7 Some of the findings in this section are reported from Bhatti (1995, 2000).

8 Note that $T^{-1}(\rho)$ obtained by Cholesky decomposition of the covariance matrix, $\Delta^{-1}(\rho) = (T^{-1}(\rho))'T^{-1}(\rho)$ is not unique.

Appendix A1: Sampling Design

The survey is based on two-stage blocksampling. The first-stage sampling units are districts of Khulna and Rajshahi division. From each district 20 farms are randomly selected. The districtwise farm distribution of each division is given below:

Division/district	Number of farms
Khulna	
Jessore	78
Khulna	92
Kushtia	79
Satkhira	80
Subtotal	329
Raishahi	
Natore	87
Nawabgunj	85
Rajshahi	99
Subtotal	271
Total	600

Appendix A2: The Measurements of the Variables

The measurements of the variables used in this experiment are as follows:

1 *gross output*: this is the money value of all the crops grown during the year 1986–87. It has been evaluated at the relevant crop-wise market prices (in thousand of Taka).
2 *biological-chemical (BC) input*: this includes both high yielding variety (HYV) and local variety of seeds, the chemical fertilizers, pesticides and insecticides. BC input per acre is measured in money terms, i.e. in thousands of Taka.
3 *human labour*: the data on human labour are given in adult man-days. This includes family as well as hired labour. In order to compute the wage-bill, family labour is assigned imputed value which is equal to the average of the wages of casual hired labour and permanently hired labour.
4 *size of the farm (land)*: this is measured in terms of acres. We take care of the differences in land quality across blocks partly by applying the random coefficient method in estimating the production functions.

Appendix A3: The Power Comparison of Various Tests

Table A3.1 Powers of the DW, LM1, LM2 and POI-tests for the n×4 design matrix of cross-sectional data for 1961 and 1976, n=32, p=4 and α=.05

Tests	*ρ=0.1*	*0.2*	*0.3*	*0.4*	*0.5*	*Average power*
			Block size 2			
PE	.099	.178	.294	.446	.620	–
s(0.3)	.099	.178	.294	.446	.619	.3272
LM1	.099	.178	.294	.445	.617	.3266
LM2	.066	.112	.196	.324	.492	.2380
d^*	.081	.126	.186	.265	.363	.2042
d	.081	.125	.184	.260	.356	.2012
			Block size 4			
PE	.140	.272	.430	.590	.734	–
s(0.3)	.139	.272	.430	.589	.732	.4324
LM1	.139	.271	.423	.577	.715	.4250
LM2	.094	.190	.323	.475	.627	.3418
d^*	.100	.175	.272	.390	.522	.2918
d	.099	.172	.268	.384	.516	.2878
			Block size 8			
PE	.164	.303	.442	.571	.686	–
s(0.3)	.163	.302	.442	.571	.684	.4321
LM1	.163	.296	.427	.547	.656	.4178
LM2	.118	.224	.343	.463	.578	.3452
d^*	.095	.162	.246	.345	.454	.2604
d	.095	.161	.245	.343	.452	.2592

Table A3.2 Powers of the DW, LM1, LM2 and the POI-tests for the n×4 design matrix of cross-sectional data for 1966 and 1971, n=32, p=4 and α=.05

Tests	*ρ=0.1*	*0.2*	*0.3*	*0.4*	*0.5*	*Average power*
			Block size 2			
PE	.099	.179	.295	.447	.620	–
s(0.3)	.099	.179	.295	.447	.620	.3280
LM1	.099	.178	.295	.446	.618	.3074
LM2	.066	.112	.196	.324	.493	.2250
d*	.082	.126	.187	.266	.365	.2052
d	.081	.125	.185	.262	.359	.1862
			Block size 4			
PE	.140	.274	.433	.595	740	–
s(0.3)	.140	.274	.433	.594	.738	.4358
LM1	.140	.272	.427	.582	.721	.4284
LM2	.095	.191	.326	.480	.632	.3448
d*	.102	.178	.278	.398	.533	.2978
d	.101	.175	.274	.394	.528	.2944
			Block size 8			
PE	.168	.309	.449	.579	.691	–
s(0.3)	.167	.309	.449	.577	.690	.4384
LM1	.167	.303	.435	.555	.661	.4242
LM2	.121	.230	.352	.472	.585	.3520
d*	.098	.167	.255	.357	.468	.2690
d	.097	.166	.254	.356	.466	.2678

Table A3.3 Powers of the DW, LM1, LM2 and the POI-tests for the n×4 design matrix of cross-sectional data for 1961 and 1976, n=64, p=4 and α=.05

Tests	*ρ=0.1*	*0.2*	*0.3*	*0.4*	*0.5*	*Average power*
			Block size 2			
PE	.134	.288	.505	.732	.900	–
s(0.3)	.134	.288	.505	.732	.899	.5116
LM1	.134	.288	.505	.732	.899	.5116
LM2	.084	.191	.379	.618	.832	.4208
d*	.102	.186	.307	.460	.630	.3370
d	.102	.185	.305	.456	.624	.3344
			Block size 4			
PE	.220	.485	.731	.891	.966	–
s(0.3)	.219	.485	.731	.890	.966	.6582
LM1	.220	.483	.728	.887	.963	.6562
LM2	.146	.373	.632	.830	.940	.5842
d*	.143	.298	.493	.687	.842	.4926
d	.142	.295	.489	.683	.839	.4896
			Block size 8			
PE	.297	.575	.772	.889	.952	–
s(0.3)	.295	.574	.772	.889	.951	.6962
LM1	.296	.596	.763	.880	.944	.6958
LM2	.215	.473	.689	.833	.919	.6258
d*	.148	.304	.486	.657	.797	.4784
d	.147	.303	.485	.657	.797	.4778

Table A3.4 Powers of the DW, LM1, LM2 and the POI-tests for the n×4 design matrix of cross-sectional data for 1966 and 1971, n=64, p=4 and α=.05

Tests	*ρ=0.1*	*0.2*	*0.3*	*0.4*	*0.5*	*Average power*
			Block size 2			
PE	.134	.288	.505	.732	.900	–
s(0.3)	.134	.288	.505	.732	.899	.5116
LM1	.134	.288	.505	.731	.899	.5114
LM2	.084	.191	.379	.618	.832	.4208
d*	.102	.186	.307	.460	.630	.3370
d	.102	.185	.305	.456	.624	.3344
			Block size 4			
PE	.220	.486	.733	.891	.967	–
s(0.3)	.220	.486	.733	.890	.966	.6592
LM1	.220	.484	.729	.888	.964	.6570
LM2	.147	.374	.634	.831	.940	.5852
d*	.144	.299	.495	.689	.844	.4942
d	.143	.297	.492	.686	.841	.4918
			Block size 8			
PE	.298	.577	.774	.890	.952	–
s(0.3)	.296	.576	.774	.890	.952	.6976
LM1	.297	.571	.764	.881	.945	.6916
LM2	.216	.476	.691	.834	.920	.6274
d*	.149	.306	.489	.661	.800	.4810
d	.149	.306	.489	.661	.801	.4812

Table A3.5 Powers of the DW, LM1, LM2 and the POI-tests for the n×4 design matrix of cross-sectional data for 1961 and 1976, n=96, p=4 and α=.05

Tests	*ρ=0.1*	*0.2*	*0.3*	*0.4*	*0.5*	*Average power*
			Block size 2			
PE	.165	.386	.664	.881	.977	–
s(0.3)	.165	.386	.664	.881	.977	.6146
LM1	.165	.386	.664	.881	.977	.6146
LM2	.103	.272	.542	.806	.954	.5354
d*	.120	.242	.415	.616	.800	.4386
d	.120	.240	.412	.612	.796	.4360
			Block size 4			
PE	.289	.639	.879	.973	.996	–
s(0.3)	.288	.639	.879	.973	.996	.7550
LM1	.289	.638	.877	.972	.996	.7544
LM2	.198	.528	.814	.951	.992	.6966
d*	.178	.398	.648	.843	.950	.6034
d	.177	.396	.645	.840	.949	.6014
			Block size 8			
PE	.406	.747	.913	.974	.993	–
s(0.3)	.404	.747	.913	.974	.993	.8062
LM1	.404	.744	.909	.972	.992	.8042
LM2	.306	.660	.868	.956	.988	.7556
d*	.194	.429	.664	.836	.935	.6116
d	.193	.427	.663	.835	.934	.6104

Table A3.6 Powers of the DW, LM1, LM2 and the POI-tests for the n×4 design matrix of cross-sectional data for 1966 and 1971, n=96, p=4 and α=.05

Tests	*ρ=0.1*	*0.2*	*0.3*	*0.4*	*0.5*	*Average power*
			Block size 2			
PE	.165	.386	.664	.881	.977	–
s(0.3)	.165	.386	.664	.881	.977	.6146
LM1	.165	.386	.664	.881	.977	.6146
LM2	.103	.272	.542	.806	.954	.5354
d*	.120	.242	.415	.616	.800	.4386
d	.120	.241	.412	.612	.796	.4362
			Block size 4			
PE	.289	.640	.879	.973	.996	–
s(0.3)	.288	.640	.879	.973	.996	.7554
LM1	.289	.639	.877	.972	.996	.7546
LM2	.199	.529	.815	.951	.992	.6972
d*	.178	.400	.650	.845	.951	.6048
d	.177	.398	.647	.843	.950	.6030
			Block size 8			
PE	.408	.750	.914	.975	.994	–
s(0.3)	.407	.750	.914	.975	.994	.8080
LM1	.407	.746	.911	.973	.993	.8060
LM2	.309	.664	.870	.957	.988	.7576
d*	.196	.434	.670	.840	.937	.6154
d	.196	.433	.669	.839	.936	.6146

Table A3.7 Some optimal tests for two-stage SSMN and SMN distributions

Name of tests	Null hypothesis	Alternative hypothesis	Form of covariance matrix	Test statistics
SSMN model				
1 LB	$\rho=0$	$\rho>0$	$\Delta(\rho_0)$	$s = Y'(I_n - D)Y < c_\alpha$
2 BO	$\rho=0$	$\rho>0$	$\Delta(\rho_1)$	$r(\rho_1) = Y'(\Delta^{-1}(\rho_1) - I_n)Y$
3 LMMP	$\rho_i=0$ $i=1,\ldots,m$	$\rho_i\geq 0$ $i=1,\ldots,m$	$\Delta(\rho_i)$	$d = Y'(I_n - D)Y < c_2$
SMN				
4 POI	$\rho=0$	$\rho>0$	$\sigma^2\Delta(\rho_i)$	$s(\rho_1) = \dfrac{Y'(\Delta^{-1}(\rho_1)Y}{Y'Y} < c_\alpha$
6 LMMPI	$\rho_i=0$ $i=1,\ldots,m$	$\rho_i\geq 0$ $i=1,\ldots,m$	$\sigma^2\Delta(\rho_i)$	$s = \dfrac{Y'(I_n - D)Y}{Y'Y} < c_2$

Table A3.8 Some optimal tests for three-stage SSMN and SMN distributions

Name of tests	Null hypothesis	Alternative hypothesis	Form of covariance matrix	Test statistics
SSMN				
1 LMMP	$\rho_1=\rho_2=0$	$\rho_1\geq 0,\rho_2\geq 0$	$\Omega(\rho_1,\rho_2)$	$d^* = Y'\{2I_n-(D_1+D_2)\}Y < c_3$
2 PO	$\rho_1=\rho_2=0$	$\rho_1=\rho_{11}>0$ $\rho_2=\rho_{22}>0$	$\Omega(\rho_{11},\rho_{22})$	$r(\rho_{11},\rho_{22}) = Y'(\Omega^{-1}(\rho_{11},\rho_{22})-I_n)Y < c$
3 PO (sub-block effects)	$\rho_2=0,\rho_1>0$	$\rho_1=\rho_{11}>0$ $\rho_2=\rho_{21}>0$	under $H_0{:}\Omega_{10}=\Omega(\rho_{10},0)$ under $H_a{:}\Omega_{11}=\Omega(\rho_{11},\rho_{21})$	$r(\rho_{10},\rho_{11},\rho_{21}) = Y'(\Omega_{11}^{-1}-\Omega_{10}^{-1})Y < c_\alpha$
SMN				
4 LMMPI	$\rho_1=\rho_2=0$	$\rho_1\geq 0,\rho_2\geq 0$	$\sigma^2\Omega(\rho_1,\rho_2)$	$d = 2-\frac{Y'(D_1+D_2)Y}{Y'Y} < c_\alpha$
5 POI	$\rho_1=\rho_2=0$	$\rho_1=\rho_{11}>0$ $\rho_2=\rho_{22}>0$	$\sigma^2\Omega(\rho_{11},\rho_{22})$	$s(\rho_{11},\rho_{22}) = \frac{Y'\Omega(\rho_{11},\rho_{22})Y}{Y'Y} < c_\alpha$
6 POI (sub-block effects)	$\rho_2=0,\rho_1>0$	$\rho_1=\rho_{11}>0$ $\rho_2=\rho_{22}>0$	$\sigma^2\Omega_{10}$ $\sigma^2\Omega_{11}$	$s(\rho_{10},\rho_{11},\rho_{21}) = \frac{Y'\Omega_{11}Y}{Y\Omega_{10}Y} < c_\alpha$

Appendix A4: Some Useful Matrix Results

This appendix gives some important matrix results which are useful in Chapters 3, 4, 5 and 6.

Lemma 1

Let $\Delta(\rho) = (1 - \rho)I_n + \rho.D$, where $\frac{-1}{n-1} < \rho < 1$, D is given by (3.5) and n = mk, then one can have the following expressions:

1 $|\Delta(\rho)| = \left[(1-\rho)^{k-1}[1+(k-1)]\rho\right]^n$;

2 $\Delta^{-1}(\rho) = (1-\rho)^{-1}\left[I_n - \rho\{1+(k-1)\rho\}^{-1}D\right]$;

3 The eigenvalues of $\Delta^{-1}(\rho)$ and $\frac{1}{(1-\rho)}$ and $\frac{1}{[1+(k-1)\rho]}$ with multiplicity $m(k-1)$ and m, respectively;

4 The eigenvalues of $\Delta(\rho)$ are $(1-\rho)$ and $[1+(k-1)\rho]$ with multiplicity $m(k-1)$ and m, respectively;

5 The matrix $\Delta(\rho)$, can be expressed in functional form as

$$\Delta(\rho) = (f_1(\rho)I_n + f_2(\rho)D)^{-1}, \text{ where}$$

$$f_1(\rho) = (1-\rho)^{-1}, f_1(\rho) = -\rho[(1-\rho)\{1+(k-1)\rho\}]^{-1}.$$

The proof is straightforward and is therefore omitted. For the special case when m = 1, this lemma reduces to Rao (1973, p. 67, problem 1.1).

Lemma 2

If A is n × n and B is n × n, then the eigenvalues of AB are the eigenvalues of BA, although the eigenvectors of the two matrices need not be the same (see Graybill, 1969, p. 208).

Lemma 3

Let $D_1 = I_m \otimes E_{sT}$, $D_2 = I_{ms} \otimes E_T$, $n = msT$ and $\lambda_i(A)$ denote the ith eigenvalue of the matrix A, then:

$$\lambda_i(D_1 + D_2) = \lambda_i(D_1) + \lambda_i(D_2)$$

for $i = 1,\ldots,n$. These eigenvalues are $T(s + 1)$, T and zeroes with multiplicities of m, $m(s - 1)$, and $ms(T - 1)$, respectively.

Chapter 4

Model Selection Procedures

4.1 Introduction

Much of the literature in econometrics is mainly concerned with the problems of estimation and inference from a sample of data. The properties of estimation techniques, and the quality of inferences, are heavily dependent on the correct specification of the model under consideration. For example, if a relevant variable is omitted, estimators are typically biased. If the disturbances are autocorrelated or heteroscedastic, there is typically a loss of efficiency in the estimators and the standard errors may be biased. This can lead to incorrect inferences. Thus, it is of paramount importance to invest considerable effort in checking the correctness of the specification of the model under consideration. In other words, we need to search for the best model from a set of alternative possible models using the available data. This is typically known as model selection in the econometrics literature.

The term *model* is quite familiar to economists, econometricians, statisticians and to researchers of various other disciplines. It is, in a simple sense, an approximation of the real data which represents the relevance of a particular phenomenon. An econometric model, as defined by Grassa (1989, p. 1), is 'an analytical characterisation of the joint probability distribution of some random variables of interest which yields some information on how the actual economy works'. In fact, it is slightly different from a mathematical economic model, which approximately describes the behaviour of an economy within the framework of a set of assumptions. In other words, an economic model typically involves some degree of abstraction from reality whereas an econometric model reflects this abstraction in practice (see, for example, Zarembka, 1974).

Unfortunately, as indicated by Bergstrom (1993), economic models are usually less precise than necessary in order to be used for statistical fitting and testing. In such a situation, econometricians usually ask questions such as: What are the attributes of a good model? What sorts of specification errors are likely to be made in practice? What are the consequences of the various specification errors? What remedies can one adopt to get back to the correct model if a specification error has been made? Thus, econometric models are usually more precise in the sense that parameters of such models can be estimated and tested through statistical techniques using available data. In other words, we are able to see how well the model fits the data. There is still the problem that for one modelling situation there might be different specifications which constitute different models in the literature. Thus an obvious question arises as to which model provides the best characterization from the viewpoint of the data. The term *model selection* emerges from this simple preliminary idea.

For many research problems we always want a good approximation of the data through a simple model so that we can easily understand it and apply it. From a statistical viewpoint, we wish to select the model that is closest to reality as represented by the data, or equivalently we wish to reject models that contain large errors due to approximations and random fluctuations. The question is, how can we select such a desirable model in practice? In most practical situations we get a limited number of observations which involve partial information regarding the underlying phenomena. In dealing with such poor information there may be many ways to make mistakes in deciding the best possible model. Moreover, if a bad choice of model is made it may lead to practitioners being misguided in many ways. For example, it may provide inaccurate parameter estimates and hence may yield misleading forecasts. In order to avoid these unwelcome problems, at least partially, our view is that good model selection strategies can be extremely useful in helping choose an adequate model rather than making a more arbitrary choice of model.

As stated in earlier chapters, econometricians, unlike physical, chemical or biological scientists, are often forced to work with non-experimental data, which adds various complications to econometric model building in practice. Econometricians usually expect that economic theory will help them to find causal links and formulate desired models. Unfortunately, existing economic theory often fails to suggest an adequate functional form of such relationships. Because of this weakness in economic theory, econometricians often use their own subjective judgement in deciding on the functional forms of models. In doing so, they have proposed different alternative forms to reflect the relationship between dependent and independent variables. However, the question again arises; how should one model be selected as the 'correct' form from a number of alternative possible models? This is a problem that can also be solved through good model selection procedures.

In addition to the above problem of functional forms, econometricians often ask questions such as which regressors should be included in a regression equation? What is the appropriate order of a time series model, say, an autoregressive (AR), or moving average (MA), or autoregressive moving average (ARMA), or autoregressive integrated moving average (ARIMA) or autoregressive fractionally integrated moving average (ARFIMA) model? What lags should be included in a vector autoregressive (VAR) model, or in a distributed lag model, or in an autoregressive conditional heteroscedasticity (ARCH) or generalized autoregressive conditional heteroscedasticity (GARCH) model? What error structure is appropriate for a model? These are questions which the data can often be used to answer. Today model selection has become an important area of research in econometrics. In reality, the selection of a model based on the data is almost always made in applied econometric research. As discussed in Körösi et al. (1992), model selection strategies should be properly employed in all phases of a model building process. Körösi et al. also argue that the concept of model selection does not necessarily mean that a particular model should be regarded as the only one possible and an *a priori* true model. Rather a good model selection procedure evaluates the model under investigation compared to other alternative models. The evaluation might be based on some statistical criteria, say, accuracy, parsimony, goodness of fit, predictive power, etc. Nevertheless, it is not unlikely that different investigators could easily end up with different models for the same set of data only because they use different methodologies (see for example, Granger et al., 1995). This is simply because different methodologies are based on different principles and therefore these may lead to different results.

There are a number of model selection techniques in the literature. Generally these techniques may be classified into four broad categories:

1 classical hypothesis testing based procedures;
2 residual error sum of squares rules;
3 criteria for forecast evaluation;
4 information criteria (IC) including Bayesian and non-Bayesian approaches.

However, if we look at the development of the model selection literature, we see that the list of contributors who have worked in this area is very rich and long. They have covered a wide range of research on model selection most of which is related to IC-based procedures. These particular procedures are probably the most viable, popular and widely used methods for model selection in econometrics. As shown in Clayton et al. (1986), IC-based procedures can be regarded as a more substantial approach to model selection than any other procedures. Furthermore, Granger et al. (1995) note that IC-based procedures involve fewer limitations than hypothesis test-based procedures, and hence have become more popular with practitioners. Thus, the focus in this chapter will be on IC-based procedures, which can be defined as maximizing the log-likelihood function minus a penalty term, where the penalty term is a function of the number of parameters included in the model and possibly dependent on sample size. The nature of IC-based procedures is that if the penalty is large, all other things being equal, then smaller models are favoured, whereas for smaller penalties, the larger models are favoured. Thus the IC which is best for a given problem, can be difficult to determine.

There has been a long debate about the proper form of the penalty function in IC-based model selection procedures in the literature. This is because, by slightly changing the form of penalty function, one can come up with a new criterion. Often asymptotic techniques have been used to justify the different choices of penalty functions. But this justification may not always be helpful in small samples. For example, Grose and King (1994) have shown that the form of likelihood functions can, sometimes, influence the choice of model rather than the choice being made purely by the information in the data. In this regard, King et al. (1995) point out that the vast hypothesis testing literature has some successful strategies, e.g., good use of parameter restrictions and proper handling of nuisance parameters to improve the inferences. In hypothesis testing, it is often very hard to find the best possible test for a given size. This is because a good test mainly depends on the appropriate knowledge of the true parameter value which is, most of the time, unknown. As a result the best test is also unknown. The more we can narrow the range in which the true parameter value lies under the alternative, the more powerful we can make our test.

Akaike's (1973) information criterion (AIC) has been found to be an efficient model selection criterion both in small and large samples. As a result, this has been considered as one of the leading and very commonly used selection criteria in the literature (see for example, Mills and Prasad, 1992; Hurvich and Tsai, 1993; Ishiguro et al.; 1994; and Fox, 1995). In this context, Hughes (1997), Hughes and King (2003) and Hughes et al. (2004) reports that due to the good properties of AIC in small and large samples, it has been used very frequently in many physical sciences to select the best-specified model. The author also makes the point that AIC can be used because it does better when the number of parameters increases with sample size. Obviously this can be regarded as an important part of an econometrician's toolkit.

The organisation of the chapter is as follows. In section 4.2, a brief review of general model selection procedures is given. Section 4.3 presents a survey of IC-based model selection work, aiming to prove that there are still some promising areas yet to be done within IC-based procedures. Section 4.4 describes the importance of the Box-Cox transformation technique in econometric analysis. The role of bootstrap technique in econometrics and statistics is presented in section 4.5. Some concluding remarks are given in the final section.

4.2 A Brief Review of General Model Selection Procedures

Over the last two decades various testing mechanisms, empirical rules, search procedures and information criteria have been proposed for model selection in the literature. Among others, a partial list includes Akaike (1973), Gaver and Geisel (1974), Hocking (1976), Leamer (1978), Thompson (1978), Schwarz (1978), Hannan and Quinn (1979), Amemiya (1980), Akaike (1981), White (1982a, 1982b, 1983, 1990), MacKinnon (1983), McAleer (1987), Rissanen (1986, 1987, 1988), Quinn (1988), Nishi (1988), Pötscher (1991), Sin et al. (1992), Maddala (1992), Hurvich et al. (1993), Shah (1994), Fox (1995), King et al. (1995) and Granger et al. (1995), Grose (1998), Rahman and King (1997, 1999), Atukorola (1999), Bose (2002), Hossain (2002), Hossain and King (1996, 1997, 2000, 2003), Hossain and Bhatti (2003) and King and Bose (2003) are among others. Let us consider a simple LR model of the form (3.27) and express it in terms of time series structure as:

$$Y = X\beta + u \tag{4.1}$$

where in (4.1) y is a $T \times 1$ vector of dependent observations, X is a $T \times (k-1)$ matrix of the independent observations, β is a $(k-1) \times 1$ vector of coefficients and u is a $T \times 1$ vector of independent disturbance terms each assumed to follow the normal distribution with mean zero and variance σ^2. Note that the structure (4.1) is almost similar to that discussed in Chapter 3 while addressing the testing issues in the 2SLR model. Here we will briefly discuss some of the important model selection criteria, mainly based on (4.1). In the history of econometrics, perhaps the first model selection criteria were R^2 and adjusted R^2, which are given as:

$$R^2 = 1 - \frac{RSS}{TSS} \tag{4.2}$$

and:

$$\bar{R}^2 = 1 - (1 - R^2)\frac{T-1}{T-k+1} \qquad (4.3)$$

respectively, where RSS is the residual sum of squares, TSS is the total sum of squares, T is the sample size and k is the total number of parameters included in the model under consideration. It is well known that addition of an extra regressor in a model usually increases the value of R^2. Thus, Theil (1961) proposed the adjusted R^2 for model comparison yielding a criterion which is sensitive to the number of remaining degrees of freedom. Theil (1971) showed that a decision rule which favours the model with the largest adjusted R^2 will result 'on average' in the correct choice of model. As can be seen from the definition of the adjusted R^2, it takes into account the goodness of fit of the model, as well as its parsimony. But a difficulty arises when the model which fitted the data well does not seem to have a good predictive performance. In particular, Schmidt (1973, 1975) has shown that the adjusted R^2 criterion does not help us in selecting the true model when a regression contains both the variables of the true model plus some extra irrelevant independent variables. Moreover, it has been suggested that the adjusted R^2 does not penalise the loss of degrees of freedom heavily enough in practice (see, for example, Amemiya, 1985). As shown in Fox (1995), the other equivalent form of adjusted R-squared through the likelihood function is given by:

$$\bar{R}^2 = L(\hat{\theta}) - \frac{T}{2}\ln(T-k). \qquad (4.4)$$

Here in (4.4), $L(\hat{\theta})$ is the maximized log likelihood function of the regression model (1) and $\theta' = (\beta', \sigma^2)$.

After Theil suggested his adjusted R^2 a number of other model selection criteria have been proposed in the literature. Some noteworthy examples include Schmidt's cross-validation criterion (1971), Amemiya's PC criterion (1972), Akaike information criterion (AIC) (1973), Mallows' C_p criterion (1973), Hocking's S_p criterion (1976), Schwarz's Bayesian information criterion (BIC) (1978) and Hannan and Quinn's HQ criterion (1979). Among these, Akaike information criterion is one of the most commonly used criteria in economics and econometrics (see for example, Hurvich et al., 1991; Mills et al., 1992 and Fox, 1995). Akaike (1973) proposes this criterion as a combination of the use of the maximized likelihood function through the familiar Kullback-Leibler information theory and the use of an appropriate penalty function which for (4.1) is given as:

$$AIC = L(\hat{\theta}) - k. \tag{4.5}$$

Like (4.4), this criterion is also in a penalized maximized log likelihood form, with the penalty term being k, the number of parameters included in the model. This is a good criterion for the best fit of a model rather than its parsimony. In fact, this is not a serious defect of AIC because when we try to estimate the true distribution from a finite data set, the concept of parsimony is not so useful (see, for example, Sakamoto et al., 1986). However, recently there has been strong evidence about the tendency of AIC to overfit the data (Hurvich and Tsai, 1989; Mills et al., 1992). Hurvich and Tsai (1989), on the other hand, found that AIC is a negatively biased estimate of the Kullback-Liebler information when the dimension of the candidate model increases in comparison to the sample size. To overcome this problem, they propose a bias corrected version of AIC for regression and autoregressive time series models, denoted by AIC_c, which is the sum of AIC and a penalty term given by:

$$AIC_c = \text{AIC} + \frac{2k(k+1)}{T-k-1} \tag{4.6}$$

However, the additional penalty, as claimed by the authors, leads to a choice of substantially less biased and more parsimonious models rather than those chosen by the usual AIC. The authors also found that AIC_c significantly outperforms AIC in the case of approximating models. However, this criterion is of most use when the sample size is small because, when T is large enough relative to k, the second term in (4.6) becomes negligible.

Another important problem with AIC is inconsistency, in the sense that it does not select the model having maximum information with probability tending to one as T tends to infinity. This problem seems to be overcome by Schwarz's Bayesian information criterion (BIC), which is usually recommended for large sample cases. As with the AIC, BIC is also a widely used criterion in econometrics today and is given by:

$$\text{BIC} = L(\hat{\theta}) - \frac{k\ln(T)}{2}. \tag{4.7}$$

Similar to AIC, this criterion is also in penalized log likelihood form, where the penalty term is $k\ln(T)/2$. The main aim of AIC and BIC is to select the model with the maximum information (or minimum loss of information) available, but they are not particularly concerned about whether a true model exists or not. However, one important point to note is that Schwarz's

BIC assumes a proper prior distribution for the parameters of the proposed model and is derived from a consideration of the asymptotic behaviour of the Bayes estimators. Akaike (1981) indicates that the use of BIC in many situations has been problematic because its use is possible under the strong assumptions of prior distribution of the parameters. However, this difficulty has been solved by Rissanen (1986, 1987, 1988), who derived a criterion based on stochastic complexity and the associated minimum description length (MDL) principle which is similar to Schwarz's BIC but with more general applicability.

Mallows (1964) suggested another criterion which has been extensively used in economics, econometrics and many other social sciences. The criterion is given in the following penalized log form:

$$C_p = L(\hat{\theta}) - \frac{T}{2}\ln\left(1 + \frac{2k}{T-k}\right). \tag{4.8}$$

Based on a slightly different form from the above, Rothman (1968) has proposed another criterion which can be expressed in penalized log likelihood form such as:

$$J_p = L(\hat{\theta}) - \frac{T}{2}\ln(T+k) + \frac{T}{2}\ln(T-k). \tag{4.9}$$

Later, Akaike (1969) calls this criterion the Final Prediction Error (FPE), whereas Amemiya (1972, 1980) calls it the Prediction Criterion (PC). On the other hand, Hocking (1976) suggests a criterion which is reviewed thoroughly by Thompson (1978) and can be expressed in log form as:

$$S_p = L(\hat{\theta}) + \frac{T}{2}\ln(T-k) + \frac{T}{2}\ln(T-k-1). \tag{4.10}$$

An alternative justification for Hocking's S_p criterion has been given by Breiman and Freedman (1983). However, our main purpose is not to go through the derivation and justification of these three predictive criteria given in (4.8), (4.9) and (4.10), for details of which, refer to Thompson (1978). One major limitation of Hocking's S_p criterion is it is not applicable for nonstochastic regressors like other criteria mentioned above. One important point is the criteria C_p, PC and S_p, in contrast to adjusted R-squared, are specifically more interested in parsimony of a model, which improves the mean square error (MSE) of prediction.

The criterion due to Hannan and Quinn (1979), which is less commonly used but useful for comparison to AIC and BIC, can be written in penalized log form as:

$$HQ = L(\hat{\theta}) - k\ln(\ln(T)). \tag{4.11}$$

This procedure is particularly employed to choose the overall lag length in a vector autoregressive model. Another criterion for model selection mainly pointed out by Schmidt (1971) is called cross-validation (CV) and involves splitting the sample into roughly two equal parts, where the first part is used for fitting a model and the second part is reserved for assessing the predictive ability of the model (often called model validation). In fact, the CV procedure is used to determine the loss of efficiency in parameter estimation of the model by providing a measure of future prediction error. But one important problem is, like AIC and C_p, this criterion is inconsistent. Another problem is that calculation of CV is really cumbersome. Moreover, this criterion is rather different in nature from the other criteria mentioned above. However, a good approximation to CV, called the generalized cross-validation (GCV) criterion, has been derived recently by Fox (1995) in penalized log likelihood form, which is given as:

$$GCV = L(\hat{\theta}) + T\ln\left(1 - \frac{k}{T}\right). \tag{4.12}$$

Note that the criteria (except AIC and BIC) which have been presented here in typical penalized log likelihood form are due to Fox (1995). Also note that some practitioners have considered Theil's adjusted R^2 criterion and Schmidt's CV criterion as informal decision rules for model selection (see for example, Zarembka, 1974).

In summary, the model selection procedures discussed above belong to, as indicated by Grassa (1989), parametric methods where it is assumed that the observations come from a particular family of parametric distributions. However, these parametric methods roughly fall into two categories, namely, Bayesian and non-Bayesian, where the former considers prior information about the parameter of the proposed model and the latter explicitly specifies a loss function. See for example Linhart and Zuchini (1986). Again the non-Bayesian procedure may be of two types where the first depends on the selection problems under a decision framework whereas the second depends on data to discriminate among models instead of saying anything about loss functions (see, for example, Grassa, 1989).

4.3 A Survey of IC-Based Model Selection Procedures

The range of work on the development of model selection procedures in econometrics is very wide today. It ranges from stepwise hypothesis testing to IC-based model selection procedures. In this section, our purpose is to present a brief discussion on IC-based work so far reported in the model selection literature during the last two decades. We will highlight an important point that there are still some promising areas of research yet to be done on this topic. However, after this discussion, a brief survey on the BCT technique will be presented in the next section indicating the significance of using this technique for our problem.

Akaike (1973) was the pioneer who introduced the famous information criterion, AIC, on which a large amount of research has been conducted since it was first proposed. He showed in the paper how the classical maximum likelihood principle can be considered to be an effective method in estimating the distance between the proposed and the true probability distributions through an information-based criterion. The author claims that his proposed method can be applied to the choice of the estimate of a finite parameter model when a number of alternative possible ML estimates are obtained corresponding to the various restrictions of that model. This can also provide solutions for various practical problems related to statistical hypothesis testing rather than statistical decision or estimation. The paper presents some numerical examples which prove that the proposed method can eventually be replaced by many of the conventional statistical procedures.

In connection with the above work, Akaike (1974) pointed out that the hypothesis testing procedure is not a proper means of statistical model identification. Rather, he proposed another procedure called minimum AIC estimate (MAICE) for model identification which provides a more capable procedure and is free from many shortcomings involved in conventional hypothesis testing procedure. The author also claims that although MAICE can be widely useful in every field of statistical model building, its practical utility in time series analysis is especially significant. Several numerical examples are given in the paper to show how MAICE provides better answers to the problems of time series analysis than the conventional approach.

Tong (1975) developed a procedure for determining the order of the AR signal process from noisy data by employing AIC. The procedure is illustrated through some numerical examples using both artificially generated and real data. Interestingly, Tong's problem is almost equivalent to the classical statistical problem of factor analysis where the parameters are estimated by the ML method and the order is determined by the MAICE procedure given by Akaike (1974). Thus, Tong's procedure can be broadly viewed as an extension of the MAICE procedure for order determination in factor analysis. Using AIC, Tong (1975) also proposed another procedure for the determination of the order for an ergodic Markov chain process where the number of states is finite. His proposed procedure explains the asymptotic properties of the ML ratio statistics and Kullback-Liebler information for discriminating between two distributions. Numerical examples are also presented in the paper.

Shibata (1976), on the other hand, analysed the statistical properties of Akaike's (1973, 1974) proposed method for statistical model fitting. In particular, the author examined the asymptotic distributions of the selected order when the order is determined by this method. He also evaluated the asymptotic quadratic risks of estimates for regression parameters. The paper presents some computational experiments in the case of small samples. Bhansali and Downham (1977) also examined some properties of the distribution of the order of an autoregressive model selected by Akaike's final prediction error (FPE) criterion. A range of simulation experiments were conducted using this criterion.

What set of regressors should be included in a regression model is an obvious model selection problem sometimes known as the variable selection problem. Thompson (1978) examined methods for variable selection according to whether the regressors included in the models are fixed or random. For fixed regressors he recommended Mallows' C_p criterion or Allen's A_p criterion whereas for random regressors he preferred Hocking's S_p procedure for variable selection in multiple regression. Sawa (1978), on the other hand, proposes some statistical criteria for general model selection in regression analysis. His main intention was to see the discrepancy between the true and the candidate model. However, in his paper, he pointed out that although a complicated model usually provided a better approximation to reality, in most cases simple or parsimonious models are likely to be preferred by practitioners. The author also argues that in general, closeness to the true distribution is incompatible with parsimony, which means there is a clear trade off between these two properties. However, to satisfy these two properties simultaneously, Theil's adjusted R^2 and AIC among others, have been well proposed criteria in the literature. The author suggested a new procedure which is considerably different from these two criteria and is based on the minimum attainable Bayes risk to identify the most adequate model from a number of alternative possible models.

Kipnis (1989) considers the problem of estimating the predictive performance of a model from a class of regression models. In his paper, he argues that the theory behind usual estimators is no longer valid when model selection and estimation are from the same set of data because the former usually affects the estimators of the parameters. Holmes et al. (1989) have also conducted a simulation experiment for comparison of five different model selection criteria, namely, Theil's (1961) adjusted R^2 criterion, AIC, BIC, Amemiya's (1980) PC and Hannan's (1981) HC criterion. Their results indicate that when the true relationship between dependent and independent variables is weak, Theil's (1961) adjusted R^2 criterion is most likely to result in the correct inference.

Hurvich et al. (1990) explore the impact of model selection on inference in the linear regression model. In their paper, they suggest that model selection and inference should be treated as separate stages of the data rather than using the same data set for both. They also suggest that the available data set should not be split into two parts where one part is used for model selection and the other used for inference. Bai et al. (1990) proposed a different approach called generalized information criterion for selecting among nested and non-nested models. They used gamma, Weibull and log-normal distributions to compare their selection procedures with traditional methods.

Pollak et al. (1991), suggest a new approach to model selection which is based on two new concepts: the dominance ordering (DO) and the likelihood dominance criterion (LDC). The DO is constructed by nesting two hypotheses in a composite of a given size and examining the possible outcomes of testing them against the composite. This procedure simply requires maximum likelihood estimates of the two hypotheses, but not of the composite, although it does require specifying its parametric size. The LDC generalizes the DO by considering a set of admissible composite parametric sizes rather than a single composite parametric size which may usually include all sizes of practical interest. When the DO corresponding to different admissible composite parametric sizes disagrees, the LDC is regarded as indecisive. However, in most practical situations, the LDC has been decisive for model selection. Symbolically the three different decisions made by the LDC are as follows:

1 the LDC prefers H_1 to H_2 if $L_2 - L_1 < [C(n_2+1) - C(n_1+1)]/2$;
2 the LDC is indecisive between H_1 and H_2;
3 if $[C(n_2-n_1+1) - C(1)]/2 > L_2 - L_1 > [C(n_2+1) - C(n_1+1)]/2$
the LDC prefers H_2 to H_1 if $L_2 - L_1 > [C(n_2-n_1+1) - C(1)]/2$.

Here L_1 and L_2 are log likelihoods and n_1 and n_2 are the number of parameters for two competing hypotheses H_1 and H_2, respectively. *C(n)* are the critical values of the chi-square distribution with n degrees of freedom at some significance level. However, when two hypotheses contain the same number of parameters, the DO and the LDC both prefer the one with the higher likelihood whereas for different numbers of parameters both provide a generalisation of this procedure for model selection. The authors also proved that their proposed approach is consistent with the classical statistical approach. This approach seems to be more related to modelling through hypothesis testing rather than modelling through some information criteria.

Zhang (1992) has given a common form for all information criteria such as:

$$C(k,\lambda) = RSS(k) + \lambda k, \qquad 0 \leq k \leq K, \tag{4.13}$$

where RSS(k) is the residual sum of squares for a general linear regression model, K is the total number of covariates included in the model, some of which (say, k_1) possess zero values. So, the remaining $k(K-k_1)$ are entered in the model and λ is the penalty for overfitting. The criterion (4.13) is commonly known as the final prediction error (FPE) criterion. For different values of λ, this criterion corresponds to different criteria. For example, C_p criterion and AIC correspond to (4.13) with $\lambda = 2$, and the Bayesian information criterion (BIC) corresponds to $\lambda = log(T)$. In the paper, the author mainly studied the distributional properties of $\hat{k}$ and $C(\hat{k},\lambda)$ where $\hat{k} = arg\ min\ C(k,\lambda)$, to see how the criterion works in terms of recovering the truth. There is a strong controversy regarding the value of λ for which the criterion is optimal. In this context, the author indicates that a penalty term of $\lambda > 5$ gains very little in performance. On the other hand, one can easily notice that small λ values are clearly unsatisfactory. Therefore, the author recommends that the penalty terms should be chosen between 1.5 and 5 for most practical situations. While discussing the distributional properties of (4.13), the author deals with the so-called grouped CV criterion, where he found some insights about how the partition should be done in this method. He also discusses the small sample performance of his proposed method through simulation experiments.

Hurvich and Tsai (1989) note that the cause of the overfitting problem for AIC has been clearly evident when one examines plots of AIC and the actual Kullback-Leibler information for the various candidate models. As the dimension of the candidate model increases in comparison to the size of sample, AIC becomes a strongly negatively biased estimate of the information and hence causes a severe overfitting problem. In order to remove this problem the authors have derived a bias corrected version of AIC (AIC_c) for regression and autoregressive time series models. This corrected version is particularly useful when the sample size is ample, or when the number of parameters of the model and a moderate to large fraction of the sample size. Their proposed method, as claimed by the authors, is asymptotically efficient if the true model is infinite dimensional. Even when the true model is of finite dimension, AIC_c has been found to provide better model choices than any other asymptotically efficient method. Hurvich and Tsai (1993) also extend the results of AIC_c for vector AR(p) models which contain many more unknown parameters than the univariate AR models. A simulation study shows that AIC_c has superior bias properties and strongly outperforms AIC for such model selection in small samples. They have also investigated the relationship between AIC and AIC_c in their paper.

Sin et al. (1992) consider the use of penalized log likelihood forms of criteria for selecting models of various forms such as nested, non-nested, correctly specified or misspecified. They provide some conditions on the penalty term to guarantee the selecting of the true model with probability close to one when competing models have the same KLIC and have similar parsimonious criteria. Their results also describe the properties of the well known AIC, BIC and HQ criteria.

Shao (1993) considers a model selection problem for the predictive ability among a class of linear regression models. In such a particular situation the author proves that the CV method for model selection is asymptotically equivalent to many other methods such as AIC, C_p, the jackknife and the bootstrap (we will be discussing these issues later) in terms of inconsistency, which means the probability of selecting a model with the best predictive ability does not converge to unity as the sample size goes to infinity. However, Shao also showed that this inconsistency can be overcome by satisfying a condition T_v/T tends to unity as the sample size T tends to infinity, where T_v is the sample size for the second part of the total sample T. Ibrahim et al. (1994), on the other hand, have introduced a Bayesian criterion for model selection based on the predictive density of a replicate experiment (PDRE). They have shown that the proposed criterion is competitive to other prevalent criteria, such as AIC, BIC and Mallow's C_p.

Granger et al. (1995) discuss some obvious difficulties involved in testing economic theories. In this regard, they recommend that for choosing an adequate model specification for particular economic relationships it is better to use model selection procedures rather than formal hypothesis testing. King et al. (1995) develop general model selection procedures in which one can calculate the penalties by controlling the probabilities of correct selection so that no one model is unnecessarily favoured. In doing so they proposed two methods; one is called the common model approach and the other the representative fixed points approach. They also provide an algorithm for calculating the penalties based on fixing probabilities of correct selection according to both of these approaches. However, the paper does not provide a concrete strategy on how the probabilities of the correct selection should be controlled, although they are hoping to be able to present some more convincing strategies in the near future. Forbes et al. (1995), on the other hand, present three IC-based model selection procedures of which the first two (one is called FIC and the other is called QFIC) are explicitly designed for regressor selections and the third is for general model selection. For the procedure FIC, they derive a new penalty function on the basis of sums of critical values from particular F distributions, whilst for QFIC they calculate penalties from particular chi-squared distributions. Both penalties come from a desire to control the probability of incorrectly choosing additional regressors.

From the above discussion, we see that a wide range of research on IC-based model selection procedures has been done during the last two decades. In this regard, as King et al. (1995) note, the most popular range of IC-based model selection procedures involve choosing the model with the largest penalized maximized log likelihood function. Obviously, models with a larger number of parameters are penalized more heavily because adding parameters typically increases the maximized log likelihood function. Pötscher (1991) indicates that using a model selection criterion such as AIC or BIC amounts to testing any model against all other models by means of likelihood ratio tests and selecting that model which is accepted against all other models where the critical values are determined by the penalty terms of the criteria. Unfortunately, there is little agreement about the form of the penalty function in the literature. This is because by slightly changing the form of the penalty function, one can come up with a new criterion. So, an obvious question asks what the proper form of the penalty function for the IC-based model selection procedures should be. Our view is that this is an important issue to look at within the model selection context. As we shall be using the Box-Cox transformation (BCT) and bootstrap techniques in later chapters of the book, brief discussions of these techniques are also presented.

4.4 Importance of the Box-Cox Transformation in Econometric Analysis

The basic assumption behind econometric and many other statistical analyses is that the population from where the sample data is drawn should be normally and independently distributed with a common variance and additive error structure. But unfortunately, in many instances, this assumption does not hold. In such a situation, transformation of variables may be an alternative consideration. In fact, the purpose of a transformation is to improve the quality of approximation of the proposed models. For example, the transformed variable may lead to a more nearly linear model, may stabilise the error variance, and/or may lead to a model for which a symmetrically, perhaps normally distributed, error term is acceptable (see, for example, Tukey, 1957).

There has been proposed a number of transformation techniques in the literature such as linear transformation, log transformation, reciprocal transformation, power transformation, etc. (see, for example, Spitzer, 1978). For several reasons, econometricians often use logarithmic transformation. One of these reasons is that it may produce relationships with more homogeneous residuals. Over the last few years, on the other hand, there has been keen interest in using a broader class of power transformations, introduced by many researchers such as Tukey (1957), Box and Cox (1964), Manly (1976), John and Draper (1980) and Bickel and Doksum (1981), which has been found more useful in the empirical determination of functional relationships in many economic applications, especially in econometrics. Among these power transformations, the Box-Cox transformation (BCT) is the most commonly used power transformation in statistics and econometrics (see, for example, Davidson and MacKinnon, 1993) which can be defined for equation (4.1) as:

$$\begin{aligned} y(\lambda) &= \frac{y^{\lambda}-1}{\lambda}, && \text{when } \lambda \neq 0 \\ &= \ln y, && \text{when } \lambda = 0 \\ &= y - 1, && \text{when } \lambda = 1 \end{aligned} \qquad (4.14)$$

where the dependent variable must be greater than zero and the transformation parameter λ can take any real values.

Recently, Sakia (1992) argued that among these various power transformations the Box-Cox transformation technique could be more successfully applied in the functional relationship between variables of interest for economic models. Gujarati (1992), on the other hand, indicates that by using this transformation technique, one can easily apply specification error tests to determine the actual functional form of a regression model. In general, it is assumed that for each λ, $y(\lambda)$ is a monotonic function of y over the admissible range (Box and Cox, 1964). Spitzer (1978) comments that the Box-Cox transformation can be regarded as a valuable tool in order to counter the problem of subjectivity in a model building process. The author also indicates that for forecasting purposes, the use of the BCT has emerged as a very promising procedure. Particularly, in the context of model selection problems, he argues that the estimation of the parameters of a BCT model is, in fact, an expensive iterative procedure which involves the maximization of a non-linear function. The process itself generates a ranking value which can discriminate between the effectiveness of alternative models. Even so, few difficulties remained in the procedure. For example, the error term cannot be strictly normal since a power transformation does not in general permit negative real values. In such cases one possible solution is to assume approximate normality for the successful implementation of the procedure.

There has been much work using the BCT in hypothesis testing and inferences. Sargan (1964) was perhaps the pioneer in proposing a criterion for choosing between two linear regression models based upon the ratio of the maximized likelihoods, which is, in fact, the likelihood ratio test and can be defined as:

$$S=\left(\frac{\hat{\sigma}_1}{g\hat{\sigma}_2}\right)^T \tag{4.15}$$

where $\hat{\sigma}_1$ and $\hat{\sigma}_2$ are two estimated standard deviations of random terms and included in the linear and log-linear models respectively, g is the geometric mean of the dependent variable y of the linear regression model. The main advantage of Sargan's criterion is that it is very simple to compute from the OLS estimates of the two competing models, which leads to a clear-cut decision between them. However, the criterion becomes less useful if neither model is correct. This is one of the main drawbacks of this approach. Andrews (1971) proposed a test for the consistency of the data with a postulated transformation within a given family. As claimed by the author, the test is exact, simple, easy to calculate and the power of the test may be useful to predict the inferences. This test was formulated by ignoring the Jacobian of the transformation. Later, this omission was investigated by Atkinson (1973), who proposed another test by incorporating the Jacobian term. The test was found to be more powerful than the Andrews test. A robust method for testing transformation to achieve normality has been proposed by Carroll (1980) and found to be competitive to these tests.

We have already mentioned one major problem with Sargan's approach to model selection. Another problem with this approach is the assumption that both error terms of the competing models are normally distributed. Aneuryn-Evans and Deaton (1980) indicated that if the model is linear with normal errors then there is some probability that negative values of the dependent variable may occur. This is not appropriate for the log-linear model and hence must be incorrect. In order to overcome this problem they proposed that the error terms be assumed to have a suitable truncated normal distribution. Then applying the important results due to Cox (1961, 1962) on testing non-nested models, one can easily derive an alternative to Sargan's procedure for choosing between two competing models. However, their tests need to estimate only two competing models and are capable of rejecting both when neither is true. One important demerit of their approach is that it involves two test statistics which are rather difficult to calculate. To overcome this, Godfrey and Wickens (1981) propose a more general test procedure which allows both models, either models or neither models to be rejected. Therefore, as claimed by the authors, their proposed procedure is a more useful addition to existing procedures.

Lawrance (1987a) has modified the Atkinson's (1973) test statistic to test whether the estimate of the BCT parameter conforms to a hypothesised value or not and reported a simulation experiment to compare his proposed test with Atkinson's test. The study indicates that the modified statistic has improved standard normal behaviour more than Atkinson's test. Lawrance (1987b) has also given a more reasonable expression for the estimated variance of the parameter λ that leads to more efficient hypothesis tests on λ than Atkinson's test procedure (see, for example, Sakia, 1992). However, a more recent improvement of Atkinson's test and Lawrance's test has been suggested by Wang (1987). He claims that his suggested method gives more accurate approximations to the standard normal. Another simulation experiment conducted by Atkinson and Lawrance (1989) shows that, in general, both of their tests are very similar to each other, although for small samples the Lawrance test was found to be superior to Atkinson's test.

We now turn to the roles of the BCT technique in determining the functional relationships between some variables of interest in economics and econometrics. Zarembka (1968) was, perhaps, the pioneer in considering the functional forms in the demand for money with the same λ for dependent and independent variables. Heckman and Polachek (1974) examined the relationship between earning, schooling and experience with the same λ for all variables. Spitzer (1976) studied the relationship between demand and the liquidity trap with a generalized Box-Cox parameter. Khan and Ross (1977), on the other hand, determined the aggregate form of the import demand equation with the same λ. Newman (1977) considered the relationship between the incidence of malaria and mortality rate and concluded that the functional form obtained by using the Box-Cox procedure has been superior to earlier forms. In this context, some other notable examples may include White (1972), Kau and Lee (1976), Mills (1978), Chang (1980), Boylan et al. (1980), Hwang (1981), Spitzer (1982a, 1982b) and Lin and Huang (1983).

However, the introduction of the BCT technique has resulted in a much wider range of applications compared with other techniques. Unfortunately, this technique has not attracted interest in model selection problems, particularly when using certain parameter restrictions to improve the accuracy of the existing procedures. Considering this view, we have been motivated to apply the BCT technique to a simple linear regression model and to see how the forms of the usual AIC look when the Box-Cox parameter is restricted in the range [0,1]. In particular, we investigate whether taking full account of such a restriction can improve the AIC in terms of accuracy of model selection. Consequently the aim of the next section of this chapter is to examine this issue briefly.

4.5 The Role of Bootstrap Technique and its Applications

Recently, the popularity of the bootstrap method has been increasing in a wide range of fields, particularly in econometrics and statistics. In conventional Monte Carlo experiments, we need to specify the data generating process (DGP) for each experiment, which is mainly used to supplement theoretical work on the properties of estimators and test statistics. In contrast, the bootstrap technique is a computationally intensive assumption free method designed for empirical work to provide statistical estimates such as standard errors, biases, confidence intervals, etc. In other words, as shown in Mooney and Duval (1993), it is one kind of data-based simulation which involves 'resampling' the data with replacement many, many times in order to generate an empirical estimate of the entire sampling distribution of a statistic. As defined in Davidson and MacKinnon (1993), the idea of bootstrapping is to use a single available data set to design a sort of Monte Carlo experiment in which the data themselves are used to approximate the distribution of the error terms where the error terms are drawn from the empirical distribution function of their sample counterparts.

Efron (1979) notes, the jackknife is an intriguing nonparametric method for estimating the bias and variance of a statistic of interest, and also for testing the null hypothesis that the distribution of a statistic is centred at some prespecified point. In the same paper the author explained the jackknife technique in a more primitive way by considering a random sample which is chosen from an unknown probability distribution and estimated the sampling distribution of some prespecified random variable based on the observed data. He named it bootstrap method and comments that this method can be more dependable and applicable in correctly estimating the variance of the sample median where the jackknife technique often fails to work. The author also shows that the bootstrap method works satisfactorily on some other estimation problems such as estimating the error rates in a linear discriminant analysis and estimating bootstrap distribution of regression parameters.

Efron (1983) constructs a prediction rule and estimates the true error rate of this rule in classifying future observations. The author finds that the CV procedure provides a nearly unbiased estimate and is closely related to the bootstrap estimate of the error rate. Basically, the paper highlights two important points; one is the theoretical basis of the prediction problem which relates to CV and the bootstrap and the other is to investigate some related estimators which seem to offer considerably improved estimation in small samples. In general, it has been found that the existing nonparametric methods for estimating the true error rate in the case of a dichotomous prediction problem are closely related to the bootstrap method. However, the author has shown that the bootstrap estimate of the error rate outperforms the CV estimate. However, some other techniques such as double bootstrap and randomized bootstrap outperform both CV and the ordinary bootstrap methods.

Econometricians often fit a regression model to an observed set of data. Questions may arise as to how well the model fits the data and how accurately this model can predict future observations? In order to provide answers to such questions, Efron (1986) suggested a theory which provides simple estimates for the downward bias of the error rate. The theory allows more general measures of prediction error which leads to a nice corroboration of AIC and can be extended to linear models for general exponential families with prediction error measured by squared Euclidean distance where the bias estimate is equivalent to Mallows's C_p criterion. The Efron paper also presents comparative discussion of several closely related ideas such as CV, GCV, bootstrap estimate of prediction error, Mallows's C_p and AIC.

The problem of consistency and asymptotic normality of bootstrap methods has been discussed in Bickel and Freedman (1981) and Freedman (1981). Shorack (1982) introduces bootstrap methods in a robust regression case. Bickel and Freedman (1983) also studied the multiparameter bootstrap regression. Morey and Schenck (1984), on the other hand, report the results of small sample simulation studies of bootstrap and jackknife regression. Note that the bootstrap prediction intervals in regression have been earlier investigated by Stine (1985). Wu (1986) discusses how bootstrap methods can be useful in the presence of heteroscedastic error disturbances. Shao (1988) analyzes resampling (Khan et al., 1999) techniques for variance and bias estimation in a simple linear regression setting. A general theory for the bootstrap hypothesis testing is discussed in detail by Hinkley's (1989) paper.

An excellent book on the topic has also been written by Efron and Tibshirani (1986), which elaborately describes the bootstrap technique and other methods for assessing the accuracy of statistical estimates. In particular, the book exposes the researcher to many exciting and useful statistical techniques through real data examples. Some of the major areas described in the book include regression analysis, density estimation, construction of confidence intervals, bias estimation, hypothesis testing, cross-validation method and jackknife-after-bootstrapping. All of these topics are illustrated in the light of how the bootstrap can be used in these problems. Some other notable examples regarding bootstrap may be Efron (1982), Efron and Gong (1983), Hall (1986a), Hall (1986b), Efron and Tibshirani (1986), Efron (1987), Hall (1988a) and Hall (1988b).

During the current decade the applications of this method have greatly widened in a variety of fields. Stine (1990) introduces the bootstrap method illustrating several important points, such as estimating the variance of a sample mean, bootstrap distribution and confidence interval, bootstrapping in a regression model, bootstrapping with heteroscedasticity, etc. Fisher and Hall (1990) treat bootstrap hypothesis testing through an example of analysis of variance. Hall and Wilson (1991) describe two guidelines of pivoting and sampling under the null hypothesis by employing bootstrap tests to a specific data set. Mammen (1991) studies the properties of the bootstrap when moments are infinite. Ishiguro and Sakamoto (1991) suggest a new information criterion WIC by employing the bootstrap method to simulate the data, which can be applied to the regression models whose parameters are estimated by the penalized maximum likelihood method as well as the ordinary maximum likelihood method.

Hall (1992) discusses methods for bootstrapping curve estimates and Edgeworth expansion giving a number of examples and references. The use of cross-validation and the bootstrap for model selection is studied by Breiman (1992), Breiman and Spector (1992), Zhang (1992) and Shao (1993). Discussion of the basic theory and practice of bootstrapping method by Mooney and Duval (1993) mainly comprised statistical inference using bootstrap and its applications in various fields. Ishiguro et al. (1994) propose a new information criterion EIC which is constructed by employing the bootstrap method to simulate the data, which can be regarded as an extension of AIC. The performance of EIC is demonstrated by some typical numerical examples. Vinod (1995) provides two solutions to the lack of a pivot problem in ridge regression and related shrinkage estimators,one of which is the modification of Efron's (1987) bias corrected percentiles, in which he suggests an approximate pivoting transformation for ridge regression. The second solution involves some practical aspects of Beran's (1987) double bootstrap designed for solutions where there is nonnormality and a lack of a pivot.

Diebold and Chen (1996) compare the performance of two alternative approximations to the finite sample distributions of test statistics for structural change, one is based on asymptotic argument and the other is based on the bootstrap. They find that the bootstrap approximations to the finite sample distribution appear consistently more accurate than the asymptotic approximation. Shao (1996) investigated the procedure that selects a model by minimizing Efron's (1982, 1983) estimators of prediction error is not consistent in the sense that the probability of selecting the optimal subset of variables does not converge to one as the sample size T tends to infinity. In the author's view, this inconsistency can be easily rectified by modifying the sampling method used in drawing bootstrap observations. Consequently, two modified bootstrap selection procedures which have been proved to be consistent have been proposed. The consistency of these procedures has been established in various situations, including linear models, non-linear models, generalized linear models and autoregressive time series models. Some other notable recent work on bootstrapping may include Swanepoel (1990), Stine (1990), Efron (1992), Jeong and Maddala (1993), and Young (1994). However, it appears that much work has been reported on regression analysis, density estimation, construction of confidence intervals, bias estimation and hypothesis testing through using bootstrap techniques. Unfortunately, not much work has been done on model selection by employing similar techniques. Moreover, the importance of the method has been increasing day by day and to avoid some obvious difficulties involved with the estimates of nuisance parameters in simulation experiments for our particular problem we have been interested in using this technique to determine the empirical penalties for our proposed CIC model selection procedure.

4.6 Concluding Remarks

The aim of this chapter has been to survey the model selection problems in econometrics. This survey reveals that there is a large body of literature on model selection ranging from stepwise hypothesis testing to IC-based model selection procedures. The evidence so far supports basing the model selection decision on some well-thought-out model selection criteria rather than classical hypothesis tests. However, the discussion on IC-based procedures mainly focuses on the penalty term, which is one of the main ingredients of such procedures. The major problem with these procedures is that by slightly changing the form of penalty function one can come up with a new criterion. As a result, the number of IC-based procedures has been increasing. Unfortunately, it appears that not much work has yet been reported on the IC-based model selection problems by employing the technique of parameter restrictions to improve the accuracy of these procedures. This chapter aims to concentrate on this particular issue. The previous sections have provided the motivation of the construction of new information criterion. Consequently, in the next chapter we focus in depth on the theoretical developments of new AIC with restricted parameters.

Chapter 5

Information Criteria for Model Selection

5.1 Introduction

As a result of our discussions in Chapter 4, we noticed that the model selection has been playing a significant role in econometric model building. In this regard, a number of different procedures were reviewed in sections 4.2 and 4.3. The literature review of Chapter 4 reveals that the IC-based procedures are the most popular and useful procedures. IC procedures are based on choosing the model with the largest maximized log of the likelihood function minus a penalty term where the models with larger numbers of parameters are penalized more heavily than the models with smaller numbers of parameters. There is nonetheless little agreement about what the form of the penalty function should be.

In econometric and statistical analyses, we sometimes have some prior information regarding the values of certain parameters. For example, in statistics, correlation coefficients should be between minus one and one, and variances are always positive. In economic applications, on the other hand, economic theory can be helpful in providing information about the sign and/or range of values of some regression coefficients. For example, the parameter of a partial adjustment model should be non-negative and less than one. This sort of knowledge provides important information about the parameter space that enables researchers to draw more efficient inferences. For example, it is well known that one-sided testing (in place of two-sided testing) improves explanatory power when the information of the parameter restriction is correct. To the best of our knowledge, Hughes (1997) is, perhaps, the pioneer who worked with model selection procedures that use one-sided information for parameters in dispute.

In particular, Hughes (1997) developed a class of one-sided AIC procedures called OSAIC, where the author used the strategy of making use of one-sided parameter restrictions such as $\theta > 0$ of a candidate model. In this chapter, we are interested in examining the effect of making an interval restriction on the form of parameters of interest θ within a model selection framework. More clearly speaking, our aim is to see whether such restrictions imposed on parameter(s) can improve AIC in terms of accuracy of selection. In that sense, our work, discussed in the present chapter, may be partially regarded as an extension of Hughes' work.

The plan of this chapter is as follows. A brief description of IC-based model selection procedures is given in section 5.2. Section 5.3 derives the UAIC for a simple one parameter regression model. Derivation of AIC for the one restricted parameter case is presented in section 5.4. Section 5.5 generalizes section 5.4. An example of new AIC with the Box-Cox transformation model is discussed in section 5.6. The final section contains some concluding remarks.

5.2 Information Criteria-Based Model Selection

Suppose $y = (y_1, y_2, \ldots, y_T)'$ is a realization of a random vector y, which may have been taken from one of m possible models each with probability density function $f_i(\theta)$ where $i = 1, 2, \ldots, m$. We assume that there are no restrictions on these parameters, i.e., the number of free parameters in each model is k_i. Let the log-likelihood function of $f_i(\theta)$ be $L_i(\theta)$ and the maximized value of $L_i(\theta)$ be $L_i(\hat{\theta})$, where $\hat{\theta}$ is the maximum likelihood estimator of θ. The usual form of almost all information criteria-based model selection procedures is to select the model with the largest penalized maximized log-likelihood function, namely:

$$IC_i = L_i(\hat{\theta}) - p_i \tag{5.1}$$

where p_i is the penalty function dependent on the number of parameters, among other things. More specifically, we select the model which possesses the maximum value of IC_i within the set of models under consideration.

5.3 AIC-Based Model Selection

The AIC procedure aims to characterize the goodness of fit and parsimony of a model by measuring the KL information using the mean expected log-likelihood of the model of interest. This is because of the fact that AIC is an estimate of the mean expected log-likelihood, which can be defined as the mean of the expected log-likelihood of the maximum likelihood model where the mean is measured with respect to the data. The larger the mean expected log-likelihood the better the fit of the model. Thus we would consider the mean expected log-likelihood as the measure of AIC throughout its derivation. Let

$\theta^* = (\theta_1^*, \theta_2^*, \ldots, \theta_k^*)'$ be the true parameter vector and $f_i(y|\theta^*)$ be the DGP of the model. In describing the derivation of AIC, Akaike (1973) and later on Sakamoto et al. (1986) defined the mean expected log-likelihood as:

$$\bar{\bar{L}}_i(\theta) = \int \bar{L}_i(\hat{\theta}) f_i(y|\theta^*) dy \tag{5.2}$$

where $\bar{L}_i(\hat{\theta})$ is the expected log-likelihood evaluated at the maximum likelihood estimate $\hat{\theta}$. In order to evaluate the integral (5.2), by using a Taylor's series expansion around the true parameter θ^*, the expected log-likelihood $\bar{L}_i(\theta)$ can be approximated as:

$$\begin{aligned} \bar{L}_i(\theta) &\approx \bar{L}_i(\theta^*) + (\theta - \theta^*) E_y\{q_i(\theta)|_{\theta=\theta^*}\} \\ &\quad + \tfrac{1}{2}(\theta - \theta^*)' E_y\{H_i(\theta)|_{\theta=\theta^*}\}(\theta - \theta^*) \end{aligned} \tag{5.3}$$

where $\bar{L}_i(\theta)$ is the expected log-likelihood evaluated at θ, $L_i(\theta^*)$ is the expected log-likelihood evaluated at the true parameter vector θ^*, E_y indicates the operation of taking expectation with respect to the variable y, $q_i(\theta)$ is the score vector and $H_i(\theta)$ is the Hessian matrix. Validity of this Taylor's series expansion needs the regularity conditions discussed in Gouriéroux et al. (1980) to be satisfied. Of them, two conditions that are particularly important for our case are:

1 $L(\theta)$ is a continuous function;
2 If $\theta = (\theta_1^*, \theta_2^*, \ldots, \theta_k^*)'$, then $\dfrac{\partial L(\theta)}{\partial \theta_j}$ and $\dfrac{\partial^2 L(\theta)}{\partial \theta_i \partial \theta_j}$ exist, and are continuous at all points of parameter space regardless of i and j. We also need to satisfy the following assumption:

$$\frac{1}{\sqrt{T}} \left(\frac{\partial L(\theta)}{\partial \theta}\bigg|_{\theta=\theta^*} \right) \xrightarrow{\ a\ } N\left(0, \lim_{T\to\infty} \left[\frac{1}{T} I(\theta)\bigg|_{\theta=\theta^*} \right]\right)$$

where 'a' indicates 'is asymptotically distributed as' and $I(\theta)$ is Fisher's information matrix, which can be defined as:

$$I(\theta) = -E\left(\frac{\partial^2 L(\theta)}{\partial \theta \partial \theta'}\right) \tag{5.4}$$

As the expected score vector evaluated at the true parameter value is zero, the second term of (5.3) vanishes and we obtain:

$$\begin{aligned}\bar{L}_i(\theta) &\approx \bar{L}_i(\theta^*) + \tfrac{1}{2}(\theta - \theta^*)' E_y\{H_i(\theta)|_{\theta=\theta^*}\}(\theta - \theta^*) \\ &\approx \bar{L}_i(\theta^*) - \tfrac{1}{2}(\theta - \theta^*)' I_i(\theta)|_{\theta=\theta^*}(\theta - \theta^*)\end{aligned} \tag{5.5}$$

where $I_i(\theta)$ is Fisher's information matrix defined in (5.4). Now we consider the case where $\theta = \hat{\theta}$. Under certain standard regularity conditions see for example, Lehmann (1983), Amemiya (1985) and Greene (1993), as the sample size $T \to \infty$:

$$\sqrt{T}(\hat{\theta} - \theta^*) \xrightarrow{\ a\ } N\left\{0, \left[\lim_{T\to\infty} \frac{1}{T} I_i(\theta)\Big|_{\theta=\theta^*}\right]^{-1}\right\}. \tag{5.6}$$

Due to the asymptotic normality of the maximum likelihood estimator and the relationship between normal random variables and chi-squared random variables, twice the second term of (5.5) (which is regarded as the Wald test statistic providing a measure of closeness between $\hat{\theta}$ and θ^* as shown by King, 1991) with $\theta = \hat{\theta}$ is asymptotically distributed as a chi-squared distribution with k_i degrees of freedom. Thus taking expectations on both sides of (5.5) with $\theta = \hat{\theta}$ we obtain:

$$\bar{\bar{L}}_i(\theta) \approx \bar{L}_i(\theta^*) - \frac{k_i}{2}. \tag{5.7}$$

Again considering the Taylor's series expansion, the log-likelihood $L_i(\theta)$, around the maximum likelihood estimate $\hat{\theta}$, can be approximated as:

$$L_i(\theta) \approx L_i(\hat{\theta}) + (\theta - \hat{\theta}) q_i(\theta)|_{\theta=\hat{\theta}} + \tfrac{1}{2}(\theta - \hat{\theta})' II_i(\theta)|_{\theta=\hat{\theta}}(\theta - \hat{\theta}). \tag{5.8}$$

Here the second term vanishes because the log-likelihood takes its maximum value at $\hat{\theta}$. Thus equation (5.8) becomes:

$$\begin{aligned}L_i(\theta) &\approx L_i(\hat{\theta}) + \tfrac{1}{2}(\theta - \hat{\theta})' H_i(\theta)|_{\theta=\theta^*}(\theta - \hat{\theta}) \\ &= L_i(\hat{\theta}) + \tfrac{1}{2}(\theta - \hat{\theta})' \left(\frac{\partial^2 L_i(\theta)}{\partial\theta\,\partial\theta'}\right)_{\theta=\hat{\theta}} (\theta - \hat{\theta}).\end{aligned} \tag{5.9}$$

Now we use asymptotic arguments to simplify the second term of (5.9). On its right-hand side, the term $\partial^2 L_i(\theta)/\partial\theta\,\partial\theta'$ is, in fact, sums of independent identical variates, and as $T\to\infty$ it converges to its expectation by the strong law of large numbers (see for example, Kendall and Stuart, 1973). Thus for $T \rightarrow \infty$, we can rewrite equation (5.9) as:

$$L_i(\theta) \approx L_i(\hat{\theta}) + \frac{1}{2}(\theta - \hat{\theta})' \mathrm{E}\left(\frac{\partial^2 L_i(\theta)}{\partial\theta\,\partial\theta'} \right)\Bigg|_{\theta=\hat{\theta}} (\theta - \hat{\theta}) + L_i(\hat{\theta}) - \frac{1}{2}(\theta - \hat{\theta})' I_i(\theta)|_{\theta=\hat{\theta}}(\theta - \hat{\theta}) \tag{5.10}$$

which is almost similar to equation (5.5) for the second term. Thus by applying the same arguments as given in (5.5) and substituting θ^* for θ and then taking expectations on both sides of (5.10) we asymptotically obtain:

$$\bar{L}_i(\theta) \approx \bar{L}_i(\theta^*) - \frac{k_i}{2}. \tag{5.11}$$

As the maximized log-likelihood $L_i(\hat{\theta})$ is an asymptotically unbiased estimator of $\bar{L}_i(\hat{\theta})$ we can combine (5.7) and (5.11) and obtain the AIC decision rule which is to select the model for which:

$$AIC_i = L_i(\hat{\theta}) - k_i \tag{5.12}$$

is maximum. Note that a similar proof is also found in Sakamoto et al. (1986) and in Hughes (1997).

5.4 AIC-Based Model Selection with One Restricted Parameter

Let us consider a simple density function $f_i(y|\theta)$ of a $T \times 1$ random vector y, where θ is the only scalar parameter of our model under the restriction of the form $a \leq \theta \leq b$, where a and b are two boundary values of the parameter θ. We are assuming that the model considered here is taken from one of m possible models, $i = 1, 2, \ldots, m$. Let $L_i(\theta)$ be the log-likelihood function of $f_i(y|\theta)$ and $L_i(\hat{\theta})$ be the maximized value of $L_i(\theta)$. Here our problem is to derive the AIC for such a density function taking into account the constraint of the parameter given above. To do this, we are required to fulfil one important assumption, which is that each of the competing models represents a logical alternative hypothesis model with respect to Gouriéroux et al.'s (1980) one-sided Wald type test. However, to derive AIC, we use the general Kuhn-Tucker inequality constrained optimization framework considered by Gouriéroux et al. (1982) for a one-sided hypothesis testing problem, such as:

$$H_0 : \theta = a \quad \text{versus} \quad H_1 : \theta > a,$$

or

$$H_0 : \theta = b \quad \text{versus} \quad H_1 : \theta < b. \tag{5.13}$$

Let θ^* be the true value of θ and $f_i(y|\theta^*)$ be the DGP of the model. Due to similar arguments about the definition of AIC given in the previous section, the expected log-likelihood can be approximated as:

$$\bar{L}_i(\theta) \approx L_i(\theta^*) - \tfrac{1}{2}\,(\theta - \theta^*)^2 I_i(\theta)\big|_{\theta=\theta^*} \tag{5.14}$$

where $I_i(\theta)$ is Fisher's information matrix. Now considering the case where $\theta = \hat{\theta}$, which is the maximized value of $\hat{\theta}$, under appropriate regularity conditions, see for example, Gouriéroux et al. (1980), Sweeting (1980), Schneider (1986), and Cressie and Lahiri (1993); when $a < \theta^* < b$, the estimator $\hat{\theta}$ is asymptotically distributed as:

$$\sqrt{T}(\hat{\theta} - \theta^*) \xrightarrow{\ a\ } N\left\{0, \left[\lim_{T\to\infty} \frac{1}{T} I_i(\theta)\Big|_{\theta=\theta^*}\right]^{-1}\right\}.$$

Thus, twice the second term of (5.15) is asymptotically distributed as a chi-squared distribution with one degree of freedom (see the arguments given in section 5.3). Thus, after taking expectations on both sides of (5.15) with θ replaced by $\hat{\theta}$ we obtain:

$$\bar{\bar{L}}_i(\theta) \approx \bar{L}_i(\theta^*) - \tfrac{1}{2}\,. \tag{5.15}$$

On the other hand, when θ^* takes the boundary values such as $\theta^* = a$ or $\theta^* = b$, then the estimator $\hat{\theta}$ cannot follow an asymptotic normal distribution because approximately half of the time it will fall on the boundary due to the constraint on θ. Thus in such cases we may assume that approximately half of the time the estimator follows an asymptotically truncated normal (which is truncated within the given admissible range) distribution and the remaining half of the time it takes the boundary value. When the estimator takes the boundary value, the second term of (5.8) automatically vanishes as $\hat{\theta} = \theta$. When the estimator takes a value away from the boundary this second term is also zero because the score evaluated at is zero when the constant is not binding.

In order to understand the next step in the derivation, we now wish to refer to some important work of Plackett (1954) and Bartholomew (1959a, 1959b and 1961) which is related to the problem of one-sided hypothesis testing such as $H_0 : \mu = 0$ versus $H_1 : \mu_j \geq 0, j = 1, 2, \ldots, k$ with at least one inequality strict, where the independent observations are taken from a k-dimensional normal distribution with mean vector μ and the variance-covariance matrix Σ. Following Plackett and Bartholomew, similar problems have been studied by several other authors (see for example, Chacko, 1963; Kudô, 1963; Perlman, 1969; and Sweeting, 1980). In particular, within the framework of testing the problem given in (5.13), Gouriéroux et al. (1980) showed that the Kuhn-Tucker test statistic is asymptotically equal to one version of the Wald test for this problem, i.e.:

$$(\theta - \theta^*)^2 I_i(\theta) \xrightarrow{a} (\hat{\lambda} - \lambda^*)^2 (I_i(\theta))^{-1}$$

where $I_i(\theta)$ is Fisher's information matrix, λ is the corresponding scalar Lagrange multiplier, and $\hat{\lambda}$ and λ^* are the estimated and true values of λ, respectively.

As shown in Gouriéroux et al. (1980), under the null hypothesis, this test statistic follows a probability weighted mixture of chi-squared distributions of the form:

$$\sum_{j=0}^{k} w(k,j)\chi^2_{(j)} \tag{5.16}$$

where $\sum_{j=0}^{k} w(k,j) = 1$ and $w(k,j), j = 0, 1, \ldots, k$, are the probability weights of the chi-squared distributions. Essentially, these weights represent the asymptotic probability of the event that under H_0 any j elements of $\hat{\theta} - \theta^*$ are strictly positive, and the remaining $k - j$ elements are zeros. More formally, the weights can be defined for variance-covariance matrix $\Sigma = I$ and for the case of symmetry, as:

$$w(k,j) = \binom{k}{j} 2^{-k}, j = 0,1,\ldots,k.$$

For a more general definition of weights, see Kudô (1963) and Wu and King et al. (1995). Note that the first integer within the bracket on the left hand side denotes the total number of restricted parameters and the second indicates the degrees of freedom of the chi-squared distribution to which the weights are attached. However, the calculation of the weights is somewhat difficult, particularly when the number of restrictions k_i is greater than 5 (see for example, Bartholomew (1959a, 1959b, 1961), Kudô (1963), Barlow et al. (1972), and Wu and King (1995)). However, Gouriéroux et al. (1982) considered a particular problem with one and two parameter restrictions where they found for the former that the asymptotic distribution under the null hypothesis of the Wald, likelihood ratio and Kuhn-Tucker test statistics are identical and are a probability weighted mixture of chi-squared distributions of the form:

$$w(1,0)\chi^2_{(0)} + w(1,1)\chi^2_{(1)}. \tag{5.17}$$

In fact, this is an analogue to our particular problem set out for the first part in (5.13). Here $\chi^2_{(0)}$ and $\chi^2_{(1)}$ denote chi-squared distributions with 0 and 1 degrees of freedom respectively, where $\chi^2_{(0)}$ is the unit mass at the origin. However, in the one constraint case, due to symmetry:

$$w(1,0) = w(1,1) = \tfrac{1}{2} \tag{5.18}$$

(see for example, Gouriéroux et al. (1982)). Thus twice the second term of (5.15) with $\theta = \hat{\theta}$ is asymptotically distributed as the probability weighted mixture of the form $\frac{1}{2}\chi^2_{(0)} + \frac{1}{2}\chi^2_{(1)}$. Taking expectations on both sides of (5.15) we obtain:

$$\begin{aligned} \bar{\bar{L}}_i(\theta) &\approx \bar{L}_i(\theta^*) - \tfrac{1}{2}\left[\tfrac{1}{2}E\left(\chi^2_{(0)}\right) + \tfrac{1}{2}E\left(\chi^2_{(1)}\right)\right] \\ &= \bar{L}_i(\theta^*) - \tfrac{1}{2}\left[\tfrac{1}{2}\times 0 + \tfrac{1}{2}\times 1\right] \\ &= \bar{L}_i(\theta^*) - \tfrac{1}{4}. \end{aligned} \tag{5.19}$$

In order to substitute the value of $\bar{L}_i(\theta^*)$ in (5.15) and (5.19), we consider again the Taylor's series expansion of the log-likelihood $L_i(\theta)$, around the maximum likelihood estimate $\hat{\theta}$ and setting $\theta = \theta^*$, $L_i(\theta^*)$ can be approximated as:

$$L_i(\theta) \approx L_i(\hat{\theta}) + (\theta^* - \hat{\theta})q_i(\theta)|_{\theta=\theta^*} + \tfrac{1}{2}(\theta^* - \hat{\theta})^2 H_i(\theta)|_{\theta=\theta^*}. \tag{5.20}$$

Now let us consider three simple situations. First, consider $\theta^* = a$. Due to the consistency property of the ML estimator, the value of $\hat{\theta}$ would be asymptotically *a* half of the time and be greater than *a* half of the time. In both of these situations the second term of (5.20) vanishes and asymptotically we obtain for large T as before (see, for example, the arguments given in equation (5.10)):

$$L_i(\theta^*) \approx L_i(\hat{\theta})\, \tfrac{1}{2}\, (\theta^* - \hat{\theta})^2 I_i(\theta)\big|_{\theta=\theta^*}. \tag{5.21}$$

We again wish to use similar arguments for the distributional form of the second term of (5.21) where what follows, as before in (5.17), under H_0 we can express the probability weighted mixture of chi-squared distributions of the form:

$$w(1,0)\chi^2_{(0)} + w(1,1)\chi^2_{(1)}.$$

Thus after taking into account expectations on both sides of (5.21) we obtain:

$$\begin{aligned}\bar{L}_i(\theta^*) &\approx \bar{L}_i(\hat{\theta}) - \tfrac{1}{2}\left[w(1,0)E\left(\chi^2_{(0)}\right) + w(1,1)E\left(\chi^2_{(1)}\right)\right] \\ &= \bar{L}_i(\hat{\theta}) - \tfrac{1}{2}\left[\tfrac{1}{2} \times 0 + \tfrac{1}{2} \times 1\right] \\ &= \bar{L}_i(\hat{\theta}) - \tfrac{1}{4}\,.\end{aligned} \tag{5.22}$$

We substitute the value of $\bar{L}_i(\theta^*)$ in (5.19) and obtain a different form of $\bar{\bar{L}}_i(\theta^*)$ such as:

$$\begin{aligned}\bar{\bar{L}}_i(\theta) &\approx L_i(\hat{\theta}) - \tfrac{1}{4} - \tfrac{1}{4} \\ &= \bar{L}_i(\hat{\theta}) - \tfrac{1}{2}\end{aligned}$$

As the maximized log-likelihood $L_i(\hat{\theta})$ is an asymptotically unbiased estimator of $\bar{L}_i(\hat{\theta})$, the above expression can be written as:

$$\bar{\bar{L}}_i(\theta) \approx L_i(\hat{\theta}) - \tfrac{1}{2}\,. \tag{5.23}$$

This is a new form of AIC due to the change of penalty and hereafter we will call it proposed AIC (PAIC). Similarly for $\theta^* = b$, we get the same result as (5.23). It is evident from (5.23) that PAIC counts restricted parameters as less than one, which seems reasonable because a totally restricted parameter, that is, $\theta^* = a$ or $\theta^* = b$, counts as zero.

Now let us consider the situation when $a < \theta^* < b$. Because of similar arguments given in the unrestricted case, the value of the ML estimator $\hat{\theta}$ would asymptotically fall between a and b, as it is assumed that the estimator $\hat{\theta}$ is consistent. Thus the second term of (5.20) vanishes because the score function has been evaluated at the maximum likelihood estimate $\hat{\theta}$ and hence asymptotically we obtain equation (5.21) as before:

$$L_i(\theta^*) \approx L_i(\hat{\theta}) - \frac{1}{2}\left(\theta^* - \hat{\theta}\right)^2 I_i(\theta)\Big|_{\theta=\theta^*}.$$

Similarly as before, twice the second term of the above expression follows a chi-squared distribution with one degree of freedom. Thus taking expectations on both sides of the above expression we obtain:

$$\bar{L}_i(\theta^*) \approx \bar{L}_i(\hat{\theta}) - \frac{1}{2}\,. \tag{5.25}$$

Substituting this value in (5.15) and using $L_i(\hat{\theta})$ instead of $\bar{L}_i(\hat{\theta})$ as a result of similar arguments as before, we obtain the usual AIC form (hereafter we will often call it usual AIC (UAIC)) for the one parameter model, as:

$$\begin{aligned}\bar{\bar{L}}_i(\theta) &\approx L_i(\hat{\theta}) - \frac{1}{2} - \frac{1}{2} \\ &\approx L_i(\hat{\theta}) - 1.\end{aligned} \tag{5.25}$$

In fact, here we obtain the normal penalty despite the parameter being restricted because in such cases the true value of the parameter θ, i.e., θ^*, falls at any point between two boundary values. Thus asymptotically the parameter is being considered as free from any restrictions in such a case. On the other hand, when one takes either boundary values, for example, $\theta^* = a$ or $\theta^* = b$, the form of AIC looks different with respect to the penalty which we named PAIC. That means, the PAIC penalizes additional restricted parameters less heavily than the UAIC indicating that if the restrictions imposed on the parameter are present in the model then the UAIC penalty function may be misspecified.

It is clear from (5.23) and (5.25) that for one parameter restriction, we obtain two possible versions of the AIC procedure depending on where the true parameter lies. Unfortunately we do not have this information when we are about to apply a model selection procedure. Thus the question is which version should we apply in practice. We recommend the use of PAIC given by (5.23) because it uses the appropriate penalty in the case when θ is an unnecessary extra parameter. As we know, the value of the maximized log-likelihood function can generally be increased by the addition of an extra (extraneous) parameter. The penalty function is designed to compensate for this increase. Equation (5.23) gives the appropriate penalty in the case of adding an extraneous but restricted parameter because in this case there is less chance of increasing the maximized log-likelihood function than in the unrestricted case.

5.5 Generalization to more than One Restricted Parameter

5.5.1 AIC-Based Model Selection with Two Restricted Parameters

Consider a density function $f_i(y|\theta)$ of a $T \times 1$ random vector y, where $\theta = (\theta_1, \theta_2)'$ is a 2×1 parameter vector of our model of interest under the restriction of the form $a \leq \theta \leq b$, or equivalently, $a_1 \leq \theta_1 \leq b_1$ and $a_2 \leq \theta_2 \leq b_2$. Assume that the model considered here is taken from one of m possible models, $i = 1,2,\ldots,$m, and let $L_i(\theta)$ be the log-likelihood function of $f_i(y|\theta)$ and $L_i(\hat{\theta})$ be the maximized value of $L_i(\theta)$. Here our aim is to derive the AIC for this two restricted parameter model.

To solve this problem, we can follow similar arguments used by Gouriéroux et al. (1982) for a one-sided hypothesis testing problem within the Kuhn-Tucker inequality constrained optimization framework as given in the one restriction case. Let $\theta^* = (\theta_1^*, \theta_2^*)$ be the true value of the parameter θ and $f_i(y|\theta)^*$ be the DGP of the model. Because of the same arguments about the definition of AIC given in section 4.3 (see equation 4.5, for example), the expected log-likelihood can be approximated as:

$$\bar{L}_i(\theta) \approx L_i(\theta^*) - \frac{1}{2}(\theta - \hat{\theta})' I_i(\theta)\big|_{\theta=\theta^*}(\theta - \theta^*). \tag{5.26}$$

For our problem, there are $3^2 = 9$ possible combinations of boundary/non-boundary values of the parameters. Of these nine models, four models lie on the four corner points in parameter space Θ, each having both parameters restricted. Another four models lie on any part (except the four corner points) of the four boundary lines, each containing one unrestricted parameter and one restricted parameter. The remaining model lies in the interior of the parameter space containing two unrestricted parameters. Thus we can categorize all these nine models into three types. Now, let us consider the first type of model, which has both parameters restricted to be on a boundary. In fact, this particular problem is analogous to the problem of one-sided hypothesis testing in multivariate analysis (see for example, Plackett (1954), Bartholomew (1961) and Gupta (1963)). In such a problem we deal with some observations which are taken from a two-dimensional (bivariate) normal distribution with a one-sided testing problem such as:

$$\begin{aligned} &H_0 : \theta^* \text{ lies on the prescribed boundary of the parameter space } \Theta; \\ &H_1 : \theta^* \text{ does not lie on the prescribed boundary.} \end{aligned} \tag{5.27}$$

As shown by Bartholomew (1959a, 1959b, 1961), Barlow et al. (1972) and Gouriéroux et al. (1982), among others, under the null hypothesis, the Wald test statistic for such a problem is distributed as a probability weighted mixture of chi-squared distributions of thc form:

$$\sum_{j=0}^{2} w(2,j)\chi^2_{(j)} = w(2,0)\chi^2_{(0)} + w(2,1)\chi^2_{(1)} + w(2,2)\chi^2_{(2)} \tag{5.28}$$

where $w(2,0) = \frac{1}{4} - \frac{\sin^{-1}\rho_{12}}{2\pi}$; $w(2,1) = \frac{1}{2}$; $w(2,2) = \frac{1}{4} + \frac{\sin^{-1}\rho_{12}}{2\pi}$ and ρ_{12}

is the correlation coefficient generated from the variance-covariance matrix of the unconstrained maximum likelihood estimates of the parameters which can be set up, in general, as:

$$\rho_{ij} = \frac{\text{cov}\left(\hat{\theta}_i, \hat{\theta}_j\right)}{\sqrt{\text{var}(\hat{\theta}_i)\text{var}(\hat{\theta}_j)}}, \; i \neq j = 1, 2, \ldots, k.$$

Therefore, twice the second term of (5.26) with $\theta = \hat{\theta}$ is asymptotically distributed as a probability weighted mixture of chi-squared distributions of the form (5.28). Taking expectations on both sides of (5.26) we obtain:

$$\begin{aligned} \bar{\bar{L}}_i(\hat{\theta}) &\approx \bar{L}_i(\theta^*) - \frac{1}{2}\left[\sum_{j=0}^{2} w(2,j)E(\chi^2_{(j)})\right] \\ &= \bar{L}_i(\theta^*) - \frac{1}{2}\left[w(2,0)E(\chi^2_{(0)}) + w(2,1)E(\chi^2_{(1)}) + w(2,2)E(\chi^2_{(2)})\right] \\ &= \bar{L}_i(\theta^*) - \frac{1}{2}\left[0 + \frac{1}{2} + \left(\frac{1}{4} + \frac{1}{2\pi}\sin^{-1}\rho_{12}\right) \times 2\right] \end{aligned}$$

$$= \bar{L}_i(\theta^*) - \frac{1}{2}\left[\frac{1}{2} + \frac{1}{2} + \frac{\sin^{-1}\rho_{12}}{\pi}\right]$$

$$= \bar{L}_i(\theta^*) - \frac{1}{2} - \frac{\sin^{-1}\rho_{12}}{2\pi}. \qquad (5.29)$$

By using similar arguments as before, we can also prove that:

$$\bar{L}_i(\theta^*) \approx \bar{L}_i(\hat{\theta}) - \frac{1}{2} - \frac{\sin^{-1}\rho_{12}}{2\pi}. \qquad (5.30)$$

Substituting the value of $\bar{L}_i(\theta^*)$ in (5.29) and using similar arguments about $\bar{L}_i(\hat{\theta})$ as before, we obtain PAIC which is to select the model for which:

$$\bar{\bar{L}}_i(\theta^*) \approx L_i(\hat{\theta}) - \left(1 + \frac{\sin^{-1}\rho_{12}}{\pi}\right) \qquad (5.31)$$

is a maximum.

Now we consider the second type of model which lies on any points of the five boundary lines except the corner points. Here each model contains only one unrestricted parameter, which means out of two parameters for each model one is restricted and the other is unrestricted. Thus, such a problem is analogous to a partially one-sided hypothesis testing problem and the Wald test statistic for such a problem can be approximated to a probability weighted mixture of chi-squared distributions of the form:

$$\sum_{j=1}^{2} w(1, j-1)\chi^2_{(j)}. \qquad (5.32)$$

See the earlier references in this context. Thus, twice the second term of (5.26) is asymptotically distributed as a probability weighted mixture of chi-squared distributions of the form (5.32). Taking expectations on both sides of (5.26) with $\theta = \hat{\theta}$ we obtain:

$$\bar{\bar{L}}_i(\theta) \approx \bar{L}_i(\theta^*) - \frac{1}{2}\left[\sum_{j=0}^{2} w(1, j-1)E(\chi^2_{(j)})\right]$$

$$= \bar{L}_i(\theta^*) - \frac{1}{2}\left[w(1,0)E(\chi^2_{(1)}) + w(1,1)E(\chi^2_{(2)})\right]$$

$$= \bar{L}_i(\theta^*) - \frac{1}{2}\left[\frac{1}{2} + 1\right]$$

$$= \bar{L}_i(\theta^*) - \frac{3}{4}. \tag{5.33}$$

By using similar arguments as before, we can also prove that:

$$\bar{L}_i(\theta^*) \approx L_i(\hat{\theta}) - \frac{3}{4}. \tag{5.34}$$

Substituting the value of $\bar{L}_i(\theta^*)$ in (5.33) and using $L_i(\hat{\theta})$ instead of $\bar{L}_i(\hat{\theta})$ due to similar arguments as before, we obtain a different form of AIC which is to select the model for which:

$$\bar{\bar{L}}_i(\theta) \approx L_i(\hat{\theta}) - 1\,\frac{1}{2} \tag{5.35}$$

is a maximum. This is a different form from the previous PAIC form in terms of penalty. In fact, this is a less penalized AIC form than the usual one only because between the two parameters of the model one is assumed to be on the boundary of the parameter space.

Finally, we consider the third type of model which lies in the interior of the parameter space or equivalently $a < \theta^* < b$ and which possesses two free parameters. Under appropriate regularity conditions, the estimator is asymptotically distributed as:

$$\sqrt{T}(\hat{\theta} - \theta^*) \xrightarrow{\ a\ } N\left\{0, \left[\lim_{T\to\infty} \frac{1}{T} I_i(\theta)\Big|_{\theta=\theta^*}\right]^{-1}\right\}.$$

Therefore, twice the second term of (5.26) with $\theta = \hat{\theta}$ is asymptotically distributed as a chi-squared distribution with two degrees of freedom. Taking expectations on both sides of (5.26) we obtain:

$$\bar{\bar{L}}_i(\theta) \approx L_i(\theta^*) - 1. \tag{5.36}$$

Similarly we can prove that:

$$\bar{L}_i(\theta^*) \approx L_i(\hat{\theta}) - 1. \tag{5.37}$$

Substituting the value of $\bar{L}_i(\theta^*)$ in (5.36) and using $L_i(\hat{\theta})$ instead of $\bar{L}_i(\hat{\theta})$ due to similar arguments as before, we obtain the UAIC decision rule which is to select the model for which:

$$\bar{\bar{L}}_i(\theta) \approx L_i(\hat{\theta}) - 2. \tag{5.38}$$

is a maximum. Here we also obtain the normal penalty for a model with two parameters simply because it is assumed that the true value of the parameter vector θ, i.e., θ^*, lies at any point in the interior of the parameter space Θ. Thus asymptotically the parameters are being considered as free from any restrictions in such a case.

Here for two parameter restrictions, we obtain three different versions of the AIC procedure which are given in (5.31), (5.35) and (5.38), respectively. Of these, (5.38) provides the usual AIC procedure for a two parameter model where both parameters are considered as unrestricted asymptotically. The other two criteria provide two different penalties depending on where the true parameter lies. Unfortunately, this information is unknown at the time of application of the model selection procedure. We argue for the use of PAIC (i.e. (5.31)) in this situation because it uses the appropriate penalty in the case of the addition of two unnecessary extra restricted parameters. It thus provides the appropriate penalty function for a likelihood function which may contain two unnecessary restricted parameters.

5.5.2 *AIC-Based Model Selection with Three Restricted Parameters*

In this subsection we wish to derive the AIC for a three parameter model whose parameters are all restricted. Let $f_i(y|\theta)$ be a density function of a $T \times 1$ random vector y, taken from one of m possible models, 1, 2,..., m, where $\theta = (\theta_1,\theta_2,\theta_3)'$ is a 3×1 parameter vector under the restriction of the form $a \leq \theta \leq b$ or equivalently $a_1 \leq \theta_1 \leq b_1$, $a_2 \leq \theta_2 \leq b_2$ and $a_3 \leq \theta_3 \leq b_3$. Obviously, in this problem the parameter vector θ can take any value from the three dimensional parameter space Θ. Consequently, we assume that $L_i(\theta)$ is the log-likelihood function of $f_i(y|\theta)$, $L_i(\hat{\theta})$ is the maximized value of $L_i(\theta)$ and $\theta^* = (\theta_1^*,\theta_2^*,\theta_3^*)'$ is the true value of θ. Therefore, by definition, the expected log-likelihood for such a model can be approximated as:

$$\bar{L}_i(\theta) \approx L_i(\theta^*) - \frac{1}{2}(\theta - \theta^*)' I_i(\theta)\big|_{\theta=\theta^*}(\theta - \theta^*) \tag{5.39}$$

where the notation has its usual meaning as in previous sections.

In this case we have $3^3 = 27$ possible combinations of boundary/non-boundary values of the parameters. Among these 27 models, eight models lie on eight corner points in the parameter space Θ where all parameters are restricted to be particular boundary values. Twelve models lie on points of the boundary edges (lines) excluding the corner points, each containing two restricted parameters and one unrestricted parameter. Another six models lie on any points of the six planes, each having one restricted and two unrestricted parameters. Finally one model falls at any point in the interior of the parameter space containing no restricted parameters. Thus we can categorise all these 27 models into five types.

Let us first consider the first type of model. This problem, like the two parameter case, can be compared to a problem of one-sided hypothesis testing in multivariate analysis (see the references given in the two restriction case). In such a situation we actually deal with the observations which are taken from a three-dimensional (trivariate) normal distribution with a particular testing problem such as (5.27). However, as before, the Wald test statistic for this problem, under the null hypothesis, is distributed as a probability weighted mixture of chi-squared distributions of the form:

$$\sum_{j=0}^{3} w(3,j)\chi^2_{(j)} \tag{5.40}$$

where $w(3,0) = \frac{1}{2}\ w(3,2)$;

$$w(3,1) = \frac{1}{2}\ w(3,3);$$

$$w(3,2) = \frac{3}{8} + \frac{1}{4\pi}\left(\sin^{-1}\rho_{12.3} + \sin^{-1}\rho_{23.1} + \sin^{-1}\rho_{13.2}\right);$$

$$w(3,3) = \frac{1}{8} + \frac{1}{4\pi}\left(\sin^{-1}\rho_{12} + \sin^{-1}\rho_{23} + \sin^{-1}\rho_{13}\right)$$

and ρ_{ls} is the correlation coefficient generated from the asymptotic covariance matrix of the unconstrained maximum likelihood estimates of the parameters, $l \neq s = 1$, 2 and 3, and $\rho_{ls.k_i}$ is the partial correlation coefficient keeping the effect of the estimate of the k_ith parameter as fixed and can be expressed as:

$$\rho_{ls.k_i} = \frac{\rho_{ls} - \rho_{lk_i}\rho_{sk_i}}{\sqrt{\left(1-\rho^2_{lk_i}\right)\left(1-\rho^2_{sk_i}\right)}}$$

(see, for example, Plackett (1955), Bartholomew (1959a, 1959b, 1961) and Barlow et al. (1972)). Therefore, twice the second term of (5.39) with $\theta = \hat{\theta}$ is asymptotically distributed as a probability weighted mixture of chi-squared distributions of the form (5.40). Taking expectations on both sides of (5.39) with $\theta = \hat{\theta}$ we obtain:

$$\bar{\bar{L}}_i(\theta) \approx \bar{L}_i(\theta^*) - \tfrac{1}{2}\left[\sum_{j=0}^{3} w(3,j)E(\chi^2_{(j)})\right]$$

$$= \bar{L}_i(\theta^*) - \tfrac{1}{2}\left[w(3,0)E(\chi^2_{(0)}) + w(3,1)E(\chi^2_{(1)}) + w(3,2)E(\chi^2_{(2)}) + w(3,3)E(\chi^2_{(3)})\right]$$

$$= \bar{L}_i(\theta^*) - \tfrac{1}{2}\Bigg[\tfrac{1}{2} - \tfrac{1}{8} - \tfrac{1}{4\pi}\left(\sin^{-1}\rho_{12} + \sin^{-1}\rho_{23} + \sin^{-1}\rho_{13}\right)$$
$$+ \tfrac{3}{4} + \tfrac{1}{2\pi}\left(\sin^{-1}\rho_{12.3} + \sin^{-1}\rho_{23.1} + \sin^{-1}\rho_{13.2}\right)$$
$$+ \tfrac{3}{8} + \tfrac{1}{4\pi}\left(\sin^{-1}\rho_{12} + \sin^{-1}\rho_{23} + \sin^{-1}\rho_{13}\right)\Bigg],$$

$$= \bar{L}_i(\theta^*) - \tfrac{3}{4} - \tfrac{1}{4\pi}\left(\sin^{-1}\rho_{12} + \sin^{-1}\rho_{23} + \sin^{-1}\rho_{13}\right)$$
$$- \tfrac{1}{4\pi}\left(\sin^{-1}\rho_{12.3} + \sin^{-1}\rho_{23.1} + \sin^{-1}\rho_{13.2}\right). \qquad (5.41)$$

In order to find the value of the first term of (5.51), we use similar arguments as before and can prove that:

$$\bar{L}_i(\theta^*) \approx \bar{L}_i(\hat{\theta}) - \tfrac{3}{4} - \tfrac{1}{4\pi}\left(\sin^{-1}\rho_{12} + \sin^{-1}\rho_{23} + \sin^{-1}\rho_{13}\right)$$
$$- \tfrac{1}{4\pi}\left(\sin^{-1}\rho_{12.3} + \sin^{-1}\rho_{23.1} + \sin^{-1}\rho_{13.2}\right). \qquad (5.42)$$

Substituting the value of (5.42) in (5.41) and using $L_i(\hat{\theta})$ instead of $\bar{L}_i(\hat{\theta})$ due to similar arguments as before, we obtain a new AIC form which we will call PAIC, namely:

$$\bar{\bar{L}}_i(\theta) \approx L_i(\hat{\theta}) - 1\tfrac{1}{2} - \tfrac{1}{2\pi}\left(\sin^{-1}\rho_{12.3} + \sin^{-1}\rho_{23.1} + \sin^{-1}\rho_{13.2}\right)$$
$$- \tfrac{1}{2\pi}\left(\sin^{-1}\rho_{12.3} + \sin^{-1}\rho_{23.1} + \sin^{-1}\rho_{13.2}\right). \qquad (5.53)$$

Now we consider the second type of model which falls on any points along 12 boundary edges except the corner points. In this case, among the three parameters, two are restricted and one is unrestricted. The problem is also related to a partially one-sided hypothesis testing problem and hence as before the Wald test statistic for such a problem can be approximated by a probability weighted mixture of chi-squared distributions of the form:

$$\sum_{j=1}^{3} w(2,j-1)\chi^2_{(j)}. \tag{5.45}$$

Thus twice the second term of (5.39) with $\theta = \hat{\theta}$ is asymptotically distributed as a probability weighted mixture of chi-squared distributions of the form (5.45). Therefore, taking expectations on both sides of (5.39) with $\theta = \hat{\theta}$ we obtain:

$$\begin{aligned}
\bar{\bar{L}}_i(\theta) &\approx \bar{L}_i(\theta^*) - \tfrac{1}{2}\left[\sum_{j=1}^{3} w(3,j-1)E(\chi^2_{(j)})\right] \\
&= \bar{L}_i(\theta^*) - \tfrac{1}{2}\left[w(2,0)E(\chi^2_{(1)}) + w(2,1)E(\chi^2_{(2)}) + w(2,2)E(\chi^2_{(3)})\right] \\
&= \bar{L}_i(\theta^*) - \tfrac{1}{2}\left[\tfrac{1}{4} - \frac{\sin^{-1}\rho_{12}}{2\pi} + \tfrac{1}{2} \times 2 + \left(\tfrac{1}{4} + \frac{\sin^{-1}\rho_{12}}{2\pi} \times 3\right)\right] \\
&= \bar{L}_i(\theta^*) - \tfrac{1}{2}\left[\tfrac{1}{4} - \frac{\sin^{-1}\rho_{12}}{2\pi} + 1 + \tfrac{3}{4} + \frac{3\sin^{-1}\rho_{12}}{2\pi}\right] \\
&= \bar{L}_i(\theta^*) - \tfrac{1}{2}\left[2 + \frac{\sin^{-1}\rho_{12}}{\pi}\right] \\
&= \bar{L}_i(\theta^*) - \left[1 + \frac{\sin^{-1}\rho_{12}}{2\pi}\right].
\end{aligned} \tag{5.45}$$

In order to find the value of $L_i(\theta^*)$, by using similar arguments as before, we can also prove that:

$$\bar{L}_i(\theta^*) \approx L_i(\hat{\theta}) - \left[1 + \frac{\sin^{-1}\rho_{12}}{2\pi}\right]. \tag{5.46}$$

Substituting the value of $\bar{L}_i(\theta^*)$ in (5.45) and using $L_i(\hat{\theta})$ instead of $\bar{L}_i(\hat{\theta})$ due to similar arguments as before we obtain a different form of AIC such as:

$$\bar{\bar{L}}_i(\theta) \approx L_i(\hat{\theta}) - \left[2 + \frac{\sin^{-1}\rho_{12}}{\pi}\right] \tag{5.47}$$

where ρ_{12} has its usual meaning as before.

We now consider the third type of model which falls on any point of the six boundary planes of the three dimensional parameter space Θ. Here, out of the three parameters for each model, only one is restricted and the other two are unrestricted. Thus, the problem can be related to a problem of partially one-sided hypothesis testing and the Wald test statistic for such a problem can be approximated to a probability weighted mixture of chi-squared distributions of the form:

$$\sum_{j=2}^{3} w(2, j-2)\chi^2_{(j)}. \tag{5.48}$$

Therefore, twice the second term of (5.39) with $\theta = \hat{\theta}$ is asymptotically distributed as a probability weighted mixture of chi-squared distributions of the form (5.48). Taking expectations on both sides of (5.39) we obtain:

$$\bar{\bar{L}}_i(\theta) \approx \bar{L}_i(\theta^*) - \frac{1}{2}\left[\sum_{j=2}^{3} w(1, j-2)E(\chi^2_{(j)})\right]$$

$$= \bar{L}_i(\theta^*) - \frac{1}{2}\left[w(1,0)E(\chi^2_{(2)}) + w(1,1)E(\chi^2_{(3)})\right]$$

$$= \bar{L}_i(\theta^*) - 1\,\frac{1}{4}. \tag{5.49}$$

Similarly we can obtain:

$$\bar{L}_i(\theta^*) \approx L_i(\hat{\theta}) - 1\,\frac{1}{4}. \tag{5.50}$$

Combining the equations (5.49) and (5.50) and using $L_i(\hat{\theta})$ instead of $\bar{L}_i(\hat{\theta})$ due to similar arguments as before we obtain a new form of AIC which is to select the model for which:

$$\bar{\bar{L}}_i(\theta)) \approx L_i(\hat{\theta}) - 2\,\frac{1}{2} \tag{5.51}$$

is maximum.

Finally, we consider the fourth type of model which lies in the interior of the parameter space, meaning that all the parameters in the model are asymptotically unrestricted. In this particular case, under appropriate regularity conditions, the estimator is $\hat{\theta}$ asymptotically distributed as:

$$\sqrt{T}(\hat{\theta}-\theta^*) \xrightarrow{a} N\left\{0, \left[\lim_{T\to\infty}\frac{1}{T} I_i(\theta)\Big|_{\theta=\theta^*}\right]^{-1}\right\}.$$

Therefore, twice the second term of (5.39) is asymptotically distributed as a chi-squared distribution with three degrees of freedom. Thus, taking expectations on both sides of (5.39) we obtain:

$$\bar{\bar{L}}_i(\theta) \approx \bar{L}_i(\theta^*) - \frac{3}{2}. \tag{5.52}$$

Similarly we can also show that:

$$\bar{L}_i(\theta^*) \approx \bar{L}_i(\hat{\theta}) - \frac{3}{2}. \tag{5.53}$$

Combining (5.52) and (5.53) and using $L_i(\hat{\theta})$ instead of $\bar{L}_i(\hat{\theta})$ due to similar arguments as before, we obtain the UAIC form as:

$$\bar{\bar{L}}_i(\theta^*) \approx L_i(\hat{\theta}) - 3. \tag{5.54}$$

Here we obtain the normal penalty for a model with three parameters. This is due to the fact that the true value of the parameter lies at any point in the interior of the parameter space Θ. Thus asymptotically the parameters are being considered as free from any restrictions.

We see from the above discussion that for three restricted parameters, there are four different versions of AIC which are given in (5.43), (5.47), (5.51) and (5.55), respectively. Of these four versions, (5.55) provides the usual AIC form for a model with three free parameters. The other three versions give three different penalties depending on where the true parameters lie. But this information is not known at the time of using the model selection procedure. We recommend the use of PAIC (that is (5.53)) in this circumstance because it provides the appropriate penalty in the case of the addition of three unnecessary but restricted parameters.

5.5.3 Generalization to More Than Three Restricted Parameters

In the case of four parameter restrictions, we obtain $3^4 = 81$ possible combinations of boundary/non-boundary values of the parameters under consideration. As before, all these 81 possible models can be categorised into five types in which the first five types of models are related to a problem of one-sided hypothesis testing, and the Wald test statistic for such a problem can be approximated to a probability weighted mixture of chi-squared distributions of the following forms:

$$\sum_{j=2}^{4} w(4,j)\chi^2_{(j)};$$

$$\sum_{j=1}^{4} w(3,j-1)\chi^2_{(j)};$$

$$\sum_{j=2}^{4} w(2,j-2)\chi^2_{(j)};$$

$$\sum_{j=3}^{4} w(1,j-3)\chi^2_{(j)}$$

respectively. Here for the last three types of models, the weights are already known as we used them in previous cases. But for the first type of model in which all the parameters are restricted, the weights are not so available in practice. However, a good approximation can be found in McFadden (1960), Abrahamson (1965) and Childs (1967). Plackett (1954), on the other hand, also gave the following approximation formula (usually called a reduction formula) discussed in Barlow et al. (1972):

$$w(5,5) = \frac{1}{16} + \frac{1}{4\pi^2}\left(\sin^{-1}\rho_{12}\sin^{-1}\rho_{34}\right) + \frac{1}{8\pi}\left(\sin^{-1}\rho_{12} + \sin^{-1}\rho_{23} + \sin^{-1}\rho_{34}\right); \tag{5.55}$$

$$\begin{aligned} w(4,3) = \frac{1}{4} + \frac{1}{8\pi}\left(\sin^{-1}\rho_{12} + \sin^{-1}\rho_{34}\right) &+ \frac{1}{8\pi}\left(\sin^{-1}\rho_{12.3} + \sin^{-1}\rho_{23.1} + \sin^{-1}\rho_{34.2}\right. \\ &\left. + \sin^{-1}\rho_{13.2} + \sin^{-1}\rho_{23.4} + \sin^{-1}\rho_{24.3}\right); \end{aligned} \tag{5.56}$$

$$\begin{aligned} w(4,2) = \frac{1}{2} + \frac{1}{8\pi}\Big(&\sin^{-1}\rho_{12.34} + \sin^{-1}\rho_{13.24} + \sin^{-1}\rho_{14.23} \\ &+ \sin^{-1}\rho_{23.14} + \sin^{-1}\rho_{24.13} + \sin^{-1}\rho_{34.12}\Big) \end{aligned}$$

$$
\begin{aligned}
&-\frac{1}{8\pi}\left(\sin^{-1}\rho_{12}+\sin^{-1}\rho_{23}+\sin^{-1}\rho_{34}\right)\\
&-\frac{1}{4\pi^2}\left(\sin^{-1}\rho_{12}\sin^{-1}\rho_{34,12}+\sin^{-1}\rho_{23}\sin^{-1}\rho_{14.23}\right.\\
&\left.+\sin^{-1}\rho_{34}\sin^{-1}\rho_{12.34}\right); \qquad (5.57)
\end{aligned}
$$

$$w(4,1)=\frac{1}{2}-w(4,3) \qquad (5.58)$$

and

$$w(4,0)=\sum_{j=1}^{4} w(4,j) \qquad (5.59)$$

where the correlation coefficients and the partial correlation coefficients are defined as before. Plackett (1955) also provides a table of exact values for the case of the five restriction case for several combinations of large correlation coefficients. However, as indicated by Bartholomew (1959b), the values of such weights are very small so any error due to using such approximate formulae may be insignificant.

However, by using the above weights and the weights used in the previous cases (without going into detailed explanations as they are similar to all the other cases), we can obtain different AIC forms for the first, second, third, fourth and fifth types of models which are given below.

For the first type of model (all five are restricted parameters):

$$
\begin{aligned}
\bar{\bar{L}}_i(\theta)\approx \bar{L}_i(\hat{\theta})-\Bigg(2\,\frac{1}{4}&+\frac{\sin^{-1}\rho_{12}\sin^{-1}\rho_{34}}{\pi^2}+\frac{2\sin^{-1}\rho_{12}+\sin^{-1}\rho_{23}+2\sin^{-1}\rho_{34}}{4\pi}\\
&+\frac{\sin^{-1}\rho_{12.3}+\sin^{-1}\rho_{23.1}+\sin^{-1}\rho_{34.2}+\sin^{-1}\rho_{13.2}+\sin^{-1}\rho_{23.4}+\sin^{-1}\rho_{24.3}}{4\pi}\\
&+\frac{\sin^{-1}\rho_{12.34}+\sin^{-1}\rho_{13.24}+\sin^{-1}\rho_{14.23}+\sin^{-1}\rho_{23.14}+\sin^{-1}\rho_{24.13}+\sin^{-1}\rho_{34.12}}{4\pi}\\
&-\frac{\sin^{-1}\rho_{12}\sin^{-1}\rho_{34.12}+\sin^{-1}\rho_{23}\sin^{-1}\rho_{14.23}+\sin^{-1}\rho_{34}\sin^{-1}\rho_{12.34}}{2\pi^2}\Bigg). \qquad (5.60)
\end{aligned}
$$

For the second type of model (three restricted parameters and one unrestricted):

$$\bar{\bar{L}}_i(\theta) \approx \bar{L}_i(\hat{\theta}) - \left(2\tfrac{1}{2} + \frac{\sin^{-1}\rho_{12} + \sin^{-1}\rho_{23} + \sin^{-1}\rho_{13} + \sin^{-1}\rho_{12.3} + \sin^{-1}\rho_{23.1} + \sin^{-1}\rho_{13.2}}{2\pi}\right). \tag{5.61}$$

For the third type of model (two restricted parameters and two unrestricted):

$$\bar{\bar{L}}_i(\theta^*) \approx L_i(\hat{\theta}) - \left(3 + \frac{\sin^{-1}\rho_{12}}{\pi}\right). \tag{5.62}$$

For the fourth type of model (one restricted parameter and three unrestricted):

$$\bar{\bar{L}}_i(\theta^*) \approx L_i(\hat{\theta}) - 3\tfrac{1}{2}\,. \tag{5.63}$$

Finally, for the fifth type of model (all five are unrestricted parameters):

$$\bar{\bar{L}}_i(\theta^*) \approx L_i(\hat{\theta}) - 4. \tag{5.64}$$

Equation (5.64) shows a usual AIC form for a model with four parameters. This is because in this particular situation the true value of the parameter lies at any point in the interior of the parameter space Θ. Thus asymptotically the parameters are considered to be free from any restrictions.

Here for four parameter restrictions, we obtain five different versions of AIC which are given by (5.60), (5.61), (5.62), (5.63) and (5.64), respectively. Of these, (5.64) gives the ususal AIC form for the four parameter model. The other four versions provide four different penalties depending on where the true parameter lies. Unfortunately, this information is unavailable at the time of model selection. Our view is to use PAIC in this situation as it does use the appropriate penalty in the case of the addition of four unnecessary restricted parameters.

Now we wish to generalise the derivation of AIC to the k restriction case. To do this, we again consider a model of k parameters, say, $\theta = (\theta_1, \theta_2, \ldots, \theta_k)'$ all of which are under restrictions of the form $a \le \theta \le b$ or equivalently $a_1 \le \theta_1 \le b_1$, $a_2 \le \theta_2 \le b_2, \ldots, a_k \le \theta_k \le b_k$. For this problem, the parameter vector θ can take any value from the k dimensional parameter space Θ. As before, we consider $f_i(y|\theta)$ to be a density function of a $T \times 1$ random vector y, taken from one of m possible models, $1, 2, \ldots, m$. We also consider that $L_i(\theta)$ is the log-likelihood function of $f_i(y|\theta)$, $L_i(\hat{\theta})$ is the maximized value of $L_i(\theta)$ and θ^*

$= (\theta_1^*, \theta_2^*, \ldots, \theta_k^*)'$ is the true value of θ. Therefore, by definition, the expected log-likelihood for such a model can be approximated as:

$$\bar{L}_i(\theta) \approx \bar{L}_i(\theta^*) - \frac{1}{2}\,(\theta - \theta^*)' I_i(\theta)\big|_{\theta=\theta^*}(\theta - \theta^*) \tag{5.65}$$

where the notation has its usual meaning as in previous sections. Now considering the case $\theta = \hat{\theta}$ and taking expectations on both sides of (5.65) we obtain:

$$\bar{\bar{L}}_i(\theta) \approx \bar{L}_i(\theta^*) - \frac{1}{2}\,E\left[(\hat{\theta} - \theta^*)' I_i(\hat{\theta})\big|_{\hat{\theta}=\theta^*}(\hat{\theta} - \theta^*)\right]. \tag{5.66}$$

By using similar arguments we can also obtain:

$$L_i(\theta) \approx L_i(\hat{\theta}) - \frac{1}{2}\,(\theta - \hat{\theta})' I_i(\theta)\big|_{\theta=\hat{\theta}}(\theta - \hat{\theta}). \tag{5.67}$$

Substituting $\theta = \theta^*$ and taking expectations on both sides of (5.67) we obtain:

$$\bar{L}_i(\theta^*) \approx L_i(\hat{\theta}) - \frac{1}{2}\,E\left[(\theta^* - \hat{\theta})' I_i(\theta^*)\big|_{\theta^*=\hat{\theta}}(\theta^* - \hat{\theta})\right]. \tag{5.68}$$

Combining (5.66) and (5.68) and using $L_i(\hat{\theta})$ instead of $\bar{L}_i(\hat{\theta})$ due to similar arguments as before, we obtain:

$$\bar{\bar{L}}_i(\theta) \approx L_i(\hat{\theta}) - E\left[(\hat{\theta} - \theta^*)' I_i(\hat{\theta})\big|_{\hat{\theta}=\theta^*}(\hat{\theta} - \theta^*)\right]. \tag{5.69}$$

For k parameter restrictions, using similar arguments as before, we can obtain 3^k possible combinations of boundary/nonboundary values of the parameters under consideration, which constitute 3^k possible models. All of these models can be categorised into $k + 1$ types. Of these $k + 1$ types of models, the last type comprises only one model which falls at any point in the interior of the parameter space and hence contains no restricted parameters at all. As a result, for such a model, we obtain the UAIC form for k parameters such as:

$$\bar{\bar{L}}_i \approx L_i(\hat{\theta}) - k_i. \tag{5.70}$$

For the remaining k types of models, the first type of model contains k restricted parameters, the second type of model contains $k - 1$ restricted parameters, the third type of model contains $k - 2$ restricted parameters, and so on. As before, this problem is related to a problem of one-sided hypothesis testing and the Wald test statistic for such a problem can be approximated to probability weighted mixtures of chi-squared distributions of the following forms:

$$\sum_{j=0}^{k} w(k,j)\chi^2_{(j)};$$

$$\sum_{j=1}^{k} w(k-1,j-1)\chi^2_{(j)};$$

$$\sum_{j=2}^{k} w(k-2,j-2)\chi^2_{(j)};$$

....

..........................;

and

$$\sum_{j=k-1}^{k} w(1,j-(k-1)\chi^2_{(j)} \qquad (5.71)$$

for the first, second, …, k^{th} type of models, respectively.

Now the essential step in the derivation of new forms of AIC for such a k restriction case is to calculate the above probability weights. In the inequality constraints literature, there has been much discussion about the calculation of the probability weights during the last few decades. The calculation of probability weights up to five is not that difficult and is already provided with due references in this chapter. But the difficulty arises when the number of restrictions becomes greater than five. Although several attempts have been made for $k > 5$ in terms of correlation coefficients these do not provide a satisfactory form for practical use unless the coefficients are small enough (see, for example, Kendall, 1941; Moran, 1948; and Barlow et al., 1972). Bartholomew (1961) provided a table for numerical values of the probability weights up to the number of restrictions equalling 11 but under the following assumptions:

1 all the diagonal elements of the correlation matrix are unity;
2 the off diagonal elements of the correlation matrix are determined by the formula $1/(k-j+2)$;
3 the weights are equal.

In most practical situations the above-mentioned assumptions do not hold exactly and hence the table provided by Bartholomew may not generally be useful. Rather, because of the huge advancement in computing technology these days, the best possible solution to calculating the probability weights for any number of parameter restrictions may be to apply computer simulation techniques. A computer program for this purpose has already been written by Bohrer and Chow (1978). Wolak (1987), on the other hand, has also discussed how the probability weights can be generated by Monte Carlo simulation. See Wu and King (1995) and Hughes (1997) for further discussion regarding this issue.

Once the probability weights are available, then following (5.69), we can easily derive the proposed forms of AIC for such k parameter restrictions as follows:

$$\overline{\overline{L}}_i(\theta) \approx L_i(\hat{\theta}) - \left[\sum_{j=0}^{k} w(k, j) j\right];$$

$$\overline{\overline{L}}_i(\theta) \approx L_i(\hat{\theta}) - \left[\sum_{j=1}^{k} w(k-1, j-1) j\right];$$

$$\overline{\overline{L}}_i(\theta) \approx L_i(\hat{\theta}) - \left[\sum_{j=2}^{k} w(k-2, j-2) j\right];$$

....

..........................;

and $\overline{\overline{L}}_i(\theta) \approx L_i(\hat{\theta}) - \left[\sum_{j=k-1}^{k} w(1, j-(k-1)) j\right]$, respectively. (5.72)

It is clear from equations (5.70) and (5.72) that for k parameter restrictions, we obtain $k+1$ different versions of AIC procedure. Of these versions, (5.70) provides the UAIC procedure for a model with k parameters. This is due to the fact that here the true value of the parameter is assumed to lie at any point in the interior of the parameter space Θ. Thus, asymptotically the parameters are being considered as free from any restrictions. The other k possible versions expressed in (5.72), on the other hand, provide k different penalties depending on where the true parameter value lies. But at the time of model selection this information is not available. Thus we recommend the use of the form of AIC for the case in which all k parameters are on the boundary because it gives the actual penalty when adding k unnecessary but restricted parameters.

5.5.4 Derivation of New AIC Forms for Partially Restricted Parameters

In the previous sections we derived new AIC forms for one, two, three and four restricted parameters and then generalized this for k restricted parameters assuming all the parameters involved in the model are restricted. Now, we wish to derive new AIC forms when the parameters involved in the model are partially restricted, that is, some of the parameters are restricted and some are unrestricted.

We first consider a density function $f_i(y|\theta)$ of a $T \times 1$ random vector y, where $\theta = (\theta_1', \theta_2')'$ is a $k \times 1$ vector of unknown parameters partitioned such that θ_1 is $(k-r) \times 1$ and θ_2 is $r \times 1$, where r is the number of restricted parameters and hence $(k-r)$ is the number of free parameters in the candidate model. We assume that the vector of restricted parameters θ_2 is under the restriction of the form $\theta_2 \in [a,b]$. Here our problem is to derive the AIC form taking into account the restrictions on the parameter θ_2. To do this, we follow a similar situation discussed in Kodde and Palm (1986) and Wu and King (1995) who considered techniques for the one-sided testing problem such as:

$$\begin{aligned} & H_0 : \theta_1 = \theta_{10}, \theta_2 = a \quad \text{versus} \quad \theta_2 > a, \theta \neq (\theta_{10}', a')', \\ \text{or} \quad & H_0 : \theta_1 = \theta_{10}, \theta_2 = b \quad \text{versus} \quad \theta_2 < b, \theta \neq (\theta_{10}', b')'. \end{aligned} \tag{5.73}$$

They found for such partial restrictions that the LR, W and KT test statistics have an asymptotic distribution under H_0 that is a probability weighted mixture of chi-squared distributions of the form:

$$\sum_{j=0}^{r} w(k,j)\chi^2_{(k-r+j)} \tag{5.74}$$

where the probability weights have a similar interpretation as in the case of full restrictions. It is clear from (5.74) that in the case of partial restrictions, the distributional forms are slightly different in terms of probability weights and degrees of freedom of chi-squared distributions. However, to derive AIC for such a model, to avoid repetition, we follow the similar procedure discussed in the full restriction case. As such we take expectations on both sides of either (5.26) or (5.39) and obtain:

$$\bar{\bar{L}}_i(\theta) \approx \bar{L}_i(\theta^*) - \frac{1}{2}\left[\sum_{j=0}^{r} w(r,j)(k-r+j)\right]. \tag{5.75}$$

Similarly we can also obtain:

$$\bar{L}_i(\theta) \approx \bar{L}_i(\hat{\theta}) - \frac{1}{2}\left[\sum_{j=0}^{r} w(r,j)(k-r+j)\right]. \tag{5.76}$$

Combining (5.75) and (5.76) and replacing $L_i(\hat{\theta})$ instead of $\bar{L}_i(\hat{\theta})$ due to similar arguments as before we obtain:

$$\bar{\bar{L}}_i(\theta) \approx \bar{L}_i(\hat{\theta}) - \left[\sum_{j=0}^{r} w(r,j)(k-r+j)\right]. \tag{5.77}$$

This is the general form of PAIC for the partial restrictions case.

From (5.77) one can derive the PAIC form for any combination of restricted and unrestricted parameters' model. For example, suppose we have a model containing one parameter of interest which is restricted to the similar form discussed earlier and one nuisance parameter which is unrestricted. In such a case the new form of AIC form will be:

$$\begin{aligned}
\bar{\bar{L}}_i(\theta) &\approx L_i(\hat{\theta}) - \left[\sum_{j=0}^{r} w(r,j)(k-r+j)\right] \\
&= L_i(\hat{\theta}) - \left[\sum_{j=0}^{r} w(1,j)(2-r+j)\right] \\
&= L_i(\hat{\theta}) - \left[\sum_{j=0}^{1} w(1,j)(1+j)\right] \\
&= L_i(\hat{\theta}) - \left[w(1,0) \times 1 + w(1,1) \times 2\right] \\
&= L_i(\hat{\theta}) - \left[\frac{1}{2} \times 1 + \frac{1}{2} \times 2\right] \\
&= L_i(\hat{\theta}) - 1\frac{1}{2}.
\end{aligned} \tag{5.78}$$

This is similar to (5.35), which is a new form of AIC for one restricted and one unrestricted parameter. Following a similar procedure as above, the new AIC forms for the models containing one restricted with two unrestricted parameters and one restricted with three unrestricted parameters are:

$$\bar{\bar{L}}_i(\theta) \approx L_i(\hat{\theta}) - 2\frac{1}{2} \tag{5.79}$$

and:

$$\bar{\bar{L}}_i(\theta) \approx L_i(\hat{\theta}) - 3\,\tfrac{1}{2} \tag{5.80}$$

respectively. Here (5.79) is similar to (5.51), and (5.80) is similar to (5.63). Similarly, different AIC forms can easily be derived for any number of restricted and unrestricted combinations of parameters involved in the model. It is also apparent from the above expressions that the case of partial restrictions is a particular version of a full restrictions case.

5.6 An Example of a New AIC for the Box-Cox Transformation Model

5.6.1 Use of the Box-Cox Transformation Model

Often, econometricians construct models to estimate economic behavioural relationships. Since economic theory is hardly useful in providing the appropriate functional relationships among the variables of interest, econometricians have become more dependable in their personal choice in the construction of the model. Such personal choice leads them to construct different possible models. The question arises as to which one is the best possible model to use. This is a problem for model building researchers which is often known as the problem of subjectivity. Spitzer (1978) argued that the BCT technique may be a useful tool to solve this problem in econometric modelling. This author also reported that the employment of such transformations has been found to be very fruitful for forecasting purposes. In addition, Gujarati (1992) advocated the use of this technique in order to specify the actual functional form of a regression model. On top of this, the BCT technique was originally proposed to overcome some anomalies involved in the data, such as non-additivity, non-normality and heteroscedasticity.

Recently, the use of such Box-Cox transformations has been widened for many other purposes. Of them, the BCT technique is mostly used to determine the proper functional relationship in many economic, econometric and statistical applications. One possible reason for the popularity of the Box-Cox transformation may be that it allows both the possibility of a log transformation (when $\lambda = 0$) and the possibility of no transformation at all (when $\lambda = 1$). For a detailed discussion about this technique, see the literature survey on this issue in Chapter 4. However, we observe that there has been much work using such a transformation in estimation, testing and prediction, and there has been some work on model selection through testing. For example, see Spitzer (1978), Aneuryn-Evans and Deaton (1980), Hinkley (1988), Collins (1991) and Kim and Hill (1993). Unfortunately, so far as we are aware, almost nothing has been reported about using this BCT technique in the IC-based model selection literature. Therefore, in this chapter, we developed a new class of model selection procedures by making appropriate use of parameter restrictions. Our main aim is to investigate whether our proposed procedure (developed in the previous chapter) works well in terms of accuracy of model selection, through a range of Monte Carlo experiments, involving the restriction $0 \leq \lambda \leq 1$, on the Box-Cox parameter.

5.6.2 Derivation of AIC for the Box-Cox Transformation Model

Before deriving the AIC of this model, let us first define the general BCT model that can be expressed as follows:

$$y_t(\lambda) = \beta_0 + \beta_1 x_1(\lambda) + \ldots + \beta_{k-3} x_{k-3}(\lambda) + u_t.. \tag{5.81}$$

In matrix form, model (5.81) can be written as:

$$y(\lambda) = X(\lambda)\beta + u \tag{5.82}$$

where $y(\lambda)$ is a $T \times 1$ vector of transformed observations on the dependent variable and can be defined as follows:

$$\begin{aligned} y_t(\lambda) &= \frac{y_t^\lambda - 1}{\lambda} && \text{when } \lambda \neq 0 && \text{(BCT model or Model-3)} \\ &= \ln(y_t) && \text{when } \lambda = 0 && \text{(log-linear model or Model-2)} \\ &= y_t - 1 && \text{when } \lambda = 1 && \text{(linear model or Model-1).} \end{aligned}$$

Note that $y \geq 0$ is required for the first case and $y > 0$ for other cases. X is a $T \times (k-2)$ matrix of transformed observations of the independent variables, β is a $(k-2) \times 1$ vector of parameters and u is a $T \times 1$ vector of disturbance terms. Here λ is our parameter of interest which is restricted to the form $\lambda \in [0,1]$ and the other parameters, namely, $\beta = (\beta_0, \beta_1, \ldots, \beta_{k-3})'$ and σ^2, are not our parameters of interest (often called nuisance parameters) and which are unrestricted in our case.

One of the major drawbacks of the Box-Cox transformation technique is that the distribution of u_t is truncated and hence it cannot be normally distributed. See for example, Fomby et al. (1984), Judge et al. (1985) and Bairam (1992). In order to work with maximum likelihood estimation, here we assume that the truncation effect is insignificant and that the disturbance term u_t is an approximately independently and normally distributed random variable with mean 0 and variance σ^2, that is, $u_t \sim IN(0,\sigma^2)$. Under such an assumption, the appropriate log-likelihood function of (5.82) is:

$$L(\theta) = -\left(\frac{T}{2}\right)\ln(2\pi) - \left(\frac{T}{2}\right)\ln(\sigma^2) - \frac{1}{2\sigma^2}\left(y(\lambda) - X(\lambda)\beta\right)' \times \left(y(\lambda) - X(\lambda)\beta\right) + (\lambda - 1)\sum_{t=1}^{T}\ln(y_t). \tag{5.83}$$

Here $\theta = (\beta',\sigma^{2\prime},\lambda')'$ and the last term of (5.83) is due to the Jacobian of the transformation from u to y, which is given by:

$$J = \prod_{t=1}^{T}\left|\frac{\partial y_t(\lambda)}{\partial y_t}\right| = \prod_{t=1}^{T} y_t^{\lambda-1}. \tag{5.84}$$

As the same constant terms are involved in all the competing models, they have the equal influence for each of the competing models in determining the size of the maximized log-likelihood. Thus, we can ignore the constant terms, and obtain the concentrated log-likelihood function as:

$$L(\theta) = -\left(\frac{T}{2}\right)\ln(\hat{\sigma}^2(\lambda)) + (\lambda - 1)\sum_{t=1}^{T}\ln(y_t) \tag{5.85}$$

where $\hat{\sigma}^2(\lambda) = \left[\left(y(\lambda) - X(\lambda)\hat{\beta}\right)'\left(y(\lambda) - X(\lambda)\hat{\beta}\right)\right]T$ is the estimated variance of u conditional on λ and $\beta = \left[X(\lambda)'X(\lambda)\right]^{-1}\left[X(\lambda)'y(\lambda)\right]$. Here the elements of $X(\lambda)$ are defined similar to the elements of $y(\lambda)$.

Now, instead of using the above general form of the BCT model, we wish to derive the AIC for a simple form of the BCT model where λ is the only restricted parameter of the form $\lambda \in [0,1]$, and β_0, β_1 and $\hat{\sigma}^2$ are three unrestricted (nuisance) parameters of our model of interest. We assume that the model considered here is taken from one of m possible models, $i = 1, 2, \ldots, m$.

Let $L_i(\theta)$ be the log-likelihood function of our considered model and $L_i(\hat{\theta})$ be the maximized value of $L_i(\theta)$. However, to derive AIC for such a model, and to avoid repetition, we just follow (5.80) where one parameter is restricted and the other three parameters are unrestricted outlined in the subsection 3.5.5 in Chapter 3. Consequently, we obtain similar formulae for AIC in this case as we obtained in (5.80), that is, for $\lambda^* = 0$ or 1 (λ^* is the true value of λ), the PAIC decision rule which is to select the model for which:

$$PAIC_i \approx L_i(\hat{\theta}) - \left(k_i - \frac{1}{2}\right) \tag{5.86}$$

is a maximum, over $i = 1,2,\ldots,m$, where k_i (which is 5 in our case) is the total number of parameters in the ith model. For $0 < \lambda^* < 1$, on the other hand, we obtain the UAIC form namely:

$$UAIC_i \approx L_i(\hat{\theta}) - k_i \tag{5.87}$$

where k_i is the number of parameters in the ith model. It is clear from (5.86) and (5.87) that for one parameter restriction, we obtain two different versions of AIC procedure one of which (5.87) is the usual criterion and the other the PAIC (5.86). The difference between these two versions is the only penalty which depends on where the true parameter lies. Questions may arise as to which penalty to apply in practice. Our view is to use the new penalty because in the case of the addition of extraneous but restricted parameters, it is a more appropriate penalty for the maximized log-likelihood function. This is because the expected increase in the maximized log-likelihood is much less when restricted but extraneous parameters are added to the likelihood.

5.6.3 *Extension of the Idea of New AIC to BIC for BCT Model*

As discussed in the previous chapter, both AIC and BIC are widely used criteria in model selection for various purposes under different situations. Because of the parallel importance of these two criteria we consider AIC for the theoretical development of our proposed AIC and then extend the arguments to BIC for our simulation experiments for comparison purposes. As PAIC counts restricted parameters as less than one in the penalty (which is $k_i - 1/2$ where one out of k_i parameters is restricted), we can apply the same count of parameters to BIC (which we call PBIC). For the one restriction case, the PBIC for the ith model is considered as below:

$$PBIC_i \approx L_i(\hat{\theta}) - \left(k_i - \frac{1}{2}\right)\frac{\ln(T)}{2}. \quad (5.88)$$

Similar to PAIC, the loss associated with PBIC is also less heavy than that of regular BIC.

5.6.4 Monte Carlo Simulation

In order to investigate the small sample properties of the PAIC and PBIC, we conducted a Monte Carlo experiment. Due to the use of some non-sample information in the estimation of a restricted model we may expect PAIC and PBIC to perform better in the Monte Carlo simulation than their usual counterparts. This experiment aims to examine such expectations in terms of probabilities of correct selection (PCS) of the true models for different sample sizes, different design matrices and different values of the transformation parameter λ.

5.6.4.1 Experimental design For any model selection problem, the main objective is to select the correct model from a set of competing models. We consider the following three competing models in our choice set for the Monte Carlo experiment:

$$\begin{aligned} &y_t = \beta_0 + \beta_1 x_t + u_t && \text{Model-1} \\ &\ln(y_t) = \beta_0 + \beta_1 x_t + u_t && \text{Model-2} \\ &(y_t^{\lambda} - 1) = \beta_0 + \beta_1 x_t + u_t && \text{Model-3} \end{aligned} \quad (5.89)$$

where y_t is the tth observation of the dependent variable, x_t is the tth observation of the independent variable and u_t is the disturbance term in period t. Here Model-1, Model-2 and Model-3 are called the simple linear regression models, the log-linear model and the BCT model respectively. The data is generated from each of the above three models in turn. For data generation in each case, the disturbance term u_t is assumed to be distributed as independently normal with mean zero and variance σ^2, that is, $u_t \sim IN(0,\sigma^2)$ where $t = 1, 2, \ldots, T$, x_t is generated from an AR(1) process such as $x_t = \rho x_{t-1} + v_t$, where $v_t \sim IN(0,\sigma_v^2)$. We set $\beta_0 = 10.0$, $\beta_1 = 1.0$, $\sigma^2 = 1.0$ for each data generating case and five different values of ρ such as 0, 0.25, 0.95, 1.00 and 1.05 for design matrices $X1$, $X2$, $X3$, $X5$ and $X5$, respectively. In each case x_t is generated artificially and then held fixed from iteration to iteration. The regressors chosen here are influenced by Engle et al.'s (1985) Monte Carlo study. However, the five ρ

values cover five different types of economic data, namely white-noise, low autoregressive, high autoregressive, random walk and explosive processes. Four different sample sizes of $T = 20, 50, 100$ and 500 are used for comparison purposes. The number of replications for each experiment is 1,000.

Note that the Jacobian of the transformation from u_t to y_t for Model-2 and Model-3 are y_t^{-1} and $y_t^{\lambda-1}$, respectively. However, for the estimation of probabilities of selecting the competing models, the concentrated log-likelihood of observing the sample $y_1, y_2, \ldots, y_T$ for Model-1, Model-2 and Model-3 without considering the constant terms (since the constant terms are the same for each model, they are unaffected for model selection in our case) are:

$$L_1(\hat{\theta}_1) = -(T/2)\ln\hat{\sigma}^2;$$

$$L_2(\hat{\theta}_2) = -(T/2)\ln\hat{\sigma}^2(l) - \sum \ln(y_t);$$

and

$$L_3(\hat{\theta}_3) = -(T/2)\ln\hat{\sigma}^2(\lambda) + (\lambda - 1)\sum \ln(y_t) \tag{5.90}$$

respectively, where:

$$\hat{\theta}_1 = \left(\hat{\beta}(1)', \hat{\sigma}^{2\prime}\right); \tag{5.91}$$

$$\hat{\theta}_2 = \left(\hat{\beta}(2)', \hat{\sigma}^2(l)'\right)'; \tag{5.92}$$

$$\hat{\theta}_3 = \left(\hat{\beta}(3)', \hat{\sigma}^2(\lambda)'\right)'; \tag{5.93}$$

$$\hat{\sigma}^2 = \sum_{t=1}^{T}(y_t - \hat{\beta}_0 - \hat{\beta}_1 x_t)^2/T; \tag{5.95}$$

$$\hat{\sigma}^2(l) = \sum_{t=1}^{T}(\ln(y_t) - \hat{\beta}_0 - \hat{\beta}_1 x_t)^2/T; \tag{5.95}$$

and

$$\hat{\sigma}^2(\lambda) = \sum_{t=1}^{T}(y_t(\lambda) - \hat{\beta}_0 - \hat{\beta}_1 x_t)^2/T. \tag{5.96}$$

Here $\hat{\beta}_0$s and $\hat{\beta}_1$s are all different as they are derived from three different models and can be defined in matrix notation as:

$$\hat{\beta}(1) = \left(\hat{\beta}_0, \hat{\beta}_1\right)' = \left(X_1'X_1\right)^{-1} X_1'y \qquad \text{(for Model-1);} \qquad (5.97)$$

$$\hat{\beta}(2) = \left(\hat{\beta}_0, \hat{\beta}_1\right)' = \left(X_1'X_1\right)^{-1} X_1'\mathrm{y}(y) \qquad \text{(for Model-2);} \qquad (5.98)$$

$$\hat{\beta}(3) = \left(\hat{\beta}_0, \hat{\beta}_1\right)' = \left(X_1'X_1\right)^{-1} X_1'\mathrm{y}(\lambda) \qquad \text{(for Model-3);} \qquad (5.99)$$

$$\text{where } X_1 = \begin{bmatrix} 1 & x_1 \\ 1 & x_2 \\ \vdots & \vdots \\ 1 & x_T \end{bmatrix}, y = \begin{bmatrix} y_1 \\ y_2 \\ \vdots \\ y_T \end{bmatrix}, \ln(y) = \begin{bmatrix} \ln(y_1) \\ \ln(y_2) \\ \vdots \\ \ln(y_T) \end{bmatrix} \text{ and } y(\lambda) = \begin{bmatrix} \left(y_1^{\lambda} - 1\right)/\lambda \\ \left(y_2^{\lambda} - 1\right)/\lambda \\ \vdots \\ \left(y_2^{\lambda} - 1\right)/\lambda \end{bmatrix}. \qquad (5.100)$$

We consider Model-1 (when data are generated for $\lambda = 1.0$), Model-2 (when data are generated for $\lambda = 0$) and Model-3 (when data are generated for $\lambda = 0.1$, $\lambda = 0.3$, $\lambda = 0.5$, $\lambda = 0.7$, $\lambda = 0.9$) as true models for the first, second and third set of experiments, respectively. That means that the simple linear regression model, log-model and the Box-Cox transformation model are considered as true models for the first, second and third set, respectively. The values of λ for when Model-3 is assumed true were estimated by maximizing the likelihood using the Gauss Constrained Optimization technique (GAUSS Documentation Version, 1996) for λ constrained between zero and one in all experiments. In each iteration, the values of AIC and BIC for three competing models were calculated. Among them, Model-3 in all cases displays two different types of penalty values; one is for UAIC and the other is for PAIC, which are 5 and 3.5, respectively. At each step we select the model whose value of UAIC, PAIC, UBIC or PBIC is a maximum.

5.6.4.2 Results of the Monte Carlo experiments Table 5.1 presents a comparison between PAIC, UAIC, PBIC and UBIC by estimating probabilities of choosing Model-1, Model-2 and Model-3 for design matrices *X*1, *X*2, *X*3, *X*4 and *X*5 when Model-1 is true. Several interesting phenomena are apparent in Table 5.1. As expected the probabilities of selecting the true model (Model-1) are much higher than the probabilities of incorrectly selecting Model-2 or -3. Moreover, the PCS gradually increase as the sample size T increases in almost all the cases and which is desirable. Among the four procedures considered in this study, PBIC and UBIC show an almost similar but slightly

Table 5.1 Comparison between PAIC, UAIC, PBIC and UBIC based on estimated probabilities of choosing competing models Model-1, Model-2 and Model-3 for design matrices *X*1, *X*2, *X*3, *X*4 and *X*5 when Model-1 is true

	Model	**Model-1**				**Model-2**				**Model-3**			
X	*T*	*PAIC*	*UAIC*	*PBIC*	*UBIC*	*PAIC*	*UAIC*	*PBIC*	*UBIC*	*PAIC*	*UAIC*	*PBIC*	*UBIC*
	20	.607	.611	.610	.611	.387	.389	.389	.389	.006	.000	.001	.000
*X*1	50	.755	.765	.765	.766	.231	.235	.235	.235	.015	.001	.001	.000
	100	.799	.826	.826	.826	.159	.173	.173	.175	.052	.001	.001	.000
	500	.852	.921	.969	.988	.000	.001	.003	.012	.158	.078	.028	.000
	20	.559	.559	.556	.559	.532	.539	.536	.550	.019	.002	.005	.001
*X*2	50	.738	.758	.758	.758	.233	.252	.252	.252	.029	.000	.000	.000
	100	.778	.812	.815	.815	.157	.185	.185	.186	.065	.003	.001	.000
	500	.833	.915	.960	.975	.002	.005	.015	.026	.165	.080	.025	.000
	20	.793	.885	.850	.925	.000	.000	.000	.000	.207	.115	.150	.076
*X*3	50	.857	.921	.920	.973	.000	.000	.000	.000	.153	.079	.080	.027
	100	.831	.902	.929	.983	.000	.000	.000	.000	.169	.098	.071	.017
	500	.832	.912	.952	.992	.000	.000	.000	.000	.168	.088	.058	.008
	20	.806	.897	.861	.933	.000	.000	.000	.000	.195	.103	.139	.067
*X*4	50	.838	.933	.931	.982	.000	.000	.000	.000	.162	.067	.069	.018
	100	.816	.911	.925	.981	.000	.000	.000	.000	.185	.089	.076	.019
	500	.850	.923	.952	.989	.000	.000	.000	.000	.160	.077	.058	.011
	20	.815	.900	.861	.936	.000	.000	.000	.000	.185	.100	.139	.065
*X*5	50	.857	.931	.930	.979	.000	.000	.000	.000	.153	.069	.070	.021
	100	.856	.908	.927	.980	.000	.000	.000	.000	.155	.092	.073	.020
	500	1.00	1.00	1.00	1.00	.000	.000	.000	.000	.000	.000	.000	.000

Table 5.2 Comparison between PAIC, UAIC, PBIC and UBIC based on estimated probabilities of choosing competing models Model-1, Model-2 and Model-3 for design matrices *X*1, *X*2, *X*3, *X*4 and *X*5 when Model-2 is true

	Model	Model-1				Model-2				Model-3			
X	*T*	*PAIC*	*UAIC*	*PBIC*	*UBIC*	*PAIC*	*UAIC*	*PBIC*	*UBIC*	*PAIC*	*UAIC*	*PBIC*	*UBIC*
*X*1	20	.000	.000	.000	.000	.892	.957	.932	.978	.108	.053	.068	.022
	50	.000	.000	.000	.000	.865	.952	.950	.986	.135	.058	.060	.015
	100	.000	.000	.000	.000	.853	.937	.951	.990	.157	.063	.059	.010
	500	.000	.000	.000	.000	.838	.925	.966	.995	.162	.076	.035	.005
*X*2	20	.000	.000	.000	.000	.933	.973	.957	.985	.067	.027	.053	.016
	50	.000	.000	.000	.000	.890	.957	.955	.985	.110	.053	.055	.016
	100	.000	.000	.000	.000	.858	.950	.959	.991	.152	.060	.051	.009
	500	.000	.000	.000	.000	.857	.927	.962	.997	.153	.073	.038	.003
*X*3	20	.000	.000	.000	.000	.822	.906	.867	.953	.178	.095	.133	.057
	50	.000	.000	.000	.000	.820	.907	.902	.965	.180	.093	.098	.036
	100	.000	.000	.000	.000	.853	.921	.936	.988	.157	.079	.065	.012
	500	.000	.000	.000	.000	.850	.939	.972	.993	.150	.061	.028	.007
*X*4	20	.000	.000	.000	.000	.820	.910	.869	.951	.180	.090	.131	.059
	50	.000	.000	.000	.000	.827	.915	.915	.972	.173	.085	.086	.028
	100	.000	.000	.000	.000	.859	.921	.933	.983	.151	.079	.067	.017
	500	.000	.000	.000	.000	.907	.969	.978	1.00	.093	.031	.022	.000
*X*5	20	.000	.000	.000	.000	.832	.901	.877	.952	.168	.099	.123	.058
	50	.000	.000	.000	.000	.853	.922	.933	.981	.157	.078	.067	.019
	100	.000	.000	.000	.000	.887	.967	.968	1.00	.113	.033	.032	.000
	500	.000	.000	.000	.000	.925	.989	1.00	1.00	.075	.011	.000	.000

better performance than PAIC and UAIC. The average probability of correct selection (APCS) of PAIC, UAIC, PBIC and UBIC over all design matrices and sample sizes are 0.8056, 0.8595, 0.8658 and 0.8975, respectively. Thus according to their APCS, they can be ranked as UBIC > PBIC > UAIC > PAIC. However, by looking forward to the probabilities of selecting Model-3, we see that both PAIC and PBIC are always better than their usual counterparts. Of the five design matrices considered, $X3$, $X4$ and $X5$ seem to be more effective than $X1$ and $X2$ in producing higher PCS.

Table 5.2 presents similar comparisons where Model-2 is now the true model. Here the probabilities of selecting the true model are consistently higher than those of Models 1 and 3 in all respects. Over the whole experiment, the PCS are very close to one for all matrices considered. In contrast to the previous case, here the matrices $X1$ and $X2$ seem more effective than the other three matrices in producing higher PCS. As the sample size increases, the PCS also increase for all procedures for matrices $X3$, $X4$ and $X5$. But for matrices $X1$ and $X2$, we find some surprising results for the PAIC and UAIC procedures, where the probabilities of choosing the true model slightly decrease as the sample size increases. For PBIC and UBIC, we find no anomalies in the results in connection with sample size. Here the PCS are relatively higher than those of the previous case (see Table 5.1). For example, the APCS for PAIC, UAIC, PBIC and UBIC overall design matrices and sample sizes are 0.8606, 0.9357, 0.9376 and 0.9811, respectively, each of which is much higher than that of the corresponding figures when Model-1 is true. Interestingly, in accordance with the APCS, the ranking which we obtained for four competing methods in the above is still the same in this case.

Finally, Tables 5.3, 5.4, 5.5, 5.6 and 5.7 show similar comparisons when Model-3 is the true model. These tables present results for design matrices $X1$, $X2$, $X3$, $X4$ and $X5$, respectively, for $\lambda = 0.1, 0.3, 0.5, 0.7$ and 0.9. Unlike the previous two cases, here the PCS for the true model vary significantly for different design matrices and for different values of λ. For example, for matrix $X1$ with sample sizes of 20, 50 and 100, the probabilities of choosing the true model are lower, and in some cases much lower. For sample size $T = 500$, on the other hand, we find the probabilities of correctly choosing the true model are much higher in most of the cases considered. As the value of λ tends to zero (which converges to a log-linear model) the probability of choosing Model-2 becomes larger. Similarly, when λ tends to one (which converges to a linear regression model) the probability of choosing Model-1 becomes larger; both of these are to be expected. Among the competing procedures for design matrix $X1$, PAIC performs better than all other procedures for lower

Table 5.3 Comparison between PAIC, UAIC, PBIC and UBIC based on estimated probabilities of choosing competing models Model-1, Model-2 and Model-3 for design matrix $X1$ when $\lambda = 0.1, 0.3, 0.5, 0.7$ and 0.9 and Model-3 is true

		Design matrix $X1$ when $\rho = 0$											
Model		Model-1				Model-2				Model-3			
λ	*T*	*PAIC*	*UAIC*	*PBIC*	*UBIC*	*PAIC*	*UAIC*	*PBIC*	*UBIC*	*PAIC*	*UAIC*	*PBIC*	*UBIC*
λ=0.1	20	.002	.005	.003	.012	.765	.869	.825	.915	.233	.126	.172	.073
	50	.000	.000	.000	.000	.589	.737	.731	.883	.511	.263	.269	.117
	100	.000	.000	.000	.000	.518	.658	.688	.858	.582	.352	.312	.152
	500	.000	.000	.000	.000	.109	.210	.325	.612	.891	.790	.675	.388
λ=0.3	20	.117	.167	.158	.193	.662	.758	.725	.773	.221	.085	.127	.035
	50	.022	.060	.058	.157	.539	.575	.572	.739	.539	.365	.370	.115
	100	.000	.008	.015	.058	.308	.558	.503	.695	.692	.535	.583	.257
	500	.000	.000	.000	.000	.009	.030	.055	.190	.991	.970	.955	.810
λ=0.5	20	.357	.382	.370	.388	.565	.606	.593	.611	.089	.012	.037	.001
	50	.301	.533	.529	.573	.392	.589	.588	.525	.307	.078	.083	.003
	100	.180	.320	.355	.567	.258	.393	.528	.521	.562	.287	.217	.012
	500	.001	.005	.019	.105	.003	.011	.027	.107	.996	.985	.955	.788
λ=0.7	20	.593	.502	.501	.502	.586	.596	.593	.597	.021	.002	.006	.001
	50	.572	.625	.623	.627	.338	.370	.369	.373	.090	.005	.008	.000
	100	.527	.658	.663	.672	.235	.315	.320	.328	.238	.038	.017	.000
	500	.230	.375	.521	.803	.002	.006	.019	.075	.768	.619	.560	.122
λ=0.9	20	.561	.563	.563	.565	.535	.536	.535	.536	.005	.001	.002	.000
	50	.698	.708	.708	.708	.287	.292	.292	.292	.015	.000	.000	.000
	100	.750	.769	.769	.770	.207	.230	.230	.230	.053	.001	.001	.000
	500	.705	.837	.907	.966	.002	.006	.013	.035	.293	.157	.080	.000

Table 5.4 Comparison between PAIC, UAIC, PBIC and UBIC based on estimated probabilities of choosing competing models Model-1, Model-2 and Model-3 for Design Matrix $X2$ when $\lambda = 0.1, 0.3, 0.5, 0.7$ and 0.9 and Model-3 is true

		Design matrix $X2$ when $\rho = 0.25$											
Model		Model-1				Model-2				Model-3			
λ	*T*	*PAIC*	*UAIC*	*PBIC*	*UBIC*	*PAIC*	*UAIC*	*PBIC*	*UBIC*	*PAIC*	*UAIC*	*PBIC*	*UBIC*
λ=0.1	20	.003	.007	.005	.016	.807	.895	.863	.905	.190	.098	.132	.079
	50	.000	.000	.000	.000	.596	.730	.727	.868	.505	.270	.273	.132
	100	.000	.000	.000	.000	.505	.630	.663	.819	.596	.370	.337	.181
	500	.000	.000	.000	.000	.118	.225	.350	.603	.882	.776	.660	.397
λ=0.3	20	.072	.116	.099	.137	.677	.780	.755	.818	.251	.105	.157	.055
	50	.015	.056	.055	.109	.519	.553	.559	.710	.567	.501	.506	.181
	100	.000	.006	.008	.055	.296	.525	.566	.656	.705	.570	.526	.309
	500	.000	.000	.000	.000	.023	.059	.089	.238	.977	.951	.911	.762
λ=0.5	20	.255	.310	.290	.323	.610	.661	.657	.673	.136	.029	.063	.005
	50	.215	.357	.355	.556	.363	.575	.570	.529	.523	.169	.176	.025
	100	.135	.261	.293	.551	.255	.365	.389	.506	.622	.375	.318	.053
	500	.001	.011	.031	.155	.010	.026	.057	.150	.989	.963	.922	.705
λ=0.7	20	.517	.535	.527	.538	.552	.559	.556	.562	.051	.006	.017	.000
	50	.510	.598	.597	.613	.328	.375	.375	.387	.162	.027	.029	.000
	100	.575	.605	.631	.662	.228	.302	.315	.338	.297	.093	.055	.000
	500	.256	.515	.555	.813	.005	.020	.039	.115	.739	.566	.507	.073
λ=0.9	20	.502	.508	.508	.508	.586	.591	.591	.592	.012	.001	.001	.000
	50	.679	.702	.701	.703	.279	.297	.297	.297	.052	.001	.002	.000
	100	.707	.759	.762	.765	.208	.235	.235	.235	.085	.007	.005	.000
	500	.713	.835	.912	.950	.005	.016	.035	.050	.283	.159	.053	.000

Table 5.5 Comparison between PAIC, UAIC, PBIC and UBIC based on estimated probabilities of choosing competing models Model-1, Model-2 and Model-3 for design matrix $X3$ when $\lambda = 0.1, 0.3, 0.5, 0.7$ and 0.9 and Model-3 is true

		Design matrix $X3$ when $\rho = 0.95$											
Model		Model-1				Model-2				Model-3			
λ	*T*	*PAIC*	*UAIC*	*PBIC*	*UBIC*	*PAIC*	*UAIC*	*PBIC*	*UBIC*	*PAIC*	*UAIC*	*PBIC*	*UBIC*
λ=0.1	20	.000	.000	.000	.000	.000	.000	.000	.000	1.00	1.00	1.00	1.00
	50	.000	.000	.000	.000	.000	.000	.000	.000	1.00	1.00	1.00	1.00
	100	.000	.000	.000	.000	.000	.000	.000	.000	1.00	1.00	1.00	1.00
	500	.000	.000	.000	.000	.000	.000	.000	.000	1.00	1.00	1.00	.100
λ=0.3	20	.000	.000	.000	.000	.000	.000	.000	.000	1.00	1.00	1.00	1.00
	50	.000	.000	.000	.000	.000	.000	.000	.000	1.00	1.00	1.00	1.00
	100	.000	.000	.000	.000	.000	.000	.000	.000	1.00	1.00	1.00	1.00
	500	.000	.000	.000	.000	.000	.000	.000	.000	1.00	1.00	1.00	.100
λ=0.5	20	.000	.000	.000	.000	.000	.000	.000	.000	1.00	1.00	1.00	1.00
	50	.000	.000	.000	.000	.000	.000	.000	.000	1.00	1.00	1.00	1.00
	100	.000	.000	.000	.000	.000	.000	.000	.000	1.00	1.00	1.00	1.00
	500	.000	.000	.000	.000	.000	.000	.000	.000	1.00	1.00	1.00	.100
λ=0.7	20	.000	.000	.000	.000	.000	.000	.000	.000	1.00	1.00	1.00	1.00
	50	.000	.000	.000	.000	.000	.000	.000	.000	1.00	1.00	1.00	1.00
	100	.000	.000	.000	.000	.000	.000	.000	.000	1.00	1.00	1.00	1.00
	500	.000	.000	.000	.000	.000	.000	.000	.000	1.00	1.00	1.00	.100
λ=0.9	20	.078	.170	.127	.275	.000	.000	.000	.000	.922	.830	.873	.726
	50	.000	.000	.000	.003	.000	.000	.000	.000	1.00	1.00	1.00	.997
	100	.000	.000	.000	.000	.000	.000	.000	.000	1.00	1.00	1.00	1.00
	500	.000	.000	.000	.000	.000	.000	.000	.000	1.00	1.00	1.00	.100

Table 5.6 Comparison between PAIC, UAIC, PBIC and UBIC based on estimated probabilities of choosing competing models Model-1, Model-2 and Model-3 for design matrix $X4$ when $\lambda = 0.1, 0.3, 0.5, 0.7$ and 0.9 and Model-3 is true

		Design matrix $X4$ when $\rho = 1.00$											
Model		Model-1				Model-2				Model-3			
λ	*T*	*PAIC*	*UAIC*	*PBIC*	*UBIC*	*PAIC*	*UAIC*	*PBIC*	*UBIC*	*PAIC*	*UAIC*	*PBIC*	*UBIC*
λ=0.1	20	.000	.000	.000	.000	.000	.000	.000	.000	1.00	1.00	1.00	1.00
	50	.000	.000	.000	.000	.000	.000	.000	.000	1.00	1.00	1.00	1.00
	100	.000	.000	.000	.000	.000	.000	.000	.000	1.00	1.00	1.00	1.00
	500	.000	.000	.000	.000	.000	.000	.000	.000	1.00	1.00	1.00	1.00
λ=0.3	20	.000	.000	.000	.000	.000	.000	.000	.000	1.00	1.00	1.00	1.00
	50	.000	.000	.000	.000	.000	.000	.000	.000	1.00	1.00	1.00	1.00
	100	.000	.000	.000	.000	.000	.000	.000	.000	1.00	1.00	1.00	1.00
	500	.000	.000	.000	.000	.000	.000	.000	.000	1.00	1.00	1.00	1.00
λ=0.5	20	.000	.000	.000	.000	.000	.000	.000	.000	1.00	1.00	1.00	1.00
	50	.000	.000	.000	.000	.000	.000	.000	.000	1.00	1.00	1.00	1.00
	100	.000	.000	.000	.000	.000	.000	.000	.000	1.00	1.00	1.00	1.00
	500	.000	.000	.000	.000	.000	.000	.000	.000	1.00	1.00	1.00	1.00
λ=0.7	20	.000	.000	.000	.000	.000	.000	.000	.000	1.00	1.00	1.00	1.00
	50	.000	.000	.000	.000	.000	.000	.000	.000	1.00	1.00	1.00	1.00
	100	.000	.000	.000	.000	.000	.000	.000	.000	1.00	1.00	1.00	1.00
	500	.000	.000	.000	.000	.000	.000	.000	.000	1.00	1.00	1.00	1.00
λ=0.9	20	.003	.006	.006	.015	.000	.000	.000	.000	.997	.995	.995	.986
	50	.000	.000	.000	.000	.000	.000	.000	.000	1.00	1.00	1.00	1.00
	100	.000	.000	.000	.000	.000	.000	.000	.000	1.00	1.00	1.00	1.00
	500	.000	.000	.000	.000	.000	.000	.000	.000	1.00	1.00	1.00	1.00

Table 5.7 Comparison between PAIC, UAIC, PBIC and UBIC based on estimated probabilities of choosing competing models Model-1, Model-2 and Model-3 for design matrix $X5$ when $\lambda = 0.1, 0.3, 0.5, 0.7$ and 0.9 and Model-3 is true

		Design matrix $X5$ when $\rho = 1.05$											
Model		Model-1				Model-2				Model-3			
λ	T	*PAIC*	*UAIC*	*PBIC*	*UBIC*	*PAIC*	*UAIC*	*PBIC*	*UBIC*	*PAIC*	*UAIC*	*PBIC*	*UBIC*
λ=0.1	20	.000	.000	.000	.000	.000	.000	.000	.000	1.00	1.00	1.00	1.00
	50	.000	.000	.000	.000	.000	.000	.000	.000	1.00	1.00	1.00	1.00
	100	.000	.000	.000	.000	.000	.000	.000	.000	1.00	1.00	1.00	1.00
	500	.000	.000	.000	.000	.000	.000	.000	.000	1.00	1.00	1.00	1.00
λ=0.3	20	.000	.000	.000	.000	.000	.000	.000	.000	1.00	1.00	1.00	1.00
	50	.000	.000	.000	.000	.000	.000	.000	.000	1.00	1.00	1.00	1.00
	100	.000	.000	.000	.000	.000	.000	.000	.000	1.00	1.00	1.00	1.00
	500	.000	.000	.000	.000	.000	.000	.000	.000	1.00	1.00	1.00	1.00
λ=0.5	20	.000	.000	.000	.000	.000	.000	.000	.000	1.00	1.00	1.00	1.00
	50	.000	.000	.000	.000	.000	.000	.000	.000	1.00	1.00	1.00	1.00
	100	.000	.000	.000	.000	.000	.000	.000	.000	1.00	1.00	1.00	1.00
	500	.000	.000	.000	.000	.000	.000	.000	.000	1.00	1.00	1.00	1.00
λ=0.7	20	.000	.000	.000	.000	.000	.000	.000	.000	1.00	1.00	1.00	1.00
	50	.000	.000	.000	.000	.000	.000	.000	.000	1.00	1.00	1.00	1.00
	100	.000	.000	.000	.000	.000	.000	.000	.000	1.00	1.00	1.00	1.00
	500	.000	.000	.000	.000	.000	.000	.000	.000	1.00	1.00	1.00	1.00
λ=0.9	20	.000	.000	.000	.000	.000	.000	.000	.000	1.00	1.00	1.00	1.00
	50	.000	.000	.000	.000	.000	.000	.000	.000	1.00	1.00	1.00	1.00
	100	.000	.000	.000	.000	.000	.000	.000	.000	1.00	1.00	1.00	1.00
	500	.000	.000	.000	.000	.000	.000	.000	.000	1.00	1.00	1.00	1.00

levels of λ values. The APCS for PAIC, UAIC, PBIC and UBIC overall design matrices and sample sizes are 0.395, 0.283, 0.261 and 0.153, respectively indicating that, on average, our PAIC and PBIC perform better than their usual counterparts by 39.2 per cent and 82.5 per cent, respectively. A similar superiority of the proposed methods is also evident in design matrix $X2$. For example, the APCS for PAIC, UAIC, PBIC and UBIC in matrix $X2$ are 0.515, 0.296, 0.272 and 0.157, respectively. As before, here the PAIC and PBIC also outperform their usual counterparts, on average, by 50.2 per cent and 85 per cent, respectively. The other characteristics of the overall results for matrix $X2$ are found to be very similar to the case of matrix $X1$. This may be due to the fact that the values of ρ in these two matrices ($\rho = 0$ for $X1$ and $\rho = 0.25$ for $X2$) are very close to each other.

For design matrices $X3$ and $X4$, we find the same results (except one case, that is, $\lambda - 0.9$ with $T = 20$) for all procedures considered in the study. In these cases, the PCS are almost always 1. For matrix $X5$, on the other hand, the results for each procedure are identical, that is, the PCS are always 1. Closeness of the values of ρ for these three matrices ($\rho = 0.95$. 1.00 and 1.05 for matrices $X3$, $X4$ and $X5$, respectively) may be the cause of such similarity. We find clear evidence from this study that our proposed procedures PAIC and PBIC perform better when the larger model is true. On the other hand, if the true process is one of the smaller models, then the usual procedures outperform the proposed procedures. We also find evidence that the probability of choosing a particular model depends not only on the size of the sample but also on the nature of the data in the design matrix. However, among the four competing methods, UBIC seems the best method in terms of choosing a correct model when Model-1 and Model-2 (smaller models) are true. This is true almost for all design matrices and all sample sizes. On the other hand, when Model-3 (larger model) is true, PAIC performs best in all cases. Of the other two methods UAIC and PBIC, UAIC defeats PBIC sometimes and vice versa. That means of these two methods, no one method has been found to be absolutely dominating in our study. As mentioned in Chapter 2, if the true model is one of the larger models then AIC will outperform BIC and conversely if the true model is one of the smaller models then BIC will outperform AIC in choosing the correct model. Our simulation results support this theory.

5.7 Concluding Remarks

The aim of this chapter has been to examine the effect of making certain restrictions on parameters of interest within a model selection framework. In particular, our intention has been to investigate whether we can improve the widely used AIC in terms of accuracy of model selection by using some non-sample information. However, we obtained different forms of AIC for different numbers of restricted parameters and found that the new AIC forms possess smaller penalties than the usual forms. As noted previously, the new form of AIC may be regarded as one more interpretation of the usual AIC with a particular respecification of the penalty function. As the new form of AIC penalizes additional restricted parameters less heavily than the usual AIC, we may claim that our new AIC forms provide more accurate penalties for judging whether the addition of extra parameters increases the maximized log-likelihood function more than it should if these parameters are extraneous. This is of course a good property of a model selection procedure in the presence of parameter restrictions. It is worthwhile to note that the expressions for new AIC forms presented in this chapter are based on two important assumptions, namely, (i) $\rho_{ij} = 0$ for $i - j \rightarrow 1$ and (ii) ρs are small, particularly when the number of restrictions is greater than four. One more important point is that there can be difficulties in calculating the resulting probability weights when the number of restrictions is greater than four. Several attempts have been made for the more than four restrictions case but unfortunately these do not always provide satisfactory solutions. One possible solution to calculating such weights for larger numbers of restrictions is to apply computer simulation techniques.

We examined whether the new form has the potential for improvement in small samples through a range of Monte Carlo experiments within the framework of the Box-Cox transformation when the parameter is restricted as $\lambda \in [0,1]$. For such a transformation, our PAIC has been found to be less penalized than the regular AIC, which indicates that the use of a restricted parameter can lead to improvements in information criteria in terms of tending to penalize additional parameters less heavily than the usual criteria. This is because a restricted parameter often counts as less than one in the penalty. The simulation results demonstrate that PAIC and PBIC perform much better than their usual counterparts when the larger model is true. Conversely, the usual procedures dominate the proposed procedures when the true process is one of the smaller models. The theoretical achievement gained in AIC has been extended to BIC in Monte Carlo experiments for comparison purposes only. However, our results raise one important question which invites more investigation, namely the probability of correct selection of the competing models. We found from our analysis that the probabilities of selecting the true models in all cases are much higher than the probabilities of selecting either of the other two competing models which is highly desirable. However, these probabilities vary significantly for different sets of contesting models and for different design matrices. Our view is that these variations may be due to the different nature of data matrices used in the experiment and also to lack of control of the probability of correct selection. Thus, it may be worth proposing some alternative methods which would reduce these deficiencies. Chapter 6 will be devoted to this aim.

Chapter 6

Controlled Information Criteria for Model Selection

6.1 Introduction

In Chapter 5, we were mainly concerned with the respecification of AIC where the parameter of interest is restricted to be in a closed interval such as $\lambda\in[0,1]$. We obtained an improved AIC (called PAIC) form in terms of penalty in the presence of such parameter restrictions. A range of simulation experiments has been conducted to see the small sample properties of PAIC, where the probabilities of correct selection from a set of three competing models were calculated and found to vary from one particular design matrix to another. As a result, one could conjecture that these probabilities sometimes can get undesirably uneven (that is, very large for some models while being undesirably small for other models). Consequently, the idea of controlling the probability of correct or incorrect selection seems attractive in the model selection context.

The issue of controlling the probability of wrongly choosing the null hypothesis has already initiated a considerable amount of research in the hypothesis testing literature. It is well known that in hypothesis testing, there is a clear trade-off between the size (also called the probability of Type I error) and power of a test. This trade-off is controlled by fixing the probability of a Type I error or level of significance of the test. In our view, this argument can also be useful in model selection, as there is a close connection between critical values in hypothesis testing and penalty terms in model selection. For example, as Pötscher (1991) notes, using a model selection criterion such as AIC or BIC amounts to testing any model against all other models by means of likelihood ratio tests and selecting that model which is accepted against all other models, where the critical values are determined by the penalty terms of the criteria.

Forbes et al. (1995) considered these issues in the model selection context and suggested methods to determine the penalties in such a way that the probability of choosing one particular model over the other is controlled, at least partially. In their paper, they proposed three IC-based model selection procedures of which the first two (one is called FIC and the other is called

QFIC) are explicitly designed for regressor selection and hence are not relevant for our general model selection problem. The third procedure, on the other hand, is relevant to our particular problem, although it is mainly based on an asymptotic justification. The penalties obtained by this procedure are approximate penalties.

Following almost similar principles as above, King et al. (1995), on the other hand, proposed a general model selection procedure in which the penalties are calculated by controlling the probabilities of correct selection in such a way that no one model is unnecessarily favoured. To do this, they suggested two approaches, one is called the common model approach and the other the representative fixed points approach. They also proposed an algorithm for calculating the penalties based on fixing probabilities of correct selection according to both of these two approaches.

To the best of our knowledge, very little is known about the properties of these approaches in the presence of parameter restrictions. Our view is that the use of restrictions on some parameters may help to improve the above procedures in terms of their probabilities of correct selection, or at least may provide some procedures which are competitive with existing procedures. The purpose of this chapter is to investigate the performance of the above-mentioned approaches in the case of parameter restrictions, with particular reference to the BCT model.

The plan of this chapter is as follows. The proposed methods for determining the penalties by controlling the probability of choosing one particular model over the other are outlined in section 6.2. Section 6.3 presents the Monte Carlo simulation and corresponding results for the proposed methods along with a discussion of the effect of choice of nuisance parameters' values on the probability of correct selection (PCS) for our choice set. Section 6.4 describes the extension of controlled information criterion to the case of two restrictions. The design of experiment and Monte Carlo simulation results are discussed in section 6.5. Some concluding remarks are made in section 6.6.

6.2 Our Proposed Methods

6.2.1 Method 1

In connection with Chapter 5, here our main purpose is to develop a new class of model selection procedures for the same set of three competing models as we considered in Chapter 5 (see equation (5.82)). In our previously proposed method discussed in Chapter 3, we worked with the penalty function which probably has the most important bearing on the small sample properties of the IC-based model selection procedures, as there is little agreement about its functional form (see for example, King, et al., 1995). In this chapter we are mainly interested in estimating penalties for the competing models in such a way that the probability of correct selection is controlled in some way. To do this, we follow the representative fixed points approach (see for detailed discussion about this approach, King et al., 1995), under which we determine the penalties of the competing models so that the probabilities of correct selection for the true models at chosen parameter points are equal. This is because the main objective of a good model selection procedure should be to make the correct decision without unnecessarily favouring one model over others, that is, we must be indifferent among the competing models and should treat them equally in every respect. To achieve this, we aim to make the probability of correctly selecting the true model for the three parameter points equal. However, the main question is, how can we calculate these penalties?

It is worth noting that a major contribution of King et al. (1995) has been to show how computer simulation methods can be used to determine penalty values when choosing between *m* models, each of which can be represented by a representative fixed point in its parameter space. For example, King et al.'s algorithm can be used to find penalties such that the *m* probabilities of correctly choosing the right model at each of these representative points are equal. This is the philosophy we employ in our first proposed method. The remaining question is, how should these representative points be chosen? For our particular problem and our parameter of interest, λ, the answer is quite simple. $\lambda = 1.0$ for Model-1 (called the linear model), $\lambda = 0$ for Model-2 (called the log-linear model) and $\lambda = 0.6$ for Model-3 (called the BCT model). Note that since λ can take any value between zero and one for the BCT model, it seems sensible to choose the mid-point $\lambda = 0.6$ as a representative point. For each model, however, there are three nuisance parameters, namely β_0, β_1 and σ^2, which are not known. This is, of course, a problem and to overcome this, we employed the parametric bootstrap approach. Under this approach, we first calculate the maximum likelihood estimates of the nuisance parameters for a given data set and then use them to generate data many times for each of the models represented by the fixed points. The samples obtained by this procedure are called bootstrap samples. The procedure mainly involves penalty calculations based on the bootstrap samples using King et al.'s equal probability algorithm applied to the representative fixed points approach mentioned earlier.

Let p_1, p_2 and p_3 be the penalties and L_1, L_2 and L_3 be the maximized log-likelihood values for Model-1, Model-2 and Model-3, respectively. Note that in our model selection case, the comparisons are made based on the relative penalties of the competing models and thus we can set $p_1 = 0$ without loss of generality in the whole experiment. We consider all three sets of models, each of which requires estimating each of the three competing models. Sample data are generated simultaneously for $\lambda = 1.0$, $\lambda = 0$ and $\lambda = 0.6$ for the first, second and third set, respectively. Therefore, Model-1, Model-2 and Model-3 would be regarded as the true models for the first, second and third set, respectively. By definition, Model-1 will be chosen if:

$$L_1 - L_2 + p_2 > 0$$

and: $$L_1 - L_3 + p_3 > 0. \tag{6.1}$$

Model-2 will be chosen if:

$$L_2 - L_1 - p_2 > 0$$

and: $$L_2 - L_3 - p_2 + p_3 > 0. \tag{6.2}$$

And Model-3 will be chosen if:

$$L_3 - L_1 - p_3 > 0$$

and: $$L_3 - L_2 - p_3 + p_2 > 0. \tag{6.3}$$

Now, according to King et al.'s equal probability algorithm, our main purpose is to make probabilities of choosing all these true models equal, that is:

$$\begin{aligned}\Pr(\text{correctly choosing Model-1}) &= \Pr(\text{correctly choosing Model-2}) \\ &= \Pr(\text{correctly choosing Model-3}) \quad (6.4)\end{aligned}$$

or at least:

$$\begin{aligned}\Pr(\text{correctly choosing Model-1}) &\approx \Pr(\text{correctly choosing Model-2}) \\ &\approx \Pr(\text{correctly choosing Model-3}). \quad (6.5)\end{aligned}$$

In equations (6.1), (6.2) and (6.3), the values of all likelihoods are known but the penalties are unknown. Consequently, in order to satisfy equations (6.4) or (6.5), of course, a new set of penalties will be needed for all competing models instead of the usual penalties, as it is almost certain that (6.4) or

(6.5) cannot be met with the usual penalties. The criterion involving these new penalties is called the controlled information criterion–1 (CIC-1) as the probability of choosing the true models is controlled in some way by this method. However, we now feel that a brief discussion is still necessary about how we calculate these two penalties, p_2 and p_3, to satisfy (6.4) or (6.5). This is done in the following way.

In order to calculate p_2 and p_3 for Model-2 and Model-3 (see equation (5.82) in Chapter 5) respectively, for our proposed CIC-1 method, we first estimate β_0, β_1 and σ^2 for Model-1 (see equation), assuming Model-1 is true by the maximum likelihood method (see 5.83–5.85) and use these estimates as true values to generate the required number of bootstrap samples for which the maximized log-likelihood values for each of the three competing models is computed. Note that the error term u_t is assumed to be distributed as independently normal with mean zero and variance σ^2. For the first set where samples are generated from Model-1, we count how many times equation (6.1) is satisfied. We call this number Count-1 which indicates how many times Model-1 is chosen from the total number of bootstrap replications when it is the true model. In other words, we count how many bootstrap samples support Model-1 as the true model when it is the true model.

Following a similar procedure as above for the second set where the bootstrap samples are generated assuming $\lambda = 0$ and the estimated values of β_0, β_1 and σ^2 are for Model-2 and hence Model-2 is the true model, we count how many times equation (6.2) is satisfied. We call this number Count-2, which shows how many bootstrap samples support Model-2 as the best model. Similarly for the third set, the parameters β_0, β_1, σ^2 and λ are jointly estimated and the resultant estimates of β_0, β_1, σ^2 are used with $\lambda = 0.5$ to generate bootstrap samples and consequently Model-3 is the true model. Note that for λ, the Gauss Constrained Optimization technique was used and for the remaining three other parameters, the ML method was used. However, here we count how many times equation (6.3) is satisfied. We call this number Count-3. As before, this Count-3 indicates how many bootstrap samples support Model-3 as the best model. In fact, Count-1, Count-2 and Count-3 represent the probabilities of correctly choosing Model-1, Model-2 and Model-3, respectively. Note that the equations (6.1), (6.2) and (6.3) are all met with estimated penalties for p_2 and p_3.

Now according to our proposed method we wish to make:

$$\text{Count-1} = \text{Count-2} = \text{Count-3}$$

or at least:

$$\text{Count-1} \approx \text{Count-2} \approx \text{Count-3} \tag{6.6}$$

by adjusting the values of only p_2 and p_3 to ensure that the probabilities of correctly selecting the true models are the same. To achieve this, we employ the simple bisection method iteratively so that the p_2 and p_3 values will lead to selection of models which satisfies the above condition. The question is how do we adjust these p_2 and p_3 values to satisfy the condition? The answer is as follows. First we check if Count-1 = Count-3. If Count-1 is greater than Count-3, p_3 is reduced. On the other hand, if Count-3 is greater than Count-1, p_3 is increased. After fixing up the value of p_3 one can then check if Count-1 = Count-2. If not, one adjusts p_2 iteratively for this given value of p_3 to make Count-1 = Count-2. Each time p_2 is changed, then we have to change p_3 until Count-1 = Count-3. The whole process is repeated until equation (6.6) is met. We then have found the required p_2 and p_3 values.

6.2.2 Method 2

Forbes et al. (1996) presented three IC-based model selection procedures of which the first two are explicitly designed for regressor selections and the third one is for general model selection. For the first procedure, called FIC, they derived a new penalty function on the basis of sums of critical values from particular *F* distributions, whilst for the second procedure, called QFIC, they calculate penalties from particular chi-squared distributions. Both penalties come from a desire to control the probability of incorrectly choosing additional regressors. However, as we are interested in general model selection for restricted parameter models rather than any procedure for regression selection, we follow Forbes et al.'s (1996) third approach for general model selection. Suppose we want to choose between m possible models, say, M_1, M_2,..., M_m, where model M_j, $j = 1, 2,..., m$, is characterised by a class of probability distributions $F(y|\theta_j)$, indexed by a k_j-dimensional parameter $\theta_j \in \Theta_j$. For such a general problem, Forbes et al. (1996) construct the penalty function for an IC-based procedure by controlling the probability of correct selection for a particular pairwise situation so that no one model is unfairly favoured. However, in general, their proposed IC procedure for selecting among models M_1, M_2,..., M_m is to choose model M_{j-1} where:

$$L_{j-1} - p_{j-1} > L_j - p_j \text{ or } L_{j-1} - L_j > p_{j-1} - p_j \tag{6.7}$$

$$\text{for } j = 1, 2, \ldots, m \text{ with penalty } p_j = \frac{k_j}{2}\chi^2_{(1)}(\alpha) \tag{6.8}$$

where $\chi^2_{(1)}(\alpha)$ is the upper α^{th} percentile of the chi-squared distribution with one degree of freedom.

Now let us concentrate on our particular problem where we are interested in determining penalties p_j, for $j = 1, 2$ and 3, as set out in (5.82) in Chapter 5 by using the above principles. In this case Model-1 and Model-2 contain the same number of parameters and Model-3 contains one additional parameter over the other two. Note that among these three competing models, Model-1 and Model-2 are unrestricted models and Model-3 is a restricted model. However, the procedures which have been discussed before are mainly derived for unrestricted models, and for such unrestricted models the relative penalties were calculated considering the likelihood ratio (LR) tests of the hypothesis M_{j-1} versus M_j under the assumption that model M_{j-1} is the true data generating process. Under such an assumption the test statistic follows a distribution for a large sample size. For our particular case where both restricted and unrestricted models are involved, we argue that the relative penalties can also be determined by the likelihood ratio tests, as there is nothing wrong with the basic principles of such tests. Of course, the distributional form of the test statistic may be slightly different in this case. Now the next step is to see what distributional form we can obtain for such a particular problem.

To solve the distributional function dilemma, we refer to our previous two chapters where we discussed the distributional form of an estimator of a restricted parameter. There we derived the AIC form for such a model which included a restricted parameter of the form $\lambda \in [0,1]$, where 0 and 1 are two boundary values of the parameter λ. For our derivation of AIC, we used the general Kuhn-Tucker inequality constrained optimization framework considered by Gouriéroux et al. (1982) for a one sided hypothesis testing problem such as:

$$\begin{aligned} & H_0 : \lambda = 0 \quad \text{versus} \quad H_1 : \lambda > 0 \\ \text{or} \quad & H_0 : \lambda = 1 \quad \text{versus} \quad H_1 : \lambda < 1. \end{aligned} \tag{6.9}$$

We have seen, for such a restricted parameter case that, under the null hypothesis, instead of the usual chi-squared distribution, the Wald test statistic follows a probability weighted mixture of chi-squared distributions asymptotically. It is worth mentioning that under the null hypothesis the Wald, the LR and the Kuhn-Tucker test statistics have their common asymptotic distribution which is the probability weighted mixture of chi-squared distribution. See for example, Gouriéroux et al. (1982).

Due to the restriction placed on the parameter of interest λ and under certain appropriate regularity conditions such as listed in Gouriéroux et al. (1980), the probability distribution of the left hand side of (6.7) converges weakly to a probability weighted mixture of chi-squared distribution as the sample size T tends to infinity. Thus, we define the relative penalties $p_j - p_{j-1}$ by setting the probability of incorrectly selecting model M_j under M_{j-1} to be α and write:

$$\text{PR}\left[2(L_j - L_{j-1}) > 2(p_j - p_{j-1})\right] = \alpha \tag{6.10}$$

or equivalently, $2(p_j - p_{j-1})$ equals the $(1-2\alpha)100$ percentile of the distribution which has probability 1/2 of 0 and probability 1/2 of $\chi^2_{(1)}$. Thus we can write:

$$2(p_j - p_{j-1}) = \chi^2_{(1)}(2\alpha)$$

$$\Rightarrow p_j - p_{j-1} = \tfrac{1}{2}\,\chi^2_{(1)}(2\alpha). \tag{6.11}$$

This is the penalty function we recommend for our particular problem, which is slightly different from the Forbes et al.'s approach given in (2.14). We call the procedure using the penalty function in (6.11) asymptotically controlled information criterion – 2 (CIC-2). Note that in both situations the penalty values depend on the choice of α values.

6.3 Monte Carlo Simulation

In order to evaluate the performance of our proposed methods, we conducted a Monte Carlo experiment which involved estimating the probabilities of choosing each of the competing models. Remember that for our proposed method CIC-1, we obtained different penalties rather than any conventional penalties for each replication of the simulation experiment. As for CIC-1, CIC-2 uses penalties which are different from those of any existing procedures. The penalties obtained in both methods are dependent on the observed data. In the simulation experiments, we compared the results of our proposed methods with those results we obtained in Chapter 5.

6.3.1 Experimental Design

We use the same experimental design in this chapter as used in Chapter 4. We just apply the different penalties for three competing models as obtained in our proposed methods. That is, for CIC-1, we use zero for penalty p_1 for Model-1 and empirically estimated penalties for Model-2 and Model-3. For CIC-2, we use zeroes for Model-1 and Model-2, and for Model-3, we obtain 2.7806, 1.3628 and 0.8920 when $\alpha = 0.01$, $\alpha = 0.06$ and $\alpha = 0.10$, respectively. These values have been calculated by using the formula given in (6.11). We use zeroes for Model-1 and Model-2 simply because both of these two models contain the same number of parameters and Model-3 contains one additional parameter over the other two. According to our proposed CIC-2, we just need to calculate the penalty for Model-3 (restricted model) in comparison to Model-2. For the CIC-1 method, we used 500 bootstrap samples in each replication because in some preliminary experiments, this delivered an appropriate degree of accuracy. The total number of replications used is 200. This low number was forced upon us by the high amount of computation required to complete one iteration for CIC-1. Essentially we are simulating a simulation under this approach. For CIC-2 we use 1,000 replications; as we used this number in Chapter 5 it will allow an appropriate comparison of the two sets of results.

6.3.2 Results of the Monte Carlo Experiments

Table 6.1 presents a comparison between the PAIC, UAIC, PBIC, UBIC, CIC-1 and CIC-2 methods by estimating probabilities of selecting Model-1, Model-2 and Model-3 for design matrix $X1$. We consider three different α values for the CIC-2 method and four different sample sizes over the whole experiment. As we have already discussed and compared the procedures PAIC, UAIC, PBIC and UBIC in Chapter 5, we do not repeat that discussion here. Rather, we wish to highlight CIC-1 and CIC-2 in our discussion and to compare them with each other and also with the previous procedures. The table shows that among the information criteria considered in our analysis, CIC-1 performs best as the probabilities of choosing the true models for this procedure are higher than for all other procedures in almost all cases. For example, the APCS for CIC-1, CIC-2 with $\alpha = 0.01$, CIC-2 with $\alpha = 0.05$, CIC-2 with $\alpha = 0.10$, PAIC, UAIC, PBIC and UBIC for design matrix $X1$ are 0.826, 0.798, 0.790, 0.778, 0.761, 0.781, 0.793 and 0.798, respectively when Model-1 is true. With respect to these APCS, the competing procedures can be ranked as: CIC-1 > CIC-2 (with $\alpha = 0.01$) > UBIC > PBIC > CIC-2 (with $\alpha = 0.05$) > UAIC > CIC-2 (with α

Table 6.1 Comparison between controlled and other methods for design matrix *X*1 based on calculated probabilities of selecting different models

T=20	Method →	CIC-1	CIC-2			PAIC	UAIC	PBIC	UBIC
			$\alpha = .01$	$\alpha = .05$	$\alpha = .10$				
Penalties	P_1	0	0	0	0	0	0	0	0
	P_2		0	0	0	0	0	0	0
	P_3		2.7805	1.3528	0.892	0.5	1.00	0.7489	1.4979
Model-1 is true	Model-1	.665	.611	.611	.611	.607	.611	.610	.611
	Model-2	.005	.389	.389	.389	.387	.389	.389	.389
	Model-3	.330	.000	.000	.000	.006	.000	.001	.000
Model-2 is true	Model-1	.000	.000	.000	.000	.000	.000	.000	.000
	Model-2	1.00	.997	.971	.950	.892	.957	.932	.978
	Model-3	.000	.003	.029	.050	.108	.043	.068	.022
Model-3 is true with $\lambda = 0.1$	Model-1	.030	.025	.012	.005	.002	.005	.003	.012
	Model-2	.960	.963	.900	.849	.765	.869	.825	.915
	Model-3	.010	.012	.088	.146	.233	.126	.172	.073
Model-3 is true with $\lambda = 0.3$	Model-1	.035	.209	.185	.162	.117	.167	.148	.193
	Model-2	.645	.789	.769	.743	.662	.748	.725	.773
	Model-3	.320	.002	.046	.095	.221	.085	.127	.034
Model-3 is true with $\lambda = 0.5$	Model-1	.330	.389	.388	.379	.347	.382	.370	.388
	Model-2	.070	.611	.611	.601	.564	.606	.593	.611
	Model-3	.600	.000	.001	.020	.089	.012	.037	.001
Model-3 is true with $\lambda = 0.7$	Model-1	.365	.502	.502	.501	.493	.502	.501	.502
	Model-2	.090	.498	.497	.496	.486	.496	.493	.497
	Model-3	.545	.000	.001	.003	.021	.002	.006	.001
Model-3 is true with $\lambda = 0.9$	Model-1	.535	.564	.564	.563	.561	.563	.563	.564
	Model-2	.205	.436	.436	.435	.434	.436	.435	.436
	Model-3	.260	.000	.000	.002	.005	.001	.002	.000

Table 6.1 (cont'd)

T=50	Method →	CIC-1	CIC-2 $\alpha = .01$	$\alpha = .05$	$\alpha = .10$	PAIC	UAIC	PBIC	UBIC
Penalties	P_1	0	0	0	0	0	0	0	0
	P_2		0	0	0	0	0	0	0
	P_3		2.7805	1.3528	0.892	0.5	1.00	0.978	1.956
Model-1 is true	Model-1	.790	.766	.766	.765	.755	.765	.765	.766
	Model-2	.005	.234	.234	.234	.231	.234	.234	.234
	Model-3	.205	.000	.000	.001	.014	.001	.001	.000
Model-2 is true	Model-1	.000	.000	.000	.000	.000	.000	.000	.000
	Model-2	1.00	.995	.962	.932	.865	.942	.940	.986
	Model-3	.000	.005	.038	.068	.135	.058	.060	.014
Model-3 is true with $\lambda = 0.1$	Model-1	.000	.000	.000	.000	.000	.000	.000	.000
	Model-2	.930	.935	.805	.711	.589	.737	.731	.883
	Model-3	.070	.065	.195	.289	.411	.263	.269	.117
Model-3 is true with $\lambda = 0.3$	Model-1	.030	.181	.091	.051	.022	.060	.058	.147
	Model-2	.440	.780	.653	.560	.439	.575	.572	.739
	Model-3	.530	.039	.256	.389	.539	.365	.370	.114
Model-3 is true with $\lambda = 0.5$	Model-1	.270	.474	.458	.419	.301	.433	.429	.473
	Model-2	.035	.526	.512	.472	.392	.489	.488	.524
	Model-3	.695	.000	.030	.109	.307	.078	.083	.003
Model-3 is true with $\lambda = 0.7$	Model-1	.430	.627	.627	.619	.572	.625	.623	.627
	Model-2	.015	.373	.373	.367	.338	.370	.369	.373
	Model-3	.555	.000	.000	.014	.090	.005	.008	.000
Model-3 is true with $\lambda = 0.9$	Model-1	.565	.708	.708	.708	.698	.708	.708	.708
	Model-2	.130	.292	.292	.292	.287	.292	.292	.292
	Model-3	.305	.000	.000	.000	.015	.000	.000	.000

Table 6.1 (cont'd)

T=100	Method →	CIC-1	CIC-2			PAIC	UAIC	PBIC	UBIC
			$\alpha = .01$	$\alpha = .05$	$\alpha = .10$				
Penalties	P_1	0	0	0	0	0	0	0	0
	P_2		0	0	0	0	0	0	0
	P_3		2.7805	1.3528	0.892	0.5	1.00	1.1513	2.3026
Model-1 is true	Model-1	.850	.826	.826	.825	.799	.826	.826	.826
	Model-2	.030	.174	.174	.173	.159	.173	.173	.174
	Model-3	.120	.000	.000	.002	.042	.001	.001	.000
Model-2 is true	Model-1	.000	.000	.000	.000	.000	.000	.000	.000
	Model-2	1.00	.994	.966	.922	.853	.937	.951	.990
	Model-3	.000	.006	.034	.078	.147	.063	.049	.010
Model-3 is true with $\lambda = 0.1$	Model-1	.000	.000	.000	.000	.000	.000	.000	.000
	Model-2	.865	.896	.731	.633	.518	.658	.688	.858
	Model-3	.135	.104	.269	.367	.482	.342	.312	.142
Model-3 is true with $\lambda = 0.3$	Model-1	.000	.086	.018	.005	.000	.008	.014	.058
	Model-2	.310	.749	.550	.434	.308	.458	.503	.695
	Model-3	.690	.165	.432	.561	.692	.534	.483	.247
Model-3 is true with $\lambda = 0.5$	Model-1	.215	.473	.399	.294	.180	.320	.355	.467
	Model-2	.000	.526	.458	.362	.258	.393	.428	.521
	Model-3	.785	.001	.143	.344	.562	.287	.217	.012
Model-3 is true with $\lambda = 0.7$	Model-1	.325	.672	.666	.642	.527	.648	.663	.672
	Model-2	.005	.328	.324	.302	.235	.314	.320	.328
	Model-3	.670	.000	.010	.056	.238	.038	.017	.000
Model-3 is true with $\lambda = 0.9$	Model-1	.580	770	770	768	740	769	769	770
	Model-2	.000	230	230	230	207	230	230	230
	Model-3	.420	000	000	002	053	001	001	000

Table 6.1 (cont'd)

T=500	Method →	CIC-1	CIC-2 $\alpha = .01$	$\alpha = .05$	$\alpha = .10$	PAIC	UAIC	PBIC	UBIC
Penalties	P_1	0	0	0	0	0	0	0	0
	P_2		0	0	0	0	0	0	0
	P_3		2.7805	1.3528	0.892	0.5	1.00	1.5537	3.1073
Model-1 is true	Model-1	1.00	.988	.955	.910	.842	.921	.969	.988
	Model-2	.000	.012	.002	.001	.000	.001	.003	.012
	Model-3	.000	.000	.043	.089	.158	.078	.028	.000
Model-2 is true	Model-1	.000	.000	.000	.000	.000	.000	.000	.000
	Model-2	1.00	.994	.957	.909	.838	.924	.966	.995
	Model-3	.000	.006	.043	.091	.162	.076	.034	.005
Model-3 is true with $\lambda = 0.1$	Model-1	.000	.000	.000	.000	.000	.000	.000	.000
	Model-2	.140	.552	.279	.183	.109	.210	.325	.612
	Model-3	.860	.448	..721	.817	.891	.790	.675	.388
Model-3 is true with $\lambda = 0.3$	Model-1	.000	.000	.000	.000	.000	.000	.000	.000
	Model-2	.005	.158	.044	.024	.009	.030	.055	.190
	Model-3	.995	.842	.956	.976	.991	.970	.945	.810
Model-3 is true with $\lambda = 0.5$	Model-1	.000	.076	.013	.005	.001	.005	.019	.105
	Model-2	.000	.087	.021	.009	.003	.011	.027	.107
	Model-3	1.00	.837	.966	.986	.996	.984	.954	.788
Model-3 is true with $\lambda = 0.7$	Model-1	.235	.755	.468	.338	.230	.375	.521	.803
	Model-2	.000	.057	.012	.006	.002	.006	.019	.075
	Model-3	.765	.188	.520	.656	.768	.619	.460	.122
Model-3 is true with $\lambda = 0.9$	Model-1	.625	.965	.889	.823	.705	.837	.907	.966
	Model-2	.000	.034	.009	.004	.002	.006	.013	.034
	Model-3	.375	.001	.102	.173	.293	.157	.080	.000

= 0.10) > PAIC. Almost similar evidence is found when Model-2 is true. For example, the corresponding APCS for the above procedures are 1.00, 0.995, 0.964, 0.928, 0.826, 0.940, 0.947 and 0.987, which can be ranked as: CIC-1 > CIC-2 (with $\alpha = 0.01$) > UBIC > CIC-2 (with $\alpha = 0.05$) > PBIC > UAIC > CIC-2 (with $\alpha = 0.10$) > PAIC. In both of the above situations, the CIC-1 ranked top and CIC-2 with $\alpha = 0.01$ is ranked in the second top position. In terms of percentage counts, CIC-1 has been the best criterion 100 per cent of the time when Model-1 and Model-2 are true.

Now let us discuss the situations when Model-3 is the true model. The APCS for the same competing methods for matrix $X1$ are 0.629, 0.136, 0.239, 0.300, 0.394, 0.283, 0.261 and 0.143, respectively. In accordance with these figures, the methods can be ranked as: CIC-1 > PAIC > CIC-2 with $\alpha = 0.10$ > UAIC > PBIC > CIC-2 with $\alpha = 0.05$ > UBIC > CIC-2 with $\alpha = 0.10$. In this particular case the ranking positions of the competing methods have changed considerably except for CIC-1. For example, here both PAIC and PBIC are much better than their corresponding usual counterparts, which indicates our proposed methods always perform well when the larger models are true. However, CIC-1 still dominates the other methods by a large margin. But unlike the other two cases, here CIC-1 is the best criterion 66 per cent of the time. Unlike the two previous cases when Model-1 and Model-2 were true, this percent is lower because CIC-1 does not perform well for boundary values of λ, for example, $\lambda = 0.1$ and $\lambda = 0.9$. Note that the probabilities of correctly choosing the true models for three considered cases are significantly different, and this is not desirable. However, this difference becomes smaller as the sample size gets larger. Interestingly, for sample size $T = 500$ this difference is nearly zero for all competing methods. That means for the large sample case, both of our proposed methods, including other proposed and usual versions of AIC and BIC, perform very well. In general, we find clear evidence that the PCS for the true models are much higher than those of the other two competing models in all cases when the smaller models are true. When the larger model (Model-3) is true, on the other hand, the table shows comparatively less attractive results in terms of PCS. That means the PCS are smaller, and in some cases much smaller for small sample cases. This deficiency is relatively less for the CIC-1 method, which indicates its superiority in all ways over the other methods. However, the deficiencies, with respect to PCS for all methods, are gradually overcome as the sample size T gets larger. This is desirable.

Table 6.2, where we used design matrix $X2$, exhibits similar characteristics as Table 6.1 in almost every respect, and hence we wish to avoid the repetition of the discussion of this table. Table 6.3 presents similar comparisons for design matrix *X*3, where we find that the PCS are much larger than other competing models in all three situations. It is apparent from the table that the proposed method CIC-1 is still performing best, through exhibiting the highest probability of correct selection among all other competing procedures. The table reveals that the probabilities of selecting the true models for all three cases for this method are very high, and for sample size $T = 50$ and larger, they are the same. Like the other two design matrices *X*1 and *X*2, the CIC-2 method seems competitive to existing AIC and BIC in the sense that it performs better in some cases and worse in other cases. Table 6.3 exhibits quite distinctive results from the results shown in Tables 6.1 and 6.2, particularly in the case where Model-3 is true. Here the table clearly indicates that the probabilities of correctly selecting the true models are much higher (close to one) than the other two competing models when Model-1 and Model-2 are true and exactly one when Model-3 is true. As a matter of fact, the differences of the selection probabilities among the true models are found to be almost negligible for this design matrix and this is desirable. Furthermore, these differences become more negligible as the sample size T gets larger. In terms of percentage counts, here CIC-1 was the best criterion 100 per cent of the time in all three situations. Interestingly, Table 6.4 and Table 6.5 show a similar pattern of results as Table 6.3 in every respect and hence we need not repeat our previous discussion.

6.3.3 *Effect of Nuisance Parameters on the Probability of Correct Selection for the True Model*

We considered the Box-Cox model for our problem, which consists of four parameters, namely, β_0, β_1, σ^2 and λ. Of these, λ is our parameter of interest while the others are not of primary interest and hence can be regarded as nuisance parameters. Their presence often causes unexpected complications in many econometric analyses, particularly in inferences (see for example, Ara, 1995). Proper handling of nuisance parameters has attracted considerable interest in econometric inferences. The purpose of this subsection is not to tackle the problem of such nuisance parameters in the model selection context; rather we wish to see the effect of these parameters on the PCS in our Monte Carlo experiment. Our aim is to see how important our choice of β_0, β_1 and σ^2 values is for our Monte Carlo results. However, it is not practical to consider all possible combinations of parameter values with various sample sizes to see the effect of nuisance parameters on our model selection problem within the time frame available. Thus we consider only one design matrix, *X*1, with sample size $T = 20$, for our convenience.

Table 6.2 Comparison between controlled and other methods for design matrix *X*2 based on calculated probabilities of selecting different models

T=20	Methods →	CIC-1	CIC-2 $\alpha = .01$	CIC-2 $\alpha = .05$	CIC-2 $\alpha = .10$	PAIC	UAIC	PBIC	UBIC
Penalties	P_1	0	0	0	0	0	0	0	0
	P_2		0	0	0	0	0	0	0
	P_3		2.7805	1.3528	0.892	0.5	1.00	0.7489	1.4979
Model-1 is true	Model-1	.600	.560	.559	.559	.549	.559	.556	.559
	Model-2	.000	.440	.440	.439	.432	.439	.439	.440
	Model-3	.400	.000	.001	.002	.019	.002	.005	.001
Model-2 is true	Model-1	.000	.000	.000	.000	.000	.000	.000	.000
	Model-2	.1.00	.995	.981	.969	.933	.973	.957	.984
	Model-3	.000	.005	.019	.031	.067	.027	.043	.016
Model-3 is true with $\lambda = 0.1$	Model-1	.020	.016	.009	.006	.003	.007	.005	.016
	Model-2	.975	.973	.921	.878	.807	.895	.863	.905
	Model-3	.005	.011	.070	.116	.190	.098	.132	.079
Model-3 is true with $\lambda = 0.3$	Model-1	.030	.156	.133	.107	.072	.116	.099	.137
	Model-2	.710	.839	.813	.770	.677	.780	.744	.818
	Model-3	.260	.005	.054	.123	.251	.104	.157	.045
Model-3 is true with $\lambda = 0.5$	Model-1	.310	.325	.321	.299	.254	.310	.290	.323
	Model-2	.085	.675	.673	.655	.610	.661	.647	.673
	Model-3	.605	.000	.006	.046	.136	.029	.063	.004
Model-3 is true with $\lambda = 0.7$	Model-1	.380	.438	.438	.434	.417	.435	.427	.438
	Model-2	.220	.562	.561	.557	.542	.559	.556	.562
	Model-3	.400	.000	.001	.009	.041	.006	.017	.000
Model-3 is true with $\lambda = 0.9$	Model-1	.500	.508	.508	.508	.502	.508	.508	.508
	Model-2	.275	.492	.491	.491	.486	.491	.491	.492
	Model-3	.225	.000	.001	.001	.012	.001	.001	.000

Table 6.2 (cont'd)

T=50	Methods →	CIC-1	CIC-2 α = .01	CIC-2 α = .05	CIC-2 α = .10	PAIC	UAIC	PBIC	UBIC
Penalties	P_1	0	0	0	0	0	0	0	0
	P_2		0	0	0	0	0	0	0
	P_3		2.7805	1.3528	0.892	0.5	1.00	0.978	1.956
Model-1 is true	Model-1	.765	.758	.758	.757	.738	.758	.758	.758
	Model-2	.000	.242	.242	.240	.233	.242	.242	.242
	Model-3	.235	.000	.000	.003	.029	.000	.000	.000
Model-2 is true	Model-1	.000	.000	.000	.000	.000	.000	.000	.000
	Model-2	1.00	.996	.967	.939	.890	.947	.945	.984
	Model-3	.000	.004	.033	.061	.110	.053	.055	.016
Model-3 is true with λ = 0.1	Model-1	.000	.000	.000	.000	.000	.000	.000	.000
	Model-2	.925	.921	.788	.704	.596	.730	.727	.868
	Model-3	.075	.079	.212	.296	.404	.270	.273	.132
Model-3 is true with λ = 0.3	Model-1	.020	.149	.060	.034	.014	.046	.045	.109
	Model-2	.435	.765	.631	.533	.419	.553	.549	.710
	Model-3	.545	.086	.309	.433	.567	.401	.406	.181
Model-3 is true with λ = 0.5	Model-1	.255	.456	.404	.324	.214	.357	.354	.446
	Model-2	.035	.538	.503	.459	.363	.474	.470	.529
	Model-3	.710	.006	.093	.217	.423	.169	.176	.025
Model-3 is true with λ = 0.7	Model-1	.455	.613	.612	.588	.510	.598	.597	.613
	Model-2	.120	.387	.382	.370	.328	.375	.374	.387
	Model-3	.425	.000	.006	.042	.162	.027	.029	.000
Model-3 is true with λ = 0.9	Model-1	.645	.703	.703	.701	.679	.702	.701	.703
	Model-2	.180	.297	.297	.296	.279	.297	.297	.297
	Model-3	.175	.000	.000	.003	.042	.001	.002	.000

Table 6.2 (cont'd)

T=100	Methods →	CIC-1	CIC-2 $\alpha = .01$	$\alpha = .05$	$\alpha = .10$	PAIC	UAIC	PBIC	UBIC
Penalties	P_1	0	0	0	0	0	0	0	0
	P_2	0	0	0	0	0	0	0	0
	P_3		2.7805	1.3528	0.892	0.5	1.00	1.1513	2.3026
Model-1 is true	Model-1	.825	.814	.814	.811	.778	.812	.814	.814
	Model-2	.000	.186	.185	.184	.157	.157	.185	.186
	Model-3	.175	.000	.001	.005	.065	.003	.001	.000
Model-2 is true	Model-1	.000	.000	.000	.000	.000	.000	.000	.000
	Model-2	1.00	.997	.962	.932	.858	.940	.949	.991
	Model-3	.000	.003	.038	.068	.142	.060	.051	.009
Model-3 is true with $\lambda = 0.1$	Model-1	.000	000	000	000	000	000	000	000
	Model-2	.870	.872	.698	.618	.504	.630	.663	.819
	Model-3	.130	.128	.302	.382	.496	.370	.337	.181
Model-3 is true with $\lambda = 0.3$	Model-1	.010	065	.014	.004	.000	.006	.008	.045
	Model-2	.275	.688	.510	.401	.296	.424	.466	.646
	Model-3	.715	.247	.476	.595	.704	.570	.526	.309
Model-3 is true with $\lambda = 0.5$	Model-1	.200	463	.333	.228	.134	.261	.293	.441
	Model-2	.005	.517	.423	.340	.244	.365	.389	.506
	Model-3	.795	.020	.244	.432	.622	.374	.318	.053
Model-3 is true with $\lambda = 0.7$	Model-1	.380	662	.646	.592	.475	.605	.631	.662
	Model-2	.050	.338	.327	.291	.228	.302	.314	.338
	Model-3	.570	.000	.027	.117	.297	.093	.055	.000
Model-3 is true with $\lambda = 0.9$	Model-1	.685	765	.764	.757	.707	.759	.762	.765
	Model-2	.085	.235	.235	.234	.208	.234	.234	.235
	Model-3	.230	.000	.001	.009	.085	.007	.004	.000

Table 6.2 (cont'd)

T=500	Method →	CIC-1	CIC-2 $\alpha = .01$	$\alpha = .05$	$\alpha = .10$	PAIC	UAIC	PBIC	UBIC
Penalties	P_1	0	0	0	0	0	0	0	0
	P_2		0	0	0	0	0	0	0
	P_3		2.7805	1.3528	0.892	0.5	1.00	1.5537	3.1073
Model-1 is true	Model-1	1.00	.974	948	.908	.833	.915	.960	.974
	Model-2	.000	.025	.011	.004	.002	.005	.015	.026
	Model-3	.000	.001	.041	.088	.165	.080	.025	.000
Model-2 is true	Model-1	.000	.000	.000	.000	.000	.000	.000	.000
	Model-2	1.00	.992	.956	.913	.847	.927	.962	.997
	Model-3	.000	.008	.044	.087	.153	.073	.038	.003
Model-3 is true with $\lambda = 0.1$	Model-1	.000	.000	.000	.000	.000	.000	.000	.000
	Model-2	.150	.558	.293	.200	.118	.224	.340	.603
	Model-3	.850	.442	.707	.800	.882	.776	.660	.397
Model-3 is true with $\lambda = 0.3$	Model-1	.000	.000	.000	.000	.000	.000	.000	.000
	Model-2	.050	.198	.070	.041	.023	.049	.089	.238
	Model-3	.950	.802	.930	.959	.977	.951	.911	.762
Model-3 is true with $\lambda = 0.5$	Model-1	.000	.111	.022	.009	.001	.011	.031	.145
	Model-2	.000	.126	.041	.025	.010	.026	.047	.150
	Model-3	1.00	.763	.937	.966	.989	.963	.922	.705
Model-3 is true with $\lambda = 0.7$	Model-1	.150	.783	.510	.379	.256	.414	.554	.813
	Model-2	.000	.103	.031	.017	.005	.020	.039	.114
	Model-3	.850	.114	.459	.604	.739	.566	.407	.073
Model-3 is true with $\lambda = 0.9$	Model-1	.705	.950	.894	.817	.713	.835	.912	.950
	Model-2	.000	.050	.026	.011	.004	.016	.035	.050
	Model-3	.295	.000	.080	.172	.283	.149	.053	.000

Table 6.3 Comparison between controlled and other methods for design matrix *X*3 based on calculated probabilities of selecting different models

T=20	Methods →	CIC-1	CIC-2			PAIC	UAIC	PBIC	UBIC
			$\alpha = .01$	$\alpha = .05$	$\alpha = .10$				
Penalties	P_1	0	0	0	0	0	0	0	0
	P_2		0	0	0	0	0	0	0
	P_3		2.7805	1.3528	0.892	0.5	1.00	0.7489	1.4979
Model-1 is true	Model-1	.995	.982	.912	.872	.793	.885	.850	.924
	Model-2	.000	.000	.000	.000	.000	.000	.000	.000
	Model-3	.005	.018	.088	.128	.207	.115	.150	.076
Model-2 is true	Model-1	.000	.000	.000	.000	.000	.000	.000	.000
	Model-2	1.00	.986	.938	.889	.822	.906	.867	.953
	Model-3	.000	.014	.062	.111	.178	.094	.133	.047
Model-3 is true with $\lambda = 0.1$	Model-1	.000	.000	.000	.000	.000	.000	.000	.000
	Model-2	.000	.000	.000	.000	.000	.000	.000	.000
	Model-3	1.00	1.00	1.00	1.00	1.00	1.00	1.00	1.00
Model-3 is true with $\lambda = 0.3$	Model-1	.000	.000	.000	.000	.000	.000	.000	.000
	Model-2	.000	.000	.000	.000	.000	.000	.000	.000
	Model-3	1.00	1.00	1.00	1.00	1.00	1.00	1.00	1.00
Model-3 is true with $\lambda = 0.5$	Model-1	.000	.000	.000	.000	.000	.000	.000	.000
	Model-2	.000	.000	.000	.000	.000	.000	.000	.000
	Model-3	1.00	1.00	1.00	1.00	1.00	1.00	1.00	1.00
Model-3 is true with $\lambda = 0.7$	Model-1	.000	.000	.000	.000	.000	.000	.000	.000
	Model-2	.000	.000	.000	.000	.000	.000	.000	.000
	Model-3	1.00	1.00	1.00	1.00	1.00	1.00	1.00	1.00
Model-3 is true with $\lambda = 0.9$	Model-1	.000	.525	.247	.157	.078	.170	.127	.274
	Model-2	.000	.000	.000	.000	.000	.000	.000	.000
	Model-3	1.00	.475	.753	.843	.922	.830	.873	.726

Table 6.3 (cont'd)

T=50	Methods →	CIC-1	CIC-2 $\alpha = .01$	$\alpha = .05$	$\alpha = .10$	PAIC	UAIC	PBIC	UBIC
Penalties	P_1	0	0	0	0	0	0	0	0
	P_2		0	0	0	0	0	0	0
	P_3		2.7805	1.3528	0.892	0.5	1.00	0.978	1.956
Model-1 is true	Model-1	1.00	.989	.949	.909	.847	.921	.920	.973
	Model-2	.000	.000	.000	.000	.000	.000	.000	.000
	Model-3	.000	.011	.051	.091	.153	.079	.080	.027
Model-2 is true	Model-1	.000	.000	.000	.000	.000	.000	.000	.000
	Model-2	1.00	.984	.938	.893	.820	.907	.902	.964
	Model-3	.000	.016	.062	.107	.180	.093	.098	.036
Model-3 is true with $\lambda = 0.1$	Model-1	.000	.000	.000	.000	.000	.000	.000	.000
	Model-2	.000	.000	.000	.000	.000	.000	.000	.000
	Model-3	1.00	1.00	1.00	1.00	1.00	1.00	1.00	1.00
Model-3 is true with $\lambda = 0.3$	Model-1	.000	.000	.000	.000	.000	.000	.000	.000
	Model-2	.000	.000	.000	.000	.000	.000	.000	.000
	Model-3	1.00	1.00	1.00	1.00	1.00	1.00	1.00	1.00
Model-3 is true with $\lambda = 0.5$	Model-1	.000	.000	.000	.000	.000	.000	.000	.000
	Model-2	.000	.000	.000	.000	.000	.000	.000	.000
	Model-3	1.00	1.00	1.00	1.00	1.00	1.00	1.00	1.00
Model-3 is true with $\lambda = 0.7$	Model-1	.000	.000	.000	.000	.000	.000	.000	.000
	Model-2	.000	.000	.000	.000	.000	.000	.000	.000
	Model-3	1.00	1.00	1.00	1.00	1.00	1.00	1.00	1.00
Model-3 is true with $\lambda = 0.9$	Model-1	.000	.012	.000	.000	.000	.000	.000	.003
	Model-2	.000	.000	.000	.000	.000	.000	.000	.000
	Model-3	1.00	.988	1.00	1.00	1.00	1.00	1.00	.997

Table 6.3 (cont'd)

T=100	Methods →	CIC-1	CIC-2 $\alpha = .01$	CIC-2 $\alpha = .05$	CIC-2 $\alpha = .10$	PAIC	UAIC	PBIC	UBIC
Penalties	P_1	0	0	0	0	0	0	0	0
	P_2		0	0	0	0	0	0	0
	P_3		2.7805	1.3528	0.892	0.5	1.00	1.1513	2.3026
Model-1 is true	Model-1	1.00	.990	.945	.892	.831	.902	.929	.983
	Model-2	.000	.000	.000	.000	.000	.000	.000	.000
	Model-3	.000	.010	.055	.108	.169	.098	.071	.017
Model-2 is true	Model-1	.000	.000	.000	.000	.000	.000	.000	.000
	Model-2	1.00	.993	.954	.908	.843	.921	.936	.988
	Model-3	.000	.007	.046	.092	.157	.079	.064	.012
Model-3 is true with $\lambda = 0.1$	Model-1	.000	.000	.000	.000	.000	.000	.000	.000
	Model-2	.000	.000	.000	.000	.000	.000	.000	.000
	Model-3	1.00	1.00	1.00	1.00	1.00	1.00	1.00	1.00
Model-3 is true with $\lambda = 0.3$	Model-1	.000	.000	.000	.000	.000	.000	.000	.000
	Model-2	.000	.000	.000	.000	.000	.000	.000	.000
	Model-3	1.00	1.00	1.00	1.00	1.00	1.00	1.00	1.00
Model-3 is true with $\lambda = 0.5$	Model-1	.000	.000	.000	.000	.000	.000	.000	.000
	Model-2	.000	.000	.000	.000	.000	.000	.000	.000
	Model-3	1.00	1.00	1.00	1.00	1.00	1.00	1.00	1.00
Model-3 is true with $\lambda = 0.7$	Model-1	.000	.000	.000	.000	.000	.000	.000	.000
	Model-2	.000	.000	.000	.000	.000	.000	.000	.000
	Model-3	1.00	1.00	1.00	1.00	1.00	1.00	1.00	1.00
Model-3 is true with $\lambda = 0.9$	Model-1	.000	.000	.000	.000	.000	.000	.000	.000
	Model-2	.000	.000	.000	.000	.000	.000	.000	.000
	Model-3	1.00	1.00	1.00	1.00	1.00	1.00	1.00	1.00

Table 6.3 (cont'd)

T=500	Methods →	CIC-1	CIC-2 $\alpha = .01$	$\alpha = .05$	$\alpha = .10$	PAIC	UAIC	PBIC	UBIC
Penalties	P_1	0	0	0	0	0	0	0	0
	P_2		0	0	0	0	0	0	0
	P_3		2.7805	1.3528	0.892	0.5	1.00	1.5537	3.1073
Model-1 is true	Model-1	1.00	.985	.934	.897	.832	.912	.952	.992
	Model-2	.000	.000	.000	.000	.000	.000	.000	.000
	Model-3	.000	.015	.066	.103	.168	.088	.048	.008
Model-2 is true	Model-1	.000	.000	.000	.000	.000	.000	.000	.000
	Model-2	1.00	.992	.959	.923	.850	.939	.972	.993
	Model-3	.000	.008	.041	.077	.150	.061	.028	.007
Model-3 is true with $\lambda = 0.1$	Model-1	.000	.000	.000	.000	.000	.000	.000	.000
	Model-2	.000	.000	.000	.000	.000	.000	.000	.000
	Model-3	1.00	1.00	1.00	1.00	1.00	1.00	1.00	1.00
Model-3 is true with $\lambda = 0.3$	Model-1	.000	.000	.000	.000	.000	.000	.000	.000
	Model-2	.000	.000	.000	.000	.000	.000	.000	.000
	Model-3	1.00	1.00	1.00	1.00	1.00	1.00	1.00	1.00
Model-3 is true with $\lambda = 0.5$	Model-1	.000	.000	.000	.000	.000	.000	.000	.000
	Model-2	.000	.000	.000	.000	.000	.000	.000	.000
	Model-3	1.00	1.00	1.00	1.00	1.00	1.00	1.00	1.00
Model-3 is true with $\lambda = 0.7$	Model-1	.000	.000	.000	.000	.000	.000	.000	.000
	Model-2	.000	.000	.000	.000	.000	.000	.000	.000
	Model-3	1.00	1.00	1.00	1.00	1.00	1.00	1.00	1.00
Model-3 is true with $\lambda = 0.9$	Model-1	.000	.000	.000	.000	.000	.000	.000	.000
	Model-2	.000	.000	.000	.000	.000	.000	.000	.000
	Model-3	1.00	1.00	1.00	1.00	1.00	1.00	1.00	1.00

Table 6.4 Comparison between controlled and other methods for design matrix *X*4 based on calculated probabilities of selecting different models

T=20	Methods →	CIC-1	CIC-2 α = .01	CIC-2 α = .05	CIC-2 α = .10	PAIC	UAIC	PBIC	UBIC
Penalties	P_1	0	0	0	0	0	0	0	0
	P_2		0	0	0	0	0	0	0
	P_3		2.7805	1.3528	0.892	0.5	1.00	0.7489	1.4979
Model-1 is true	Model-1	.990	.982	.924	.882	.806	.897	.861	.933
	Model-2	.000	.000	.000	.000	.000	.000	.000	.000
	Model-3	.010	.018	.076	.118	.194	.103	.139	.067
Model-2 is true	Model-1	.000	.000	.000	.000	.000	.000	.000	.000
	Model-2	1.00	.985	.935	.890	.820	.910	.869	.941
	Model-3	.000	.015	.065	.110	.180	.090	.131	.059
Model-3 is true with $\lambda = 0.1$	Model-1	.000	.000	.000	.000	.000	.000	.000	.000
	Model-2	.000	.000	.000	.000	.000	.000	.000	.000
	Model-3	1.00	1.00	1.00	1.00	1.00	1.00	1.00	1.00
Model-3 is true with $\lambda = 0.3$	Model-1	.000	.000	.000	.000	.000	.000	.000	.000
	Model-2	.000	.000	.000	.000	.000	.000	.000	.000
	Mode	1.00	1.00	1.00	1.00	1.00	1.00	1.00	1.00
	Models 1–3								
Model-3 is true with $\lambda = 0.5$	Model-1	.000	.000	.000	.000	.000	.000	.000	.000
	Model-2	.000	.000	.000	.000	.000	.000	.000	.000
	Model-3	1.00	1.00	1.00	1.00	1.00	1.00	1.00	1.00
Model-3 is true with $\lambda = 0.7$	Model-1	.000	.000	.000	.000	.000	.000	.000	.000
	Model-2	.000	.000	.000	.000	.000	.000	.000	.000
	Model-3	1.00	1.00	1.00	1.00	1.00	1.00	1.00	1.00
Model-3 is true with $\lambda = 0.9$	Model-1	.000	.066	.009	.006	.003	.006	.006	.014
	Model-2	.000	.000	.000	.000	.000	.000	.000	.000
	Model-3	1.00	.934	.991	.994	.997	.994	.994	.986

Table 6.4 (cont'd)

T=50	Methods →	CIC-1	CIC-2 α = .01	CIC-2 α = .05	CIC-2 α = .10	PAIC	UAIC	PBIC	UBIC
Penalties	P_1	0	0	0	0	0	0	0	0
	P_2		0	0	0	0	0	0	0
	P_3		2.7805	1.3528	0.892	0.5	1.00	0.978	1.956
Model-1 is true	Model-1	1.00	.994	.959	.923	.838	.933	.931	.982
	Model-2	.000	.000	.000	.000	.000	.000	.000	.000
	Model-3	.000	.006	.041	.077	.162	.067	.069	.018
Model-2 is true	Model-1	.000	.000	.000	.000	.000	.000	.000	.000
	Model-2	1.00	.987	.944	.905	.827	.915	.914	.972
	Model-3	.000	.013	.056	.095	.173	.085	.086	.028
Model-3 is true with λ = 0.1	Model-1	.000	.000	.000	.000	.000	.000	.000	.000
	Model-2	.000	.000	.000	.000	.000	.000	.000	.000
	Model-3	1.00	1.00	1.00	1.00	1.00	1.00	1.00	1.00
Model-3 is true with λ = 0.3	Model-1	.000	.000	.000	.000	.000	.000	.000	.000
	Model-2	.000	.000	.000	.000	.000	.000	.000	.000
	Model-3	1.00	1.00	1.00	1.00	1.00	1.00	1.00	1.00
Model-3 is true with λ = 0.5	Model-1	.000	.000	.000	.000	.000	.000	.000	.000
	Model-2	.000	.000	.000	.000	.000	.000	.000	.000
	Model-3	1.00	1.00	1.00	1.00	1.00	1.00	1.00	1.00
Model-3 is true with λ = 0.7	Model-1	.000	.000	.000	.000	.000	.000	.000	.000
	Model-2	.000	.000	.000	.000	.000	.000	.000	.000
	Model-3	1.00	1.00	1.00	1.00	1.00	1.00	1.00	1.00
Model-3 is true with λ = 0.9	Model-1	.000	.000	.000	.000	.000	.000	.000	.000
	Model-2	.000	.000	.000	.000	.000	.000	.000	.000
	Model-3	1.00	1.00	1.00	1.00	1.00	1.00	1.00	1.00

Table 6.4 (cont'd)

T=100	Methods →	CIC-1	CIC-2 α = .01	α = .05	α = .10	PAIC	UAIC	PBIC	UBIC
Penalties	P_1	0	0	0	0	0	0	0	0
	P_2		0	0	0	0	0	0	0
	P_3		2.7805	1.3528	0.892	0.5	1.00	1.1513	2.3026
Model-1 is true	Model-1	1.00	.990	.941	.896	.816	.911	.924	.981
	Model-2	.000	.000	.000	.000	.000	.000	.000	.000
	Model-3	.000	.010	.059	.104	.184	.089	.076	.019
Model-2 is true	Model-1	.000	.000	.000	.000	.000	.000	.000	.000
	Model-2	1.00	.988	.955	.913	.849	.921	.933	.983
	Model-3	.000	.012	.045	.087	.151	.079	.067	.017
Model-3 is true with λ = 0.1	Model-1	.000	.000	.000	.000	.000	.000	.000	.000
	Model-2	.000	.000	.000	.000	.000	.000	.000	.000
	Model-3	1.00	1.00	1.00	1.00	1.00	1.00	1.00	1.00
Model-3 is true with λ = 0.3	Model-1	.000	.000	.000	.000	.000	.000	.000	.000
	Model-2	.000	.000	.000	.000	.000	.000	.000	.000
	Model-3	1.00	1.00	1.00	1.00	1.00	1.00	1.00	1.00
Model-3 is true with λ = 0.5	Model-1	.000	.000	.000	.000	.000	.000	.000	.000
	Model-2	.000	.000	.000	.000	.000	.000	.000	.000
	Model-3	1.00	1.00	1.00	1.00	1.00	1.00	1.00	1.00
Model-3 is true with λ = 0.7	Model-1	.000	.000	.000	.000	.000	.000	.000	.000
	Model-2	.000	.000	.000	.000	.000	.000	.000	.000
	Model-3	1.00	1.00	1.00	1.00	1.00	1.00	1.00	1.00
Model-3 is true with λ = 0.9	Model-1	.000	.000	.000	.000	.000	.000	.000	.000
	Model-2	.000	.000	.000	.000	.000	.000	.000	.000
	Model-3	1.00	1.00	1.00	1.00	1.00	1.00	1.00	1.00

Table 6.4 (cont'd)

T=500	Methods →	CIC-1	CIC-2 $\alpha = .01$	CIC-2 $\alpha = .05$	CIC-2 $\alpha = .10$	PAIC	UAIC	PBIC	UBIC
Penalties	P_1	0	0	0	0	0	0	0	0
	P_2		0	0	0	0	0	0	0
	P_3		2.7805	1.3528	0.892	0.5	1.00	1.5537	3.1073
Model-1 is true	Model-1	1.00	.988	.948	.909	.840	.923	.952	.989
	Model-2	.000	.000	.000	.000	.000	.000	.000	.000
	Model-3	.000	.012	.052	.091	.160	.077	.048	.011
Model-2 is true	Model-1	.000	.000	.000	.000	.000	.000	.000	.000
	Model-2	1.00	.992	.973	.918	.907	.969	.978	1.00
	Model-3	.000	.008	.027	.082	.093	.031	.022	.000
Model-3 is true with $\lambda = 0.1$	Model-1	.000	.000	.000	.000	.000	.000	.000	.000
	Model-2	.000	.000	.000	.000	.000	.000	.000	.000
	Model-3	1.00	1.00	1.00	1.00	1.00	1.00	1.00	1.00
Model-3 is true with $\lambda = 0.3$	Model-1	.000	.000	.000	.000	.000	.000	.000	.000
	Model-2	.000	.000	.000	.000	.000	.000	.000	.000
	Model-3	1.00	1.00	1.00	1.00	1.00	1.00	1.00	1.00
Model-3 is true with $\lambda = 0.5$	Model-1	.000	.000	.000	.000	.000	.000	.000	.000
	Model-2	.000	.000	.000	.000	.000	.000	.000	.000
	Model-3	1.00	1.00	1.00	1.00	1.00	1.00	1.00	1.00
Model-3 is true with $\lambda = 0.7$	Model-1	.000	.000	.000	.000	.000	.000	.000	.000
	Model-2	.000	.000	.000	.000	.000	.000	.000	.000
	Model-3	1.00	1.00	1.00	1.00	1.00	1.00	1.00	1.00
Model-3 is true with $\lambda = 0.9$	Model-1	.000	.000	.000	.000	.000	.000	.000	.000
	Model-2	.000	.000	.000	.000	.000	.000	.000	.000
	Model-3	1.00	1.00	1.00	1.00	1.00	1.00	1.00	1.00

Table 6.5 Comparison between controlled and other methods for design matrix *X5* based on calculated probabilities of selecting different models

T=20	Methods →	CIC-1	CIC-2 $\alpha = .01$	CIC-2 $\alpha = .05$	CIC-2 $\alpha = .10$	PAIC	UAIC	PBIC	UBIC
Penalties	P_1	0	0	0	0	0	0	0	0
	P_2		0	0	0	0	0	0	0
	P_3		2.7805	1.3528	0.892	0.5	1.00	0.7489	1.4979
Model-1 is true	Model-1	.985	.981	.925	.885	.815	.900	.861	.936
	Model-2	.000	.000	.000	.000	.000	.000	.000	.000
	Model-3	.015	.019	.075	.115	.185	.100	.139	.064
Model-2 is true	Model-1	.000	.000	.000	.000	.000	.000	.000	.000
	Model-2	1.00	.984	.930	.890	.832	.901	.877	.942
	Model-3	.000	.016	.070	.110	.168	.099	.123	.058
Model-3 is true with $\lambda = 0.1$	Model-1	.000	.000	.000	.000	.000	.000	.000	.000
	Model-2	.000	.000	.000	.000	.000	.000	.000	.000
	Model-3	1.00	1.00	1.00	1.00	1.00	1.00	1.00	1.00
Model-3 is true with $\lambda = 0.3$	Model-1	.000	.000	.000	.000	.000	.000	.000	.000
	Model-2	.000	.000	.000	.000	.000	.000	.000	.000
	Model-3	1.00	1.00	1.00	1.00	1.00	1.00	1.00	1.00
Model-3 is true with $\lambda = 0.5$	Model-1	.000	.000	.000	.000	.000	.000	.000	.000
	Model-2	.000	.000	.000	.000	.000	.000	.000	.000
	Model-3	1.00	1.00	1.00	1.00	1.00	1.00	1.00	1.00
Model-3 is true with $\lambda = 0.7$	Model-1	.000	.000	.000	.000	.000	.000	.000	.000
	Model-2	.000	.000	.000	.000	.000	.000	.000	.000
	Model-3	1.00	1.00	1.00	1.00	1.00	1.00	1.00	1.00
Model-3 is true with $\lambda = 0.9$	Model-1	.000	.000	.000	.000	.000	.000	.000	.000
	Model-2	.000	.000	.000	.000	.000	.000	.000	.000
	Model-3	1.00	1.00	1.00	1.00	1.00	1.00	1.00	1.00

Table 6.5 (cont'd)

T=50	Methods →	CIC-1	CIC-2 $\alpha = .01$	$\alpha = .05$	$\alpha = .10$	PAIC	UAIC	PBIC	UBIC
Penalties	P_1	0	0	0	0	0	0	0	0
	P_2		0	0	0	0	0	0	0
	P_3		2.7805	1.3528	0.892	0.5	1.00	0.978	1.956
Model-1 is true	Model-1	1.00	.990	.949	.918	.847	.931	.930	.979
	Model-2	.000	.000	.000	.000	.000	.000	.000	.000
	Model-3	.000	.010	.051	.082	.153	.069	.070	.021
Model-2 is true	Model-1	.000	.000	.000	.000	.000	.000	.000	.000
	Model-2	1.00	.989	.948	.911	.853	.922	.933	.981
	Model-3	.000	.011	.052	.089	.147	.078	.067	.019
Model-3 is true with $\lambda = 0.1$	Model-1	.000	.000	.000	.000	.000	.000	.000	.000
	Model-2	.000	.000	.000	.000	.000	.000	.000	.000
	Model-3	1.00	1.00	1.00	1.00	1.00	1.00	1.00	1.00
Model-3 is true with $\lambda = 0.3$	Model-1	.000	.000	.000	.000	.000	.000	.000	.000
	Model-2	.000	.000	.000	.000	.000	.000	.000	.000
	Model-3	1.00	1.00	1.00	1.00	1.00	1.00	1.00	1.00
Model-3 is true with $\lambda = 0.5$	Model-1	.000	.000	.000	.000	.000	.000	.000	.000
	Model-2	.000	.000	.000	.000	.000	.000	.000	.000
	Model-3	1.00	1.00	1.00	1.00	1.00	1.00	1.00	1.00
Model-3 is true with $\lambda = 0.7$	Model-1	.000	.000	.000	.000	.000	.000	.000	.000
	Model-2	.000	.000	.000	.000	.000	.000	.000	.000
	Model-3	1.00	1.00	1.00	1.00	1.00	1.00	1.00	1.00
Model-3 is true with $\lambda = 0.9$	Model-1	.000	.000	.000	.000	.000	.000	.000	.000
	Model-2	.000	.000	.000	.000	.000	.000	.000	.000
	Model-3	1.00	1.00	1.00	1.00	1.00	1.00	1.00	1.00

Table 6.5 (cont'd)

T=100	Methods →	CIC-1	CIC-2 $\alpha = .01$	$\alpha = .05$	$\alpha = .10$	PAIC	UAIC	PBIC	UBIC
Penalties	P_1	0	0	0	0	0	0	0	0
	P_2		0	0	0	0	0	0	0
	P_3		2.7805	1.3528	0.892	0.5	1.00	.1513	2.3026
Model-1 is true	Model-1	1.00	.989	.943	.900	.846	.908	.927	.980
	Model-2	.000	.000	.000	.000	.000	.000	.000	.000
	Model-3	.000	.011	.057	.100	.154	.092	.073	.020
Model-2 is true	Model-1	.000	.000	.000	.000	.000	.000	.000	.000
	Model-2	1.00	.990	.957	.914	.887	.967	.968	1.00
	Model-3	.000	.010	.043	.086	.113	.033	.032	.000
Model-3 is true with $\lambda = 0.1$	Model-1	.000	.000	.000	.000	.000	.000	.000	.000
	Model-2	.000	.000	.000	.000	.000	.000	.000	.000
	Model-3	1.00	1.00	1.00	1.00	1.00	1.00	1.00	1.00
Model-3 is true with $\lambda = 0.3$	Model-1	.000	.000	.000	.000	.000	.000	.000	.000
	Model-2	.000	.000	.000	.000	.000	.000	.000	.000
	Model-3	1.00	1.00	1.00	1.00	1.00	1.00	1.00	1.00
Model-3 is true with $\lambda = 0.5$	Model-1	.000	.000	.000	.000	.000	.000	.000	.000
	Model-2	.000	.000	.000	.000	.000	.000	.000	.000
	Model-3	1.00	1.00	1.00	1.00	1.00	1.00	1.00	1.00
Model-3 is true with $\lambda = 0.7$	Model-1	.000	.000	.000	.000	.000	.000	.000	.000
	Model-2	.000	.000	.000	.000	.000	.000	.000	.000
	Model-3	1.00	1.00	1.00	1.00	1.00	1.00	1.00	1.00
Model-3 is true with $\lambda = 0.9$	Model-1	.000	.000	.000	.000	.000	.000	.000	.000
	Model-2	.000	.000	.000	.000	.000	.000	.000	.000
	Model-3	1.00	1.00	1.00	1.00	1.00	1.00	1.00	1.00

Table 6.5 (cont'd)

T=500	Methods →	CIC-1	CIC-2 $\alpha = .01$	$\alpha = .05$	$\alpha = .10$	PAIC	UAIC	PBIC	UBIC
Penalties	P_1	0	0	0	0	0	0	0	0
	P_2		0	0	0	0	0	0	0
	P_3		2.7805	1.3528	0.892	0.5	1.00	1.5537	3.1073
Model-1 is true	Model-1	1.00	1.00	1.00	1.00	1.00	1.00	1.00	1.00
	Model-2	.000	.000	.000	.000	.000	.000	.000	.000
	Model-3	.000	.000	.000	.000	.000	.000	.000	.000
Model-2 is true	Model-1	.000	.000	.000	.000	.000	.000	.000	.000
	Model-2	1.00	.995	.972	.919	.925	.989	1.00	1.00
	Model-3	.000	.005	.028	.081	.075	.011	.000	.000
Model-3 is true with $\lambda = 0.1$	Model-1	.000	.000	.000	.000	.000	.000	.000	.000
	Model-2	.000	.000	.000	.000	.000	.000	.000	.000
	Model-3	1.00	1.00	1.00	1.00	1.00	1.00	1.00	1.00
Model-3 is true with $\lambda = 0.3$	Model-1	.000	.000	.000	.000	.000	.000	.000	.000
	Model-2	.000	.000	.000	.000	.000	.000	.000	.000
	Model-3	1.00	1.00	1.00	1.00	1.00	1.00	1.00	1.00
Model-3 is true with $\lambda = 0.5$	Model-1	.000	.000	.000	.000	.000	.000	.000	.000
	Model-2	.000	.000	.000	.000	.000	.000	.000	.000
	Model-3	1.00	1.00	1.00	1.00	1.00	1.00	1.00	1.00
Model-3 is true with $\lambda = 0.7$	Model-1	.000	.000	.000	.000	.000	.000	.000	.000
	Model-2	.000	.000	.000	.000	.000	.000	.000	.000
	Model-3	1.00	1.00	1.00	1.00	1.00	1.00	1.00	1.00
Model-3 is true with $\lambda = 0.9$	Model-1	.000	.000	.000	.000	.000	.000	.000	.000
	Model-2	.000	.000	.000	.000	.000	.000	.000	.000
	Model-3	1.00	1.00	1.00	1.00	1.00	1.00	1.00	1.00

Tables 6.6 and 6.7 reflect the effect of nuisance parameters, β_0, β_1, and σ on PCS for the true models *M*1 and *M*2, respectively, for all methods considered, namely, CIC-1, CIC-2, PAIC, UAIC, PBIC and UAIC. Tables 6.8 to 6.12 show the effect of the same nuisance parameters on PCS for the true model *M*3 where the data were generated from five different values of λ, namely 0.1, 0.3, 0.5, 0.7 and 0.9. We fix $\beta_0 = 10$, $\beta_1 = 1$ and $\sigma = 1$ throughout all our experiments. In order to examine the effect of these parameters, we first consider three different values of β_1, namely 6, 10 and 100 keeping $\beta_0 = 10$ and $\sigma^2 = 1$ fixed. Similarly we consider $\beta_0 = 20$, 50 and 100 and $\sigma = 0.5$, 0.1 and 0.01, keeping the values of the other two nuisance parameters fixed.

As mentioned earlier, Table 6.6 presents the effect of nuisance parameters when *M*1 is the true model. The table indicates that the effect of β_1 on PCS for the true model is moderately significant. As the value of β_1 increases, the PCS slightly increase for all methods although their relative ranks remain the same. In contrast, as the value of β_0 increases, the PCS decrease. The overall rankings of the competing methods, except CIC-1, also slightly change due to the negative effect of β_0. Similarly, as the value of σ decreases, the PCS increase, and this is true for all methods. Because of this, we find no remarkable change in the rankings of the different methods. With respect to average PCS, the eight competing methods can be ranked as: CIC-1 > CIC-2 ($\alpha = 0.01$) > UBIC > CIC-2 ($\alpha = 0.05$) > UAIC > CIC-2 ($\alpha = 0.10$) > PBIC > PAIC. In terms of PCS and corresponding rank, the CIC-1 holds the first position 100 per cent of the time, the CIC-2 with $\alpha = 0.01$ holds the second position 90 per cent of the time, UBIC holds the third position 60 per cent of the time, CIC-2 with $\alpha = 0.06$ holds the fourth position 60 per cent of the time, UAIC holds the fifth position 60 per cent of the time, the CIC-2 with $\alpha = 0.10$ holds the sixth position 60 per cent of the time, PBIC holds the seventh position 70 per cent of the time and finally PAIC holds the eighth position 70 per cent of the time. Interestingly, the overall rank of each of the eight competing methods mostly coincides with the individual rank obtained by three different values of β_1 and σ. But in the case of constant intercept β_0, we find a small anomaly between individual ranks of PCS and the rank of APCS in all methods except CIC-1. In looking to the ranks of all competing methods, we find clear evidence from the first row and the row of average PCS that the ranks obtained by the newly developed methods CIC-1, CIC-2 with $\alpha = 0.01$, PAIC and PBIC are invariant to the nuisance parameters.

Table 6.7 shows the effect of the same set of three nuisance parameters, β_0, β_1, and σ, when model *M*2 is now the true model. The table demonstrates a clearer picture of the effect of nuisance parameters on the PCS. Here the effect of β_1 on the PCS seems very mild. That means, the PCS are almost identical, although the value of β_1 increases a lot. For example, the PCS for the CIC-2 with $\alpha = 0.01$ shifts from 0.992 to 0.991 for the change of value of $\beta_1 = 6$ to $\beta_1 = 100$. Similarly, we find very negligible changes for all other methods as well. In the case of the constant intercept term β_0, we find no change in the PCS in any method, which clearly indicates that the PCS are invariant to the value of β_0. Finally, in the case of the standard deviation σ, the table shows, in a way which seems unexpected, that as the value of σ decreases, the PCS also slightly decrease. However, the degree of change in the PCS is almost negligible with the change of σ. It is important to note that in this particular case, the PCS of the true model are almost invariant to the nuisance parameters. With respect to average PCS, the eight competing methods can be ranked as: CIC-1 > CIC-2 ($\alpha = 0.01$) > UBIC > CIC-2 ($\alpha = 0.06$) > UAIC > CIC-2 ($\alpha = 0.10$) > PBIC > PAIC. This is exactly the same as the case when model *M*1 was true. Interestingly, according to average PCS, the rank held by each of the competing methods is exactly the same as their individual rank obtained for different values of nuisance parameters. That means each of the competing methods holds their respective position 100 per cent of the time.

Tables 6.8 to 6.12 present the effect of the same nuisance parameters on the PCS involved in the model in question when model *M*3 is now the true model and when the data were generated from five λ values, namely 0.1, 0.3, 0.6, 0.7 and 0.9. The tables show an almost similar pattern of results for all methods considered. It is apparent from these tables that the effects of nuisance parameters on the PCS are almost the same as the two other (when *M*1 and *M*2 were true) previous cases. That means the effect of β_1 on the PCS is always positive and that of β_0 and σ is always negative. This is true for all competing methods and for all five versions of the data generating processes as well. In looking to the ranks of individual PCS and average PCS in Table 6.8 (when $\lambda = 0.1$), we find that the ranks obtained by eight different methods in the original setting (see the first row of the third section) are very close to those of the average PCS except in one case (CIC-1). This is also true for the other three cases, namely when $\lambda = 0.3$, $\lambda = 0.7$ and $\lambda = 0.9$. Interestingly, when $\lambda = 0.5$, the ranks in both cases are exactly the same, indicating that the effect of nuisance parameters on the rankings of the PCS has been proven to be invariant in this case and almost invariant in the other four cases. Thus the results we obtained for our particular setting could be claimed to be representative, at least in terms of relative rankings, over the whole parameter space.

Table 6.6 **Effect of choice of β_1, β_0 and σ values on the probabilities of selecting competing models for different methods when model *M*1 with $T = 20$ is true**

Nuisance parameters			CIC-1	CIC-2			PAIC	UAIC	PBIC	UBIC
				$\alpha = .01$	$\alpha = .05$	$\alpha = .10$				
β_0	β_1	σ			**Probability of choosing *M*1 when *M*1 is true**					
10	1	1	.665(1)	.6112=	.6112=	.6112=	.607(8)	.6112=	.610(7)	.6112=
10	5	1	.995(1)	.977(2)	.902(4)	.845(6)	.757(8)	.868(5)	.823(7)	.913(3)
10	10	1	1.00(1)	.979(2)	.908(4)	.862(6)	.773(8)	.873(5)	.839(7)	.925(3)
10	100	1	1.00(1)	.981(2)	.922(4)	.874(6)	.789(8)	.886(5)	.849(7)	.938(3)
20	1	1	.575(1)	.5012=	.5012=	.5012=	.5012=	.5012=	.5012=	.5012=
50	1	1	.520(1)	.4374=	.4374=	.4374=	.4392=	.4374=	.4374=	.4392=
100	1	1	.510(1)	.4192=	.4192=	.4192=	.4192=	.4192=	.4192=	.4192=
10	1	.5	.775(1)	.709(2)	.7083=	.706(6)	.680(8)	.7083=	.702(7)	.7083=
10	1	.1	1.00(1)	.982(2)	.916(4)	.864(6)	.788(8)	.876(5)	.843(7)	.931(3)
10	1	.01	1.00(1)	.983(2)	.924(4)	.872(6)	.801(8)	.881(5)	.855(7)	.940(3)
Average PCS			.804(1)	.758(2)	.725(4)	.699(6)	.655(8)	.706(5)	.688(7)	.733(3)
					Probability of choosing *M*2 when *M*1 is true					
10	1	1	.005	.389	.389	.389	.387	.389	.389	.389
10	5	1	.000	.000	.000	.000	.000	.000	.000	.000
10	10	1	.000	.000	.000	.000	.000	.000	.000	.000
10	100	1	.000	.000	.000	.000	.000	.000	.000	.000
20	1	1	.045	.499	.499	.499	.499	.499	.499	.499
50	1	1	.060	.563	.563	.563	.563	.563	.563	.563

Table 6.6 (cont'd)

Nuisance parameters			Methods							
			CIC-1	CIC-2			PAIC	UAIC	PBIC	UBIC
				$\alpha = .01$	$\alpha = .05$	$\alpha = .10$				
β_0	β_1	σ			Probability of choosing *M2* when *M1* is true					
100	1	1	.060	.581	.581	.581	.581	.581	.581	.581
10	1	.5	.050	.291	.292	.291	.281	.291	.288	.291
10	1	.1	.000	.000	.000	.000	.000	.000	.000	.000
10	1	.01	.000	.000	.000	.000	.000	.000	.000	.000
					Probability of choosing *M3* when *M1* is true					
10	1	1	.330	.000	.000	.000	.006	.000	.001	.000
10	5	1	.005	.023	.098	.155	.243	.132	.177	.087
10	10	1	.000	.021	.092	.138	.227	.127	.161	.075
10	100	1	.000	.019	.078	.126	.211	.114	.151	.062
20	1	1	.380	.000	.000	.000	.000	.000	.000	.000
50	1	1	.420	.000	.000	.000	.000	.000	.000	.000
100	1	1	.430	.000	.000	.000	.000	.000	.000	.000
10	1	.5	.175	.000	.000	.003	.039	.001	.010	.001
10	1	.1	.000	.018	.084	.136	.212	.124	.157	.069
10	1	.01	.000	.017	.076	.128	.199	.119	.145	.060

Note: The values within brackets indicate rank. The right extreme digit in smaller font with equals sign indicates a similar rank within the row.

Table 6.7 Effect of choice of β_1, β_0 and σ values on the probabilities of selecting competing models for different methods when model *M2* with $T = 20$ is true

Nuisance parameters			Methods							
			CIC-1	CIC-2			PAIC	UAIC	PBIC	UBIC
				$\alpha = .01$	$\alpha = .05$	$\alpha = .10$				
β_0	β_1	σ	Probability of choosing *M1* when *M2* is true							
10	1	1	.000	.000	.000	.000	.000	.000	.000	.000
10	5	1	.000	.000	.000	.000	.000	.000	.000	.000
10	10	1	.000	.000	.000	.000	.000	.000	.000	.000
10	100	1	.000	.000	.000	.000	.000	.000	.000	.000
20	1	1	.000	.000	.000	.000	.000	.000	.000	.000
50	1	1	.000	.000	.000	.000	.000	.000	.000	.000
100	1	1	.000	.000	.000	.000	.000	.000	.000	.000
10	1	.5	.000	.000	.000	.000	.000	.000	.000	.000
10	1	.1	.000	.000	.000	.000	.000	.000	.000	.000
10	1	.01	.000	.000	.000	.000	.000	.000	.000	.000
			Probability of choosing *M2* when *M2* is true							
10	1	1	1.00(1)	.997(2)	.971(4)	.950(6)	.892(8)	.957(5)	.932(7)	.978(3)
10	5	1	1.00(1)	.992(2)	.942(4)	.913(6)	.855(8)	.918(5)	.901(7)	.950(3)
10	10	1	1.00(1)	.990(2)	.937(4)	.906(6)	.846(8)	.916(5)	.893(7)	.946(3)
10	100	1	1.00(1)	.991(2)	.945(4)	.904(6)	.840(8)	.912(5)	.887(7)	.953(3)
20	1	1	1.00(1)	.997(2)	.971(4)	.950(6)	.892(8)	.957(5)	.932(7)	.978(3)
50	1	1	1.00(1)	.997(2)	.971(4)	.950(6)	.892(8)	.957(5)	.932(7)	.978(3)
100	1	1	1.00(1)	.997(2)	.971(4)	.950(6)	.892(8)	.957(5)	.932(7)	.978(3)

Table 6.7 (cont'd)

Nuisance parameters			Methods							
			CIC-1	CIC-2			PAIC	UAIC	PBIC	UBIC
				$\alpha = .01$	$\alpha = .05$	$\alpha = .10$				
					Probability of choosing *M2* when *M2* is true					
β_0	β_1	σ								
10	1	.5	1.00(1)	.991(2)	.958(4)	.924(6)	.879(8)	.936(5)	.911(7)	.966(3)
10	1	.1	1.00(1)	.990(2)	.937(4)	.906(6)	.846(8)	.916(5)	.893(7)	.946(3)
10	1	.01	1.00(1)	.990(2)	.933(4)	.902(6)	.839(8)	.911(5)	.885(7)	.942(3)
Average PCS			1.00(1)	.993(2)	.954(4)	.926(6)	.867(8)	.934(5)	.910(7)	.962(3)
					Probability of choosing *M3* when *M2* is true					
10	1	1	.000	.003	.029	.050	.108	.043	.068	.022
10	5	1	.000	.008	.058	.087	.145	.082	.099	.050
10	10	1	.000	.010	.063	.094	.154	.084	.107	.054
10	100	1	.000	.009	.055	.096	.160	.088	.113	.047
20	1	1	.000	.003	.029	.050	.108	.043	.068	.022
50	1	1	.000	.003	.029	.050	.108	.043	.068	.022
100	1	1	.000	.003	.029	.050	.108	.043	.068	.022
10	1	.5	.000	.009	.042	.076	.121	.064	.089	.034
10	1	.1	.000	.010	.063	.094	.154	.084	.107	.054
10	1	.01	.000	.010	.067	.098	.161	.089	.115	.058

Note: The values within brackets indicate rank.

Table 6.8 **Effect of choice of β_1, β_0 and σ values on the probabilities of selecting competing models for different methods when $\lambda = 0.1$ and model $M3$ with $T = 20$ is true**

Nuisance parameters			Methods							
			CIC-1	CIC-2			PAIC	UAIC	PBIC	UBIC
				$\alpha = .01$	$\alpha = .05$	$\alpha = .10$				
β_0	β_1	σ	Probability of choosing $M1$ when $M3$ is true and $\lambda = 0.1$							
10	1	1	.030	.025	.012	.005	.002	.005	.003	.012
10	5	1	.000	.000	.000	.000	.000	.000	.000	.000
10	10	1	.000	.000	.000	.000	.000	.000	.000	.000
10	100	1	.000	.000	.000	.000	.000	.000	.000	.000
20	1	1	.000	.062	.055	.047	.029	.049	.043	.056
50	1	1	.090	.163	.163	.161	.152	.163	.159	.163
100	1	1	.240	.263	.263	.263	.263	.263	.263	.263
10	1	.5	.000	.001	.000	.000	.000	.000	.000	.000
10	1	.1	.000	.000	.000	.000	.000	.000	.000	.000
10	1	.01	.000	.000	.000	.000	.000	.000	.000	.000
			Probability of choosing $M2$ when $M3$ is true and $\lambda = 0.1$							
10	1	1	.960	.963	.900	.849	.765	.869	.825	.915
10	5	1	.020	.005	.000	.000	.000	.000	.000	.000
10	10	1	.000	.000	.000	.000	.000	.000	.000	.000
10	100	1	.000	.000	.000	.000	.000	.000	.000	.000
20	1	1	.775	.937	.909	.878	.824	.888	.869	.918
50	1	1	.105	.837	.837	.833	.827	.836	.833	.837
100	1	1	.150	.737	.737	.737	.737	.737	.737	.737

Table 6.8 (cont'd)

Nuisance parameters			CIC-1	CIC-2			PAIC	UAIC	PBIC	UBIC
				$\alpha = .01$	$\alpha = .05$	$\alpha = .10$				
β_0	β_1	σ	Probability of choosing *M2* when *M3* is true and $\lambda = 0.1$							
10	1	.5	.960	.931	.823	.747	.629	.765	.703	.844
10	1	.1	.245	.107	.018	.009	.004	.010	.007	.024
10	1	.01	.000	.000	.000	.000	.000	.000	.000	.000
			Probability of choosing *M3* when *M3* is true and $\lambda = 0.1$							
10	1	1	.010(8)	.012(7)	.088(5)	.146(3)	.233(1)	.126(4)	.172(2)	.073(6)
10	5	1	.980(8)	.995(7)	1.001=	1.001=	1.001=	1.001=	1.001=	1.001=
10	10	1	1.001=	1.001=	1.001=	1.001=	1.001=	1.001=	1.001=	1.001=
10	100	1	1.001=	1.001=	1.001=	1.001=	1.001=	1.001=	1.001=	1.001=
20	1	1	.225(1)	.001(8)	.036(6)	.075(4)	.147(2)	.063(5)	.088(3)	.026(7)
50	1	1	.805(1)	.0006=	.0006=	.006(4)	.021(2)	.001(5)	.008(3)	.0006=
100	1	1	.610(1)	.0002=	.0002=	.0002=	.0002=	.0002=	.0002=	.0002=
10	1	.5	.040(8)	.068(7)	.177(5)	.253(3)	.371(1)	.235(4)	.297(2)	.156(6)
10	1	.1	.755(8)	.893(7)	.982(5)	.991(3)	.996(2)	.990(4)	.997(1)	.976(6)
10	1	.01	1.001=	1.001=	1.001=	1.001=	1.001=	1.001=	1.001=	1.001=
Average PCS			1.643(1)	.497(8)	.528(6)	.547(4)	.577(2)	.542(5)	.556(3)	.523(7)

Note: The values within brackets indicate rank. The right extreme digit in smaller font with equal signs indicates a similar rank within the row.

Table 6.9 Effect of choice of β_1, β_0 and σ values on the probabilities of selecting competing models for different methods when $\lambda = 0.3$ and model *M3* with $T = 20$ is true

Nuisance parameters			Methods							
			CIC-1	CIC-2			PAIC	UAIC	PBIC	UBIC
				$\alpha = .01$	$\alpha = .05$	$\alpha = .10$				
β_0	β_1	σ	Probability of choosing *M1* when *M3* is true and $\lambda = 0.3$							
10	1	1	.035	.209	.185	.162	.117	.167	.148	.193
10	5	1	.000	.000	.000	.000	.000	.000	.000	.000
10	10	1	.000	.000	.000	.000	.000	.000	.000	.000
10	100	1	.000	.000	.000	.000	.000	.000	.000	.000
20	1	1	.260	.279	.279	.279	.273	.279	.279	.279
50	1	1	.335	.342	.342	.342	.342	.342	.342	.342
100	1	1	.355	.369	.369	.369	.369	.369	.369	.369
10	1	.5	.125	.175	.106	.063	.029	.073	.050	.116
10	1	.1	.000	.000	.000	.000	.000	.000	.000	.000
10	1	.01	.000	.000	.000	.000	.000	.000	.000	.000
			Probability of choosing *M2* when *M3* is true and $\lambda = 0.3$							
10	1	1	.645	.789	.769	.743	.662	.748	.725	.773
10	5	1	.000	.000	.000	.000	.000	.000	.000	.000
10	10	1	.000	.000	.000	.000	.000	.000	.000	.000
10	100	1	.000	.000	.000	.000	.000	.000	.000	.000
20	1	1	.735	.721	.721	.720	.711	.720	.720	.721
50	1	1	.665	.658	.658	.658	.658	.658	.658	.658
100	1	1	.645	.631	.631	.631	.631	.631	.631	.631

Table 6.9 (cont'd)

Nuisance parameters			CIC-1	CIC-2			PAIC	UAIC	PBIC	UBIC
				$\alpha = .01$	$\alpha = .05$	$\alpha = .10$				
β_0	β_1	σ	**Probability of choosing *M2* when *M3* is true and $\lambda = 0.3$**							
10	1	.5	.805	.786	.650	.557	.466	.586	.523	.672
10	1	.1	.010	.000	.000	.000	.000	.000	.000	.000
10	1	.01	.000	.000	.000	.000	.000	.000	.000	.000
			Probability of choosing *M3* when *M3* is true and $\lambda = 0.3$							
10	1	1	.320(1)	.002(8)	.046(6)	.095(4)	.221(2)	.085(5)	.127(3)	.034(7)
10	5	1	1.001=	1.001=	1.001=	1.001=	1.001=	1.001=	1.001=	1.001=
10	10	1	1.001=	1.001=	1.001=	1.001=	1.001=	1.001=	1.001=	1.001=
10	100	1	1.001=	1.001=	1.001=	1.001=	1.001=	1.001=	1.001=	1.001=
20	1	1	.005(2)	.0006=	.0006=	.0013=	.016(1)	.0013=	.0013=	.0006=
50	1	1	.0001=	.0001=	.0001=	.0001=	.0001=	.0001=	.0001=	.0001=
100	1	1	.0001=	.0001=	.0001=	.0001=	.0001=	.0001=	.0001=	.0001=
10	1	.5	.070(7)	.039(8)	.244(5)	.380(3)	.505(1)	.341(4)	.427(2)	.212(6)
10	1	.1	.990(8)	1.001=	1.001=	1.001=	1.001=	1.001=	1.001=	1.001=
10	1	.01	1.001=	1.001=	1.001=	1.001=	1.001=	1.001=	1.001=	1.001=
Average PCS			.539(5)	.504(8)	.529(6)	.548(3)	.574(1)	.543(4)	.556(2)	.525(7)

Note: The values within brackets indicate rank. The right extreme digit in smaller font with equal signs indicates a similar rank within the row.

Table 6.10 **Effect of choice of β_1, β_0 and σ values on the probabilities of selecting competing models for different methods when $\lambda = 0.5$ and model *M3* with $T = 20$ is true**

Nuisance parameters			Methods							
			CIC-1	CIC-2			PAIC	UAIC	PBIC	UBIC
				$\alpha = .01$	$\alpha = .05$	$\alpha = .10$				
β_0	β_1	σ	Probability of choosing *M1* when *M3* is true and $\lambda = 0.5$							
10	1	1	.330	.389	.388	.379	.347	.382	.370	.388
10	5	1	.000	.000	.000	.000	.000	.000	.000	.000
10	10	1	.000	.000	.000	.000	.000	.000	.000	.000
10	100	1	.000	.000	.000	.000	.000	.000	.000	.000
20	1	1	.375	.389	.389	.389	.389	.389	.389	.389
50	1	1	.380	.393	.393	.393	.393	.393	.393	.393
100	1	1	.385	.400	.400	.400	.400	.400	.400	.400
10	1	.5	.330	.436	.395	.342	.251	.354	.320	.409
10	1	.1	.000	.000	.000	.000	.000	.000	.000	.000
10	1	.01	.000	.000	.000	.000	.000	.000	.000	.000
			Probability of choosing *M2* when *M3* is true and $\lambda = 0.5$							
10	1	1	.070	.611	.611	.601	.564	.606	.593	.611
10	5	1	.000	.000	.000	.000	.000	.000	.000	.000
10	10	1	.000	.000	.000	.000	.000	.000	.000	.000
10	100	1	.000	.000	.000	.000	.000	.000	.000	.000
20	1	1	.625	.611	.611	.611	.611	.611	.611	.611
50	1	1	.620	.607	.607	.607	.607	.607	.607	.607
100	1	1	.615	.600	.600	.600	.600	.600	.600	.600

Table 6.10 (cont'd)

Nuisance parameters			CIC-1	CIC-2			PAIC	UAIC	PBIC	UBIC
				$\alpha = .01$	$\alpha = .05$	$\alpha = .10$				
β_0	β_1	σ	**Probability of choosing *M2* when *M3* is true and $\lambda = 0.5$**							
10	1	.5	.590	.562	.528	.482	.418	.498	.465	.537
10	1	.1	.000	.000	.000	.000	.000	.000	.000	.000
10	1	.01	.000	.000	.000	.000	.000	.000	.000	.000
			Probability of choosing *M3* when *M3* is true and $\lambda = 0.5$							
10	1	1	.600(1)	.000(8)	.0016=	.020(4)	.089(2)	.012(5)	.037(3)	.0016
10	5	1	1.001=	1.001=	1.001=	1.001=	1.001=	1.001=	1.001=	1.001=
10	10	1	1.001=	1.001=	1.001=	1.001=	1.001=	1.001=	1.001=	1.001=
10	100	1	1.001=	1.001=	1.001=	1.001=	1.001=	1.001=	1.001=	1.001=
20	1	1	.0001=	.0001=	1.001=	.0001=	.0001=	.0001=	.0001=	.0001=
50	1	1	.0001=	.0001=	.0001=	.0001=	.0001=	.0001=	.0001=	.0001=
100	1	1	.0001=	.0001=	.0001=	.0001=	.0001=	.0001=	.0001=	.0001=
10	1	.5	.080(5)	.002(8)	.077(6)	.176(3)	.331(1)	.148(4)	.215(2)	.054(7)
10	1	.1	1.001=	1.001=	1.001=	1.001=	1.001=	1.001=	1.001=	1.001=
10	1	.01	1.001=	1.001=	1.001=	1.001=	1.001=	1.001=	1.001=	1.001
					1.001=					
Average PCS			.568(1)	.500(8)	.508(6)	.520(4)	.542(2)	.516(5)	.525(3)	.506(7)

Note: The values within brackets indicate rank. The right extreme digit in smaller font with equal signs indicates a similar rank within the row.

Table 6.11 **Effect of choice of β_1, β_0 and σ values on the probabilities of selecting competing models for different methods when $\lambda = 0.7$ and model $M3$ with $T = 20$ is true**

Nuisance parameters			CIC-1	CIC-2			PAIC	UAIC	PBIC	UBIC
				$\alpha = .01$	$\alpha = .05$	$\alpha = .10$				
β_0	β_1	σ	Probability of choosing $M1$ when $M3$ is true and $\lambda = 0.7$							
10	1	1	.365	.502	.502	.501	.493	.502	.501	.502
10	5	1	.000	.235	.064	.027	.006	.036	.020	.071
10	10	1	.000	.000	.000	.000	.000	.000	.000	.000
10	100	1	.000	.000	.000	.000	.000	.000	.000	.000
20	1	1	.480	.443	.443	.443	.443	.443	.443	.443
50	1	1	.390	.417	.417	.417	.417	.417	.417	.417
100	1	1	.390	.409	.409	.409	.409	.409	.409	.409
10	1	.5	.545	.562	.556	.542	.476	.546	.523	.559
10	1	.1	.510	.278	.090	.048	.021	.060	.038	.103
10	1	.01	.000	.000	.000	.000	.000	.000	.000	.000
			Probability of choosing $M2$ when $M3$ is true and $\lambda = 0.7$							
10	1	1	.090	.498	.497	.496	.486	.496	.493	.497
10	5	1	.000	.000	.000	.000	.000	.000	.000	.000
10	10	1	.000	.000	.000	.000	.000	.000	.000	.000
10	100	1	.000	.000	.000	.000	.000	.000	.000	.000
20	1	1	.520	.557	.557	.557	.557	.557	.557	.557
50	1	1	.610	.583	.583	.583	.583	.583	.583	.583
100	1	1	.610	.591	.591	.591	.591	.591	.591	.591

Table 6.11 (cont'd)

Nuisance parameters			CIC-1	CIC-2			PAIC	UAIC	PBIC	UBIC
				$\alpha = .01$	$\alpha = .05$	$\alpha = .10$				
β_0	β_1	σ	**Probability of choosing *M2* when *M3* is true and $\lambda = 0.7$**							
10	1	.5	.435	.436	.434	.425	.381	.432	.413	.435
10	1	.1	.000	.000	.000	.000	.000	.000	.000	.000
10	1	.01	.000	.000	.000	.000	.000	.000	.000	.000
			Probability of choosing *M3* when *M3* is true and $\lambda = 0.7$							
10	1	1	.545(1)	.000(8)	.0016=	.003(4)	.021(2)	.002(5)	.006(3)	.0016=
10	5	1	1.00(1)	.765(5)	.936(7)	.973(4)	.994(2)	.964(6)	.980(3)	.929(8)
10	10	1	1.001=	1.001=	1.001=	1.001=	1.001=	1.001=	1.001=	1.001=
10	100	1	1.001=	1.001=	1.001=	1.001=	1.001=	1.001=	1.001=	1.001=
20	1	1	.0001=	.0001=	.0001=	.0001=	.0001=	.0001=	.0001=	.0001=
50	1	1	.0001=	.0001=	.0001=	.0001=	.0001=	.0001=	.0001=	.0001=
100	1	1	.0001=	.0001=	.0001=	.0001=	.0001=	.0001=	.0001=	.0001=
10	1	.5	.020(5)	.002(8)	.010(6)	.033(3)	.143(1)	.022(4)	.064(2)	.006(7)
10	1	.1	.490(8)	.722(7)	.910(5)	.952(3)	.979(1)	.940(4)	.962(2)	.897(6)
10	1	.01	1.001=	1.001=	1.001=	1.001=	1.001=	1.001=	1.001=	1.001=
Average PCS			.506(2)	.449(6)	.395(8)	.401(7)	.514(1)	.493(4)	.501(3)	.483(5)

Note: The values within brackets indicate rank. The right extreme digit in smaller font with equal signs indicates a similar rank within the row.

Table 6.12 **Effect of choice of β_1, β_0 and σ values on the probabilities of selecting competing models for different methods when $\lambda = 0.9$ and model *M3* is true**

Nuisance parameters			CIC-1	CIC-2			PAIC	UAIC	PBIC	UBIC
				$\alpha = .01$	$\alpha = .05$	$\alpha = .10$				
β_0	β_1	σ	**Probability of choosing *M1* when *M3* is true and $\lambda = 0.9$**							
10	1	1	.535	.564	.564	.563	.561	.563	.563	.564
10	5	1	.000	.895	.692	.570	.457	.604	.536	.727
10	10	1	.000	.585	.323	.219	.139	.255	.198	.350
10	100	1	.000	.000	.000	.000	.000	.000	.000	.000
20	1	1	.455	.484	.484	.484	.484	.484	.484	.484
50	1	1	.410	.435	.435	.435	.435	.435	.435	.435
100	1	1	.390	.414	.414	.414	.414	.414	.414	.414
10	1	.5	.660	.645	.645	.639	.619	.641	.635	.645
10	1	.1	.930	.908	.729	.615	.492	.645	.567	.763
10	1	.01	.000	.000	.000	.000	.000	.000	.000	.000
			Probability of choosing *M2* when *M3* is true and $\lambda = 0.9$							
10	1	1	.205	.436	.436	.435	.434	.436	.435	.436
10	5	1	.000	.000	.000	.000	.000	.000	.000	.000
10	10	1	.000	.000	.000	.000	.000	.000	.000	.000
10	100	1	.000	.000	.000	.000	.000	.000	.000	.000
20	1	1	.545	.516	.516	.516	.516	.516	.516	.516
50	1	1	.590	.565	.565	.565	.565	.565	.565	.565

Table 6.12 (cont'd)

Nuisance parameters			CIC-1	CIC-2			PAIC	UAIC	PBIC	UBIC
				α = .01	α = .05	α = .10				
β_0	β_1	σ	**Probability of choosing *M2* when *M3* is true and λ = 0.9**							
100	1	1	.610	.586	.586	.586	.586	.586	.586	.586
10	1	.5	.330	.355	.355	.354	.340	.354	.349	.355
10	1	.1	.000	.000	.000	.000	.000	.000	.000	.000
10	1	.01	.000	.000	.000	.000	.000	.000	.000	.000
			Probability of choosing *M3* when *M3* is true and λ = 0.9							
10	1	1	.260(1)	.0006=	.0006=	.0023=	.005(2)	.001(5)	.0023=	.0006=
10	5	1	1.00(1)	.105(8)	.308(6)	.430(4)	.543(2)	.396(5)	.464(3)	.273(7)
10	10	1	1.00(1)	.415(8)	.677(6)	.781(4)	.861(3)	.745(5)	.882(2)	.650(7)
10	100	1	1.001=	1.001=	1.001=	1.001=	1.001=	1.001=	1.001=	1.001=
20	1	1	.000(1)	.0001=	.0001=	.0001=	.0001=	.0001=	.0001=	.0001=
50	1	1	.0001=	.0001=	.0001=	.0001=	.0001=	.0001=	.0001=	.0001=
100	1	1	.0001=	.0001=	.0001=	.0001=	.0001=	.0001=	.0001=	.0001=
10	1	.5	.010(3)	.0006=	.0006=	.007(4)	.041(1)	.005(5)	.016(2)	.0006=
10	1	.1	.070(8)	.092(7)	.271(5)	.385(3)	.508(1)	.355(4)	.433(2)	.237(6)
10	1	.01	1.001=	1.001=	1.001=	1.001=	1.001=	1.001=	1.001=	1.001=
Average PCS			.434(1)	.261(8)	.326(6)	.361(4)	.396(2)	.350(5)	.380(3)	.316(7)

Note: The values within brackets indicate rank. The right extreme digit in smaller font with equal signs indicates a similar rank within the row.

6.4 The Extension of Controlled Information Criterion-1 to the Case of Two Restrictions

Chapter 4 dealt with the general approach of our proposed new AIC for one and more than one restricted parameter and applied it to a simple version of the BCT model. In fact, the BCT model can be expressed in at least four different versions such as:

$$y_t(\lambda) = \beta_1 + \beta_2 x_{2t} + \ldots + \beta_k x_{kt} + u_t; \tag{6.12}$$

$$y_t(\lambda) = \beta_1 + \beta_2 x_{2t}(\lambda) + \ldots + \beta_k x_{kt}(\lambda) + u_t; \tag{6.13}$$

$$y_t(\lambda_1) = \beta_1 + \beta_2 x_{2t}(\lambda_2) + \ldots + \beta_k x_{kt}(\lambda_2) + u_t; \tag{6.14}$$

$$y_t(\lambda_1) = \beta_1 + \beta_2 x_{2t}(\lambda_2) + \ldots + \beta_k x_{kt}(\lambda_k) + u_t \tag{6.15}$$

where $t = 1, 2, \ldots, T$ and (6.15) is the most general case, allowing different Box-Cox transformation parameters on all the variables in the model. In Chapter 4 we also developed two new model selection procedures (CIC-1 and CIC-2) of which CIC-1 worked very well and provided much better performance than the other procedures considered. The CIC-1 method was applied to (6.12) where the number of regressors was simply one and the data employed for this analysis were generated from independent normal disturbances with mean zero and variance σ^2. In this connection some obvious questions may arise such as: CIC-1 was clearly the best procedure of all considered for one restriction and for three competing models only; is it still so clearly the best for more than one restriction and for a larger number of competing models? Along with CIC-1, how do the other approaches work for more than one restriction? In order to provide answers to these questions, we consider (6.15) but with only one regressor so that both dependent and independent variables would contain different restricted parameters. In fact, in this section we extend our CIC-1 method for its wider applications in practice.

This section is organised as follows. The theoretical set up for the BCT model in two restricted parameter cases is illustrated in subsection 6.4.1 Subsection 6.4.2 gives a description of our proposed CIC-1 method for two parameter restrictions. A range of simulation experiments is reported in subsection 6.4.3. The final part of this section points out some concluding remarks.

6.4.1 Theoretical Set-up for BCT Model with Two Parameter Restrictions

Consider the following version of a general BCT model:

$$y_t(\lambda_1) = \beta_0 + \beta_1 x_t(\lambda_2) + u_t, \qquad t = 1, 2, \ldots, T \tag{6.16}$$

where $y_t(\lambda_1)$ is a transformed observation at time t on the dependent variable, $x_t(\lambda_2)$ is a transformed observation at time t on the regressor x_t, β_0 is the constant intercept, β_1 is the coefficient of the transformed x_t variable and u_t is the disturbance term distributed $IN(0,\sigma^2)$. Both $y_t(\lambda_1)$ and $x_t(\lambda_2)$ can be defined as (5.82) given in Chapter 5. In this chapter, we investigate the construction and performance of new IC-based model selection procedures with two parameters of interest restricted in the range [0,1], that is, and $0 \leq \lambda_1 \leq 1$, $0 \leq \lambda_2 \leq 1$. For such a problem, there are $3^2 = 9$ possible combinations of boundary/non-boundary values of the parameters which are ($\lambda_1 = 1$ and $\lambda_2 = 1$), ($\lambda_1 = 1$ and $\lambda_2 = 0$), ($\lambda_1 = 0$ and $\lambda_2 = 1$), ($\lambda_1 = 0$ and $\lambda_2 = 0$), ($\lambda_1 = 1$ and $0 < \lambda_2 < 1$), ($\lambda_1 = 0$ and $0 < \lambda_2 < 1$), ($0 < \lambda_1 < 1$ and $\lambda_2 = 1$), ($0 < \lambda_1 < 1$ and $\lambda_2 = 0$) and ($0 < \lambda_1 < 1$ and $0 < \lambda_2 < 1$). For these nine possible combinations we obtain nine models to compare in our particular model selection problem:

$$M1:\; y_t = \beta_{10} + \beta_{11} x_t + u_t; \tag{6.17}$$

$$M2:\; y_t = \beta_{20} + \beta_{21} \ln(x_t) + u_t; \tag{6.18}$$

$$M3:\; \ln(y_t) = \beta_{30} + \beta_{31} x_t + u_t; \tag{6.19}$$

$$M4:\; \ln(y_t) = \beta_{40} + \beta_{41} \ln(x_t) + u_t; \tag{6.20}$$

$$M6:\; y_t = \beta_{50} + \beta_{51} \left(\frac{x_t^{\lambda_2} - 1}{\lambda_2} \right) + u_t; \tag{6.21}$$

$$M6:\; \ln(y_t) = \beta_{60} + \beta_{61} \left(\frac{x_t^{\lambda_2} - 1}{\lambda_2} \right) + u_t; \tag{6.22}$$

$$M7:\; \frac{y_t^{\lambda_1} - 1}{\lambda_1} = \beta_{70} + \beta_{71} x_t + u_t; \tag{6.23}$$

$$M8:\; \frac{y_t^{\lambda_1} - 1}{\lambda_1} = \beta_{80} + \beta_{81} \ln(x_t) + u_t \tag{6.24}$$

and:

$$M9:\ \frac{y_t^{\lambda_1}-1}{\lambda_1} = \beta_{90} + \beta_{91}\left(\frac{x_t^{\lambda_2}-1}{\lambda_2}\right) + u_t. \tag{6.25}$$

Here the disturbance terms u_t for models $M1$ to $M4$ are normally and independently distributed with mean 0 and variance σ^2, that is $u_t \sim IN(0, \sigma^2)$. Under the Box-Cox transformation scheme, the terms u_t for models $M6$ to $M9$ cannot be normally distributed because the distribution of u_t is truncated. Readers may refer to section 5.6.2 in Chapter 5 on this point. However, to overcome this problem and to proceed with maximum likelihood estimation, we assume that the truncation effect is negligible and that the terms u_t are approximately independently and normally distributed with mean 0 and variance σ^2, that is, $u_t \sim IN(0, \sigma^2)$.

However, of these nine models, the first four contain three parameters each and possess no restricted parameters at all and hence each of them has three as their usual AIC penalty. Similarly, the BIC penalties for these four models are the usual BIC penalties. The second four models, on the other hand, contain four parameters each, one of which is restricted in each model. In accordance with our proposed form of new AIC for such one restricted parameter models, the penalties were chosen as 3.5 (see for example, equation (5.63) in Chapter 5 for PAIC). Similarly the PBIC penalties for such models have been proposed as $3.5 \times \ln(T)/2$. The last model ($M9$) contains 5 parameters, two of which are restricted to be in the range [0,1]. For the new penalty of this model we follow (5.62) in Chapter 5 where PAIC in this case takes the form:

$$\text{PAIC} = \bar{L}_9(\psi) - \left(4 + \frac{\sin^{-1}\rho_{12}}{\pi}\right) \tag{6.26}$$

where $\psi = \left(\hat{\beta}_0, \hat{\beta}_1, \hat{\sigma}^2, \hat{\lambda}_1, \hat{\lambda}_2\right)$, suffix 9 stands for $M9$ and ρ_{12} is the correlation coefficient between estimates of the parameters λ_1 and λ_2 obtained from the covariance matrix (given in detail below) of the unconstrained maximum likelihood estimates of the parameters, namely:

$$\rho_{12} = \frac{\text{cov}\left(\hat{\lambda}_1, \hat{\lambda}_1\right)}{\sqrt{\text{var}\left(\hat{\lambda}_1\right)\text{var}\left(\hat{\lambda}_1\right)}}. \tag{6.27}$$

As there is no significant difference between AIC and BIC other than their penalties, the proposed BIC for $M9$ would be:

$$PBIC = L_9(\hat{\psi}) - \left(4 + \frac{\sin^{-1}\rho_{12}}{\pi}\right)\frac{\ln(T)}{2}. \quad (6.28)$$

The main purpose of this chapter is to see whether the pattern of results we obtained in Chapter 5 can be generalized for more than one restricted parameter for the BCT model or not. Note that in all of the above nine models (*M*1 to *M*9), β_0, β_1 and σ^2 are nuisance parameters and λ_1 and λ_2 (wherever they exist) are two parameters of interest. The log-likelihood function for model (6.16) assuming $u_t \sim IN(0, \sigma^2)$ is:

$$L(\psi) = -\left(\frac{T}{2}\right)\ln(2\pi) - \left(\frac{T}{2}\right)\ln(\sigma^2) - \frac{1}{2\sigma^2}\sum_{t=1}^{T}(y_t(\lambda_1) - \beta_0 - \beta_1 x_t(\lambda_2))^2$$

$$+ (\lambda_1 - 1)\sum_{t=1}^{T}\ln(y_t). \quad (6.29)$$

Here the last term of the above equation is due to the Jacobian of the transformation as defined in Chapter 4. By ignoring the constant terms, the concentrated log-likelihood is:

$$L(\psi) = -\left(\frac{T}{2}\right)\ln(\hat{\sigma}^2(\lambda)) + (\lambda_1 - 1)\sum_{t=1}^{T}\ln(y_t) \quad (6.30)$$

where $\hat{\sigma}^2(\lambda) = \sum_{t=1}^{T}(y_t(\lambda_1) - \hat{\beta}_0 - \hat{\beta}_1 x_t(\lambda_2))^2/\mathrm{T}$ is the estimated variance of u_t conditional on λ and $\hat{\beta} = (\hat{\beta}_0, \hat{\beta}_1)' = (X'X)^{-1}(X'y(\lambda_1))$, where:

$$X = \begin{bmatrix} 1 & x_1(\lambda_2) \\ 1 & x_2(\lambda_2) \\ \vdots & \vdots \\ 1 & x_T(\lambda_2) \end{bmatrix} \quad \text{and } y(\lambda_1) = \begin{bmatrix} y_1(\lambda_1) \\ y_2(\lambda_1) \\ \vdots \\ y_T(\lambda_1) \end{bmatrix}. \quad (6.31)$$

The Jacobian of the transformation from u_t to y_t for models *M*3, *M*4 and *M*6 is y_t^{-1} and for models *M*7, *M*8 and *M*9 is $y_t^{\lambda_1 - 1}$. Thus the concentrated log-likelihoods for models *M*1 to *M*4 ignoring constant terms (as they are same for all competing models) are:

$$\hat{L}_1 = -(\mathrm{T}/2)\ln(\hat{\sigma}_1^2); \quad (6.32)$$

$$\hat{L}_2 = -\,(\mathrm{T}/2)\ln(\hat{\sigma}_2^2); \tag{6.33}$$

$$\hat{L}_3 = -\,(\mathrm{T}/2)\ln(\hat{\sigma}_3^2)\sum_{t=1}^{T}\ln(y_t) \tag{6.34}$$

and:

$$\hat{L}_4 = -\,(\mathrm{T}/2)\ln(\hat{\sigma}_4^2)\sum_{t=1}^{T}\ln(y_t) \tag{6.35}$$

respectively, where:

$$\hat{\sigma}_1^2 = \sum_{t=1}^{T}\left(y_t - \hat{\beta}_{10} - \hat{\beta}_{11}x_t\right)/\mathrm{T}; \tag{6.36}$$

$$\hat{\sigma}_2^2 = \sum_{t=1}^{T}\left(y_t - \hat{\beta}_{20} - \hat{\beta}_{21}x_t\right)/\mathrm{T}; \tag{6.37}$$

$$\hat{\sigma}_3^2 = \sum_{t=1}^{T}\left(\mathrm{In}y_t - \hat{\beta}_{30} - \hat{\beta}_{31}x_t\right)/\mathrm{T} \tag{6.38}$$

and:

$$\hat{\sigma}_4^2 = \sum_{t=1}^{T}\left(\mathrm{In}y_t - \hat{\beta}_{40} - \hat{\beta}_{41}\ln(x_t)\right)/\mathrm{T}. \tag{6.39}$$

Here the betas can be defined as:

$$\hat{\beta}(1) = \left(\hat{\beta}_{10}, \hat{\beta}_{11}\right)' = (X_1'X_1)\ {}^{1}(X_1'y); \tag{6.40}$$

$$\hat{\beta}(2) = \left(\hat{\beta}_{20}, \hat{\beta}_{21}\right)' = (X_2'X_2)^{-1}(X_2'y); \tag{6.41}$$

$$\hat{\beta}(3) = \left(\hat{\beta}_{30}, \hat{\beta}_{31}\right)' = (X_1'X_1)^{-1}(X_1'\ln(y)); \tag{6.42}$$

$$\hat{\beta}(4) = \left(\hat{\beta}_{40}, \hat{\beta}_{41}\right)' = (X_2'X_2)^{-1}(X_2'\ln(y)) \tag{6.43}$$

$$\text{where } X = \begin{bmatrix} 1 & x_1 \\ 1 & x_2 \\ \vdots & \vdots \\ 1 & x_T \end{bmatrix}, \begin{bmatrix} 10 & \ln(x_1) \\ 10 & \ln(x_1) \\ \vdots & \vdots \\ 10 & \ln(x_T) \end{bmatrix} \text{ and } \ln(y) = \begin{bmatrix} \ln(y_1) \\ \ln(y_2) \\ \vdots \\ \ln(y_T) \end{bmatrix}. \tag{6.44}$$

Note that the above estimates of the error variances are not dependent on λ parameters. Similarly, the concentrated log-likelihoods for models *M6* to *M9* for fixed λs are:

$$\hat{L}_5 = -(\mathrm{T}/2)\ln\left(\hat{\sigma}_5^2(\lambda_1)\right); \tag{6.45}$$

$$\hat{L}_6 = -(\mathrm{T}/2)\ln\left(\hat{\sigma}_6^2(\lambda_2)\right) - \sum_{t=1}^{T}\ln(y_t); \tag{6.46}$$

$$\hat{L}_7 = -(\mathrm{T}/2)\ln\left(\hat{\sigma}_7^2(\lambda_1)\right) + (\lambda_1 - 1)\sum_{t=1}^{T}\ln(y_t); \tag{6.47}$$

$$\hat{L}_8 = -(\mathrm{T}/2)\ln\left(\hat{\sigma}_8^2(\lambda_1)\right) + (\lambda_1 - 1)\sum_{t=1}^{T}\ln(y_t); \tag{6.48}$$

and:

$$\hat{L}_9 = -(\mathrm{T}/2)\ln\left(\hat{\sigma}_9^2(\lambda_1,\lambda_2)\right) + (\lambda_1 - 1)\sum_{t=1}^{T}\ln(y_t) \tag{6.49}$$

respectively, where:

$$\hat{\sigma}_5^2(\lambda_2) = \sum_{t=1}^{T}\left(y_t - \hat{\beta}_{50} - \hat{\beta}_{51}x_t(\lambda_2)\right)/\mathrm{T}; \tag{6.50}$$

$$\hat{\sigma}_6^2(\lambda_2) = \sum_{t=1}^{T}\left(\ln y_t - \hat{\beta}_{60} - \hat{\beta}_{61}x_t(\lambda_2)\right)/\mathrm{T}; \tag{6.51}$$

$$\hat{\sigma}_7^2(\lambda_1) = \sum_{t=1}^{T}\left(y_t(\lambda_1) - \hat{\beta}_{70} - \hat{\beta}_{71}x_t\right)/\mathrm{T}; \tag{6.52}$$

$$\hat{\sigma}_8^2(\lambda_1) = \sum_{t=1}^{T}\left(y_t(\lambda_1) - \hat{\beta}_{80} - \hat{\beta}_{81}\ln(x_t)\right)/\mathrm{T} \tag{6.53}$$

and:

$$\hat{\sigma}_9^2(\lambda_1,\lambda_2) = \sum_{t=1}^{T}\left(y_t(\lambda_1) - \hat{\beta}_{90} - \hat{\beta}_{91}x_t(\lambda_2)\right)/\mathrm{T} \tag{6.54}$$

respectively. Here all betas are different as they are derived from different models and can be defined as:

$$\hat{\beta}(5) = \left(\hat{\beta}_{50}, \hat{\beta}_{51}\right)' = (X'X)^{-1}X'y; \tag{6.55}$$

$$\hat{\beta}(6) = \left(\hat{\beta}_{60}, \hat{\beta}_{61}\right)' = (X'X)^{-1}X'\ln(y); \tag{6.56}$$

$$\hat{\beta}(7) = \left(\hat{\beta}_{70}, \hat{\beta}_{71}\right)' = (X_1'X_1)^{-1}X_1'y(\lambda_1); \tag{6.57}$$

$$\hat{\beta}(8) = \left(\hat{\beta}_{80}, \hat{\beta}_{81}\right)' = (X_2'X_2)^{-1}X_2'y(\lambda_1) \tag{6.58}$$

and $\hat{\beta}(9) = \left(\hat{\beta}_{90}, \hat{\beta}_{91}\right)' = (X_1'X_1)^{-1}X'y(\lambda_1).$ (6.59)

Subtracting the appropriate penalties from maximized log-likelihoods for each of the above nine competing models, we obtain UAIC, PAIC, UBIC and PBIC. Here the main problem is to estimate the penalty for *M9*. To do this, we first need to calculate ρ_{12} and hence we need to estimate the Hessian matrix, which can be given as:

$$H(\psi) = \frac{\partial^2 L(\psi)}{\partial\psi\,\partial\psi'}. \tag{6.60}$$

For the purpose of notational brevity, let L denote $L(\psi|y,X)$ and thus the Hessian matrix is:

$$H(\psi) = \begin{vmatrix} \frac{\partial^2 L}{\partial\beta_0^2} & \frac{\partial^2 L}{\partial\beta_0\partial\beta_1} & \frac{\partial^2 L}{\partial\beta_0\partial\lambda_1} & \frac{\partial^2 L}{\partial\beta_0\partial\lambda_2} & \frac{\partial^2 L}{\partial\beta_0\partial\sigma^2} \\ \frac{\partial^2 L}{\partial\beta_1\partial\beta_0} & \frac{\partial^2 L}{\partial\beta_1^2} & \frac{\partial^2 L}{\partial\beta_1\partial\lambda_1} & \frac{\partial^2 L}{\partial\beta_1\partial\lambda_2} & \frac{\partial^2 L}{\partial\beta_1\partial\sigma^2} \\ \frac{\partial^2 L}{\partial\lambda_1\partial\beta_0} & \frac{\partial^2 L}{\partial\lambda_1\partial\beta_1} & \frac{\partial^2 L}{\partial\lambda_1^2} & \frac{\partial^2 L}{\partial\lambda_1\partial\lambda_2} & \frac{\partial^2 L}{\partial\lambda_1\partial\sigma^2} \\ \frac{\partial^2 L}{\partial\lambda_2\partial\beta_0} & \frac{\partial^2 L}{\partial\lambda_2\partial\beta_1} & \frac{\partial^2 L}{\partial\lambda_2\partial\lambda_1} & \frac{\partial^2 L}{\partial\lambda_2^2} & \frac{\partial^2 L}{\partial\lambda_2\partial\sigma^2} \\ \frac{\partial^2 L}{\partial\sigma^2\partial\beta_0} & \frac{\partial^2 L}{\partial\sigma^2\partial\beta_1} & \frac{\partial^2 L}{\partial\sigma^2\partial\lambda_1} & \frac{\partial^2 L}{\partial\sigma^2\partial\lambda_2} & \frac{\partial^2 L}{\partial(\sigma^2)^2} \end{vmatrix}$$

where:

$$\frac{\partial^2 L}{\partial\beta_0^2}, = -\frac{T}{\sigma^2}; \tag{6.61}$$

$$\frac{\partial^2 L}{\partial\beta_0\partial\beta_1} = -\frac{\sum_{t=1}^{T} x_t(\lambda_2)}{\sigma^2}; \tag{6.62}$$

$$\frac{\partial^2 L}{\partial\beta_0\partial\lambda_1} = -\frac{\sum_{t=1}^{T} By_t}{\sigma^2}; \tag{6.63}$$

$$\frac{\partial^2 L}{\partial\beta_0\partial\lambda_2} = -\frac{\beta_1\sum_{t=1}^{T} Bx_t}{\sigma^2}; \tag{6.64}$$

$$\frac{\partial^2 L}{\partial\beta_0\partial\sigma^2} = -\frac{\sum_{t=1}^{T} u_t}{\sigma^4}; \tag{6.65}$$

$$\frac{\partial^2 L}{\partial\beta_1^2} = -\frac{\sum_{t=1}^{T} (x_t(\lambda_2))^2}{\sigma^2}; \tag{6.66}$$

$$\frac{\partial^2 L}{\partial\beta_1\partial\lambda_1} = -\frac{\sum_{t=1}^{T} x_t(\lambda_2)By_t}{\sigma^2}; \tag{6.67}$$

$$\frac{\partial^2 L}{\partial\beta_1\partial\lambda_1} = \frac{\sum_{t=1}^{T} x_t(\lambda_2)By_t}{\sigma^2}; \tag{6.68}$$

$$\frac{\partial^2 L}{\partial\beta_1\partial\lambda_2} = -\frac{\left(\sum_{t=1}^{T} y_t(\lambda_1)Bx_t - \beta_0\sum_{t=1}^{T} Bx_t - 2\beta_1\sum_{t=1}^{T} x_t(\lambda_2)Bx_t\right)}{\sigma^2}; \tag{6.69}$$

$$\frac{\partial^2 L}{\partial \beta_1 \partial \sigma^2} = -\frac{\sum_{t=1}^{T} x_t(\lambda_2) u_t}{\sigma^4};\tag{6.70}$$

$$\frac{\partial^2 L}{\partial \lambda_1^2} = -\frac{\sum_{t=1}^{T}\left((By_t)^2 u_t + Cy_t u_t\right)}{\sigma^4};\tag{6.71}$$

$$\frac{\partial^2 L}{\partial \lambda_1 \partial \lambda_2} = \frac{\beta_1 \sum_{t=1}^{T} Bx_t By_t}{\sigma^2};\tag{6.72}$$

$$\frac{\partial^2 L}{\partial \lambda_1 \partial \sigma^2} = \frac{\sum_{t=1}^{T} By_t u_t}{\sigma^4};\tag{6.73}$$

$$\frac{\partial^2 L}{\partial \lambda_2^2} = -\frac{\beta_1^2 \sum_{t=1}^{T} (Bx_t)^2 + Cx_t u_t}{\sigma^2};\tag{6.74}$$

$$\frac{\partial^2 L}{\partial \lambda_2 \partial \sigma^2} = -\frac{\beta_1 \sum_{t=1}^{T} Bx_t Bu_t}{\sigma^4}\tag{6.75}$$

and $$\frac{\partial^2 L}{\partial (\sigma^2)^2} = \frac{T}{2\sigma^4} - \frac{\sum_{t=1}^{T} u_t}{\sigma^6}\tag{6.76}$$

where $u_t = y_t(\lambda_1) - \beta_0 - \beta_1 x_t(\lambda_2)$; (6.77)

$$By_t = \frac{\partial y_t(\lambda_1)}{\partial(\lambda_1)} = \frac{\left(\lambda_1 y_t^{\lambda_1}\log(y_t) - y_t^{\lambda_1} + 1\right)}{\lambda_1^2};\tag{6.78}$$

$$Bx_t = \frac{\partial x_t(\lambda_2)}{\partial(\lambda_2)} = \frac{\left(\lambda_2 x_t^{\lambda_2}\log(x_t) - x_t^{\lambda_2} + 1\right)}{\lambda_2^2}; \tag{6.79}$$

$$Cy_t = \frac{\partial By_t}{\partial \lambda_1} = \frac{y_t^{\lambda_1}\left(\log(y_t)\right)^2 - 2By_t}{\lambda_1}; \tag{6.80}$$

$$\text{and } Cx_t = \frac{\partial Bx_t}{\partial \lambda_2} = \frac{x_t^{\lambda_2}\left(\log(x_t)\right)^2 - 2Bx_t}{\lambda_2}. \tag{6.81}$$

Now for the calculation of ρ_{12}, we can easily find an approximate value of $\text{cov}\left(\hat{\lambda}_1, \hat{\lambda}_2\right)$ and $\sqrt{\text{var}(\hat{\lambda}_1)\text{var}(\hat{\lambda}_2)}$ from the Hessian matrix in (6.60) where the former is the (5.4) element in the inverse of the estimated Hessian matrix and the latter is the square root of the product of the (5.3) and (5.4) elements of the same matrix.

6.4.2 CIC-1 Method with Two Parameter Restrictions

Similar to the CIC-1 method in Chapter 5, here we discuss the CIC-1 method for our problem involving two parameter restrictions. Under a two parameter case, the method deals with nine competing models and hence, at each step, requires the estimation of nine models. As has already been discussed earlier, the main point of the CIC-1 method is to calculate penalties in such a way that the probability of correct selection is controlled. In doing so, we follow the representative fixed point approach as before, where each of the competing models is represented by a particular point in the parameter space. Under this approach, the estimated probabilities of correctly selecting the true model for each of the parameter points are made equal by the choice of penalty. The question is, what should be the representative points for this particular problem. The answer is simple. $\lambda_1 = 1.0$ and $\lambda_2 = 1.0$ for *M*1, $\lambda_1 = 1.0$ and $\lambda_2 = 0.0$ for *M*2, $\lambda_1 = 0.0$ and $\lambda_2 = 1.0$ for *M*3, $\lambda_1 = 0.0$ and $\lambda_2 = 0.0$ for *M*4, $\lambda_1 = 1.0$ and $\lambda_2 = 0.5$ for *M*5, $\lambda_1 = 0.0$ and $\lambda_2 = 0.5$ for *M*6, $\lambda_1 = 0.5$ and $\lambda_2 = 1.0$ for *M*7, $\lambda_1 = 0.5$ and $\lambda_2 = 0.0$ for *M*8 and $\lambda_1 = 0.5$ and $\lambda_2 = 0.5$ for *M*9.

For models *M*6 to *M*9, while λ_1 or λ_2 or both λ_1 and λ_2 can take any value between zero and one for our BCT model, we consider 0.5 as a representative point as this is the middle value of the range considered. As the nuisance parameters are unknown, we use the data to calculate maximum likelihood estimates of the parameters of that model and then use them to generate samples many times, assuming their estimated values are true. This is repeated for each of the nine models. The procedure is mainly concerned with penalty calculations based on the bootstrap samples, using King et al.'s (1995) equal probability algorithm.

Let $p_1, p_2, p_3, p_4, p_5, p_6, p_7, p_8$ and p_9 be the penalties and $L_1, L_2, L_3, L_4, L_5, L_6, L_7, L_8$ and L_9 be the maximized log-likelihood values for *M*1, *M*2, *M*3, *M*4, *M*5, *M*6, *M*7, *M*8 and *M*9, respectively, for a given data set. As in the case of one restriction discussed in Chapter 5, we set $p_1 = 0$ without loss of generality for the whole experiment. Sample data are generated simultaneously from models *M*1, *M*2, *M*3, *M*4, *M*5, *M*6, *M*7, *M*8 and *M*9, respectively. As a result, *M*1, *M*2, *M*3, *M*4, *M*5, *M*6, *M*7, *M*8 and *M*9, would be regarded as the true models for the 1st, 2nd, 3rd, 4th, 5th, 6th, 7th, 8th and 9th set, respectively. By definition, model M_i will be chosen if:

$$L_i - p_i > L_j - p_j, \text{ for all } i \neq j; j = 1, 2, \ldots, 9. \tag{6.82}$$

For example, *M*1 will be chosen if:

$$\begin{aligned}
&L_1 - p_1 > L_2 - p_2, L_1 - p_1 > L_3 - p_3;\\
&L_1 - p_1 > L_4 - p_4, L_1 - p_1 > L_5 - p_5;\\
&L_1 - p_1 > L_6 - p_6, L_1 - p_1 > L_7 - p_7;\\
&L_1 - p_1 > L_8 - p_8 \text{ and } L_1 - p_1 > L_9 - p_9.
\end{aligned}$$

According to King et al.'s equal probability algorithm, our purpose is to make probabilities of choosing all these true models equal, that is:

$$\begin{aligned}
&\Pr(\text{correctly choosing } M1) = \Pr(\text{correctly choosing } M2)\\
&\quad = \Pr(\text{correctly choosing } M3)\\
&\quad = \Pr(\text{correctly choosing } M4) = \Pr(\text{correctly choosing } M5)\\
&\quad = \Pr(\text{correctly choosing } M6)\\
&\quad = \Pr(\text{correctly choosing } M7) = \Pr(\text{correctly choosing } M8)\\
&\quad = \Pr(\text{correctly choosing } M9)
\end{aligned} \tag{6.83}$$

or at least:

$$\begin{aligned}
&\Pr(\text{correctly choosing } M1) \approx \Pr(\text{correctly choosing } M2)\\
&\quad \approx \Pr(\text{correctly choosing } M3)\\
&\quad \approx \Pr(\text{correctly choosing } M4) \approx \Pr(\text{correctly choosing } M5)\\
&\quad \approx \Pr(\text{correctly choosing } M6)
\end{aligned}$$

$\approx$ Pr(correctly choosing $M7$) $\approx$ Pr(correctly choosing $M8$)
$\approx$ Pr(correctly choosing $M9$). (6.84)

In equation (6.82), the values of all likelihoods are known for a given set of data but the penalties are unknown. As we set $p_1 = 0$, we just calculate penalties $p_2, p_3, \ldots, p_9$ in such a way that either (6.83) or at least (6.84) is satisfied. The basic way of computing these penalties will be similar to the previous case (see section 6.2 of this chapter). The only difference is, instead of working with two penalties and three competing models, we work here with eight penalties and nine competing models. However, the information criterion considering such new penalties is also called the controlled information criterion-1 (CIC-1) as the probability of correct selection for the true model is being controlled in this method.

6.5 Monte Carlo Simulation

In order to evaluate the performance of our proposed CIC-1 method for the two parameter restrictions, we conducted a range of Monte Carlo experiments. Through the simulation experiments we critically examine the probabilities of correctly selecting the true models in each case along with a comparison between the performance of our proposed methods and their usual counterparts.

6.5.1 Experimental Design

We generally follow a similar experimental design in this chapter as we used in Chapters 4 and 6. The main differences between the previous simulation experiments and the present experiment are the penalties which we obtained in our proposed methods (given in the previous section), fewer sample sizes, fewer design matrices and the values of λ_1 and λ_2. In the present Monte Carlo experiment, we use nine competing models namely, $M1$, $M2$, $M3$, $M4$, $M5$, $M6$, $M7$, $M8$ and $M9$, respectively. For the CIC-1 method we follow a slightly different design of experiments. Instead of using 600 bootstrap samples for each replication we use 200 bootstrap samples, because of the intensive computer simulation involved.[1] Unlike the previous experiments, here we consider only two design matrices, that is, $X2$ and $X4$ (already described in the two previous chapters) and two different sample sizes, that is, $T = 20$ and 100, because of the time constraint of the study. The reasons for these particular choices are that the results of the matrix *X*1 are very close to those of matrix *X*2 and similarly the results of the matrices *X*3 and *X*5 are very close to those of matrix *X*4. Thus, instead of using all five design matrices, we simply use two. In order to examine the effect of λ_1 and λ_2 on the probabilities of correct selection for the true models, we consider three different values such as 0.25, 0.50 and 0.75 for each λ used to generate data. Note that we ignore two marginal values, that is, 0.1 and 0.9, as they provide almost similar performance of log-linear (when λ equals zero, which is close to 0.1) and linear (when λ equals one, which is close to 0.9) models.

6.5.2 Results of the Monte Carlo Experiments

Tables 6.13 to 6.21 present the results of the simulation experiments for five different methods namely PAIC, UAIC, PBIC, UBIC and CIC-1 for model selection based on estimated probabilities of selecting models *M*1, *M*2, ..., *M*9 for design matrices *X*2 and *X*4 with two sample sizes $T = 20$ and 100. In Table 6.13, *M*1 is the true model and the remaining eight models (*M*2, *M*3, ..., *M*9) are the competing models. Likewise in Table 6.14, *M*2 is the true model and the other eight models (*M*1, *M*3, ..., *M*9) are the competing models. Similarly *M*3, *M*4, ..., *M*9 have been considered as the true models for Tables 6.15, 6.16, ..., 6.21, respectively. For each sample size, we use all five methods for comparison purposes.

Table 6.13 reveals that for the *X*2 matrix with $T = 20$, the PCS of the true models for all methods are higher than all other competing models except in a few cases (PAIC for *M*2, PAIC, UAIC, PBIC and UBIC for *M*3 and UAIC and UBIC for *M*4). For the CIC-1 method this probability is 0.360 which is substsantially higher than all other methods. In the case of sample size $T = 100$, the PCS get much larger than all other competing models for all methods, which is highly desirable. In the case of design matrix *X*4, the probabilities of correct selection are much higher than probabilities of selecting in all other competing models. This is true for all five methods and for both sample sizes. In terms of PCS for the true models, design matrix *X*4 shows much better performance than *X*2 in all competing methods. Interestingly, among the five methods considered in this study, we find that with respect to average probabilities of correct selection (APCS), our proposed method CIC-1 dominates the other methods with average improvements ranging from 9.2 per cent to 49.1 per cent.

Table 6.14 presents simulation results when *M*2 is now the true model. As before, here the PCS for design matrix *X*2 with $T = 20$ are in some cases

Table 6.13 Comparison between PAIC, UAIC, PBIC, UBIC and CIC-1 based on estimated probabilities of choosing competing models *M*1, *M*2, *M*3, *M*4, *M*5, *M*6, *M*7, *M*8 and *M*9 for design matrices *X*2 and *X*4 when *M*1 is true

T	*Methods*	*M*1	*M*2	*M*3	*M*4	*M*5	*M*6	*M*7	*M*8	*M*9
					Design matrix *X*2					
20	PAIC	.175	.181	.257	.138	.004	.144	.084	.006	.011
	UAIC	.246	.010	.403	.281	.000	.060	.000	.000	.000
	PBIC	.186	.179	.264	.150	.000	.063	.103	.017	.038
	UBIC	.268	.010	.418	.297	.000	.007	.000	.000	.000
	CIC-1	.360	.010	.420	.210	.000	.000	.000	.000	.000
100	PAIC	.567	.051	.118	.021	.062	.145	.031	.001	.004
	UAIC	.656	.000	.169	.035	.024	.113	.000	.002	.001
	PBIC	.673	.061	.143	.037	.014	.059	.011	.002	.000
	UBIC	.738	.000	.181	.060	.000	.020	.000	.001	.000
	CIC-1	.820	.000	.140	.020	.010	.010	.000	.000	.000
					Design matrix *X*4					
20	PAIC	.627	.002	.000	.000	.074	.003	.090	.000	.204
	UAIC	.748	.000	.000	.000	.046	.003	.046	.000	.157
	PBIC	.742	.002	.000	.000	.054	.003	.062	.000	.137
	UBIC	.872	.000	.000	.000	.018	.003	.029	.000	.078
	CIC-1	.950	.000	.000	.000	.000	.000	.010	.000	.040
100	PAIC	.721	.000	.000	.000	.068	.000	.079	.000	.132
	UAIC	.849	.000	.000	.000	.037	.000	.037	.000	.077
	PBIC	.911	.000	.000	.000	.030	.000	.031	.000	.028
	UBIC	.978	.000	.000	.000	.007	.000	.008	.000	.007
	CIC-1	.990	.000	.000	.000	.000	.000	.000	.000	.010

Average probabilities of correct selection (APCS) of the true model *M*1 for five methods

PAIC = 0.523 UAIC = 0.625 PBIC = 0.628 UBIC = 0.714 CIC-1 = 0.780

lower than selection probabilities for other competing models for all methods except CIC-1. For the CIC-1 method, the PCS for model *M2* is 0.370, which is much higher than for any competing model and method considered. For sample size $T = 100$, these selection probabilities are much higher than those for all other competing models, which indicate that as T gets larger, the PCS become higher. Among the false models, *M4* seems more often chosen than any other model. The pattern of the last five models for all methods is very similar with respect to the probability of incorrectly selecting the false model. In the case of design matrix *X4*, the PCS of the true model are always much higher than those of the other competing models. This is true for both sample sizes and for all competing methods. As the sample size increases, the PCS also increase, which is an encouraging phenomenon. In looking to the APCS for all competing methods, we find a clear pattern with the CIC-1 method uniformly dominating the other methods. In terms of percentages, the improvement in CIC-1 varies from 13.2 per cent to 51.9 per cent.

Table 6.15 exhibits the simulation results when *M3* is the true model. Unlike Tables 6.13 and 6.14, here the PCS are much higher (closer to one) than the probabilities of choosing competing models. This is uniformly true for both design matrices (*X2* and *X4*), for both sample sizes ($T = 20$ and 100) and for all methods. Among the proposed and usual AIC and BIC methods, UBIC can be ranked top with respect to APCS. The CIC-1 method on the other hand defeats the UBIC by 5.7 per cent.

Table 6.16 shows the results of the simulation experiment when *M4* is the true model. Here we find that the PCS of the true model are much higher than all other models except one single case (PAIC in *M3*). Among the proposed and usual AIC and BIC methods, the usual methods show better performance than the proposed methods in terms of PCS because here the smaller models are true. In the case of overall performance of the competing methods with respect to APCS, they can be ranked as: CIC-1 > UBIC > UAIC > PBIC > PAIC. On average, CIC-1 performs better than UBIC by 5 per cent and PAIC by 61.8 per cent.

Table 6.17(a) shows the simulation results when model *M5* is the true model and when the data is generated for $\lambda_2 = 0.25$. In contrast to the above four cases, here for design matrix *X2*, the PCS for all methods are much lower than those of many other competing models, which is not expected. Nevertheless, among the competing methods, CIC-1 is still marginally better than any other method with respect to PCS. For design matrix *X4*, on the other hand, the overall results improve significantly in the case of all competing methods. For sample size $T = 20$, these probabilities are higher than for any other competing

Table 6.14 **Comparison between PAIC, UAIC, PBIC, UBIC and CIC-1 based on estimated probabilities of choosing competing models *M1*, *M2*, *M3*, *M4*, *M5*, *M6*, *M7*, *M8* and *M9* for design matrices *X2* and *X4* when *M2* is true**

T	*Methods*	*M1*	***M2***	*M3*	*M4*	*M5*	*M6*	*M7*	*M8*	*M9*
					Design matrix *X2*					
20	PAIC	.189	.181	.166	.289	.033	.012	.082	.003	.045
	UAIC	.173	.225	.173	.428	.000	.001	.000	.000	.000
	PBIC	.175	.155	.152	.259	.031	.012	.093	.003	.120
	UBIC	.174	.225	.173	.428	.000	.000	.000	.000	.000
	CIC-1	.270	.370	.160	.200	.000	.000	.000	.000	.000
100	PAIC	.209	.425	.201	.137	.006	.004	.011	.005	.002
	UAIC	.201	.551	.062	.186	.000	.000	.000	.000	.000
	PBIC	.202	.399	.178	.131	.005	.018	.025	.000	.042
	UBIC	.201	.551	.062	.186	.000	.000	.000	.000	.000
	CIC-1	.210	.620	.070	.100	.000	.000	.000	.000	.000
					Design matrix *X4*					
20	PAIC	.015	.340	.169	.281	.065	.035	.088	.006	.001
	UAIC	.032	.508	.012	.403	.023	.019	.000	.003	.000
	PBIC	.022	.349	.174	.283	.043	.020	.101	.003	.005
	UBIC	.036	.520	.012	.420	.006	.006	.000	.000	.000
	CIC-1	.200	.560	.040	.200	.000	.000	.000	.000	.000
100	PAIC	.000	.633	.067	.111	.098	.009	.003	.079	.000
	UAIC	.000	.794	.000	.148	.048	.002	.000	.008	.000
	PBIC	.000	.737	.067	.150	.036	.002	.004	.004	.000
	UBIC	.000	.825	.000	.164	.010	.001	.000	.000	.000
	CIC-1	.000	.850	.000	.140	.010	.000	.000	.000	.000

Average probabilities of correct selection (APCS) of the true model *M2* for five methods

PAIC = 0.395 UAIC = 0.520 PBIC = 0.410 UBIC = 0.530 CIC-1 = 0.600

Table 6.15 **Comparison between PAIC, UAIC, PBIC, UBIC and CIC-1 based on estimated probabilities of choosing competing models *M*1, *M*2, *M*3, *M*4, *M*5, *M*6, *M*7, *M*8 and *M*9 for design matrices *X*2 and *X*4 when *M*3 is true**

					Design matrix *X*2					
T	*Methods*	*M1*	*M2*	*M3*	*M4*	*M5*	*M6*	*M7*	*M8*	*M9*
20	PAIC	.000	.000	.832	.072	.009	.069	.017	.001	.000
	UAIC	.000	.000	.873	.107	.000	.010	.009	.001	.000
	PBIC	.000	.000	.857	.093	.009	.027	.013	.001	.000
	UBIC	.000	.000	.883	.112	.000	.001	.003	.001	.000
	CIC-1	.000	.000	.980	.020	.000	.000	.000	.000	.000
100	PAIC	.000	.000	.791	.000	.000	.124	.085	.000	.000
	UAIC	.000	.000	.895	.000	.000	.069	.036	.000	.000
	PBIC	.000	.000	.913	.000	.000	.058	.029	.000	.000
	UBIC	.000	.000	.978	.001	.000	.015	.006	.000	.000
	CIC-1	.000	.000	1.00	.000	.000	.000	.000	.000	.000
					Design matrix *X*4					
20	PAIC	.000	.000	.792	.000	.000	.109	.099	.000	.000
	UAIC	.000	.000	.882	.000	.000	.066	.052	.000	.000
	PBIC	.000	.000	.844	.000	.000	.085	.071	.000	.000
	UBIC	.000	.000	.925	.000	.000	.037	.038	.000	.000
	CIC-1	.000	.000	1.00	.000	.000	.000	.00	.000	.000
100	PAIC	.000	.000	.832	.000	.000	.083	.084	.000	.001
	UAIC	.000	.000	.910	.000	.000	.043	.046	.000	.001
	PBIC	.000	.000	.923	.000	.000	.037	.040	.000	.000
	UBIC	.000	.000	.978	.000	.000	.012	.010	.000	.000
	CIC-1	.000	.000	1.00	.000	.000	.000	.000	.000	.000

Average probabilities of correct selection (APCS) of the true model *M*3 for five methods

PAIC = 0.812	UAIC = 0.890	PBIC = 0.884	UBIC = 0.941	CIC-1 = 0.995

Table 6.16 Comparison between PAIC, UAIC, PBIC, UBIC and CIC-1 based on estimated probabilities of choosing competing models *M*1, *M*2, *M*3, *M*4, *M*5, *M*6, *M*7, *M*8 and *M*9 for design matrices *X*2 and *X*4 when *M*4 is true

T	*Methods*	*M1*	*M2*	*M3*	*M4*	*M5*	*M6*	*M7*	*M8*	*M9*
					Design matrix *X*2					
20	PAIC	.000	.001	.359	.367	.214	.001	.034	.024	.000
	UAIC	.002	.000	.378	.593	.000	.000	.015	.012	.000
	PBIC	.001	.001	.369	.376	.214	.001	.023	.015	.000
	UBIC	.002	.000	.386	.600	.000	.000	.006	.006	.000
	CIC-1	.010	.010	.310	.650	.000	.000	.010	.010	.000
100	PAIC	.000	.000	.248	.431	.228	.000	.031	.062	.000
	UAIC	.000	.000	.261	.679	.000	.000	.016	.044	.000
	PBIC	.000	.000	.262	.469	.228	.000	.015	.026	.000
	UBIC	.000	.000	.271	.716	.000	.000	.004	.009	.000
	CIC-1	.000	.000	.210	.790	.000	.000	.000	.000	.000
					Design matrix *X*4					
20	PAIC	.020	.000	.038	.565	.168	.132	.023	.046	.014
	UAIC	.000	.000	.055	.843	.000	.056	.017	.025	.004
	PBIC	.004	.000	.043	.622	.183	.094	.024	.029	.001
	UBIC	.000	.000	.063	.888	.000	.022	.013	.014	.000
	CIC-1	.000	.000	.000	.900	.000	.070	.000	.020	.010
100	PAIC	.001	.000	.000	.701	.060	.132	.000	.091	.015
	UAIC	.000	.000	.000	.876	.000	.066	.000	.050	.008
	PBIC	.000	.000	.000	.846	.061	.052	.000	.039	.002
	UBIC	.000	.000	.000	.977	.000	.014	.000	.009	.000
	CIC-1	.000	.000	.000	1.00	.000	.000	.000	.000	.000

Average probabilities of correct selection (APCS) of the true model *M*4 for five methods

PAIC = 0.516 UAIC = 0.748 PBIC = 0.578 UBIC = 0.795 CIC-1 = 0.835

model except for model *M4*. For the true model *M5*, the performance of PAIC and PBIC seems much better than that of their usual counterparts. As the sample size increases to 100, these probabilities significantly improve (almost double) for all methods. Tables 6.17(b) and 6.17(c), where data is generated for $\lambda_2 = 0.5$ and $\lambda_2 = 0.75$, respectively, exhibit almost a similar pattern of results as Table 6.17(a) except for the case of $T = 20$ for matrix *X4*. In this case, the PCS of the true model are much higher than for any other competing models. If we look at the APCS for all competing methods considered, we find that CIC-1 dominates the other methods, with improvements ranging from 39 per cent to 59.2 per cent for Table 6.17(a), 31.7 per cent to 48.3 per cent for Table 6.17(b) and 25.9 per cent to 43.2 per cent for Table 6.17(c). From these statistical figures it is clear that as the value of λ_2 increases, the relative dominance of CIC-1 decreases.

Table 6.18(a) presents the results when *M6* is the true model and the data is generated for $\lambda_2 = 0.25$. As in the case of three different versions for model *M6*, here the design matrix *X2* does not result in good probabilities for the true model. On the other hand, the *X4* matrix works extremely well by providing very high probabilities of correct selection for the true model in comparison to other models considered. This is true for all methods and for both sample sizes. Tables 6.18(b) and 6.18(c) exhibit almost similar patterns of results for design matrix *X2*. For matrix *X4*, on the other hand, we find some somewhat surprising results. In such cases, small samples ($T = 20$) provide better performance for the true model than large samples ($T = 100$). This has occurred for all methods considered in our study. In terms of PCS, CIC-1 works better for *X2* than *X4* in all three cases. In order to assess the competing methods, we compared the APCS for all methods in three cases. It is clearly evident that CIC-1 performs better than other methods, with improvements ranging from 2.7 per cent to 6 per cent, 7.4 per cent to 9.9 per cent and 7.2 per cent to 10.4 per cent for Tables 6.18(a), 6.18(b) and 6.18(c), respectively. It emerges from these statistical measures that the performance of CIC-1 is relatively better when $\lambda_2 = 0.5$.

Table 6.19(a) presents similar comparisons when *M7* is now the true model and the data is generated for $\lambda_1 = 0.26$. Here for matrix *X2* with $T = 20$, the PCS are much lower than for many of the other competing models, which is not desirable. As the sample size T increases to 100, these probabilities get much larger, except for UBIC. For *X4* with $T = 20$, the PCS are much higher than for all other models, except model *M9* for PAIC and UAIC. As the sample size increases to 100, these probabilities slightly decrease, which is surprising. However, among the five contesting methods, our proposed CIC-1 method

Table 6.17(a) Comparison between PAIC, UAIC, PBIC, UBIC and CIC-1 based on estimated probabilities of choosing competing models *M1*, *M2*, *M3*, *M4*, *M5*, *M6*, *M7*, *M8* and *M9* for design matrices *X2* and *X4* when $\lambda_2 = 0.25$ and *M5* is true

T	*Methods*	*M1*	*M2*	*M3*	*M4*	***M5***	*M6*	*M7*	*M8*	*M9*
					Design matrix *X2*					
20	PAIC	.166	.160	.180	.285	.031	.012	.102	.003	.061
	UAIC	.160	.195	.195	.449	.000	.001	.000	.000	.000
	PBIC	.160	.143	.169	.261	.024	.007	.115	.008	.113
	UBIC	.161	.195	.195	.449	.000	.000	.000	.000	.000
	CIC-1	.200	.230	.260	.190	.120	.000	.000	.000	.000
100	PAIC	.257	.348	.171	.160	.039	.007	.010	.003	.005
	UAIC	.268	.447	.077	.208	.000	.000	.000	.000	.000
	PBIC	.269	.349	.160	.157	.009	.003	.028	.000	.025
	UBIC	.268	.447	.077	.208	.000	.000	.000	.000	.000
	CIC-1	.350	.230	.120	.100	.200	.000	.000	.000	.000
					Design matrix *X4*					
20	PAIC	.001	.050	.076	.218	.286	.143	.151	.073	.002
	UAIC	.005	.121	.000	.433	.233	.165	.000	.041	.002
	PBIC	.004	.074	.074	.260	.259	.127	.154	.047	.001
	UBIC	.016	.142	.000	.526	.186	.119	.000	.010	.001
	CIC-1	.140	.140	.000	.250	.330	.070	.070	.000	.000
100	PAIC	.000	.000	.000	.080	.574	.058	.068	.017	.203
	UAIC	.000	.000	.000	.149	.590	.064	.000	.017	.180
	PBIC	.000	.000	.000	.147	.651	.050	.068	.021	.063
	UBIC	.000	.000	.000	.257	.640	.042	.000	.020	.041
	CIC-1	.000	.000	.000	.110	.660	.010	.010	.020	.190

Average probabilities of correct selection (APCS) of the true model *M5* for five methods

PAIC = 0.233 UAIC = 0.206 PBIC = 0.236 UBIC = 0.207 CIC-1 = 0.328

Table 6.17(b) Comparison between PAIC, UAIC, PBIC, UBIC and CIC-1 based on estimated probabilities of choosing competing models *M*1, *M*2, *M*3, *M*4, *M*5, *M*6, *M*7, *M*8 and *M*9 for design matrices *X*2 and *X*4 when $\lambda_2 = 0.5$ and *M*5 is true

T	*Methods*	*M1*	*M2*	*M3*	*M4*	***M5***	*M6*	*M7*	*M8*	*M9*
					Design matrix *X*2					
20	PAIC	.176	.137	.202	.291	.027	.026	.104	.006	.031
	UAIC	.181	.132	.231	.455	.000	.001	.000	.000	.000
	PBIC	.170	.122	.189	.254	.020	.014	.128	.007	.096
	UBIC	.181	.132	.231	.455	.000	.001	.000	.000	.000
	CIC-1	.210	.160	.300	.230	.100	.000	.000	.000	.000
100	PAIC	.332	.202	.130	.175	.105	.040	.010	.005	.001
	UAIC	.386	.264	.097	.239	.008	.006	.000	.000	.000
	PBIC	.389	.234	.137	.200	.006	.014	.020	.000	.000
	UBIC	.391	.267	.101	.241	.000	.000	.000	.000	.000
	CIC-1	.400	.100	.110	.150	.240	.000	.000	.000	.000
					Design matrix *X*4					
20	PAIC	.000	.004	.009	.061	.416	.198	.089	.012	.211
	UAIC	.000	.000	.000	.108	.416	.263	.000	.018	.195
	PBIC	.000	.004	.009	.082	.441	.207	.089	.011	.157
	UBIC	.000	.000	.000	.157	.431	.264	.000	.014	.134
	CIC-1	.020	.000	.000	.120	.460	.250	.000	.020	.130
100	PAIC	.000	.000	.000	.000	.522	.000	.000	.000	.478
	UAIC	.000	.000	.000	.000	.526	.000	.000	.000	.474
	PBIC	.000	.000	.000	.000	.587	.000	.000	.000	.413
	UBIC	.000	.000	.000	.000	.592	.000	.000	.000	
	CIC-1	.000	.000	.000	.000	.610	.000	.000	.000	.390

Average probabilities of correct selection (APCS) of the true model *M*5 for five methods

PAIC = 0.268 UAIC = 0.238 PBIC = 0.264 UBIC = 0.256 CIC-1 = 0.353

Table 6.17(c) Comparison between PAIC, UAIC, PBIC, UBIC and CIC-1 based on estimated probabilities of choosing competing models *M1*, *M2*, *M3*, *M4*, *M5*, *M6*, *M7*, *M8* and *M9* for design matrices *X2* and *X4* when $\lambda_2 = 0.75$ and *M5* is true

T	*Methods*	*M1*	*M2*	*M3*	*M4*	**M5**	*M6*	*M7*	*M8*	*M9*
					Design matrix *X2*					
20	PAIC	.174	.145	.214	.268	.008	.062	.102	.008	.019
	UAIC	.194	.068	.283	.438	.000	.017	.000	.000	.000
	PBIC	.182	.177	.207	.248	.009	.026	.124	.017	.010
	UBIC	.202	.068	.287	.442	.000	.001	.000	.000	.000
	CIC-1	.220	.050	.360	.300	.070	.000	.000	.000	.000
100	PAIC	.441	.041	.093	.105	.174	.113	.021	.012	.000
	UAIC	.552	.047	.103	.186	.050	.055	.000	.007	.000
	PBIC	.571	.078	.106	.161	.032	.024	.021	.005	.002
	UBIC	.601	.067	.115	.216	.000	.001	.000	.000	.000
	CIC-1	.520	.010	.120	.080	.270	.000	.000	.000	.000
					Design matrix *X4*					
20	PAIC	.000	.001	.000	.000	.439	.038	.017	.000	.505
	UAIC	.000	.000	.000	.001	.440	.057	.000	.000	.502
	PBIC	.000	.001	.000	.002	.458	.045	.017	.000	.477
	UBIC	.000	.000	.000	.005	.460	.063	.000	.000	.472
	CIC-1	.000	.000	.000	.000	.470	.140	.000	.000	.390
100	PAIC	.000	.000	.000	.000	.473	.000	.000	.000	.527
	UAIC	.000	.000	.000	.000	.474	.000	.000	.000	.526
	PBIC	.000	.000	.000	.000	.502	.000	.000	.000	.498
	UBIC	.000	.000	.000	.000	.502	.000	.000	.000	.498
	CIC-1	.000	.000	.000	.000	.570	.000	.000	.000	.430

Average probabilities of correct selection (APCS) of the true model *M5* for five methods

PAIC = 0.274 UAIC = 0.241 PBIC = 0.250 UBIC = 0.241 CIC-1 = 0.345

Table 6.18(a) Comparison between PAIC, UAIC, PBIC, UBIC and CIC-1 based on estimated probabilities of correctly competing models *M*1, *M*2, *M*3, *M*4, *M*5, *M*6, *M*7, *M*8 and *M*9 for design matrices *X*2 and *X*4 when $\lambda_2 = 0.25$ and *M*6 is true

T	*Methods*	*M1*	*M2*	*M3*	*M4*	*M5*	***M6***	*M7*	*M8*	*M9*
					Design matrix *X*2					
20	PAIC	.000	.001	.402	.362	.188	.001	.031	.015	.000
	UAIC	.001	.000	.420	.558	.000	.000	.012	.009	.000
	PBIC	.000	.000	.413	.369	.189	.000	.021	.008	.000
	UBIC	.001	.000	.426	.562	.000	.000	.006	.005	.000
	CIC-1	.010	.010	.310	.550	.000	.100	.010	.010	.000
100	PAIC	.000	.000	.329	.386	.156	.027	.045	.057	.000
	UAIC	.000	.000	.358	.591	.000	.000	.021	.030	.000
	PBIC	.000	.000	.357	.449	.156	.000	.018	.020	.000
	UBIC	.000	.000	.369	.619	.000	.000	.007	.005	.000
	CIC-1	.000	.000	.300	.560	.000	.120	.010	.010	.000
					Design matrix *X*4					
20	PAIC	.000	.000	.005	.215	.014	.679	.026	.000	.061
	UAIC	.000	.000	.018	.314	.000	.594	.027	.000	.047
	PBIC	.000	.000	.008	.261	.014	.652	.035	.000	.030
	UBIC	.000	.000	.030	.399	.000	.516	.033	.000	.022
	CIC-1	.000	.000	.010	.280	.000	.650	.020	.000	.040
100	PAIC	.000	.000	.000	.002	.000	.854	.000	.000	.144
	UAIC	.000	.000	.000	.002	.000	.861	.000	.000	.137
	PBIC	.000	.000	.000	.002	.000	.930	.000	.000	.068
	UBIC	.000	.000	.000	.002	.000	.936	.000	.000	.062
	CIC-1	.000	.000	.000	.000	.000	.940	.000	.000	.060

Average probabilities of correct selection (APCS) of the true model *M*6 for five methods

PAIC = 0.390	UAIC = 0.364	PBIC = 0.396	UBIC = 0.363	CIC-1 = 0.423

Table 6.18(b) Comparison between PAIC, UAIC, PBIC, UBIC and CIC-1 based on estimated probabilities of correctly competing models *M*1, *M*2, *M*3, *M*4, *M*5, *M*6, *M*7, *M*8 and *M*9 for design matrices *X*2 and *X*4 when $\lambda_2 = 0.5$ and *M*6 is true

T	*Methods*	*M1*	*M2*	*M3*	*M4*	*M5*	***M6***	*M7*	*M8*	*M9*
					Design matrix *X*2					
20	PAIC	.000	.001	.492	.320	.148	.003	.023	.013	.000
	UAIC	.000	.000	.502	.485	.000	.000	.010	.003	.000
	PBIC	.000	.001	.498	.334	.148	.000	.014	.005	.000
	UBIC	.000	.000	.508	.487	.000	.000	.004	.001	.000
	CIC-1	.010	.010	.330	.500	.000	.120	.020	.010	.000
100	PAIC	.000	.000	.453	.241	.118	.088	.077	.023	.000
	UAIC	.000	.000	.531	.401	.000	.010	.045	.013	.000
	PBIC	.000	.000	.536	.296	.118	.004	.038	.008	.000
	UBIC	.000	.000	.563	.427	.000	.000	.009	.001	.000
	CIC-1	.000	.000	.460	.320	.000	.160	.050	.010	.000
					Design matrix *X*4					
20	PAIC	.000	.000	.000	.000	.000	.800	.036	.000	.164
	UAIC	.000	.000	.000	.000	.000	.803	.037	.000	.160
	PBIC	.000	.000	.000	.000	.000	.830	.050	.000	.120
	UBIC	.000	.000	.000	.000	.000	.837	.053	.000	.110
	CIC-1	.000	.000	.000	.000	.000	.840	.010	.000	.150
100	PAIC	.000	.000	.000	.000	.000	.709	.000	.000	.291
	UAIC	.000	.000	.000	.000	.000	.710	.000	.000	.290
	PBIC	.000	.000	.000	.000	.000	.784	.000	.000	.216
	UBIC	.000	.000	.000	.000	.000	.787	.000	.000	.213
	CIC-1	.000	.000	.000	.000	.000	.800	.000	.000	.200

Average probabilities of correct selection (APCS) of the true model *M6* for five methods

PAIC = 0.400 UAIC = 0.381 PBIC = 0.405 UBIC = 0.406 CIC-1 = 0.480

Table 6.18(c) Comparison between PAIC, UAIC, PBIC, UBIC and CIC-1 based on estimated probabilities of correctly competing models *M1*, *M2*, *M3*, *M4*, *M5*, *M6*, *M7*, *M8* and *M9* for design matrices *X2* and *X4* when $\lambda_2 = 0.75$ and *M6* is true

T	*Methods*	*M1*	*M2*	*M3*	*M4*	*M5*	***M6***	*M7*	*M8*	*M9*
					Design matrix *X2*					
20	PAIC	.000	.000	.644	.251	.067	.017	.018	.003	.000
	UAIC	.000	.000	.661	.329	.000	.001	.007	.002	.000
	PBIC	.000	.000	.659	.260	.067	.003	.009	.002	.000
	UBIC	.000	.000	.664	.333	.000	.000	.003	.000	.000
	CIC-1	.000	.010	.400	.380	.000	.170	.040	.000	.000
100	PAIC	.000	.000	.588	.056	.041	.207	.108	.000	.000
	UAIC	.000	.000	.736	.111	.000	.086	.067	.000	.000
	PBIC	.000	.000	.763	.076	.041	.062	.058	.000	.000
	UBIC	.000	.000	.847	.137	.000	.000	.016	.000	.000
	CIC-1	.000	.000	.590	.110	.000	.210	.090	.000	.000
					Design matrix *X4*					
20	PAIC	.000	.000	.000	.000	.000	.695	.100	.000	.205
	UAIC	.000	.000	.000	.000	.000	.697	.101	.000	.202
	PBIC	.000	.000	.000	.000	.000	.738	.115	.000	.147
	UBIC	.000	.000	.000	.000	.000	.740	.118	.000	.142
	CIC-1	.000	.000	.000	.000	.000	.750	.110	.000	.140
100	PAIC	.000	.000	.000	.000	.000	.654	.000	.000	.346
	UAIC	.000	.000	.000	.000	.000	.661	.000	.000	.339
	PBIC	.000	.000	.000	.000	.000	.725	.000	.000	.275
	UBIC	.000	.000	.000	.000	.000	.730	.000	.000	.270
	CIC-1	.000	.000	.000	.000	.000	.730	.000	.000	.270

Average probabilities of correct selection (APCS) of the true model *M6* for five methods

PAIC = 0.393 UAIC = 0.361 PBIC = 0.382 UBIC = 0.368 CIC-1 = 0.465

performs marginally better than other methods in all cases. For example, CIC-1 dominates PAIC (where the PAIC is the best among the usual and proposed AIC and BIC in this case) only by 3.3 per cent. Tables 6.19(b) and 6.19(c) reveal an almost similar pattern of results as those in Table 6.19(a), except for matrix *X2* with $T = 20$. In this particular case, we find somewhat worse results as the value of λ_1 increases. In Table 6.19(b), for *X2* with $T = 100$, CIC-1 is slightly worse than PAIC but better than all other methods. The average performance of CIC-1 is slightly better (1.4 per cent larger with respect to APCS) than PAIC, the best of the four other methods. Table 6.19(c) reveals that with respect to APCS, CIC-1 dominates the other four methods, with improvements ranging from 3.4 per cent to 8 per cent.

Table 6.20(a) provides similar comparisons when *M8* is the true model and the data is generated for $\lambda_1 = 0.25$. It is clear from the table that the PCS are much lower than the probability of choosing many of the other competing models for almost all cases, which is undesirable. The table also reveals that as the sample size gets larger, these probabilities become higher which is expected. Among the competing methods, CIC-1 is still better than other methods in terms of PCS. Tables 6.20(b) and 6.20(c) show a pattern of results almost similar to those in Table 6.20(a). In all of these cases PAIC is ranked second after CIC-1 with respect to APCS. Interestingly, the CIC-1 beats PAIC by 6.8 per cent, 4.1 per cent and 9.4 per cent for Tables 6.20(a), 6.20(b) and 6.20(c), respectively.

Finally, in the case of *M9*, we have two restricted parameters, λ_1 and λ_2, both of which possess three different values, namely 0.25, 0.5 and 0.75, in our experiment. With these three values we can have nine possible combinations for which we use nine tables to present the simulation results. As the results obtained in the nine tables are similar, we discuss them together.

There is clear evidence from Tables 6.21(a) to 6.21(i) that design matrix *X2* does not result in good probabilities for *M9*, as the PCS for this model are very low (closer to zero in some cases and exactly zero in other cases). For matrix *X4* with sample size $T = 20$, the PCS are relatively higher than the probabilities of choosing other models for the combinations $\lambda_1 = 0.25$ and $\lambda_2 = 0.5$; $\lambda_1 = 0.25$ and $\lambda_2 = 0.75$; $\lambda_1 = 0.5$ and $\lambda_2 = 0.75$ and $\lambda_1 = 0.75$ and $\lambda_2 = 0.75$, except in a few cases. This clearly indicates as the value of λ_2 increases, we obtain larger PCS, which is not equally true for increases in λ_1. This means that the PCS are more influenced by the value of λ_2 than λ_1. However, in the case of other combinations, some methods perform well as measured by PCS and some methods do not. For sample size 100 for the same matrix, the PCS are much higher than the probabilities of choosing any other models in almost all

Table 6.19(a) Comparison between PAIC, UAIC, PBIC, UBIC and CIC-1 based on estimated probabilities of choosing competing models *M1*, *M2*, *M3*, *M4*, *M5*, *M6*, *M7*, *M8* and *M9* for design matrices *X2* and *X4* when $\lambda_1 = 0.25$ and *M7* is true

T	*Methods*	*M1*	*M2*	*M3*	*M4*	*M5*	*M6*	*M7*	*M8*	*M9*
					Design matrix *X2*					
20	PAIC	.020	.143	.475	.111	.024	.182	.043	.002	.000
	UAIC	.026	.005	.658	.238	.000	.070	.002	.001	.000
	PBIC	.025	.131	.528	.146	.036	.107	.024	.001	.002
	UBIC	.027	.005	.691	.260	.000	.016	.000	.001	.000
	CIC-1	.250	.010	.470	.090	.000	.100	.080	.000	.000
100	PAIC	.000	.014	.280	.006	.000	.269	.411	.000	.020
	UAIC	.000	.000	.417	.017	.000	.231	.318	.000	.017
	PBIC	.000	.014	.451	.023	.000	.208	.304	.000	.000
	UBIC	.008	.000	.648	.052	.000	.114	.178	.000	.000
	CIC-1	.060	.000	.300	.010	.000	.180	.420	.000	.030
					Design matrix *X4*					
20	PAIC	.000	.000	.000	.000	.000	.002	.485	.000	.513
	UAIC	.000	.000	.000	.000	.000	.002	.485	.000	.513
	PBIC	.000	.000	.000	.000	.000	.002	.503	.000	.495
	UBIC	.000	.000	.000	.000	.000	.002	.503	.000	.495
	CIC-1	.000	.000	.000	.000	.000	.000	.540	.000	.460
100	PAIC	.000	.000	.000	.000	.000	.000	.441	.000	.559
	UAIC	.000	.000	.000	.000	.000	.000	.441	.000	.559
	PBIC	.000	.000	.000	.000	.000	.000	.453	.000	.547
	UBIC	.000	.000	.000	.000	.000	.000	.453	.000	.547
	CIC-1	.000	.000	.000	.000	.000	.000	.470	.000	.530

Average probabilities of correct selection (APCS) of the true model *M7* for five methods

PAIC = 0.345 UAIC = 0.312 PBIC = 0.321 UBIC = 0.284 CIC-1 = 0.378

Table 6.19(b) Comparison between PAIC, UAIC, PBIC, UBIC and CIC-1 based on estimated probabilities of choosing competing models *M1*, *M2*, *M3*, *M4*, *M5*, *M6*, *M7*, *M8* and *M9* for design matrices *X2* and *X4* when $\lambda_1 = 0.5$ and *M7* is true

T	*Methods*	*M1*	*M2*	*M3*	*M4*	*M5*	*M6*	*M7*	*M8*	*M9*
					Design matrix *X2*					
20	PAIC	.082	.256	.337	.102	.007	.157	.057	.001	.001
	UAIC	.108	.007	.551	.254	.000	.079	.001	.000	.000
	PBIC	.091	.237	.361	.131	.014	.098	.057	.003	.008
	UBIC	.116	.007	.585	.273	.000	.019	.000	.000	.000
	CIC-1	.380	.040	.470	.000	.000	.000	.110	.000	.000
100	PAIC	.144	.056	.200	.014	.000	.205	.361	.000	.020
	UAIC	.249	.000	.329	.023	.000	.210	.185	.000	.004
	PBIC	.275	.054	.332	.021	.000	.160	.158	.000	.000
	UBIC	.385	.000	.476	.045	.000	.089	.005	.000	.000
	CIC-1	.400	.000	.240	.030	.000	.050	.280	.000	.000
					Design matrix *X4*					
20	PAIC	.000	.000	.000	.000	.000	.003	.487	.000	.510
	UAIC	.000	.000	.000	.000	.000	.003	.487	.000	.510
	PBIC	.000	.000	.000	.000	.000	.003	.507	.000	.490
	UBIC	.000	.000	.000	.000	.000	.003	.507	.000	.490
	CIC-1	.000	.000	.000	.000	.000	.000	.550	.000	.450
100	PAIC	.000	.000	.000	.000	.000	.000	.438	.000	.562
	UAIC	.000	.000	.000	.000	.000	.000	.438	.000	.562
	PBIC	.000	.000	.000	.000	.000	.000	.447	.000	.553
	UBIC	.000	.000	.000	.000	.000	.000	.447	.000	.553
	CIC-1	.000	.000	.000	.000	.000	.000	.460	.000	.540

Average probabilities of correct selection (APCS) of the true model *M7* for five methods

PAIC = 0.336 UAIC = 0.278 PBIC = 0.292 UBIC = 0.240 CIC-1 = 0.350

Table 6.19(c) Comparison between PAIC, UAIC, PBIC, UBIC and CIC-1 based on estimated probabilities of choosing competing models *M1*, *M2*, *M3*, *M4*, *M5*, *M6*, *M7*, *M8* and *M9* for design matrices *X2* and *X4* when $\lambda_1 = 0.75$ and *M7* is true

T	*Methods*	*M1*	*M2*	*M3*	*M4*	*M5*	*M6*	*M7*	*M8*	*M9*
					Design matrix *X2*					
20	PAIC	.134	.237	.294	.109	.002	.135	.076	.004	.009
	UAIC	.193	.007	.484	.254	.000	.062	.000	.000	.000
	PBIC	.158	.214	.314	.134	.002	.068	.074	.008	.028
	UBIC	.214	.007	.500	.267	.000	.012	.000	.000	.000
	CIC-1	.410	.070	.370	.020	.000	.000	.130	.000	.000
100	PAIC	.462	.063	.171	.014	.008	.170	.111	.001	.000
	UAIC	.567	.000	.255	.021	.000	.153	.004	.000	.000
	PBIC	.580	.061	.235	.020	.000	.094	.010	.000	.000
	UBIC	.631	.000	.293	.039	.000	.037	.000	.000	.000
	CIC-1	.650	.000	.180	.010	.000	.020	.140	.000	.000
					Design matrix *X4*					
20	PAIC	.000	.000	.000	.000	.000	.003	.484	.000	.513
	UAIC	.000	.000	.000	.000	.000	.003	.484	.000	.513
	PBIC	.000	.000	.000	.000	.000	.003	.501	.000	.496
	UBIC	.000	.000	.000	.000	.000	.003	.502	.000	.495
	CIC-1	.000	.000	.000	.000	.000	.000	.530	.000	.470
100	PAIC	.000	.000	.000	.000	.000	.000	.451	.000	.549
	UAIC	.000	.000	.000	.000	.000	.000	.451	.000	.549
	PBIC	.000	.000	.000	.000	.000	.000	.453	.000	.547
	UBIC	.000	.000	.000	.000	.000	.000	.453	.000	.547
	CIC-1	.000	.000	.000	.000	.000	.000	.460	.000	.540

Average probabilities of correct selection (APCS) of the true model *M7* for five methods

PAIC = 0.281 UAIC = 0.235 PBIC = 0.260 UBIC = 0.239 CIC-1 = 0.315

Table 6.20(a) Comparison between PAIC, UAIC, PBIC, UBIC and CIC-1 based on estimated probabilities of choosing competing models *M1*, *M2*, *M3*, *M4*, *M5*, *M6*, *M7*, *M8* and *M9* for design matrices *X2* and *X4* when $\lambda_1 = 0.25$ and *M8* is true

T	*Methods*	*M1*	*M2*	*M3*	*M4*	*M5*	*M6*	*M7*	***M8***	*M9*
					Design matrix *X2*					
20	PAIC	.108	.075	.250	.339	.167	.011	.036	.008	.006
	UAIC	.079	.078	.278	.562	.000	.000	.002	.001	.000
	PBIC	.084	.065	.245	.346	.191	.013	.030	.001	.025
	UBIC	.079	.078	.280	.563	.000	.000	.000	.000	.000
	CIC-1	.170	.300	.380	.070	.000	.000	.000	.080	.000
100	PAIC	.089	.007	.159	.253	.113	.002	.131	.246	.000
	UAIC	.005	.008	.163	.510	.000	.000	.085	.229	.000
	PBIC	.015	.009	.202	.360	.202	.005	.067	.139	.001
	UBIC	.024	.053	.213	.661	.000	.000	.012	.037	.000
	CIC-1	.080	.090	.150	.370	.000	.000	.040	.270	.000
					Design matrix *X4*					
20	PAIC	.042	.052	.159	.471	.042	.075	.049	.108	.002
	UAIC	.039	.107	.025	.715	.011	.032	.001	.070	.000
	PBIC	.044	.069	.155	.523	.039	.050	.053	.067	.000
	UBIC	.042	.128	.029	.759	.002	.014	.001	.025	.000
	CIC-1	.140	.320	.100	.240	.000	.000	.000	.200	.000
100	PAIC	.001	.002	.079	.296	.000	.034	.001	.537	.050
	UAIC	.001	.000	.000	.440	.000	.015	.000	.507	.037
	PBIC	.001	.002	.079	.471	.003	.015	.001	.415	.013
	UBIC	.002	.002	.000	.680	.004	.003	.000	.307	.002
	CIC-1	.010	.030	.000	.340	.000	.010	.000	.580	.030

Average probabilities of correct selection (APCS) of the true model *M8* for five methods

PAIC = 0.225 UAIC = 0.202 PBIC = 0.156 UBIC = 0.092 CIC-1 = 0.283

Table 6.20(b) Comparison between PAIC, UAIC, PBIC, UBIC and CIC-1 based on estimated probabilities of choosing competing models *M*1, *M*2, *M*3, *M*4, *M*5, *M*6, *M*7, *M*8 and *M*9 for design matrices *X*2 and *X*4 when $\lambda_1 = 0.5$ and *M*8 is true

T	*Methods*	*M1*	*M2*	*M3*	*M4*	*M5*	*M6*	*M7*	***M8***	*M9*
					Design matrix *X*2					
20	PAIC	.167	.131	.185	.280	.091	.013	.084	.001	.048
	UAIC	.138	.144	.221	.497	.000	.000	.000	.000	.000
	PBIC	.141	.106	.174	.280	.100	.014	.076	.001	.108
	UBIC	.138	.144	.221	.497	.000	.000	.000	.000	.000
	CIC-1	.180	.420	.330	.000	.000	.000	.000	.070	.000
100	PAIC	.160	.132	.227	.203	.030	.008	.078	.162	.000
	UAIC	.123	.284	.129	.424	.000	.000	.013	.027	.000
	PBIC	.137	.200	.227	.287	.083	.016	.019	.007	.024
	UBIC	.128	.299	.136	.436	.000	.000	.000	.001	.000
	CIC-1	.210	.460	.110	.060	.000	.000	.000	.160	.000
					Design matrix *X*4					
20	PAIC	.036	.161	.176	.386	.059	.052	.092	.036	.002
	UAIC	.036	.300	.020	.587	.022	.027	.000	.008	.000
	PBIC	.038	.190	.172	.415	.032	.032	.104	.014	.003
	UBIC	.045	.315	.024	.603	.004	.009	.000	.000	.000
	CIC-1	.200	.430	.070	.170	.000	.000	.000	.130	.000
100	PAIC	.000	.078	.085	.207	.073	.021	.006	.516	.014
	UAIC	.000	.211	.000	.348	.053	.011	.000	.372	.005
	PBIC	.000	.209	.085	.376	.048	.007	.006	.269	.000
	UBIC	.001	.445	.000	.481	.016	.002	.000	.055	.000
	CIC-1	.010	.160	.000	.250	.040	.010	.000	.520	.010

Average probabilities of correct selection (APCS) of the true model *M*8 for five methods

PAIC = 0.179 UAIC = 0.102 PBIC = 0.073 UBIC = 0.014 CIC-1 = 0.220

Table 6.20(c) Comparison between PAIC, UAIC, PBIC, UBIC and CIC-1 based on estimated probabilities of choosing competing models *M1*, *M2*, *M3*, *M4*, *M5*, *M6*, *M7*, *M8* and *M9* for design matrices *X2* and *X4* when $\lambda_1 = 0.75$ and *M8* is true

T	*Methods*	*M1*	*M2*	*M3*	*M4*	*M5*	*M6*	*M7*	***M8***	*M9*
					Design matrix *X2*					
20	PAIC	.176	.154	.169	.246	.062	.012	.100	.003	.078
	UAIC	.152	.194	.205	.449	.000	.000	.000	.000	.000
	PBIC	.153	.134	.153	.246	.049	.013	.085	.006	.161
	UBIC	.152	.194	.205	.449	.000	.000	.000	.000	.000
	CIC-1	.160	.450	.290	.000	.000	.000	.000	.100	.000
100	PAIC	.196	.308	.244	.165	.027	.005	.030	.018	.007
	UAIC	.167	.457	.093	.283	.000	.000	.000	.000	.000
	PBIC	.168	.320	.194	.173	.028	.017	.045	.000	.055
	UBIC	.167	.457	.093	.283	.000	.000	.000	.000	.000
	CIC-1	.260	.500	.100	.030	.000	.000	.000	.110	.000
					Design matrix *X4*					
20	PAIC	.024	.267	.171	.325	.061	.042	.106	.002	.002
	UAIC	.033	.410	.016	.493	.024	.023	.000	.001	.000
	PBIC	.025	.281	.170	.337	.043	.030	.112	.000	.002
	UBIC	.037	.423	.018	.508	.006	.008	.000	.000	.000
	CIC-1	.180	.500	.060	.170	.000	.000	.000	.090	.000
100	PAIC	.000	.398	.084	.165	.113	.019	.009	.212	.000
	UAIC	.000	.628	.000	.257	.049	.008	.000	.058	.000
	PBIC	.000	.565	.084	.262	.041	.006	.009	.033	.000
	UBIC	.000	.692	.000	.296	.011	.001	.000	.000	.000
	CIC-1	.000	.390	.000	.220	.080	.000	.000	.310	.000

Average probabilities of correct selection (APCS) of the true model *M8* for five methods

PAIC = 0.059 UAIC = 0.015 PBIC = 0.010 UBIC = 0.000 CIC-1 = 0.153

cases which is expected. Only for the combination of $\lambda_1 = 0.75$ and $\lambda_2 = 0.25$, do we find some slightly surprising results, where the PCS of the true model are much lower than any other combinations considered in this study. Among the five competing methods, it is apparent from Tables 6.21(a) to 6.21(i) that with respect to APCS, our proposed CIC-1 method still performs better than other methods, with improvements ranging from 7 per cent to 18.5 per cent in Table 6.21(a), 5.4 per cent to 12.5 per cent in Table 6.21(b), 5.4 per cent to 6.2 per cent in Table 6.21(c), 6 per cent to 12.8 per cent in Table 6.21(d), 5.4 per cent to 6.3 per cent in Table 6.21(f), 12.1 per cent to 21.3 per cent in Table 6.21(g), 9 per cent to 13.3 per cent in Table 6.21(h) and 4.6 per cent to 13.5 per cent in Table 6.21(i). Only in Table 6.21(d) is CIC-1 dominated by PBIC by 4.5 per cent with respect to APCS, but CIC-1 dominates the other three methods PAIC, UAIC and UBIC by 17.8 per cent, 19.5 per cent and 25 per cent, respectively. It is worthwhile to note that in Tables 6.21(a) to 6.21(i), we use three different values of λ_1 and λ_2 in order to see the effect of these parameters on the PCS. We summarise these effects in Tables 6.22 and 6.23, which clearly indicate that the effects of λ_1 and λ_2 on the PCS are of various types and do not follow any specific pattern.

Among the four methods PAIC, UAIC, PBIC and UBIC, with respect to that of PCS, the performance of UAIC and UBIC seems better than PAIC and PBIC, when the smaller model is the true model (*M*1 to *M*4). On the other hand, as expected, PAIC and PBIC seem to be more dominating than UAIC and UBIC when larger models (*M*6 to *M*9) are true. Of the two methods UAIC and UBIC, UBIC seems to have higher PCS when the smaller model is true. When the larger model is true, PAIC seems to be better in most of the cases. In order to evaluate the overall performance of all five methods considered, we calculated the average of APCS (AAPCS) for these five methods irrespective of whether the smaller or larger model is true. The AAPCS for PAIC, UAIC, PBIC, UBIC and CIC-1 are 0.345, 0.343, 0.347, 0.329 and 0.443, respectively. According to AAPCS, the five contesting methods used in our study can be ranked as: CIC-1 > PBIC > PAIC > UAIC > UBIC. In terms of AAPCS, the CIC-1 procedure dominates PBIC, PAIC, UAIC and UBIC by 9.6 per cent, 9.8 per cent, 10 per cent and 11.4 per cent, respectively. In terms of proportions, on the other hand, for matrix *X*2 with $T = 20$ and $T = 100$, CIC-1 dominates other criteria 100 per cent and 88 per cent of the time respectively. For design matrix *X*4, CIC-1 dominates other methods 92 per cent of the time both in small ($T = 20$) and large sample ($T = 100$) cases. However, the above ranking clearly indicates that CIC-1 has proved to be a much better method than the existing AIC and BIC for model selection. PBIC and PAIC appear to be the second and

Table 6.21(a) Comparison between PAIC, UAIC, PBIC, UBIC and CIC-1 based on estimated probabilities of choosing competing models *M1*, *M2*, *M3*, *M4*, *M5*, *M6*, *M7*, *M8* and *M9* for design matrices *X2* and *X4* when $\lambda_1 = 0.25$, $\lambda_2 = 0.25$ and *M9* is true

T	*Methods*	*M1*	*M2*	*M3*	*M4*	*M5*	*M6*	*M7*	*M8*	*M9*
					Design matrix *X2*					
20	PAIC	.099	.075	.279	.323	.162	.008	.043	.007	.004
	UAIC	.071	.061	.309	.556	.000	.000	.002	.001	.000
	PBIC	.166	.050	.346	.424	.000	.014	.000	.000	.000
	UBIC	.072	.061	.310	.556	.000	.000	.000	.001	.000
	CIC-1	.210	.270	.360	.090	.000	.000	.000	.000	.070
100	PAIC	.053	.013	.182	.281	.076	.011	.189	.195	.000
	UAIC	.011	.005	.214	.487	.000	.002	.125	.156	.000
	PBIC	.211	.020	.183	.480	.022	.081	.000	.003	.000
	UBIC	.038	.044	.285	.599	.000	.000	.013	.021	.000
	CIC-1	.150	.090	.230	.400	.000	.000	.040	.040	.050
					Design matrix *X4*					
20	PAIC	.040	.025	.045	.314	.014	.349	.056	.037	.120
	UAIC	.069	.000	.000	.510	.009	.299	.009	.031	.073
	PBIC	.102	.000	.000	.301	.083	.358	.000	.000	.156
	UBIC	.114	.000	.001	.597	.006	.241	.004	.020	.017
	CIC-1	.120	.000	.010	.240	.000	.190	.000	.040	.400
100	PAIC	.000	.000	.000	.049	.000	.080	.001	.000	.870
	UAIC	.000	.000	.000	.069	.000	.075	.000	.000	.856
	PBIC	.004	.000	.000	.000	.002	.000	.000	.000	.994
	UBIC	.000	.000	.000	.226	.000	.098	.000	.001	.675
	CIC-1	.000	.000	.000	.090	.000	.000	.000	.000	.910

Average probabilities of correct selection (APCS) of the true model *M9* for five methods

PAIC = 0.249   UAIC = 0.232   PBIC = 0.288   UBIC = 0.173   CIC-1 = 0.358

Table 6.21(b) Comparison between PAIC, UAIC, PBIC, UBIC and CIC-1 based on estimated probabilities of choosing competing models *M1*, *M2*, *M3*, *M4*, *M5*, *M6*, *M7*, *M8* and *M9* for design matrices *X2* and *X4* when $\lambda_1 = 0.25$, $\lambda_2 = 0.5$ and *M9* is true

T	*Methods*	*M1*	*M2*	*M3*	*M4*	*M5*	*M6*	*M7*	*M8*	*M9*
					Design matrix *X2*					
20	PAIC	.077	.096	.308	.310	.131	.020	.055	.002	.001
	UAIC	.066	.037	.373	.518	.000	.003	.002	.001	.000
	PBIC	.078	.063	.276	.333	.184	.006	.040	.001	.019
	UBIC	.066	.037	.377	.519	.000	.000	.000	.001	.000
	CIC-1	.240	.230	.340	.110	.000	.000	.000	.000	.080
100	PAIC	.019	.022	.203	.253	.040	.103	.259	.100	.001
	UAIC	.019	.001	.280	.431	.000	.019	.173	.076	.001
	PBIC	.014	.015	.247	.377	.132	.002	.108	.105	.000
	UBIC	.070	.008	.370	.518	.000	.000	.026	.008	.000
	CIC-1	.170	.040	.240	.340	.000	.030	.090	.030	.060
					Design matrix *X4*					
20	PAIC	.000	.017	.000	.008	.001	.381	.037	.000	.556
	UAIC	.001	.000	.000	.020	.000	.397	.037	.000	.545
	PBIC	.017	.018	.042	.039	.014	.320	.017	.029	.504
	UBIC	.006	.000	.000	.029	.000	.418	.049	.000	.498
	CIC-1	.030	.000	.000	.030	.000	.300	.010	.000	.630
100	PAIC	.000	.000	.000	.000	.000	.001	.000	.000	.999
	UAIC	.000	.000	.000	.000	.000	.001	.000	.000	.999
	PBIC	.000	.000	.000	.136	.000	.113	.001	.000	.750
	UBIC	.000	.000	.000	.000	.000	.001	.000	.000	.999
	CIC-1	.000	.000	.000	.000	.000	.000	.000	.000	1.00

Average probabilities of correct selection (APCS) of the true model *M9* for five methods

PAIC = 0.389 UAIC = 0.386 PBIC = 0.318 UBIC = 0.374 CIC-1 = 0.443

Table 6.21(c) Comparison between PAIC, UAIC, PBIC, UBIC and CIC-1 based on estimated probabilities of choosing competing models *M*1, *M*2, *M*3, *M*4, *M*5, *M*6, *M*7, *M*8 and *M*9 for design matrices *X*2 and *X*4 when $\lambda_1 = 0.25$, $\lambda_2 = 0.75$ and *M*9 is true

T	*Methods*	*M1*	*M2*	*M3*	*M4*	*M5*	*M6*	*M7*	*M8*	*M9*
					Design matrix *X*2					
20	PAIC	.042	.139	.365	.260	.092	.048	.051	.003	.000
	UAIC	.041	.015	.479	.446	.000	.014	.004	.001	.000
	PBIC	.067	.081	.314	.319	.152	.004	.047	.001	.015
	UBIC	.043	.015	.488	.452	.000	.001	.000	.001	.000
	CIC-1	.300	.100	.380	.150	.000	.010	.000	.000	.060
100	PAIC	.002	.025	.214	.112	.007	.262	.351	.011	.016
	UAIC	.009	.000	.339	.202	.000	.169	.277	.003	.001
	PBIC	.024	.013	.303	.380	.065	.008	.154	.053	.000
	UBIC	.047	.000	.520	.336	.000	.009	.088	.000	.000
	CIC-1	.160	.000	.350	.180	.000	.140	.070	.000	.100
					Design matrix *X*4					
20	PAIC	.000	.001	.000	.000	.000	.061	.130	.000	.808
	UAIC	.000	.000	.000	.000	.000	.062	.131	.000	.807
	PBIC	.003	.014	.000	.017	.002	.104	.052	.000	.808
	UBIC	.000	.000	.000	.000	.000	.064	.145	.000	.791
	CIC-1	.000	.000	.000	.000	.000	.120	.000	.000	.880
100	PAIC	.000	.000	.000	.000	.000	.000	.001	.000	.999
	UAIC	.000	.000	.000	.000	.000	.000	.001	.000	.999
	PBIC	.000	.000	.000	.000	.000	.001	.000	.000	.999
	UBIC	.000	.000	.000	.000	.000	.000	.001	.000	.999
	CIC-1	.000	.000	.000	.000	.000	.000	.000	.000	1.00

Average probabilities of correct selection (APCS) of the true model *M*9 for five methods

PAIC = 0.456 UAIC = 0.452 PBIC = 0.456 UBIC = 0.448 CIC-1 = 0.510

Table 6.21(d) Comparison between PAIC, UAIC, PBIC, UBIC and CIC-1 based on estimated probabilities of choosing competing models *M1*, *M2*, *M3*, *M4*, *M5*, *M6*, *M7*, *M8* and *M9* for design matrices *X2* and *X4* when $\lambda_1 = 0.5$, $\lambda_2 = 0.25$ and *M9* is true

T	*Methods*	*M1*	*M2*	*M3*	*M4*	*M5*	*M6*	*M7*	*M8*	*M9*
					Design matrix *X2*					
20	PAIC	.161	.135	.205	.274	.087	.010	.091	.002	.035
	UAIC	.133	.121	.243	.503	.000	.000	.000	.000	.000
	PBIC	.042	.118	.386	.280	.115	.016	.042	.001	.000
	UBIC	.133	.121	.243	.503	.000	.000	.000	.000	.000
	CIC-1	.230	.360	.310	.000	.000	.000	.000	.000	.100
100	PAIC	.171	.124	.208	.234	.035	.012	.100	.116	.000
	UAIC	.178	.203	.173	.413	.000	.000	.012	.021	.000
	PBIC	.012	.025	.359	.211	.007	.133	.252	.001	.000
	UBIC	.185	.214	.177	.423	.000	.000	.000	.001	.000
	CIC-1	.320	.360	.140	.120	.000	.000	.000	.000	.060
					Design matrix *X4*					
20	PAIC	.027	.014	.052	.301	.162	.260	.106	.055	.023
	UAIC	.049	.005	.000	.503	.134	.241	.000	.058	.010
	PBIC	.000	.001	.000	.000	.000	.063	.145	.000	.791
	UBIC	.082	.009	.000	.591	.100	.181	.000	.036	.001
	CIC-1	.060	.010	.000	.230	.030	.090	.000	.040	.540
100	PAIC	.000	.000	.000	.080	.010	.055	.008	.007	.840
	UAIC	.000	.000	.000	.116	.011	.046	.000	.007	.820
	PBIC	.000	.000	.000	.000	.000	.000	.001	.000	.999
	UBIC	.000	.000	.000	.301	.040	.042	.000	.002	.615
	CIC-1	.000	.000	.000	.070	.010	.010	.000	.000	.910

Average probabilities of correct selection (APCS) of the true model *M9* for five methods

PAIC = 0.225 UAIC = 0.208 PBIC = 0.448 UBIC = 0.154 CIC-1 = 0.403

Table 6.21(e) Comparison between PAIC, UAIC, PBIC, UBIC and CIC-1 based on estimated probabilities of choosing competing models *M*1, *M*2, *M*3, *M*4, *M*5, *M*6, *M*7, *M*8 and *M*9 for design matrices *X*2 and *X*4 when $\lambda_1 = 0.5$, $\lambda_2 = 0.5$ and *M*9 is true

T	*Methods*	*M1*	*M2*	*M3*	*M4*	*M5*	*M6*	*M7*	*M8*	*M9*
					Design matrix *X2*					
20	PAIC	.132	.139	.223	.270	.073	.020	.103	.011	.029
	UAIC	.124	.082	.306	.486	.000	.002	.000	.000	.000
	PBIC	.123	.103	.230	.277	.072	.005	.102	.001	.087
	UBIC	.124	.082	.308	.486	.000	.000	.000	.000	.000
	CIC-1	.280	.250	.340	.000	.000	.000	.000	.000	.130
100	PAIC	.207	.079	.180	.231	.024	.071	.141	.067	.000
	UAIC	.275	.085	.224	.381	.000	.009	.013	.013	.000
	PBIC	.278	.102	.247	.310	.025	.002	.030	.006	.000
	UBIC	.280	.092	.234	.392	.000	.000	.000	.002	.000
	CIC-1	.410	.220	.190	.110	.000	.000	.000	.000	.070
					Design matrix *X4*					
20	PAIC	.130	.022	.001	.024	.048	.288	.044	.001	.442
	UAIC	.198	.000	.000	.042	.041	.345	.000	.001	.373
	PBIC	.213	.022	.000	.036	.056	.315	.044	.001	.313
	UBIC	.345	.000	.000	.066	.034	.355	.000	.001	.199
	CIC-1	.230	.000	.000	.030	.010	.210	.000	.010	.510
100	PAIC	.000	.000	.000	.000	.000	.000	.000	.000	1.00
	UAIC	.000	.000	.000	.000	.000	.000	.000	.000	1.00
	PBIC	.001	.000	.000	.000	.000	.000	.000	.000	.999
	UBIC	.002	.000	.000	.000	.000	.000	.000	.000	.998
	CIC-1	.000	.000	.000	.000	.000	.000	.000	.000	1.00

Average probabilities of correct selection (APCS) of the true model *M9* for five methods

PAIC = 0.368 UAIC = 0.343 PBIC = 0.350 UBIC = 0.300 CIC-1 = 0.428

Table 6.21(f) **Comparison between PAIC, UAIC, PBIC, UBIC and CIC-1 based on estimated probabilities of choosing competing models *M*1, *M*2, *M*3, *M*4, *M*5, *M*6, *M*7, *M*8 and *M*9 for design matrices *X*2 and *X*4 when $\lambda_1 = 0.5$, $\lambda_2 = 0.75$ and *M*9 is true**

T	*Methods*	*M1*	*M2*	*M3*	*M4*	*M5*	*M6*	*M7*	*M8*	***M9***
					Design matrix *X*2					
20	PAIC	.116	.192	.268	.218	.052	.042	.104	.000	.008
	UAIC	.126	.032	.389	.437	.000	.016	.000	.000	.000
	PBIC	.120	.161	.277	.234	.057	.015	.099	.002	.035
	UBIC	.129	.032	.395	.442	.000	.002	.000	.000	.000
	CIC-1	.340	.200	.360	.000	.000	.000	.000	.000	.100
100	PAIC	.246	.046	.169	.093	.006	.210	.210	.013	.007
	UAIC	.357	.004	.266	.190	.000	.125	.048	.008	.002
	PBIC	.377	.045	.279	.164	.005	.086	.040	.004	.000
	UBIC	.409	.004	.317	.261	.000	.006	.000	.003	.000
	CIC-1	.520	.010	.280	.090	.000	.010	.000	.000	.090
					Design matrix *X*4					
20	PAIC	.000	.004	.000	.001	.000	.054	.130	.000	.811
	UAIC	.000	.000	.000	.001	.000	.058	.130	.000	.811
	PBIC	.000	.004	.000	.001	.000	.057	.148	.000	.790
	UBIC	.001	.000	.000	.001	.000	.061	.148	.000	.789
	CIC-1	.010	.000	.000	.000	.000	.050	.080	.000	.860
100	PAIC	.000	.000	.000	.000	.000	.000	.001	.000	.999
	UAIC	.000	.000	.000	.000	.000	.000	.001	.000	.999
	PBIC	.000	.000	.000	.000	.000	.000	.001	.000	.999
	UBIC	.000	.000	.000	.000	.000	.000	.001	.000	.999
	CIC-1	.000	.000	.000	.000	.000	.000	.000	.000	1.00

Average probabilities of correct selection (APCS) of the true model *M*9 for five methods

PAIC = 0.456 UAIC = 0.453 PBIC = 0.456 UBIC = 0.447 CIC-1 = 0.510

Table 6.21(g) Comparison between PAIC, UAIC, PBIC, UBIC and CIC-1 based on estimated probabilities of choosing competing models *M1*, *M2*, *M3*, *M4*, *M5*, *M6*, *M7*, *M8* and *M9* for design matrices *X2* and *X4* when $\lambda_1 = 0.75$, $\lambda_2 = 0.25$ and *M9* is true

T	*Methods*	*M1*	*M2*	*M3*	*M4*	*M5*	*M6*	*M7*	*M8*	*M9*
					Design matrix *X2*					
20	PAIC	.167	.153	.177	.242	.037	.011	.130	.004	.079
	UAIC	.148	.162	.218	.471	.000	.001	.000	.000	.000
	PBIC	.151	.123	.167	.245	.030	.007	.120	.003	.154
	UBIC	.148	.162	.219	.471	.000	.000	.000	.000	.000
	CIC-1	.190	.310	.290	.000	.000	.000	.000	.000	.210
100	PAIC	.240	.261	.210	.199	.037	.007	.030	.013	.003
	UAIC	.236	.337	.123	.304	.000	.000	.000	.000	.000
	PBIC	.237	.266	.188	.206	.025	.004	.037	.000	.037
	UBIC	.236	.337	.123	.304	.000	.000	.000	.000	.000
	CIC-1	.370	.290	.140	.090	.000	.000	.000	.000	.110
					Design matrix *X4*					
20	PAIC	.003	.027	.059	.253	.255	.195	.136	.068	.004
	UAIC	.018	.043	.000	.461	.210	.211	.000	.055	.002
	PBIC	.011	.031	.057	.307	.234	.169	.142	.049	.000
	UBIC	.035	.061	.000	.556	.169	.153	.000	.026	.000
	CIC-1	.230	.050	.000	.380	.090	.090	.000	.050	.110
100	PAIC	.000	.000	.000	.113	.274	.111	.048	.006	.448
	UAIC	.000	.000	.000	.182	.286	.105	.000	.006	.421
	PBIC	.000	.000	.000	.207	.404	.101	.048	.008	.232
	UBIC	.000	.000	.000	.336	.409	.080	.000	.007	.168
	CIC-1	.000	.000	.000	.170	.210	.030	.000	.000	.590

Average probabilities of correct selection (APCS) of the true model *M9* for five methods

PAIC = 0.134 UAIC = 0.106 PBIC = 0.106 UBIC = 0.042 CIC-1 = 0.255

Table 6.21(h) Comparison between PAIC, UAIC, PBIC, UBIC and CIC-1 based on estimated probabilities of choosing competing models *M*1, *M*2, *M*3, *M*4, *M*5, *M*6, *M*7, *M*8 and *M*9 for design matrices *X*2 and *X*4 when $\lambda_1 = 0.75, \lambda_2 = 0.5$ and *M*9 is true

T	*Methods*	*M1*	*M2*	*M3*	*M4*	*M5*	*M6*	*M7*	*M8*	*M9*
					Design matrix *X*2					
20	PAIC	.163	.138	.217	.242	.034	.021	.132	.005	.048
	UAIC	.159	.111	.271	.457	.000	.002	.000	.000	.000
	PBIC	.156	.104	.215	.245	.027	.006	.125	.006	.116
	UBIC	.160	.111	.271	.457	.000	.001	.000	.000	.000
	CIC-1	.240	.280	.320	.000	.000	.000	.000	.000	.160
100	PAIC	.331	.157	.163	.187	.069	.045	.038	.010	.000
	UAIC	.366	.176	.152	.295	.003	.006	.000	.002	.000
	PBIC	.368	.173	.176	.225	.008	.001	.035	.001	.013
	UBIC	.368	.179	.154	.299	.000	.000	.000	.000	.000
	CIC-1	.440	.260	.180	.040	.000	.000	.000	.000	.080
					Design matrix *X*4					
20	PAIC	.004	.014	.004	.031	.291	.249	.070	.003	.334
	UAIC	.014	.000	.000	.067	.287	.318	.000	.002	.312
	PBIC	.011	.013	.002	.052	.311	.262	.073	.002	.274
	UBIC	.042	.000	.000	.097	.299	.328	.000	.002	.232
	CIC-1	.110	.000	.000	.040	.150	.230	.000	.010	.460
100	PAIC	.000	.000	.000	.000	.043	.001	.000	.000	.956
	UAIC	.000	.000	.000	.000	.043	.001	.000	.000	.956
	PBIC	.000	.000	.000	.000	.064	.001	.000	.000	.935
	UBIC	.000	.000	.000	.000	.065	.001	.000	.000	.934
	CIC-1	.000	.000	.000	.000	.000	.000	.000	.000	1.00

Average probabilities of correct selection (APCS) of the true model *M*9 for five methods

PAIC = 0.335 UAIC = 0.317 PBIC = 0.335 UBIC = 0.292 CIC-1 = 0.425

Table 6.21(i) Comparison between PAIC, UAIC, PBIC, UBIC and CIC-1 based on estimated probabilities of choosing competing models *M*1, *M*2, *M*3, *M*4, *M*5, *M*6, *M*7, *M*8 and *M*9 for design matrices *X*2 and *X*4 when $\lambda_1 = 0.75$, $\lambda_2 = 0.75$ and *M*9 is true

T	*Methods*	*M1*	*M2*	*M3*	*M4*	*M5*	*M6*	*M7*	*M8*	*M9*
					Design matrix *X*2					
20	PAIC	.150	.188	.220	.220	.022	.049	.124	.005	.022
	UAIC	.166	.050	.346	.424	.000	.014	.000	.000	.000
	PBIC	.151	.145	.228	.235	.018	.020	.110	.012	.081
	UBIC	.168	.050	.350	.430	.000	.002	.000	.000	.000
	CIC-1	.290	.250	.360	.000	.000	.000	.000	.000	.100
100	PAIC	.427	.060	.130	.095	.081	.148	.052	.007	.000
	UAIC	.511	.020	.183	.180	.022	.081	.000	.003	.000
	PBIC	.523	.069	.171	.153	.012	.043	.026	.002	.001
	UBIC	.542	.025	.204	.223	.000	.004	.000	.002	.000
	CIC-1	.530	.170	.210	.020	.000	.000	.000	.000	.070
					Design matrix *X*4					
20	PAIC	.274	.007	.000	.001	.109	.044	.008	.000	.557
	UAIC	.402	.000	.000	.001	.083	.058	.000	.000	.456
	PBIC	.423	.007	.000	.002	.097	.047	.007	.000	.417
	UBIC	.597	.000	.000	.002	.058	.061	.000	.000	.282
	CIC-1	.290	.000	.000	.000	.030	.090	.000	.000	.590
100	PAIC	.003	.000	.000	.000	.002	.000	.000	.000	.995
	UAIC	.004	.000	.000	.000	.002	.000	.000	.000	.994
	PBIC	.028	.000	.000	.000	.002	.000	.000	.000	.970
	UBIC	.060	.000	.000	.000	.002	.000	.000	.000	.938
	CIC-1	.000	.000	.000	.000	.000	.000	.000	.000	1.00

Average probabilities of correct selection (APCS) of the true model *M*9 for five methods

PAIC = 0.394	UAIC = 0.363	PBIC = 0.368	UBIC = 0.305	CIC-1 = 0.440

Table 6.22 Effect of changes in λ_2 and λ_1 on PCS for the true models *M5* to *M8*

Effect of λ_2	X2 with $T = 20$	PCS decrease as λ_2 increases
	X2 with $T = 100$	PCS increase as λ_2 increases
	X4 with $T = 20$	PCS increase as λ_2 increases
	X4 with $T = 100$	PCS decrease as λ_2 increases
	X2 with $T = 20$	PCS increase as λ_2 increases
	X2 with $T = 100$	PCS increase as λ_2 increases
	X4 with $T = 20$	PCS increase as λ_2 increases
	X4 with $T = 100$	PCS decrease as λ_2 increases
Effect of λ_1	X2 with $T = 20$	PCS increase as λ_1 increases
	X2 with $T = 100$	PCS decrease as λ_1 increases
	X4 with $T = 20$	No significant effect on PCS
	X4 with $T = 100$	No significant effect on PCS
	X2 with $T = 20$	No significant effect on PCS
	X2 with $T = 100$	PCS decrease as λ_1 increases
	X4 with $T = 20$	PCS decrease as λ_1 increases
	X4 with $T = 100$	PCS decrease as λ_1 increases

Table 6.23 Effect of changes in λ_1 and λ_2 on PCS for the true model *M9*

Effect of λ_2 with $\lambda_1 = 0.25$	X2 with T = 20	Almost similar pattern in all cases
	X2 with T = 100	PCS increase as λ_2 increases
	X4 with T = 20	PCS increase as λ_2 increases
	X4 with T = 100	PCS increase as λ_2 increases
Effect of λ_2 with $\lambda_1 = 0.5$	X2 with T = 20	Almost similar pattern in all cases
	X2 with T = 100	Almost similar pattern in all cases
	X4 with T = 20	PCS increase as λ_2 increases
	X4 with T = 100	PCS increase as λ_2 increases
Effect of λ_2 with $\lambda_1 = 0.75$	X2 with T = 20	PCS decrease as λ_2 increases
	X4 with T = 100	PCS decrease as λ_2 increases
	X2 with T = 20	PCS increase as λ_2 increases
	X4 with T = 100	PCS increase as λ_2 increases

third best criteria. Note that the PCS significantly vary for the different true models. These variations are mostly apparent for both the usual and proposed AIC and BIC methods rather than CIC-1 implying that the philosophy behind the CIC-1 has been successful, at least partially. However, as the sample size tends to infinity, these variations become insignificant.

6.6 Concluding Remarks

In this chapter, we propose two new information criteria one of which is called CIC-1 and the other is called CIC-2. We consider three versions of CIC-2 for three different conventional values of α. Basically, these two new procedures introduce the idea of controlling the probability of correct selection in the context of model selection. The main point of these procedures has been to show how we can set the penalties in IC-based model selection procedures and hence take control of probabilities of correct selection. In this regard, it is worthwhile to point out how such control would be maintained in practice. To do this, we employ the parametric bootstrap approach for calculating penalties for the CIC-1 method. For the CIC-2 method, on the other hand, the penalties are derived from the probability weighted mixture of chi-squared distributions and the usual Monte Carlo simulation technique was used to assess the performance of the method. The outcome of using such techniques is that our proposed CIC-1 method performs significantly better than the existing AIC and BIC in almost all cases. The CIC-2 method, on the other hand, has been found to be better than other methods (except CIC-1) in some cases and slightly worse in other cases.

We also discussed the effect of nuisance parameters on the PCS for the true model. We found that the effect of nuisance parameters on the PCS is moderately significant in some cases and insignificant in other cases. To see the overall effect of nuisance parameters, we calculated the average PCS for each of the competing methods and ranked them. We then compared this with the results obtained for our particular chosen parameter values. We found no significant dissimilarity between these two results, indicating the conclusions we have drawn from our results are almost free from the effect of our choice of nuisance parameter values.

However, we wish to mention one more point. Usually new procedures do well in some circumstances and relatively poorly in other circumstances. Unlike such a usual case, CIC-1 has been found to be a very promising model selection procedure, because it worked extremely well in almost all circumstances.

We know of no other new procedure that has been proposed in the literature and found to dominate existing procedures in such a comprehensive manner. Although the procedure itself is an extensive simulation-based method, we claim that the extra computation required to apply CIC-1 is still very much worth the effort.

Finally we investigated the performance of the CIC-1 method in the case of two parameter restrictions and hence for a larger number of models. The simulation results indicate that the performance of CIC-1, relative to both usual and proposed AIC and BIC, in this particular case is very clearly superior. We found clear evidence that the new procedure CIC-1 can easily be applied to the case of two restrictions and dominates the other methods by a large margin in most situations. Thus we wish to claim that the CIC-1 procedure may be used by applied researchers in place of existing AIC and BIC for the selection of models with restricted parameters. One small problem with this new approach is that it is a computer simulation method and hence it involves a huge amount of computation. However, our analysis demonstrates one important point, which is that the PCS vary significantly for different true models. These variations are relatively smaller for the CIC-1 procedure than for the other competing methods, which is desirable. The analysis also identifies that such variations depend on some important factors, for example, sample size, values of parameters, nature of data matrix and method used. However, for large sample cases, these variations become negligible.

Note

1 We would have liked to conduct the experiment in the same way as the previous ones but the huge amount of computation involved made it impossible. Therefore the experiment had to be cut down.

Chapter 7

Arbitrage Pricing Model

7.1 Introduction

In the rest of the book (Chapters 7 to 9), we will apply hypothesis testing and model selection procedures to models. Arbitrage pricing theory (APT) assumes that share prices are efficient in adjusting to new information in stock markets. Due to the price efficiency assumption, which implies that the current share prices are equal to their true value, the no arbitrage condition of the APT is realized. The efficient market hypothesis (EMH) and the APT share the same root as neoclassical economics and are built on some common assumptions, such as having perfect market competition in stock markets. Because of this very important inter-relationship between the APT and the EMH, we will include a section on the EMH at the start of this chapter.

Bodie, Kane and Marcus (1996) define arbitrage as, 'the exploitation of security mispricing in such a way that risk-free economic profits may be earned' (p. 288). The theory presents a testable framework for estimating prices of risk for holding financial assets in relation to a set of factors that are perceived to be important in determining these assets' returns. Elton and Gruber (1995) describe the APT in the following statement: 'it remains the newest and most promising explanation of relative returns. The theory promises to supply us with a more complete description of returns than the Capital Asset Pricing Model' (p. 388). Both the APT and the capital asset pricing model (CAPM) are equilibrium models which describe the expected returns of risky assets in terms of their risks. In an equilibrium state, the current prices of financial assets are equal to their true values.

While the CAPM considers only one source of risk, the market portfolio, the APT considers the possibility of having more than one source of risk. In fact, listed shares have two types of risk: systematic risk and idiosyncratic risk. Systematic risk is common to all shares in stock markets and cannot be diversified, whereas idiosyncratic risk is specific to a particular firm or industry and can be diversified away. In equilibrium models, only systematic risk, which is undiversifiable, is rewarded by earning a premium that compensates investors for holding risky assets.

The rest of this chapter is organized into the following sections. Section 7.2 presents an overview of the efficient market hypothesis and its three forms (weak, semi-strong and strong). The APT model will be presented in section 7.3, where two distinguished methods of empirical testing using factor analysis and observed variables will be discussed. Furthermore, this section will divide up the empirical tests of the APT model, which are based on using observed variables, into three main stages, namely, identifying the observed variables, generating innovation terms from the observed variables and estimating the prices of risk of the observed variables. Section 7.4 summarizes the literature survey of the efficient market hypothesis and the APT model.

7.2 Efficient Market Hypothesis

The efficient market hypothesis (EMH) was developed by Eugene Fama in the 1960s. This hypothesis suggests that share prices are very efficient in incorporating any new information and quickly adjust to such new information to reflect their true values. It assumes that prices are perfect, adjustment to new information is done instantaneously and the prices at any given time reflect the true intrinsic value of listed share prices. Shiller (1981) defines current share prices in the efficient markets model as the expected present discounted value of future dividends payments, as given in model (7.1) below:

$$P_t = E(D) / (1 + r) \tag{7.1}$$

where:

P_t is the current price of listed shares;
E(D) is the expected dividend;
r is the discount rate.

At the heart of the efficient market hypothesis lie the fair game model and the random walk model, which provide a framework for testing the hypothesis. The fair game model states that market participants cannot achieve above average returns based on historic information because such information has been fully incorporated into listed share prices. Any private information that might be used by some market participants would not be considered as part of the fair game model. The random walk model builds on the broad definition of the fair game model by assuming that successive returns are completely independent of each other and that they have the same distribution. Therefore, the random walk model is a restricted version of the fair game model. If the hypothesis of the random walk model holds in empirical tests, this would provide support for the efficient market hypothesis. Fama (1970) assumes that there is no transaction cost when buying shares, that public information is available to all market participants at no cost, and that market participants are uniformly interpreting the effect of any new information on current prices. The author acknowledges that even though such assumptions are not realistic in stock markets, they are sufficient for market efficiency but not necessary. In order to test the efficient market hypothesis, Fama (1970) divides the hypothesis into three forms: the weak form, the semi-strong form and the strong form of market efficiencies. These are detailed in the subsequent subsections.

7.2.1 The Weak Form of Market Efficiency

The weak form of the efficient market (WFEM) states that all past publicly available information is factored into share prices of listed firms in stock markets. As a result, market participants will not be able to use historical information of listed shares to successfully predict their future behaviour and therefore achieve above average rates of return. Many scholars have used different empirical techniques to support the presence of this form of the efficient market hypothesis in the stock markets. The WFEM has focused exclusively on using past data to predict future returns based on the serial correlation test and the run test (see Fama, 1970). The serial correlation test is based on using the random walk model to verify whether the past returns are independent of each other and have the same distribution. Because market efficiency implies that security returns are independent of each other and (as information which affect such return arrives randomly), it is expected that returns at the present period should be statistically independent from past periods. If any of the serial correlations are statistically significant, this means that current return is dependent on past returns, and that is evidence against the market efficiency hypothesis. The run test assigns positive (+) sign, negative (–) sign and zero (0) sign to changes in listed share prices. A run test could take this form: + + – – – – + + + 0 – – +, which has six runs. As long as the run test does not show a consistent pattern of similar signs, then it is possible to conclude that a particular stock market exhibits market efficiency.

In testing returns predictability in developing stock markets using serial correlations and run tests, there have been few articles that provide empirical evidence on the stock market efficiency in different countries. Articles by Barnes (1986) for the Kuala Lumpur Stock Exchange in Malaysia, and Dickinson and Muragu (1994) for the Nairobi Stock Exchange in Kenya, both analyze monthly time series data using the serial correlation test and the run test. The two articles produced empirical results that are in conformity with the market efficiency hypothesis. On the other hand, empirical evidence of stock market inefficiency was found by Butler and Malaikah (1992) in Kuwait and Saudi Arabia, and by El-Erian and Kumar (1995) in Jordan and Turkey; the first article used serial correlation and run tests, whereas the second article used only run tests.

7.2.2 The Semi-Strong Form of Market Efficiency

The semi-strong form of the efficient market hypothesis builds on the weak form and adds that share prices adjust very quickly to any newly available public information in markets. To test the presence of this form of market efficiency, researchers have used event studies techniques which deal with the announcements of listed companies. Event studies are concerned with the reaction of share prices to announcements by listed companies. Announcements include, for example, unexpected high earnings and high dividend yield. The purpose of the event studies technique is to measure whether new unexpected announcements have a significant impact on the changing share prices of listed firms. Event studies are organized in the following way (see Elton and Gruber, 1995). First of all, a set of listed firms is selected, and they are grouped into positive and negative sets based on the direction of change in their prices following announcements. Secondly, daily data are, usually, used in events studies and a zero would normally be assigned to the day of announcement. A time interval of 40 or 60 days is usually adopted for analysis. For example, in the case of using 40 days, there will be 20 days prior to the announcement, zero for the announcement day and 20 days after the announcement. Thirdly, according to the efficient market hypothesis, a positive announcement would normally lead to an immediate increase in share prices on the day of announcement, and vice versa. But it is not possible to achieve above average returns after the announcement day. The above-average returns of each firm in the sample would be computed by subtracting each firm return from its expected return, then a cumulative return would be added for all the firms in the sample. Finally, if the cumulative return of the sample exceeds its expected return, this implies that markets are not efficient. Whereas, if the cumulative return of the sample is equal to its expected return, then markets are efficient.

None of the studies has been conducted in developing stock markets, but empirical results from developed stock markets show a consistent pattern of market efficiency. That is, market participants are not likely to gain excess profit from listed shares by purchasing them immediately after a new positive announcement, because they will very quickly adjust to new levels that reflect their true value. Unlike tests of the weak form, the semi-strong form provides the most significant support and least controversial evidence in favour of the stock market efficiency hypothesis, according to Fama (1991).

7.2.3 The Strong Form of Market Efficiency

The strong form of the efficient market hypothesis goes further than the weak and semi-strong forms by stating that not only all publicly available information is rapidly factored into share prices, but privately held information is factored in also. This means, according to the strong efficient hypothesis, that stock markets are perfect in pricing listed shares. As a consequence, it is not possible for any market participant to achieve consistently above-average returns even if they have access to a private source of information about the economy, sector or particular companies.

Tests of the strong form of market efficiency are intended to verify whether the most extreme claim of the efficient market hypothesis holds. This test is concerned with measuring the performance of professional fund managers and insider corporate traders to find out if they can consistently gain abnormal returns. Empirical results on the performance of professional fund managers show no significant consistency in abnormal returns in spite of the time and resources they have in managing their holdings. This provides support to the market efficiency hypothesis. But in the case of insider corporate traders, it is possible to show that this category of market participants can achieve above-average returns, and that contradicts the market efficiency hypothesis.

If the efficient market hypothesis holds in stock markets, then it is not possible to devise a profitable investment strategy based on either technical analysis or fundamental analysis. But, apart from the empirical evidence from the semi-strong form of market efficiency, tests of the weak and strong forms provide mixed results for the efficient market hypothesis. Furthermore, stock market analysts have discovered a number of anomalies that are present in the market and contradict the efficient market hypothesis. These anomalies include the January effect, referring to the fact that stock prices tend to increase during this month; the small firm effect, in which small size listed companies tend to consistently out-perform large size listed companies and the day of the week effect, in which share prices tend to perform badly on Mondays.

Fama (1991) asserts that the efficient market hypothesis cannot be tested by itself; rather it has to be tested jointly with an equilibrium model, such as the arbitrage pricing model. The reason for the joint-hypothesis test is that the efficient market hypothesis states that all public information has to be properly incorporated into asset prices; the word 'proper' needs to be defined in the context of an equilibrium model that defines the expected return in terms of risk factors.

7.3 The APT

The development of the arbitrage pricing theory followed a major breakthrough in the field of finance that started in 1952 when Harry Markowitz introduced portfolio theory in which he demonstrated how to select an optimal portfolio of listed shares. Markowitz (1952) shows that when investors diversify their portfolio holdings by purchasing shares that have either low or negative correlation between them, they can maximize their return and minimize their risk. William Sharpe, who was a student of Markowitz, then used this foundation of portfolio selection by Markowitz to develop the CAPM in 1964. During the 1960s Eugene Fama was fine-tuning the concept of EMH, which he introduced in 1970.

Ross (1976) developed the APT as an alternative method of analysing and measuring asset returns to the one offered by the CAPM. Both APT and CAPM are rooted in neoclassical economic theory which, in this context, stipulates that the expected returns on risky assets in a perfect competitive market should equal the returns on a risk-free asset plus a premium that compensates investors for holding such risky assets. Both theories describe the relationships between expected returns of financial assets and risk but the fundamental difference between them is that while the CAPM considers the market portfolio as the only factor in determining asset prices, APT allows for more than one factor to be a source of risk. The thrust of both APT and CAPM is that only systematic variation is responsible for the expected returns of financial assets and that non-systematic variation can be diversified away in large efficient portfolios. Each theory rests on different assumptions and uses a different technique to measure such relationships. Fama (1991) argues that, 'the multi-factor asset-pricing models of Ross (1976) are rich and more flexible than their competitors; i.e. the CAPM' (p. 1590).

The fundamental assumption of the APT is based on the law of one price, which states that in an equilibrium market the price of two assets that have the same risk must be equal, otherwise an arbitrage opportunity will arise to take advantage of such disequilibrium in prices at no risk and without having to invest any capital. Thus, the theory assumes that the law of one price must hold in an equilibrium market because rational investors are expected to eliminate the possibility of arbitrage opportunity. In other words, a no arbitrage condition is essential for the theory to hold. The APT starts by stating a linear relationship between asset returns and a set of common factors that enter the return generating process of a multi-factor model, as in equation (7.2):

$$R_i = E(r_i) + b_{i1}F_1 + \ldots + b_{ij}F_j + \varepsilon_i \;;\quad (i=1, 2, \ldots, n) \tag{7.2}$$

where:

R_i is the current returns on asset i;
$E(r_i)$ is the expected returns on asset i;
F_j is the value of the jth factor that influences returns on asset i;
b_{ij} is the sensitivity of asset i to factor j;
ε_i is the random error term with usual assumptions.

The expected values of the common factors in the return generating process are equal to zero because they measure the unexpected changes or surprises due to new information about these factors, rather than their levels. By definition, new information has zero expected value. Furthermore, the common factors are assumed to be uncorrelated with each other.[1] The random error, in equation (7.2), represents the asset specific return, which also has zero expected value, and Ross (1976) assumes no correlation between the residuals of different assets; i.e., $E(\varepsilon_i\varepsilon_j) = 0$ $(i \neq j)$. The expected return $E(r_i)$ and the coefficients of regression (b_{ij}) terms are ex ante specification, and the ex post terms are R_i and F_j in the above return generation process.[2] In a well-diversified portfolio, the random error will approach zero as the number of shares increases based on the law of large numbers. The above equation indicates that the returns on asset i are subject to two sources of risk: a source of risk that is common to all assets in an economy, which will be called 'systematic risk', and a source that is specific to a particular asset or group of assets in an industry, which will be called 'idiosyncratic' or 'unsystematic' risk, represented by the random error term (ε_i). The APT assumes that the number of assets, n, must be larger than the number of common factors, j. Because of the assumption that the idiosyncratic residual term is not correlated with the common factors, this version of APT became known as the strict factor structure of returns.

Invoking the law of large numbers in a well-diversified portfolio means that the idiosyncratic risk is eliminated, and the condition of no arbitrage, which states that a portfolio that uses no wealth and has no risk earns no returns, implies that only systematic factors command a risk premium. Since investors are concerned about expected return and risk, the only important terms, in equation (7.2), are the $E(r_i)$ and b_{ij}s. Ross (1976) then introduces the APT model, as in model (7.3), which approximates the expected returns of risky assets based on their sensitivities to common factors:

$$E(r_i) \approx \lambda_0 + \lambda_1 b_{i1} + \ldots\ldots\ldots + \lambda_j b_{ij} \tag{7.3}$$

where:

λ_0 is the risk-free rates of returns;
λ_j is the price of risk associated with F_j.

The sensitivities of asset returns to common factors (b_{ij}), which represent risk exposure, are different for each asset. Some assets tend to have high exposure to particular factors and less exposure to other factors. But the prices of risk (λ_j) for each factor are the same for all assets. Sometimes, the prices of risk for some factors are equal to zero, which means that these factors are not perceived to be significant in determining asset returns. The APT's main intuition, from equation (7.3), is that the expected returns on financial assets are only determined by changes in systematic factors. It assumes homogeneity of expectation, which means that all investors are expected to agree on the number and the nature of common factors that are significant in determining the expected returns of financial assets. Harrington (1987) remarks that 'the APT is not only an ex ante, expectational model; just like the CAPM, the model can be written in ex post, realized terms' (p. 190). The theory provides a framework for identifying the existence of common factors which enter the return generating process and measuring their prices, but it is completely silent about the type and number of common factors which enter the return generating process of equation (7.2). Also, the APT does not specify the magnitude or the sign of the prices of risk (λ_j) terms, which makes it very hard to interpret, whereas the CAPM states that betas have positive correlation with the market portfolio.

The fact that the APT does not specify the number or type of systematic factors that enter the return generating process of the multi-factor model and does not indicate the magnitude or the sign of the prices of risk, makes it very difficult to apply and interpret its results. Since the theory was introduced in 1976, there have been two distinguishing approaches in applying empirical tests. The first case uses the factor analysis approach to extract the number of common factors that enter the return generating process either by using the maximum likelihood method or by using the principal components method. The second approach uses observed economic and financial variables to determine asset returns. In this case, we have a joint test of the APT model and the relevancy of the observed variables. Figure 7.1 illustrates the development of these two approaches in testing the APT model.

Factor analysis refers to statistical techniques that are used in estimating simultaneously the number of common factors and their coefficients, which are known in factor analysis terminology as 'factor loadings'. The underlying assumption of factor analysis is that the observed correlation between two or more financial assets is mainly due to a few common factors that are responsible for their co-movement. It simply relies on using asset returns to explain asset returns.

In spite of the fact that exploratory factor analysis is an elaborate and time-consuming process, it has been extensively utilized in testing the validity of APT during the 1980s. This method has been mainly applied in the US market because it requires a large sample size of listed shares over a long period of time. There have been a number of strong criticisms of using factor analysis in testing the APT. For example, Beenstock and Chan (1988) remark that 'although the APT has been exclusively tested using factor analysis, it hardly provides a satisfactory basis for empirical enquiry' (p. 27). The fact that this method does not provide any economic intuition into asset returns has led to a gradual shift in emphasis from using factor analysis in favour of using observed economic and financial variables.

Burmeister and McElroy (1988) state that:

> both the factor-analysis approach and the measured-macroeconomic factor approach have their merits. The primary advantages of using measured economic factors are: (1) the factors and their APT prices in principle can be given economic interpretations, while with a factor-analysis approach it is unknown what factors are being priced; and (2) rather than using only asset prices to explain asset prices, measured macroeconomic factors introduce additional information, linking asset-price behaviour to macroeconomic events. (p. 721)

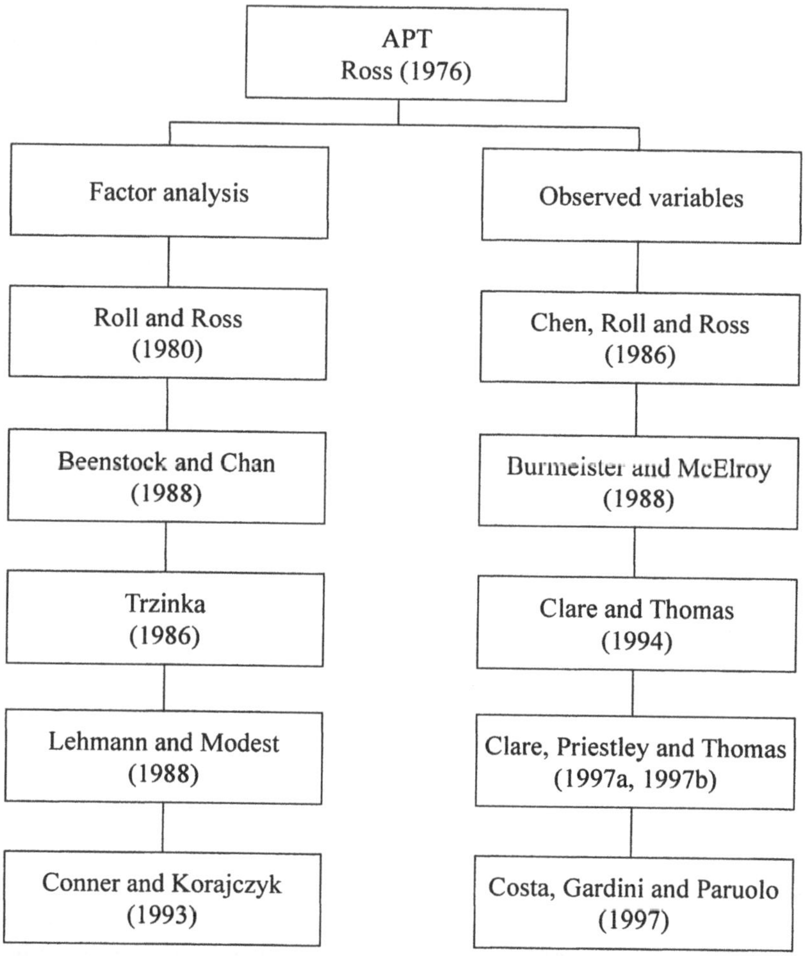

Figure 7.1 Methods of testing the arbitrage pricing theory

A number of empirical studies of the APT model using observed variables have been applied outside the US market, but these were mainly in developed financial markets, such as Europe and Japan.

Fama (1991) states that:

> the Chen, Roll and Ross approach (identifying economic factors that are correlated with returns and testing whether the factor loadings explain the cross-section of expected returns) is probably the most fruitful way to use multifactor models to improve our understanding of asset-pricing. (p. 1595)

7.3.1 *Factor Analysis Approach in Testing the APT*

Ross (1976) assumed that APT follows a strict factor structure, which means that the idiosyncratic risk is zero and only the systematic risk factors are important in determining asset returns. In other words, the residual returns of listed shares are assumed to be strictly uncorrelated among themselves and their covariance matrix is assumed to be diagonal. As a result, Roll and Ross (1980) used the maximum likelihood method in extracting the number of common factors. But Chamberlain and Rothschild (1983) proved that if Ross's strict factor structure assumption is relaxed and the residual returns can be weakly correlated with the latent factors, the same results can be achieved as in the strict factor structure assumption. This paved the way for Trzcinka (1986) to use approximate factor structure rather than strict factor structure in testing the APT. Table 7.1 presents a summary of the use of factor analysis in testing the APT.

Table 7.1 Factor analysis approach in testing the APT model

Articles	Methods	Market	Date frequencies
Roll and Ross (1980)	Maximum likelihood	US	Daily
Beenstock and Chan (1986)	Maximum likelihood	UK	Monthly
Trzcinka (1986)	Principal components	US	Weekly
Lehmann and Modest (1988)	Maximum likelihood	US	Weekly
Connor and Korajczyk (1993)	Principal components	US	Monthly

The classic article by Roll and Ross (1980) set the stage for empirical testing of the APT by investigating the existence of common factors, and then estimating their prices using the strict returns factor structure of the theory. They applied the maximum likelihood method of factor analysis to extract the number of common factors which entered the return generating process by analyzing daily returns of 1,260 listed shares in the US market during the period from 3 July 1962 to 31 December 1972, and divided them into 42 groups of 30 shares each, based on their alphabetical order. While the authors acknowledged that the sample size of 30 shares per group is a small size and the ideal size would be to include all the listed shares in their sample, they were constrained by computer processing capacity, which could not handle a larger sample size than the one they used to test the theory. Roll and Ross used a two-step procedure for testing the APT empirically. The first step involves using time series analysis to estimate the number of common factors and their coefficients (factor loadings), while the second step involves using cross-sectional analysis to estimate the risk premiums or factor prices. They pointed out that the two-step procedure would usually lead to having error-in-variables problems because of the correlation between the error term and the factor loadings when applying cross-section regression.

The Roll and Ross (1980) analysis started by constructing covariance matrices from the time series of returns for each of the 42 groups. Then, they used the maximum-likelihood method of factor analysis to extract a number of common factors, and a matrix of factor loadings for each group using their covariance matrices of returns. The objective of this step is to find out the minimum number of common factors that have the highest likelihood of explaining satisfactorily the observed correlation between listed shares in each group. This method starts by hypothesizing the presence of a number of common factors, k, which are normally much smaller than the sample size, in this case 30 listed shares per group. The maximum likelihood method of extraction uses the chi-square statistic to test the significance of the computed common factors in explaining the observed correlation between listed shares in different groups. Normally, exploratory data analysis starts from assuming one common factor and increases the number of factors until the variation between those factors and the observed variables is insignificant. In the case of the maximum likelihood method of exploratory data analysis, the chi-square test of significance is used to indicate if there is a large deviation between the common factors and the observed variables. For example, if one common factor model is hypothesized and the chi-square test indicates that the variation is significant between the one common factor and the observed variables, then we increase the hypothesized common factors to two and repeat the chi-square test until the variation becomes insignificant.

The authors then solved the first likelihood function value, which is conditional on the covariance matrix of returns that was generated by the exact number of the hypothesized factors. The second value of the likelihood function is found, also conditional on the observed covariance matrix of the sample. Then a likelihood ratio was found by dividing the first likelihood value by the second one and this ratio is used as a test for identifying the number of common factors that enter the return generating process of the APT. Further, the factor loadings for each of the listed shares within each group are estimated and used in cross-sectional regression to explain the variation in the expected return of each listed share in every group. This leads to the estimation of the magnitudes or prices of factors that are associated with the common factors, which have been estimated earlier. Finally, a cross-sectional regression method is used to estimate the risk premium or factor price of each of the statistically significant factors in the APT model.

Roll and Ross (1980) find that three and probably four common factors are significantly priced and the intercept term is constant across all 42 groups, which means that the theory is testable. They point out one main drawback of factor analysis, which is that it does not reveal whether the four common factors that are priced for the first group are the same for all other groups or if they are different for each group. They also explained that while the APT is based on the fact that only systematic risk factors are important in explaining expected returns on financial assets proving that the theory is testable, having significant non-systematic factors in the APT model would indicate that the theory might not hold. Finally, Roll and Ross tested the consistency of the intercept (λ_0) in equation (7.3) among different groups and found that it is consistent, which implies that their empirical results are supportive of the theory.

Shanken (1982) questioned the appropriateness of using the factor analysis method to extract the number of common factors that enter the return generated process from a small unrepresentative sample of assets, as in the study of Roll and Ross (1980). The reason for that, according to Shanken, is that factor analysis is a statistical tool which is only concerned with measuring the covariation between different assets and cannot account for economic forces that could be more relevant to asset returns in multi-index models. He concludes by stating that when using factor analysis for an unrepresentative set of portfolios 'the factor model can be manipulated rather arbitrarily by repackaging a given set of securities. A new set of returns and a corresponding factor model can be produced, with virtually any pre-specified random variables as the factors' (p. 1137). Based on the conclusion of Shanken (1982), Chen (1983) used daily returns for the period from 1963 to 1978, which was divided into four sub-periods of four years each. The first sub-period used 1,064 shares, the second used 1,522 shares, the third 2,580 shares and the fourth 1,378 shares. Each group used 180 shares instead of the 30 shares per group which was used by Roll and Ross (1980). Chen uses the maximum likelihood method of factor analysis to extract the number of common factors that enter the return generating process. He finds that there are five significantly priced common factors. He stresses the importance of having an economic interpretation for the common factors and predicts that future research on the empirical application of the APT will focus on this direction.

In the UK stock market, Beenstock and Chan (1986) test the APT using monthly data in the period from December 1961 to December 1981 for 220 listed companies. They divided the sample size into three groups, each with 80 listed shares, and using the maximum likelihood method to extract the number of common factors which enter the return generating process. The authors found that there were 11 significantly priced factors for the data they used.

A controversy was started by Dhrymes, Friend and Gultekin (1984), who questioned the robustness of the empirical methodology of Roll and Ross (1980) and Chen (1983) in testing the APT using the maximum likelihood method of factor analysis. They demonstrated that the number of common factors increased in proportion to the number of shares in a group. For example, when the number of shares increased from 15 to 30 shares per group, the number of common factors increased from two to three, and with a group of 90 shares the number increased to nine common factors. This leads to two main implications in their conclusions, which are: first, the sample size of the groups used by Roll and Ross is small, and second, the factor analysis method is not an appropriate tool in defining the number of common factors in the case of asset returns. Furthermore, Dhrymes, Friend, Gultekin and Gultekin (1985) add that not only are the number of factors dependent on the sample size in groups, but also on the number of observations. As the number of observations increases, the number of common factors increases in proportion. Raveh (1985) endorses the finding of Dhrymes et al. (1985) with regard to using factor analysis in empirical testing of the APT. He draws on the experience of using factor analysis in the field of psychology – which finds that the number of common factors tends to increase proportionally to the increase in the sample size, that is, the number of common factors are not stable.

Caution is recommended by Lehmann and Modest (1988) with regard to drawing inferences from using the maximum likelihood method of factor analysis on a small sample of data as in the case of Roll and Ross (1980). They state that using a small sample – by dividing the whole sample of listed shares into small groups – will lead to inexact estimations of common factors in factor analysis. The authors use weekly data for the US stock market in the period from 1963 to 1982 – which is divided into four periods of five years each – in order to test the APT. There are 1001 listed shares in the first period, 1,359 shares in the second, 1,346 shares in the third and 1,263 shares in the fourth period. They conclude by stating that when applying the maximum likelihood method for large sample size, it is possible to show that the APT provides a better measure of returns than does the CAPM.

The maximum likelihood method of factor analysis, which has been introduced above, assumes strict factor structure of the residuals, but Chamberlain and Rothschild (1983) introduced an alternative method to extract common factors, based on approximate factor structure in which the residuals are allowed to vary. Trzcinka (1986) uses the approximate factor structure in what has become known as the principal components method to extract the number of common factors. He uses weekly data of 865 listed shares returns in the US market for 20 years to analyze eigenvalues, and chi-square tests, which leads the author to conclude that there is at least one common factor that enters the return generating process. Furthermore, Connor and Korajczyk (1993) test the APT using the principal component method to estimate the number of common factors and their prices. The authors used monthly data of listed share returns in the US market in the period from 1967 to 1991 which is divided into five-year sub-periods: 1967–71 has 1,647 listed shares; 1972–76 has 1,796 listed shares; 1977–81 has 1,869 listed shares; 1982–86 has 1,651 listed shares and 1987–91 has 1,626 listed shares. Also, the authors use the monthly returns on US Treasury bills for the risk-free rates of return. Connor and Korajczyk find evidence that there are between three and six common factors that generate returns in listed shares.

Shukla and Trzcinka (1990) test the APT using both the maximum likelihood method of factor analysis and the principal components method for weekly data of 20 years in the US market. They compared the results of these two methods and conclude that in their case the principle components approach was better in estimating common factors and their prices than the maximum likelihood approach, but state that this cannot be generalized for all cases. The authors point out that there are some cases where the maximum likelihood method would be superior.

In spite of the fact that exploratory factor analysis is an elaborate and time-consuming process, it has been extensively utilized in testing the validity of APT during the 1980s. This method has been mainly applied in the US market because it requires a large sample size of listed shares over a long period of time. There have been a number of strong criticisms of using factor analysis in testing the APT. For example, Beenstock and Chan (1988) remark that 'although the APT has been exclusively tested using factor analysis, it hardly provides a satisfactory basis for empirical enquiry' (p. 27). The fact that this method does not provide any economic intuition with respect to asset returns has led to a gradual shift in emphasis from using factor analysis in favour of using observed economic and financial variables, which will be the focus of the next subsection on testing the APT.

7.3.2 Observed Variables Approach in Testing the APT

Using pre-specified economic and financial variables in the return generating process of the APT model instead of the factor analysis approach in testing the APT started to gain popularity in the late 1980s and 1990s. This approach is based on using the efficient market hypothesis model of asset prices, which states that asset prices are determined by future expected discounted dividend payments. Therefore, observed economic and financial variables that influence changes in either expected cash flows and/or discount rates can be considered as a source of systematic risk. In this approach, we are testing the APT model and the relevance of the observed variables jointly.

There are three main aspects of testing the APT model using observed variables, namely, determining the number and type of economic and financial variables that are considered as common factors, generating the unexpected changes in the observed variables and estimating the prices of risk for each of those observed variables. These three aspects will be discussed in detail in the next three subsections.

7.3.2.1 Identifying observed variables Even though Chen (1983) points out the importance of having an economic interpretation of the common factors, the first article to use observed economic and financial variables as common factors was written by Chen, Roll and Ross (1986). The authors used the following basic variables:

1 return on one-month US Treasury bill;
2 return on long-term government bonds;
3 return on corporate low-grade bonds;
4 industrial production;
5 consumer price index;
6 equally weighted stock index;
7 value-weighted stock index;
8 real per capita consumption;
9 oil prices.

The returns on the one-month Treasury bill are considered as the risk-free interest rate. Chen et al. (1986) then introduce two new series from the above list of observed variables. The first series is the term structure of interest rates which is taken as the difference between the end of the month return on long-term government bonds and the return on one-month Treasury bills.

This new interest rate variable is intended to capture the effect of changes in risk aversion. When the term structure rate is positive, it means that the price of long-term bonds is increasing and the yield is decreasing. The second series is the risk premium, which is taken as the difference between the end of the month return on the long-term government bonds and the return on low grade corporate bonds. Using the risk premium term is intended to capture the level of risk implicit in listed share prices. Furthermore, Chen et al. (1986) use the annual industrial production rate because, as they point out, monthly returns on listed shares are less likely to have a high correlation with the contemporaneous monthly rate of industrial production, but share prices are more likely to respond to expected forward changes in industrial production. The use of the two stock market indexes is intended to capture other sources of systemic risks that are not captured by the above list of observed variables during a contemporaneous month. Again, recall that share prices are assumed to be highly efficient in factoring public available information.

In the Japanese stock market, Hamao (1988) applied the APT model using nine observed variables, which are:

1 return on three month Japanese Gensaki rate;[3]
2 return on 10 year government bonds;
3 return on 10 year electricity company bonds;
4 industrial production;
5 inflation;
6 exchange rate (yen/dollar);
7 return on the value-weighted Tokyo Stock Exchange;
8 return on the equally-weighted Tokyo Stock Exchange;
9 oil prices.

The term structure of the interest rate in Japan is taken as the difference between the monthly returns on ten-year government bonds and the returns on the three-month Gensaki rate, because there is no equivalent monthly return on the Japanese Treasury bills. Further, the risk premium is calculated as the difference in monthly returns on ten-year government bonds and ten-year electricity bonds, since there were no data available on the low-grade corporate bonds in Japan at the time of the study.

There are three main empirical studies that test the APT model in the United Kingdom stock market. The first one is by Beenstock and Chan (1988), who use the following 11 observed variables:

1 return on three-month UK Treasury bill;
2 money supply (M3);
3 the fuel and material cost index for manufacturing industry;
4 the UK general index of retail prices;
5 the UK general index of wages;
6 industrial stoppage (measured in terms of total working days lost);
7 UK exports volume index;
8 UK retail volume index;
9 UK relative export price;
10 UK GDP;
11 total OECD production.

All the above list of observed variables are a monthly time series except the last three, which are quarterly. The list of observed variables in this study, for the UK stock market, differs in two ways from the first two studies. It does not include any measure of the term structure of interest rates and the risk premium variables which are both found to be statistically significant in the US and Japanese markets, and it uses three quarterly data time series instead of the all monthly series that have been used before. The second study, in the UK stock market, is by Clare and Thomas (1994), who use the following list of observed variables:

1 return on three-month UK Treasury bill;
2 return on long-term government bonds;
3 return on short-term government bonds;
4 debenture and loan redemption yield;
5 price of gold;
6 real retail sales;
7 industrial output;
8 current account balance;
9 oil prices;
10 retail price index;
11 dividend yield;
12 unemployment;
13 money supply;
14 exchange rate ($/£);
15 stock market turnover;
16 comfort index;[4]
17 private sector bank lending;

18 excess return on the FT-all share price index.

The above 18 observed variables are all monthly time series data. The authors of this study use the term structure of interest rates and the risk premium as systematic variables that enter the return generating process model, which is similar to the Chen et al. (1986) study. Chen et al. (1986), Beenstock and Chan (1988), and Hamao (1988) have used two measures of stock market indices as systematic factors in determining listed share returns, but none of the mentioned articles have found them to be statistically significant. This has led some researchers to exclude them as part of the observed systematic variables. For example, Clare and Thomas (1994) argue, 'we feel that the inclusion of a market index per se is inappropriate given our interest in identifying key economic factors which are priced in securities markets' (p. 312).

The third study in the UK stock market is by Priestley (1996), who uses ten observed variables that are found to be significant in pricing listed shares by Chen et al. (1986) in the US stock market, and Beenstock and Chan (1988), and Clare and Thomas (1994) in the UK stock market. Even though the above three studies are done in the UK stock market, the list of observed variables is not the same in each case. This demonstrates that the type of observed variables and their numbers do not have to be the same in a particular stock market, like the London Stock Exchange.

The fourth developed stock market where the APT model has been tested is the Milan Stock Exchange in Italy tested by Costa, Gardini and Paruolo (1997), who use ten basic observed variables which are:

1 return on three-month Italian Treasury bills;
2 return on long-term government bonds;
3 discount rate;
4 inflation rate;
5 industrial production index;
6 US dollar–Italian lira exchange rate;
7 Deutsche mark–lira exchange rate;
8 money supply (M2);
9 Milan Stock Exchange index;
10 oil prices.

The authors did not explicitly mention in their article if they used the term structure of interest rates, even though it is highly likely that they did. But from the list of observed variables, it is clear that there is no indication of having any systematic variable for the risk premium variable. The two exchange rates reflect the major trading partners with Italy.

Finally, the only study (which we are aware of) that tests the APT model in a developing stock market using observed variables was written by Vipul and Gianchandani (1997) for the Bombay Stock Exchange in India. The authors use weekly time series data for five observed variables as common factors, which are:

1 wholesale price index;
2 dollar–rupee exchange rate;
3 call money rate;
4 prices of gold;
5 Bombay Stock Exchange national price index.

This data frequency represents the exception to the normal monthly frequency that other researchers like Chen et al. (1986), Clare and Thomas (1994) and Costa et al. (1997) use in testing the APT model, using observed variables. Also, there are no observed variables for the term structure of interest rate and the risk premium. Table 7.2 presents a comparative summary of the articles that use observed variables in testing the APT model.

It is clear from Table 7.2 that there is no consistency in the number or type of economic and financial variables that are used as common factors in the return generating process of the APT model. Each country tends to have specific variables that are considered to be significant in determining asset prices.

Table 7.2 Summary of the number of observed variables used in testing the APT model

Articles	Number of variables	Markets
Chen, Roll and Ross (1986)	9	US
Hamao (1988)	9	Japan
Beenstock and Chan (1988)	11	UK
Clare and Thomas (1994)	18	UK
Priestley (1996)	10	UK
Costa, Gardini and Paruolo (1997)	10	Italy
Vipul and Gianchandani (1997)	5	India

7.3.2.2 Generating innovation terms After determining a set of observed economic and financial variables which will be considered as common factors in the return generating process of the APT model, the next step is to generate the unexpected changes, which are referred to as innovations, of these observed variables. This second aspect of testing the APT model is considered as a critical step. Priestley (1996) pointed out that when testing the APT using observed variables, it is important to have a reliable method of measuring the innovations or surprises. These innovations should meet two statistical conditions, firstly, to form a stationary time series with zero mean and constant variance and secondly, to be serially uncorrelated. There are three main approaches in measuring the innovations of the observed variables, which are: rate of change models, autoregressive models and vector autoregressive models.

The rate of change model of generating innovations for the observed variables was first introduced by Chen, Roll and Ross (1986) and subsequently used by Hamao (1988) and Beenstock and Chan (1988), among others. This approach is based on taking the first difference of the observed variables as an innovation, but the major drawback of this model is that most of the time series data is serially correlated and therefore one of the statistical conditions of the innovation term is violated.

To avoid the problem of serial correlation in innovation terms of the observed variable, Clare and Thomas (1994) introduced single equation autoregressive models as an alternative approach to the rate of change model. The authors use an unrestricted autoregressive model with 12 lags for monthly data that has stationary observed variables. They then drop the lags that are not statistically significant and test the restriction, using either the likelihood ratio or the F-statistic indicator. The residuals from restricted autoregressive models are then used as innovation terms of the observed variables.

The reason for using autoregressive models is to eliminate any serial correlation in the residual terms. The innovation terms from the restricted autoregressive models are then used as regressors in the return generating process of the APT model. This approach was later used by Clare, Priestley and Thomas (1997) to generate the innovation terms for the observed variables.

Priestley (1996) compares three methods of generating innovation terms from observed variables and their effect on estimating the risk premiums of systematic variables. These three methods of generating innovation terms are the rate of change model, the autoregressive model and the Kalman filter technique. Priestley criticizes the rate of change model on the basis that it fails to meet the condition of being serially uncorrelated. With regard to the autoregressive method which is used by Clare and Thomas (1994) in generating the innovation terms, Priestley finds that this method satisfies the two statistical conditions, but he points out that the parameters in the model are not stable. He shows that the innovation terms generated by the Kalman filter technique are better than the other two methods in estimating the risk premiums of the observed variables.

A different method of estimating innovations in observed variables from the one used in previous studies is the vector autoregressive model, which uses the residuals as innovations. This method was first pointed out by Chen, Roll and Ross (1986) as a possible alternative to the single equation model but they did not apply it in their article. A recent study by Costa, Gardini and Paruolo (1997) used this new approach in testing the APT. Table 7.3 shows a summary of the different methods of estimating the unexpected changes in the observed variables.

While the rate of change model approach of generating the unexpected changes in the observed variables has been deemed to be inappropriate due to the problem of serial correlation, the Kalman filter approach would be necessary only if the parameters were shown to be unstable.

Table 7.3 Methods of generating innovations terms from observed variables

Articles	Methods
Chen, Roll and Ross (1986)	Rate of change model
Hamao (1988)	Rate of change model
Beenstock and Chan (1988)	Rate of change model
Clare and Thomas (1994)	Autoregressive model
Priestley (1996)	Kalman filter technique
Clare, Priestley and Thomas (1997)	Autoregressive model
Costa, Gardini and Paruolo (1997)	Vector autoregressive model
Vipul and Gianchandani (1997)	Unspecified

On the other hand, the autoregressive and vector autoregressive approaches are considered more appropriate in estimating the innovations of the observed variables, based on the literature review of the above empirical studies. The choice between these two methods is based on the statistical properties of the innovation terms from each method.

7.3.2.3 Estimating the risk premiums Following the selection of the observed variables and generating their innovation terms, the third aspect of testing the APT model is measuring the risk premiums associated with these variables. There have been three different methods of measuring the risk premiums of the observed variables. The first one uses variance of the two-step method, the second uses the non-linear least square method and the last uses the reduced rank regression method of estimation.

Variance of the two-step method, which was introduced by Fama and MacBeth (1973), has been utilized by Chen et al. (1986) in estimating the risk premiums of the observed variables. In the first step, an ordinary least square method is used to regress the excess returns of listed share prices on the innovation terms of the observed variables. The estimated coefficients of regressions from the first step are then used as independent variables in cross-section regressions (which is the second step) to estimate the risk premiums of the observed variables. The estimated coefficients in the first step, which are used as regressors in the second step, are known to have an error-in-variable problem. To mitigate the error-in-variable problem in estimating the APT model, the authors group the listed shares on the New York Stock Exchange into 20 equally weighted portfolios, sorted by firm size, in the period from January 1953 to November 1983. Chen et al. (1986) find that the innovation terms of the term structure of interest rates, the market risk premium, the industrial production and the inflation rates are significantly priced. Other variables such as consumption and oil prices are insignificantly priced. Also, the two stock market indexes are insignificant in pricing listed shares. Furthermore, Hamao (1988) tests the APT model in the period from January 1975 to December 1984 and finds that only three variables are priced in the Japanese stock market. These three variables are the term structure of interest rates, the market risk premium and the inflation rate. Beenstock and Chan (1988) also find three variables that are significantly priced in the UK stock market in the period from October 1977 to December 1983. These variables are the interest rate, money supply and inflation rate. The two-step method is also used by Vipul and Gianchandani (1997), who find that there are no significantly priced observed variables in the Bombay Stock Exchange of India during the period from 11 January 1991 to 30 July 1993.

Clare and Thomas (1994) point out that the number of significantly priced observed variables tends to be different depending on the method used in sorting the portfolios of listed shares. To prove their point, the authors used 840 listed shares on the London Stock Exchange in the period from January 1973 to December 1990 and formed 56 portfolios. Each portfolio consisted of 15 equally weighted shares which were first sorted based on their market betas, and then on their size. The authors justified using portfolios rather than individual returns of listed firms in order to 'eliminate diversifiable risk and to reduce the well-known errors-in-variables problem' (p. 317). The portfolios are used as the dependent variables in the two-step procedure of estimating the prices of risk associated with the observed variables. When portfolios are sorted according to their market betas, the authors find that six observed variables are priced. Those priced variables are oil prices, two measures of market risk, the retail price index, UK private sector bank lending and the current account balance. Clare and Thomas also find that the market returns index is insignificantly priced when economic variables are included in the estimation, whereas in the second method of sorting portfolios according to listed share sizes they find that only the stock market return price index is significantly priced.

Even though in the two-step method of estimating the prices of risk that are associated with the observed variables has been used by a number of researchers like Beenstock and Chan (1988), Hamao (1988), Clare and Thomas (1994) and Vipul and Gianchandani (1997), the major drawback of this method is having an error-in-variable problem. To overcome this problem some researchers have suggested forming portfolios of shares. But the criteria of forming portfolios – for example, when using market beta or firm size – tend to influence the estimates of risk premiums. As a result, McElroy, Burmeister and Wall (1985), and Burmeister and McElroy (1988) demonstrate that the APT model can be solved in one step instead of the common two-step approach. They showed that the APT model can be expressed as a system of nonlinear equations, which has a number of advantages over the two-step method. The main advantages of the one-step method is that it overcomes the error-in-variable problem and provides an easy way to test the cross-section restrictions in which the risk premiums are all the same. This method was applied by Priestley (1996) and Clare, Priestley and Thomas (1997), using the non-linear three-stage least square method of estimation in the UK market.

The third method of estimating the risk premiums associated with the observed variables is introduced by Costa, Gardini and Paruolo (1997) who tested the APT using the reduced rank regression approach for the Milan Stock Exchange. They acknowledge the problem of using factor analysis in extracting the number of common factors, in line with the conclusion of Dhrymes et al. (1985). The authors state that the reduced rank regression method unifies the two different approaches of testing the APT; namely the factor analysis and the observed variables. Monthly return data of 37 listed companies in the Milan Stock Exchange during the period from December 1979 to December 1991 are used by Costa et al. (1997) to apply the reduced rank regression method. They concluded that more than four latent factors are priced, but only one observed variable is significantly priced. They attributed having fewer observed variables than latent factors to the possibility of orthogonality between the two types of factors. Table 7.4 shows the different methods used in estimating the risk premiums of the observed variables. We have presented the arguments above which show that the two-step method is inappropriate due to the error-in-variable problem. The other two methods have been applied satisfactorily in a number of empirical studies.

Table 7.4 Methods of estimating the risk premiums of the observed variables

Articles	Methods
Chen, Roll and Ross (1986)	Two-step linear regression
Hamao (1988)	Two-step linear regression
Beenstock and Chan (1988)	Two-step linear regression
Burmeister and McElroy (1988)	Non-linear three-stage least square
Clare and Thomas (1994)	Two-step linear regression
Priestley (1996)	Non-linear three-stage least square
Clare, Priestley and Thomas (1997)	Non-linear three-stage least square
Costa, Gardini and Paruolo (1997)	Reduced rank regression
Vipul and Gianchandani (1997)	Two-step linear regression

It is important to point out at this stage that the only study which is applied in a developing stock market (by Vipul and Gianchandani, 1997) is clearly out of touch with the development in the APT literature for the following reasons: firstly, it has not specified the approach used in generating the innovation terms of the observed variables in spite of the importance of this aspect in testing the APT model; secondly, it has used the two-step method in estimating the risk premiums of the observed variables in spite of the shortcomings of this method (which were presented above). As a result, it is possible to question the significance of this study in relation to the on-going research into empirical application of the APT model.

Ferson and Harvey (1993, 1994) test the significance of the following observed variables for a group of 18 countries: term structure of interest rates;

real interest rate; two measures of inflation; industrial production; oil prices; exchange rate risk and Morgan Stanley Capital International (MSCI) world stock market price index. They use the domestic capital asset pricing model of Sharpe (1964) and Lintner (1965), which they refer to as the global asset-pricing model. The authors find that only the MSCI index and the exchange rate risk are statistically significant in determining global asset prices. Furthermore, Ferson and Harvey (1998) point out that domestic factors drive out international factors. While the above mentioned articles of Ferson and Harvey apply the global asset-pricing model in the spirit of the CAPM, our focus in this study will be on using the APT model.

7.4 Concluding Remarks

The efficient market hypothesis, which was introduced by Fama (1970), is an important assumption in asset pricing models – which include the CAPM and the APT. According to the efficient market hypothesis, the prices of listed shares are very efficient in factoring in publicly available information.

The arbitrage pricing theory of Ross (1976) offers an attractive alternative in risk management of holding risky assets. Because the APT does not specify the type of factors that enter the return generation process, scholars use two different approaches in testing the theory. The first approach is based on factor analysis and the second is based on using observed economic and financial variables. Most of the empirical studies that use factor analysis have been primarily applied in the US market (with only a few exceptions) because of the need to have a large sample size and a long period of time series for asset returns in order to carry out any significant testing. In contrast to that, empirical studies of testing the APT model based on using observed variables has gained popularity, especially in the 1990s (see Burmeister and McElroy (1988, p. 721). A number of empirical studies of the APT model using observed variables have been applied outside the US market, but these were mainly in developed financial markets, such as Europe and Japan.

There are four key articles that have contributed significantly to the development of empirical testing of the APT model using the observed variables approach. The first is the article by Chen, Roll and Ross (1986), in which they use the rate of change model in generating the innovation terms of the observed variables, and apply the two-step method in estimating the risk premiums. The second article is by Burmeister and McElroy (1988), who introduced the one-step method of estimating the risk premiums instead of the two-step method. This one-step method involves solving a system of equations using the non-linear three-stage least square method of regression to estimate the risk premiums. The third article is by Clare and Thomas (1994), who introduced an alternative approach to generate the innovation terms using the autoregressive model instead of the rate of change model. Finally, the fourth article is by Costa, Gardini and Paruolo (1997), who use two different approaches in generating the innovation terms using the VAR model and in estimating the risk premiums using the reduced rank method of regression.

We are only aware of one study (published in 1997) which applied the APT model in a developing stock market, but this study is outdated in its approach. Therefore, it is possible to state that there is a gap in the literature that exists for testing the APT model in developing stock markets.

Notes

1 Having uncorrelated or independent factors leads to estimating asset returns by adding the contribution of each factor to the total return of assets.

2 Fogler (1982) explains that 'ex ante models provide equations based on expectations, or anticipated events. Ex post models provide equations based upon historical sample results' (p. 22).

3 The Japanese Gensaki rate is the interest rate on bond transactions with repurchase agreements. This is used as the risk-free rate of return.

4 Clare and Thomas (1994) define the comfort index as 'the ratio of the consol to equity market dividend yield; i.e. the relative expensiveness of the gilt and equity markets' (p. 311).

Chapter 8

Model Selection in Testing the Arbitrage Pricing Theory

8.1 Introduction

As noticed in the previous chapter, the APT offers an interesting insight into risk management of financial investment in risky assets, such as listed shares in stock markets. The main objective of this chapter is to determine the observed economic and financial variables that command a risk premium in the United Kingdom, Norway, Mexico, Venezuela and Oman (which are net oil exporting countries) in the period from January 1992 to December 1999, using the arbitrage pricing theory model (see Al-Shanfari, 2001).

The rest of this chapter is divided into the following sections. Section 8.2 provides an overview of the data. Section 8.3 provides two types of models used in generating the innovation terms which enter the return generation process of the APT model. We will use, as innovation terms, the residuals from restricted autoregressive models and then the residuals from vector autoregressive models. Finally, a summary of important results will be presented in section 8.4.

8.2 The Data

The intuition of linking share prices to economic and financial variables is based on the capital market theory of asset prices, which states that asset prices are a function of expected cash flow and the discount rate. Consequently, any observed economic and financial variable that either determines the cash flow or the discount rate of listed shares would be a good candidate for a systematic factor in the APT framework, as stated in Chen, Roll and Ross (1986).

Empirical results of testing the APT model using observed economic and financial variables in Japan, the UK and USA markets have identified a number of variables that are significantly priced – like the term structure of interest rates, inflation, market risk premium, industrial production, money supply and commercial banks' lending to the private sector (see Chen, Roll and Ross, 1986; Hamao, 1988; Clare and Thomas, 1994; Priestley, 1996; and Clare, Priestley, and Thomas, 1997 among others). All published research that applies the APT model (which we are aware of) have been focused on a single country instead of a group of countries. Therefore, since we will be testing the APT model in the UK, Norway, Mexico, Venezuela and Oman – which are net oil exporting countries – the aim of this section is to identify the appropriate economic and financial variables that are expected to be sources of systematic risks in each of the five countries. The oil prices variable is common to all countries which are either major world oil producers or where oil sector activities dominate the economic activities. Another observed variable, which we will be considering as a source of systematic risk for Norway, Mexico, Venezuela and Oman, is the *Financial Times* and Standard & Poors (FT/S&P) world stock markets price index. This observed variable represents the degree of integration between national stock markets and the major world stock markets. The higher the degree of openness or integration of the national stock market in the world financial market, the greater the expected systematic risk of this variable. For the United Kingdom, we have considered the Standard & Poors (S&P) composite price index variable as a source of systematic risk, instead of the FT/S&P world stock market price index of which the London Stock Exchange makes up a sizable proportion.

In the UK stock market we will be using the following variables: the term structure of interest rates, oil prices, money supply, commercial banks' lending to the private sector, the retail price index and the industrial production index, in addition to the S&P composite price index as the seventh variable to reflect the increasing integration between the stock markets in the UK and USA. The term structure of interest rates variable for the UK is taken as the difference between the monthly yield on long-term government bonds and the yield on three-month Treasury bills. The oil prices data is measured in US dollars per barrel and is based on the UK Brent crude one-month forward prices. These same benchmark crude oil prices will be used for Norway, Mexico, Venezuela and Oman. The money supply is the end of period stock of M4 in billions of pounds sterling. The commercial banks' lending to the private sector variable is taken as the end of the month stock in billions of pounds sterling. The UK retail price index is taken as a measure of inflation at the end of the month. Since there is a one-month lag in the announcement of the inflation rates (that is, April inflation is announced in May, which means that share prices react to the April inflation announcement in May), we will adjust this series to reflect the time lag. This means that the April inflation rate will be used in May. The same adjustment is made to the oil prices. One-month forward prices of oil are normally available to the public, so, instead of using the contemporaneous oil prices with the share prices, we will be using the one-month forward oil prices. All the variables except the commercial banks' lending to the private sector are from Datastream database; the latter is from the IMF financial statistics database. The levels and the first differences of the seven observed variables for the UK market are shown in Figure 8.1.

After identifying the economic and financial variables, which are considered as systematic factors in determining the share prices of listed companies in the UK stock market, the next step is to determine their order of integration. The purpose of determining the order of integration for each variable is to use their stationary forms – discussed later on in the next section – in unrestricted autoregressive models to generate their innovation terms. It is now common when determining the order of integration or testing the stationarity of a time-series data to use Dickey-Fuller unit root tests, which are based on equations (8.1) and (8.2):

$$\Delta Z_t = \alpha_1 + \beta Z_{t-1} + u_t; \tag{8.1}$$

$$\Delta Z_t = \alpha_1 + \alpha_2 t + \beta Z_{t-1} + u_t. \tag{8.2}$$

The value of the t statistic for the β coefficient in the above equations is known as the τ (tau) statistic, which has critical values that have been computed by Dickey and Fuller based on Monte Carlo simulations. This τ test is known as a Dickey-Fuller (DF) statistic. When testing the null hypothesis ($H_0 : \beta = 0$) for non-stationary series in the above two equations, if the estimated absolute value of τ is greater than the DF absolute critical values at the 1 per cent, 5 per cent and 10 per cent level of significance, then we reject the null hypothesis of non-stationarity in favour of stationarity. But if it is less than the critical values, we can not reject the null hypothesis of non-stationarity. When the error term (u_t) is serially correlated, in any of the above two equations, then they are modified to remove the serial correlation in the error term by introducing an appropriate number of lagged variables for ΔZ_t, as in equations (8.3) and (8.4) – which are known as the Augmented Dickey-Fuller (ADF) test and have the same critical values as the Dickey-Fuller statistic:

$$\Delta Z_t = \alpha_1 + \beta Z_{t-1} + \sum_{i=1}^{k} \vartheta_i \Delta Z_{t-i} + \delta_t; \tag{8.3}$$

$$\Delta Z_t = \alpha_1 + \alpha_2 t + \beta Z_{t-1} + \sum_{i=1}^{k} \vartheta_i \Delta Z_{t-i} + \delta_t. \tag{8.4}$$

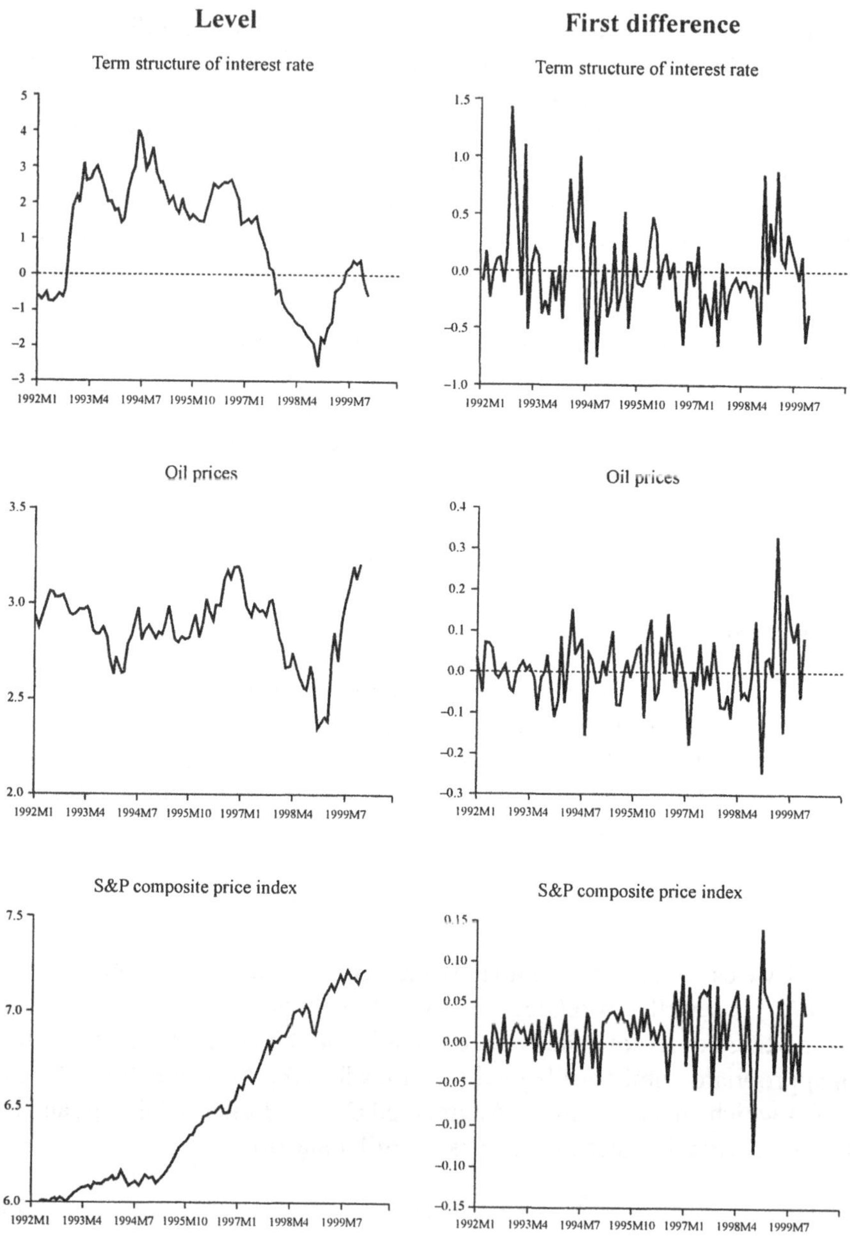

Figure 8.1 The observed variables for the UK

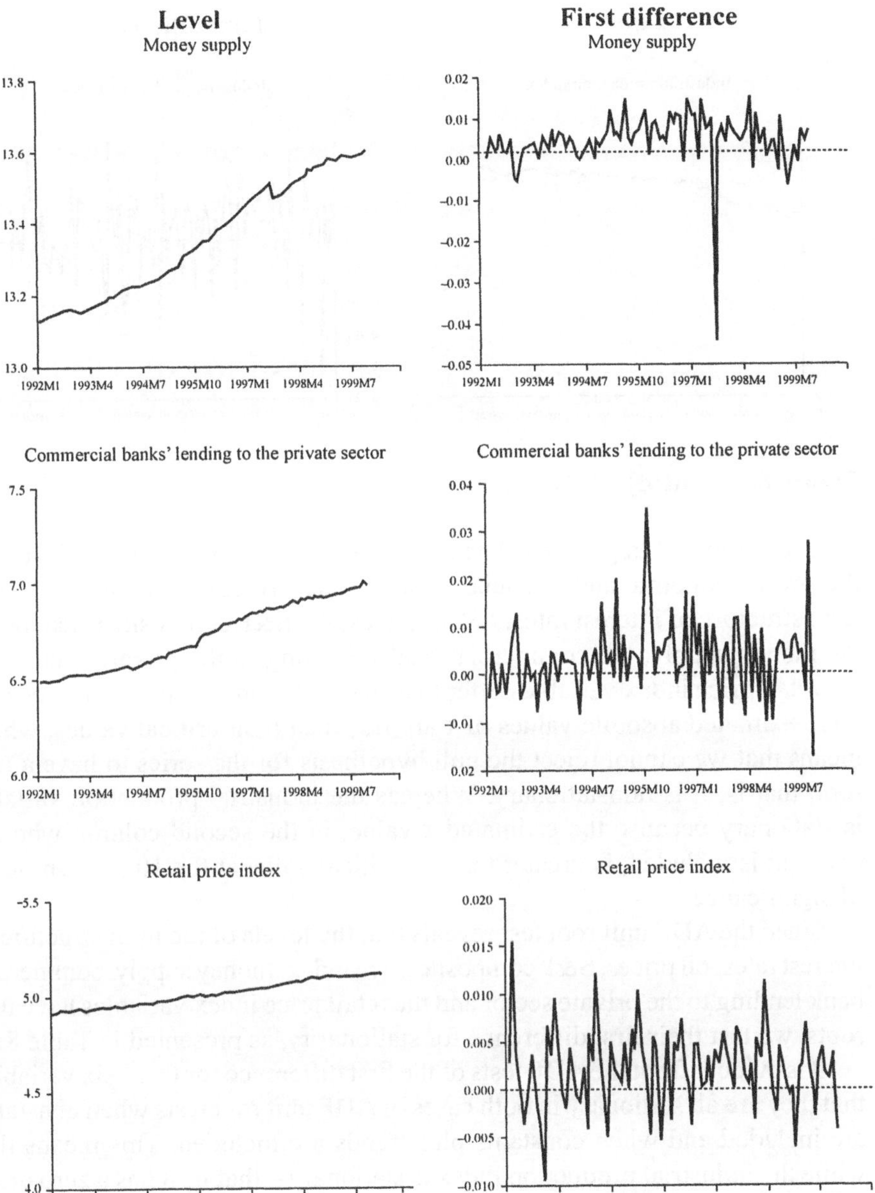

Figure 8.1 (cont'd)

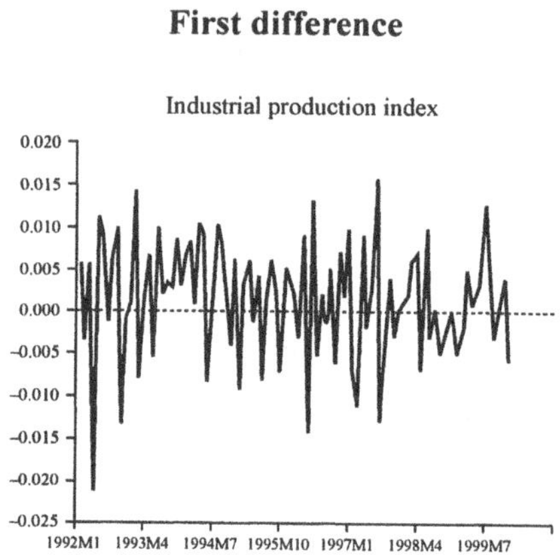

Figure 8.1 (cont'd)

The estimated augmented Dickey-Fuller unit root tests for the levels of the seven economic and financial variables are presented in Table 8.1. The term structure of interest rates, the oil prices, the S&P composite price index, the money supply, the commercial banks' lending to the private sector and the retail price index variables offer to be a nonstationary time series because their estimated absolute values of τ are less than their critical values, which means that we cannot reject the null hypothesis for the series to have a unit root; that is, it is nonstationary. Whereas the industrial production variable is stationary because the estimated τ value, in the second column where a constant is included, is greater than its critical value at the 10 per cent level of significance.

Since the ADF unit root test reveals that the levels of the term structure of interest rates, oil prices, S&P composite price index, money supply, commercial bank lending to the private sector and the retail price index variables have unit roots, we test their first difference for stationarity, as presented in Table 8.2.

It is evident from the ADF tests of the first difference for these six variables that they are all stationary in both cases of ADF unit root tests when constants are included and when constants plus trends are included. This means that while the industrial production index is stationary – that is, it has a zero order of integration – the term structure of interest rates, the oil prices, the S&P composite price index, the money supply, the commercial banks' lending to the private sector and the retail price index all have first order of integration.

For Norway, the seven observed variables are: the term structure of interest rates, FT/S&P world stock market price index, money supply,

Table 8.1 Unit root tests for the level of the observed variables in the UK

Variables	ADF test* Without trend	With trend
Term structure of interest rate	–0.98	–2.34
Oil prices	–1.96	–1.82
S&P composite price index	0.57	–2.48
Money supply	–0.37	–1.63
Commercial banks' lending to the private sector	0.23	–1.72
Retail price index	–1.06	–2.95
Industrial production	–2.86	–2.35

* The critical value of the augmented Dickey-Fuller statistic at 95% level of significance with intercept = –2.90 and with intercept and time trend is = –3.47.

Table 8.2 Unit root tests for the first difference of the observed variables in the UK

Variables	ADF test* Without trend	With trend
Term structure of interest rate	–3.50	–3.47
Oil prices	–4.23	–4.31
S&P composite price index	–6.75	–6.86
Money supply	–6.35	–6.31
Commercial banks' lending to the private sector	–6.14	–6.11
Retail price index	–7.40	–7.45

* The critical value of the augmented Dickey-Fuller statistic at 95% level of significance with intercept = –.90 and with intercept and time trend is = –3.47.

commercial banks' lending to the private sector, the consumer price index and the exchange rate (Kroner/US$). The seven variables used in the case of Mexico are: oil prices, FT/S&P world stock market price index, interest rates, money supply, commercial banks' lending to the private sector, the consumer price index and the exchange rate (Peso/US$). For Venezuela they are oil prices, FT/S&P world stock market price index, interest rates, money supply, commercial banks' lending to the private sector, the consumer price index and the exchange rate (Bolivar/US$). But for Oman, we only have a total of five observed variables due to a lack of published data. These variables are oil prices, FT/S&P world stock market price index, interest rates, money supply and commercial banks' lending to the private sector. The same procedure for identifying the order of integration in the case of the UK is applied in the other four countries.

Therefore, we have identified seven observed variables for each of the United Kingdom, Norway, Mexico and Venezuela stock markets and only five variables for Oman. We will be using monthly time series data in the period from January 1992 to December 1999 for all observed variables and using the stationary forms of the variables in the autoregressive models to generate the innovation terms in the next section.

8.3 Generating Innovation Terms

According to the efficient market hypothesis, listed share prices react only to new information regarding the state of an economy. Such information is usually unanticipated and this has led researchers to propose different models of how expectations are formed and how these models generate unanticipated components or innovations from a set of economic and financial variables that are expected to command a risk premium in stock markets. The innovations should satisfy two statistical conditions according to the APT, first, those innovations should form stationary processes, that is, they should have zero means and a constant variance, and secondly, they should be serially uncorrelated.

There have been three main methods of generating innovations from the observed economic and financial variables in the APT literature. The first method was introduced by Chen, Roll and Ross (1986) and is based on taking the first differences of the observed variables as innovation terms. The second method was introduced by Clare and Thomas (1994) and is based on using the residuals from autoregressive models of the observed variables as innovation terms. The third method was mentioned by Chen, Roll and Ross (1986) and used by Costa, Gardini and Paruolo (1997). It is based on using the residuals from vector autoregressive models of the observed variables as the innovation terms.

The first method of generating innovation terms for the observed variables by taking their first differences (which is referred to in the literature as rate of change models) has a problem which does not satisfy one of the two statistical assumptions for innovations.

This problem is based on the fact that the innovation terms generated from this method tend to be serially correlated, which renders this method unsatisfactory. Therefore, the focus will be on the other two methods of generating innovation terms for the observed variables. Each method will be discussed in detail and compared with the other method in order to select which one will be more appropriate in generating the innovation terms from the observed variables. To do that, we have selected the observed variables for Oman because there are five, whereas for the United Kingdom, Norway, Mexico and Venezuela, each has seven observed variables – which we identified earlier in section 8.3.

8.3.1 Using Autoregressive Models

Clare and Thomas (1994) use autoregressive models to generate innovation terms from observed variables that enter the return generating process of the APT model, instead of the rate of change models that are used by Chen et al. (1986). This alternative is based on using residuals from restricted autoregressive models to form expectations for the stationary observed variables by imposing restrictions on unrestricted autoregressive models. The unrestricted autoregressive models which use monthly data are normally specified with 12 lags and for quarterly data they are normally specified with four lags. Since we are using monthly data, the general autoregressive model is specified with 12 lags, as in equation (8.5):

$$X_t = \alpha + \beta_i X_{t-i} + \nu \qquad i=1, 2, \ldots\ldots, 12. \tag{8.5}$$

To derive the restricted autoregressive model from the above unrestricted model in equation (8.5), Hendry (1987) proposed a technique he called the general-to-specific approach. This approach starts from the general autoregressive model and deletes the insignificant coefficients by imposing restrictions on the coefficients, $\beta = 0$, and tests the validity of the restrictions using F tests. For zero restriction tests, if the estimated value of the F statistic is greater than its critical value, it means that the restricted model is invalid. Otherwise, the restriction is valid. The interest rate, oil prices, money supply and commercial banks' lending to the private sector variables, in Oman, all have first order of integration and the FT/S&P world stock markets price index variable is trend stationary. Therefore, the first difference of the four I (1) variables will enter the general autoregressive model, as well as the level of the I (0) variable. To check if the residuals from the restricted models are serially uncorrelated, we use the F version test of the Lagrange multiplier, and for the zero restrictions on the insignificant coefficient in the general autoregressive model we use the chi-square (χ^2) test of the likelihood ratio. Both the F tests of zero restriction and the chi-square tests of serial correlation are shown in Table 8.3.

Table 8.3 Test of linear restrictions and serial correlation of residuals from restricted autoregressive models for Oman

Variables	Model	F test	χ^2 test
Interest rate	$\Delta I_t = 0.003 + 0.28\Delta I_{t-1}$	0.92	11.91
	(0.78) (2.75)	1.55	17.12
Oil prices	$\Delta O_t = 0.002 + 0.24\Delta O_{t-6}$		
	(2.14)		
FT/S&P world Stock Market price index	$F_t = 0.04 + 0.99F_{t-1}$ (0.50)(61.66)	1.13	14.19
Money supply	First difference	1.32	15.39
Commercial bank lending to the private sector	$\Delta L_t = 0.02 - 0.47\Delta L_{t-1}$ (4.26)(–5.07)	1.20	13.87

Note: the figures in parentheses are t-statistics.

The restricted autoregressive model for the first difference of the interest rate variable only has its first lag significantly different from zero – as indicated by the t-test in Table 8.3. The residuals from this restricted model are serially uncorrelated because the estimated value of F (12, 80), in the third column, is less than its critical value, which is equal to 1.92 at the 5 per cent level of significance. Also, the estimated chi-square [χ^2 (11)] test, in the fourth column, of zero restriction on the coefficients of deleted variables in the unrestricted autoregressive model is less than its critical value of 19.68 at the 5 per cent level of significance. This means that the restricted autoregressive model for the stationary form of the interest rate variable is correctly specified and has serially uncorrelated residuals.

The second restricted autoregressive model in the above table is for the first difference of the oil prices variable, where the critical value of the F (12, 75) test of serial correlation is equal to 1.92. Since the estimated F-statistic is less than its critical value at the 5 per cent level, this means that the residuals are serially uncorrelated, and from the chi-square test it is possible to state that the restricted autoregressive model for the oil prices variable is correctly identified. Likewise, Table 8.3 shows that the restricted autoregressive model for the stationary forms of the FT/S&P world stock market price index, money supply and commercial banks' lending to the private sector, are all correctly specified.

To check the stationarity of the residual terms obtained from the restricted autoregressive models – which were presented in Table 8.3 – we use the augmented Dickey-Fuller unit root test, which is shown in Table 8.4. All the residual terms for the five observed variables offer no sign of having a unit root because the estimated values of τ are greater than their critical value at the 5 per cent level. This means that the residuals of the restricted autoregressive models are all stationary.

Table 8.4 Unit root tests of residuals from restricted autoregressive models for Oman

Variables	ADF statistic
Interest rate	–5.28
Oil price	–4.17
FT world price index	–7.07
Money supply	–5.59
Commercial banks' lending to the private sector	–7.35

Since the residuals generated by the restricted autoregressive models are serially uncorrelated and stationary, it is possible to consider them as innovation terms which could enter the return generation process of the APT model. The graphs of the residuals generated from the restricted autoregressive models in Table 8.3 are shown in Figure 8.2.

To test whether the restricted autoregressive models in Table 8.3 are correctly specified, we use two structural stability tests, first the Chow test and then the cumulative sum and cumulative sum of squares tests which use the recursive residuals.

The Chow test is a popular measure for checking the parameter stability of regressions and it follows the F distribution, as in equation (8.6). The procedure that is followed when using the Chow test can be summarised in the following steps. First, an OLS regression is used to estimate the whole period (n) from January 1992 to December 1999 and define its Residual Sum of Squares (RSS) as RSS_1. Second, the whole period is divided into two

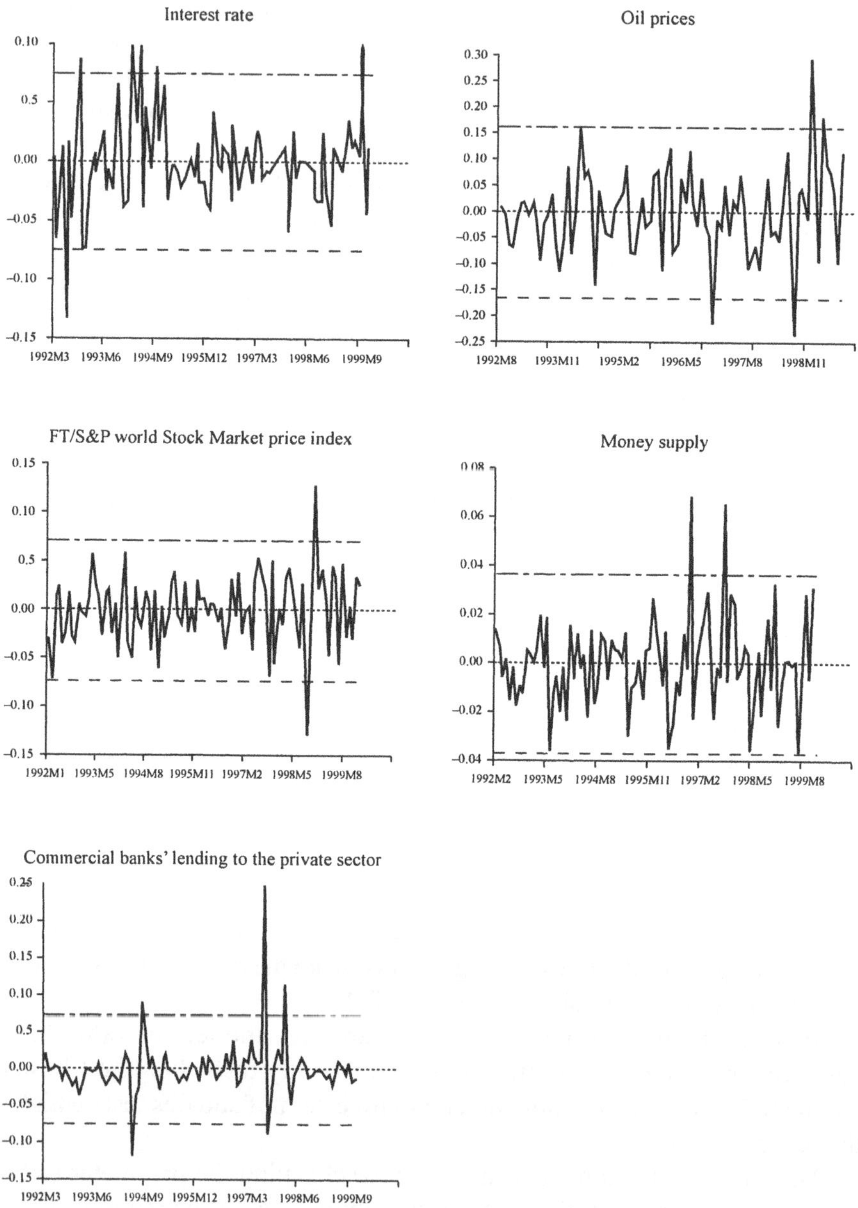

Figure 8.2 Residuals generated by restricted autoregressive models for Oman

sub-periods, which are called m_1 and m_2, and then we estimate the RSS_2 for the first sub-period from January 1992 to December 1997, and RSS_3 for the second sub-period from January 1998 to December 1999. Third, we define $RSS_4 = RSS_2 + RSS_3$, $RSS_5 = RSS_1 + RSS_4$ and $n = m_1 + m_2$. The variable k represents the number of regressors in a model:

$$F = \frac{RSS_5/k}{RSS_4/(n-2k)}. \tag{8.6}$$

Finally, provided that the residuals from the first and second periods are normally distributed, have zero means, constant variances and are independently distributed, the null hypothesis of structural stability in the parameters of regression can be tested based on the calculated value of the F statistic from equation (8.6). If the calculated F statistic is greater than its critical value, then it is possible to reject the null hypothesis of stable parameters, otherwise the parameters of the regression are stable. Table 8.5 shows the Chow tests for the restricted autoregressive models.

The null hypotheses of having stable parameters in the restricted autoregressive models cannot be rejected because the estimated F-statistics of the Chow tests are less than their critical values at the 5 per cent level of significance. Hence the restricted autoregressive models of the five stationary forms of observed variables have stable parameters according to the Chow test in Table 8.5.

Table 8.5 Chow test of parameter stability of restricted autoregressive models for Oman

Variables		Estimated F-test	Critical value*
Interest rates	F(2, 90)	0.19	3.15
Oil prices	F(2, 85)	2.22	3.15
FT/S&P world Stock Market price index	F(2, 91)	1.27	4.00
Money supply	F(1, 93)	0.19	4.00
Commercial banks' lending to the private sector	F(2 , 90)	0.04	3.15

* The critical value is at the 5 per cent level of significance.

In addition to the Chow test there are two other statistical methods to test the structural stability of the restricted autoregressive models. These are the cumulative sum and the cumulative sum of squares tests of recursive residuals, which can be shown graphically in the Microfit statistical package. In each graph of the cumulative sum and the cumulative sum of squares tests, Microfit displays two straight lines that represent the 5 per cent critical bounds where the null hypothesis of having stable parameters for each of the five observed variables is rejected if any of the straight lines is significantly crossed. Otherwise, if the plot generally remains within those two straight lines, the null hypothesis is not rejected. The cumulative sum test helps to show if the coefficients of regression are changing systematically, whereas the cumulative sum of squares test is helpful in showing if the regression coefficients are changing suddenly. Figure 8.3 shows these two tests for the recursive residuals of all the five variables, where the cumulative sum (CUSUM) tests are on the left column and the cumulative sum of squares (CUSUMSQ) tests are on the right column.

In general, the cumulative sum and the cumulative sum of squares tests of the recursive residuals for the restricted autoregressive models of interest rate, oil prices, FT/S&P world stock market price index, money supply and commercial banks' lending to the private sector variables, indicate relative stability of the parameters in the restricted autoregressive models. The cumulative sum tests show that all the residual terms are within the two straight lines. But the cumulative sum of squares tests for the recursive residual terms show a marginal change in the structural stability for interest rate, oil prices, FT/S&P world stock market price index and money supply residuals. While the Chow test shows that the parameters of the commercial banks' lending to the private sector variable are stable, the cumulative sum of squares test displays a sudden shift in the plot of its recursive residuals.

Given the results of stability tests (using the Chow, the cumulative sum, and the cumulative sum of squares tests) for the five restricted autoregressive models, it is possible to state that these models are generally stable. Hence there is no need to use other methods like the Kalman filter to generate innovations – as suggested by Priestley (1996). In addition to that, we have shown that the residual terms of the observed variables are stationary and serially uncorrelated. This leads us to conclude that the single equation autoregressive model is an appropriate method of generating the innovation terms, in the case of Oman.

8.3.2 *Using Vector Autoregressive Models*

Even though Chen, Roll and Ross (1986) were the first to suggest using the residuals from vector autoregressive models as one appropriate method of

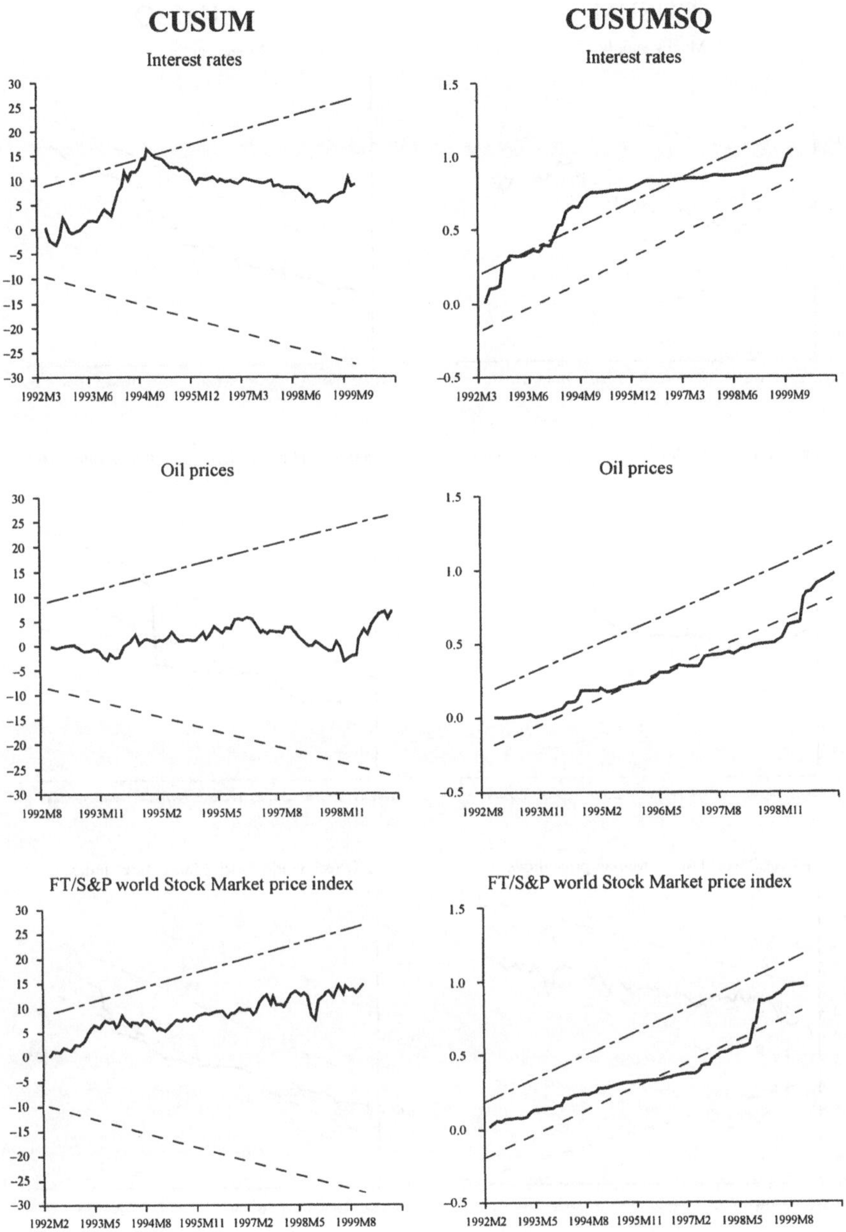

Figure 8.3 Plot of cumulative sum (CUSUM) and cumulative sum of squares (CUSUMSQ) of recursive residuals for Oman

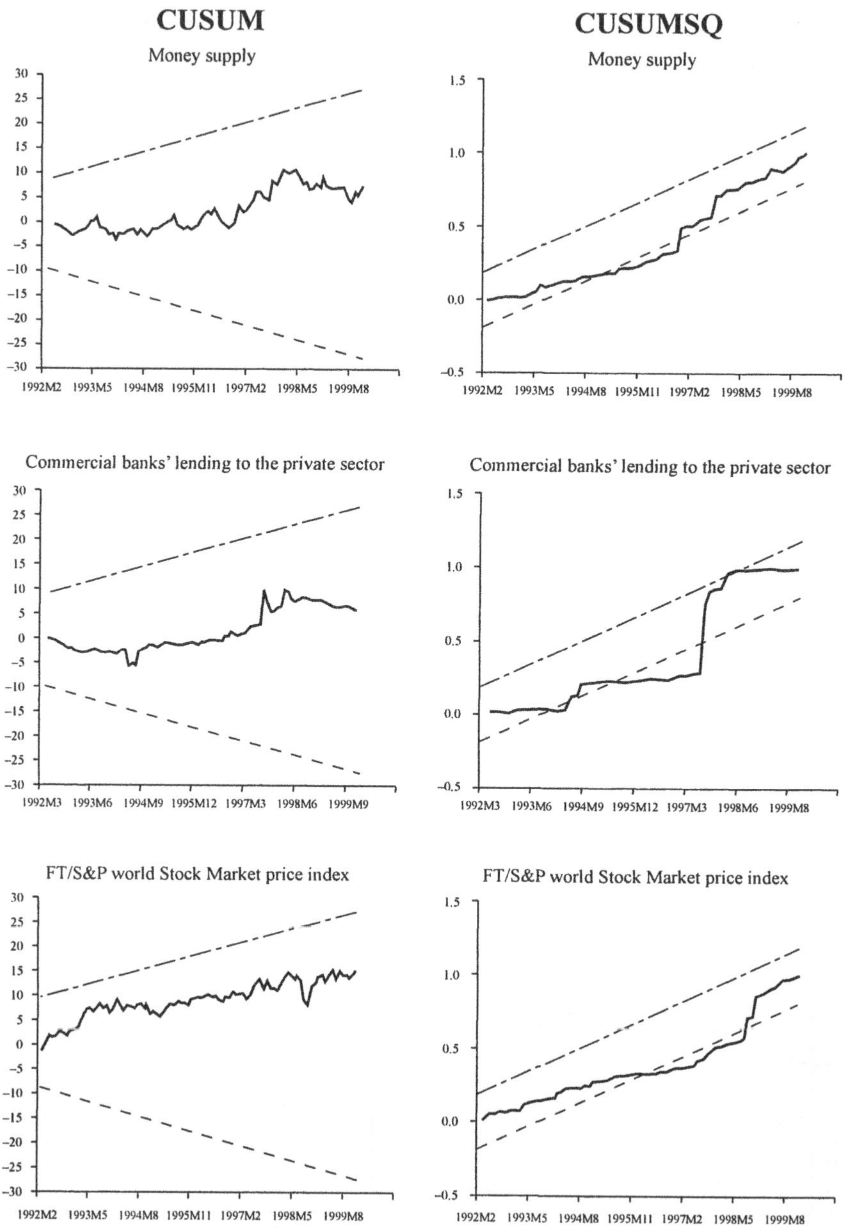

Figure 8.3 cont'd

generating innovation terms from observed economic and financial variables, they nevertheless used single equation methods. It was not until 1997 that the first article on the use of innovations from vector autoregressive (VAR) models was written by Costa, Gardini and Paruolo.

The VAR models represent one method of estimating a multi-equation system. They are dynamic models that provide a simple approach to analyzing the statistical relationship between a set of variables in a system of equations without imposing many restrictions on how the data is generated. Sims (1980) introduces the VAR model as an alternative to the traditional way of estimating a system of equations simultaneously. The emphasis of the traditional approach is based on identifying each equation in the system and determining the exogenous and endogenous variables. But Sims criticized this method of identification as an arbitrary process and he treats all variables in the system as endogenous variables where each equation has the same number of regressors. A standard VAR model for a set of variables (Z_t) in a system of n equations that have lag length p is presented in equation (8.7):

$$Z_t = A_0 + \sum_{i=1}^{p} A_t Z_{t-1} + \mu_t: \qquad i=1,\ldots, p \qquad (8.7)$$

where:

Z_t is a column vector (n × 1) of observed variables;
A_0 is a column vector (n × 1) of constants terms;
A_i are n non-zero matrixes (n × n) of coefficients;
μ_t is a column vector (n × 1) of error terms.

The standard VAR model is considered as a reduced form of the structural model because it has no current values of regressors on the right-hand side of equation (8.7), which has only lagged values of the same order in all the equations of a system. Moreover, in empirical applications of the VAR models, it is common to add a time trend and dummy variables to correct any possible mis-specification in the model. Adding dummy variables or a time trend to the standard VAR model will result in a changed distribution of the test statistics. The disturbance terms (μ_t) in the standard VAR models are assumed to be stationary, serially uncorrelated, homoskedastic, and normally distributed for a given correctly specified system. Also, the disturbance terms are assumed to be uncorrelated with the regressors. As a result, it is possible to estimate each equation in the VAR model using an OLS regression, which will be a consistent and asymptotically efficient estimator. When the residuals across equations are highly correlated and the regressors are not the same in all equations, then an efficient method of estimation would be to use seemingly unrelated regressions equations (SURE) and the system would be known as a near VAR.

The two main requirements of Sims's standard VAR model are to identify the appropriate variables and to determine the order of the lag length. Identifying the appropriate variables in empirical testing of the APT generally – and in the context of the VAR models specifically – has been mainly based on the capital market theory in finance, which relates the prices of assets to their expected cash flow and the discount rate. So, economic and financial variables that have an effect on either the expected cash flow or the discount rate can be considered as appropriate variables that enter the VAR model specification. After determining the appropriate variables in the VAR models, the next critical decision is to deal with the issue of stationarity of the variables. While Sims (1980) and Doan (1996) strongly recommend using levels and no trend variables in the VAR models (even if some of the levels are nonstationary), other researchers have suggested using only stationary forms of variables. In other words, when the level of some variables are I (1), stationarity can be achieved by taking the first differences of those variables. The argument against transforming nonstationary variables of the first order in the standard VAR models is based on the fact that using the first differences would throw away important information on the long-run relationship between the variables in the system. Furthermore, even if the levels of some variables in the system are first order nonstationary, they could be cointegrated to a low level if their residuals are integrated of lower level, that is, they are I (0). The condition for using nonstationary variables of the first order rather than their first differences – which are stationary – is that there should be at least one cointegrated vector between the nonstationary variables in the VAR system. If there are no cointegrated vectors in the multi-equation system, then it becomes necessary to use the first differences in the VAR models. The procedure used for testing for the presence of the cointegration vectors between a set of first-order variables will be presented in more detail later on in this section, but before that we will discuss how to determine the lag length or the order of the VAR models.

There are three indicators that are helpful in determining the appropriate order in the VAR models, which are the log-likelihood ratio statistic, two selection criteria and examining the statistical properties of the residuals. Determining the order of the lag length in the VAR models can be selected using the log-likelihood ratio statistic, which has a chi-square asymptotic distribution with degrees of freedom equal to the number of restrictions. If the estimated value of a chi-square is significantly less than its critical value at the 5 per cent level, then the null hypothesis of having the appropriate lag length cannot be rejected. But, in small samples, the log-likelihood ratio tends to over-reject the null hypothesis, which led Sims (1980) to propose an adjustment to this test in order to take care of such small sample problems, as in equation (8.8):

$$LR_p = (T - c)(\ln|\textstyle\sum_r| - \ln|\textstyle\sum_u|) \tag{8.8}$$

where:

LR is the likelihood ratio statistic;
T is the number of observations;
c is the number of variables in each equation of the unrestricted system;
$|\sum_r|$ is the determinant of the covariance matrix of the residuals for the restricted model;
$|\sum_u|$ is the determinant of the covariance matrix of the residuals for the unrestricted model;
$\mathrm{Ln}|\sum_r|$ is the natural logarithm of $|\sum_r|$;
$\mathrm{Ln}|\sum_u|$ is the natural logarithm of $|\sum_u|$.

In addition the log-likelihood ratio statistic, which helps in determining the order of the VAR models, there are two selection criteria that are commonly used in an empirical application of the VAR. These criteria are the Akaike information criterion (AIC) and Schwarz Bayesian criterion (SBC) called BIC in earlier chapters. The AIC is based on the formula in equation (8.9). This criterion is a particularly useful indicator in determining the appropriate lag length of the VAR models in small sample sizes:

$$AIC = T\ln|\textstyle\sum| + 2N \tag{8.9}$$

where:

$|\sum|$ is the determinant of the covariance matrix of the residuals;
N is the total number of parameters estimated in all equations.[1]

Whereas the BIC is based on equation (8.10) below. The highest values of AIC and BIC indicate the appropriate order of the VAR model:

$$BIC = T\ln\left|\sum\right| + N\ln(T). \tag{8.10}$$

In addition to the two selection criteria discussed in Chapters 4 to 6 and the log-likelihood ratio test (detailed in Chapter 3) help in determining the order of the VAR models, examining the residuals of the variables is another useful tool. If the residuals are Gaussian residuals – in other words, if they are serially uncorrelated and normally distributed with zero mean and constant variance – they imply that the order of the VAR models is likely to be optimal. In this regard, some scholars, like Lutkepohl (1991), suggest experimenting with different lag lengths of the VAR models in order to obtain an appropriate order that represents a stable system, especially in small samples of data. He also noted that the order of the VAR model is not size invariant, which implies that it is a function of the sample size. This means that the order tends to increase as the sample size increases. Having presented the procedure for selecting the appropriate variables that should enter the VAR models and the selection methods of the order for the VAR models, it is necessary at this stage to elaborate on the issue of stationarity in the VAR models.

The stationarity of the variables in the VAR model was presented briefly earlier in this section where we pointed out that some scholars have strongly recommended using levels of nonstationary variables instead of using their first differences, which are stationary. The reason for such a recommendation is that the long-run statistical equilibrium relationship between different variables can only be captured using their levels. But using the levels of nonstationary variables of first order in a multi-equation system like the VAR models will produce a spurious regression unless some of these nonstationary variables form at least one linearly independent vector which is strongly correlated to the stationary forms of the first differences. In this case the nonstationary variables are said to be cointegrated. Harris (1995) defines a spurious regression as:

> having results that suggest there are statistically significant relationships between the variables in the regression model when in fact all that is obtained is evidence of contemporaneous correlations rather than meaningful causal relations. (p. 14)

In a spurious regression the residual terms are non-stationary and tend to drift because their variance increases in direct proportion to an increase in the sample size. To avoid having spurious regressions implies formal testing procedures for cointegration vectors in multi-equation systems. When two or more variables are cointegrated, it means that they form a long-run statistical equilibrium relationship among their stochastic trends. This implies that the nonstationary cointegrated variables are combined in a linear relationship. Harris (1995) explains this link between cointegration and long-run equilibrium in the following way:

> The economic interpretation of cointegration is that if two (or more) series are linked to form an equilibrium relationship spanning the long-run, then even though the series themselves may contain stochastic trends (i.e., be non-stationary) they will nevertheless move closely together over time and the difference between them will be stable (i.e., stationary). Thus, the concept of cointegration mimics the existence of a long-run equilibrium to which an economic system converges over time, and the error terms can be interpreted as the disequilibrium error (i.e., the distance that the system is away from equilibrium at any given time). (p. 22)

Since most of the economic and financial time series data are nonstationary, it is important to determine the order of integration for each variable that enters the standard VAR models using the augmented Dickey-Fuller unit root tests. If there is a nonstationary variable of the first order, then it would be necessary to test for the presence of any cointegration relationships between these nonstationary variables. We have already determined the order of integration for the five observed variables for Oman. But, how do we test for cointegration between nonstationary variables in a multi-equation system,[2] like the VAR models?

In multi-equation systems, the test of cointegration is based on using vector error-correction models (VECM), which include information on both the long-run relationships between first-order nonstationary variables and information on their short-run adjustments. The levels of the variables represent the long-run relationships, whereas the short-run adjustments are represented by the first differences of these variables. The VECM can be derived from the standard VAR models by subtracting the variables in Z_{t-1} from both sides of equation (8.7), resulting in equation (8.11), where I is the identity matrix:

$$\Delta Z_t = A_0 + (A_1 - I)Z_{t-1} + \sum_{i=2}^{p} A_t Z_{t-i} + \mu_t. \tag{8.11}$$

Furthermore, when subtracting and adding the term $(A_1 - I)Z_{t-2}$ to the right hand side of equation (8.11), we get equation (8.12):

$$\Delta Z_t = A_0 + (A_1 - I)\Delta Z_{t-1} + (A_2 - I)\Delta Z_{t-2} + \sum_{i=3}^{p} A_t Z_{t-i} + \mu_t. \tag{8.12}$$

If we continue the process of subtracting and adding terms, like $(A_1 + A_2 - I)$ Z_{t-3} …… $(A_1 + A_2 + \ldots\ldots + A_p - I)Z_{t-p+1}$, to the right hand side of equation (8.12), we get the VECM in equation (8.13):

$$\Delta Z_t = A_0 + \sum_{i=1}^{p-1}\left[\sum_{j=1}^{i}(A_j - \mathrm{I})\right]\Delta Z_{t-1} + \left[\sum_{i=1}^{p}A_i - \mathrm{I}\right]Z_{t-p} + \mu_t. \tag{8.13}$$

To simplify equation (8.13), let:

$$\Gamma_i = \left[I - \sum_{j=1}^{i}A_j\right] \qquad \text{and} \qquad \prod = \left[I - \sum_{i=1}^{p}A_i\right].$$

Hence, the VECM shown in equation (8.14) is derived from the standard VAR model:

$$\Delta Z_t = A_0 + \sum_{i=1}^{p-1}\Gamma_i \Delta Z_{t-1} + \prod Z_{t-p} + \mu_t. \tag{8.14}$$

For the VECM in equation (8.14) to be stationary, there should be at least one cointegrated vector that forms r linearly independent columns in the $\prod$ matrix of (8.16). There are three cases when the nonstationary variables in Z_{t-p} are stationary. In the first case, there is no cointegration in the $\prod$ matrix, which means that $r = 0$, and the VECM becomes a standard VAR in first differences. In the second case, there are n cointegrated vectors, which means that $r = n$, and in this case the levels of the variables are all stationary, I (0), and we may use the standard VAR in levels rather than using the VECM. The third case is when the cointegrated vectors are more than zero and less than the number of equations in the system; i.e., $0 < r < n$. In this third case, the $\prod$ matrix has reduced rank, whereas in the first case it has zero rank and in the second case it has full rank. The numbers of linearly independent vectors, r, are known as the cointegrated rank of the variables in $Z_{t-p.}$ While the OLS method of regression is an efficient estimator of each equation in both the first and second cases, in the third case it is not an appropriate method of estimating the reduced rank because the OLS method can only determine the full rank matrix. To estimate the number of cointegrated vectors for nonstationary first order variables in the reduced rank matrix, Johansen (1988) develops a technique that uses a reduced rank regression method. Unlike the Engle-Granger (1987) method, which uses a two-step procedure to test for cointegration in single equations, the Johansen technique uses single-step maximum likelihood estimators to test for the presence of cointegration vectors in the $\prod$ matrix in equation (8.9). The number of cointegrated vectors in the $\prod$ matrix is equal to its rank r. Hence, one of the main objectives of the Johansen technique is to determine the number of cointegrated vectors that are present in the $\prod$ matrix by using two likelihood ratio statistics. The first likelihood ratio statistic is based on the maximal eigenvalue of the stochastic matrix, as in equation (8.15). The null hypothesis test of the maximal eigenvalue statistic (λ_{max}) is based on having r cointegrated vectors in the $\prod$ matrix against the alternative hypothesis of having r + 1 cointegrated vectors:

$$\lambda_{max}(r, r+1) = -T\ln(1-\hat{\lambda}_{r+1}) \tag{8.15}$$

where:

r is the number of cointegrated vectors;
T is the total number of observations;
$\hat{\lambda}$ is the eigenvalue.

The second likelihood ratio statistic is based on the trace of the stochastic matrix, as in equation (8.16). The trace statistic (λ_{trace}) tests the null hypothesis that the $\prod$ matrix has r cointegrated vectors against the alternative hypothesis of having more than r cointegrated vectors:

$$\lambda_{trace}(r) = -T\sum_{i=r+1}^{n}\ln(1-\hat{\lambda}_i). \tag{8.16}$$

To recap the discussion in this section so far, we present a summary of the procedure for testing the number of cointegrated vectors in a multi-equation system using Johansen's technique. Firstly, the order of integration for each variable that enters the VAR models, is determined using the augmented Dickey-Fuller unit root tests. Secondly, the appropriate order of the VAR models needs to be determined. This can be achieved using the log-likelihood ratio statistic and the two selection criteria; namely the AIC and the BIC. Thirdly, it is necessary to determine if a trend and/or constant term should enter the cointegration test. Plotting the levels and the first differences of the selected variables over time would help in deciding if we should include deterministic variables in the cointegration test. Finally, we use the two likelihood ratio statistics, which are based on the maximal eigenvalue and the trace of the stochastic matrices, to determine the number of cointegrated vectors in the reduced rank matrix of the VECM. This procedure will be followed to generate innovation terms of the five selected economic and financial variables from the VAR model.

The procedure that will be followed in this section for selecting the optimal lag length in the VAR model will utilise the general-to-specific approach. This will start with a lag length that is sufficiently long for the unrestricted VAR model, in order to capture the dynamics of the data generation process and to eliminate any serial correlation in the residual terms. But using a long lag length and five observed variables will lead to very high consumption of the degrees of freedoms. Thus, it is important when generating innovations using the VAR models to trade-off parsimony with an absence of serial correlation.

The maximum lag length of the VAR model, which uses the levels of the five observed variables and a constant term, for a total of 96 observations in the period from January 1992 to December 1999, is equal to 14 lags. When testing the restriction of deleting the constant in the unrestricted VAR, using the likelihood ratio statistic, the null hypothesis of zero restrictions was rejected at the 5 per cent level (the estimated chi-square with five degrees of freedom was equal to 38.69, which is greater than its critical value of 11.07). Hence we then start by decreasing the order of the lag length, starting from the fourteenth order of the VAR model and sequentially decreasing the lag length to the lowest order where the residual assumptions are not violated in order to identify the appropriate lag length of the model. The two selection criteria and the adjusted log-likelihood ratio statistics for the unrestricted VAR model are shown in Table 8.6.

Based on the two selection criteria of the lag length for the VAR model, the AIC selects the fourteenth lag, whereas the BIC selects the first lag. The log-likelihood ratio statistic when adjusted for small samples does not reject any of the lags except zero. Since the selection criteria indicate two different lag lengths and the likelihood ratio tests do not reject any of these two selection criteria, we use diagnostic tests of the residual terms from the OLS regression in order to select the appropriate lag length. Table 8.7 shows the diagnostic tests for the residual terms of the thirteenth, twelfth and eleventh lags of the VAR models. In Table 8.7, the F_1 statistic is the f-version of the Lagrange multiplier test of the residual serial correlation, F_2 is the f-version of the Ramsey's RESET test of the model specification, F_3 is the f-version of the heteroscedasticity test of the variance stability and χ^2 is the Lagrange multiplier version of the normality distribution for the residual term, which has chi-square distribution.

The diagnostic tests of the five residual terms from the VAR model of the thirteenth order reveals significant evidence of serial correlation in the

Table 8.6 Determining the order of the VAR model for Oman

Order	AIC	BIC	LR
0	585	597	$\chi^2(350) = 246$
1	1008	972	$\chi^2(325) = 126$
2	1010	943	$\chi^2(300) = 119$
3	996	900	$\chi^2(275) = 116$
4	987	861	$\chi^2(250) = 111$
5	984	827	$\chi^2(225) = 106$
6	980	793	$\chi^2(200) = 100$
7	978	761	$\chi^2(175) = 94$
8	991	744	$\chi^2(150) = 83$
9	995	718	$\chi^2(125) = 76$
10	1009	702	$\chi^2(100) = 65$
11	1027	690	$\chi^2(75) = 54$
12	1069	702	$\chi^2(50) = 36$
13	1119	722	$\chi^2(25) = 16$
14	1152	725	----

where LR is the adjusted likelihood ratio statistics, which has a chi-square distribution.

residual term of the interest rate variable at the 10 per cent level, as in part a) of Table 8.7. But there is no significant evidence of violation in the four assumptions of the residual terms at the 10 per cent level for the VAR model of the twelfth order, as in part b) of Table 8.7. In part c) of Table 8.7, the normality assumption of the residual term for the commercial banks' lending to the private sector is violated at the 10 per cent level. The estimated values of the chi-square for the residual terms of the commercial banks' lending to the private sector tends to increase as the lag length decreases. This means that only at the twelfth lag of the VAR order is the normality assumption not violated for this residual term.

As a result of examining the residual terms of the levels from the five observed variables, it is possible to select the twelfth lag order for the VAR model. The residual terms from the VAR model for this lag length are shown in Figure 8.4. All of the residual terms have zero mean and are within the two standard error bands, which are indicated by the two straight horizontal lines in Figure 8.4. This means that there is no indication of outliers in the residual terms.

So far, we have shown that the appropriate lag length of the VAR model for the levels of the five observed variables is 12 and the residual terms from

Table 8.7 Diagnostic tests of the residuals from VAR models for Oman

a) VAR (13)

Tests	OP	IR	FT	M2	LP
F1 (12, 5)	3.83	12.82**	1.83	0.78	1.65
F2 (1, 16)	0.01	0.71	0.003	2.14	0.10
F3 (1, 81)	0.81	1.60	2.64	2.27	0.56
χ^2 (2)	1.51	0.59	0.60	0.63	2.66

b) VAR (12)

Tests	OP	TS	FT	M2	LP
F1 (12, 11)	2.65	1.00	3.95*	1.17	2.09
F2 (1, 12)	1.00	0.45	0.57	3.25	0.22
F3 (1, 82)	0.19	0.15	0.78	2.57	0.27
χ^2 (2)	0.44	0.27	1.84	0.13	3.78

c) VAR (11)

Tests	OP	TS	FT	M2	LP
F1 (12, 17)	2.38	1.58	2.72	1.63	0.99
F2 (1, 28)	3.69	0.17	0.13	3.81	0.12
F3 (1, 83)	0.01	0.06	0.27	1.22	0.17
χ^2 (2)	0.14	2.33	1.07	7.59	22.30**

* The null hypothesis is rejected at the 5 per cent level of significance but not at the 10 per cent.

** The null hypothesis is rejected at the 10 per cent level of significance where:

OP is the oil prices variable;
IR is the interest rate;
FT is the FT/S&P world stock market price index;
M2 is the money supply;
LP is the commercial banks lending to private sector.

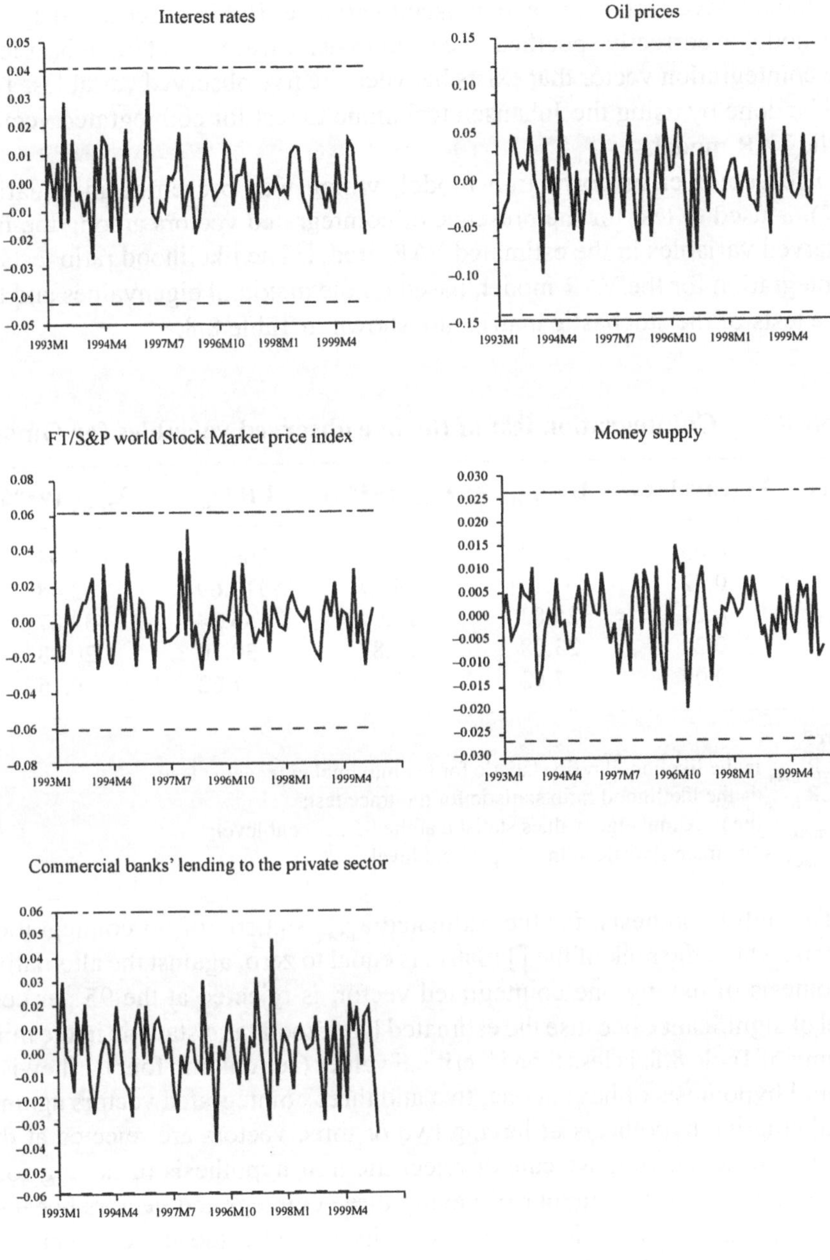

Figure 8.4 Residuals from the VAR (12) model for Oman

this model have zero mean and constant variance. But in order to verify that our model is correctly specified, we need to demonstrate that there is at least one cointegration vector that exists between the five observed variables. This can be done by using the Johansen technique to test for cointegrated vectors in the VAR model.

The vector error correction model, which was presented in equation (8.7), is used to test for the presence of cointegrated vectors among the five observed variables in the estimated VAR model. The likelihood ratio tests of cointegration for the VAR model, based on the maximal eigenvalues and the trace tests of the stochastic matrix, are shown in Table 8.8.

Table 8.8 Cointegration test of the five observed variables for Oman

Rank	Eigenvalues	LR_{max}	λ_{max} (95%)	LR_{trace}	λ_{trace} (95%)
0	0.65	89.24	34.40	206.93	75.98
1	0.52	61.15	28.27	117.69	53.48
2	0.27	25.83	22.04	56.54	34.87
3	0.24	23.08	15.87	30.70	20.18
4	0.09	7.62	9.16	7.62	9.16

where:

LR_{max} is the likelihood ratio statistic for the maximal eigenvalue test;
LR_{trace} is the likelihood ratio statistic for the trace test;
λ_{max} is the maximal eigenvalues statistic at the 95 per cent level;
λ_{trace} is the trace statistic at the 95 per cent level.

The null hypothesis, for the estimated λ_{max} statistic of no cointegration vectors, where the rank of the $\prod$ matrix is equal to zero, against the alternative hypothesis of having one cointegrated vector, is rejected at the 95 per cent level of significance because the estimated likelihood ratio statistic in the third column of Table 8.8, is less than its critical values (see column four). Likewise, the null hypothesis of having one, two and three cointegrated vectors against the alternative hypothesis of having two or three vectors are rejected at the 95 per cent level. But, we cannot reject the null hypothesis of having four cointegrated vectors in favour of having three cointegrated vectors because the estimated λ_{max} statistic is greater than its critical value at the 95 per cent level. For the second likelihood statistic, the estimated likelihood ratio statistic for the λ_{trace} test, which is shown in the fifth column of Table 8.8, rejects the null hypothesis of no cointegrated vector in favour of having one or more cointegrated vectors, at the 95 per cent level. The same thing can be stated with regard to rejecting the null hypothesis of having one, two and three cointegrated vectors in favour of having four or more cointegrated vectors. But the null hypothesis of having four cointegrated vectors cannot be rejected at the 95 per cent level. So, both the maximal eigenvalues and the trace tests, at the 95 per cent level of significance, do not reject the null hypothesis of having four cointegrated vectors in the VAR model of the twelfth order. Therefore, it is possible to confirm the existence of up to four cointegrated vectors that form a linear long-run equilibrium relationship between the five observed variables. As a result of having up to four cointegrated vectors between the observed variables, it is appropriate to use the levels of the nonstationary variables in the VAR model. Using the first differences of the four nonstationary variables in the VAR model, instead, would lead to a misspecification error.

Since the residual terms of the five observed variables from the estimated VAR model all have zero means and are serially uncorrelated, it is possible to consider them as innovations which enter the APT return generating process of listed shares. Lutkepohl (1991) argues that stationarity of the VAR model, that is, having zero means and constant variance in the residuals, would imply stability in the system of equations.

8.4 Concluding Remarks

The first method of generating innovation terms from five observed variables from Oman based on single equation autoregressive models. The unrestricted autoregressive model has 12 lags, due to the use of monthly data. Then we tested the zero restrictions on the insignificant lags to test the validity of the restricted autoregressive model. After that we tested the presence of serial correlation in the residuals of the restricted model. We have found that all the five models are correctly specified and the residuals are serially uncorrelated. Furthermore, the test of the parameter stability using the Chow test, cumulative square and cumulative sum of squares of the recursive residual tests reveal that they are generally stable.

The second method of generating innovation terms is by using the vector autoregressive model. While the residuals from the five observed variables, which are generated using the vector autoregressive model are stationary and serially uncorrelated there are two main problems with this second method.

The first problem is that this method tends to consume a large degree of freedom. When using five observed variables for Oman, the VAR model has an order of 12, which enables it to generate residual terms that possess desirable statistical properties. Since there are seven observed variables for each of the other four countries, the United Kingdom, Norway, Mexico and Venezuela, the order of the VAR model will further increase. This means that it is less likely to obtain residuals with desirable properties, because of the major increase in the degrees of freedom consumption.

The second problem with using the VAR model to generate innovation terms is that residuals of the oil prices variable, which is common in all five countries, will not be the same for each country, due to the simultaneity of the multiple equations in the VAR system.

Given the two drawbacks of the VAR model, we will be using the restricted autoregressive models to generate the innovation terms for the United Kingdom, Norway, Mexico and Venezuela in the next chapter. If these residuals for the four countries have the same desirable property as in the case of Oman, which we have shown in this chapter, then they enter the return generating process of the APT model.

Notes

1 The total number of parameters in a VAR model is equal to n2p + n, where n is the number of variables and p is the number of lags.

2 The common method of testing cointegration in single equations is the Engle-Granger (1987) method. This method is used in testing the long-run equilibrium relationship between two or more variables, which have the same first-order of integration. If the residual term of a single equation is integrated at a lower level, that is, it is stationary, then the regression is known to be cointegrated. Otherwise, the regression is known as a spurious regression. But there are a number of limitations in the Engle-Granger method which render it unsuitable in a multi-equation system like the VAR models.

Chapter 9

Modelling the Risk Premium of Listed Stocks

9.1 Introduction

Empirical testing of the arbitrage pricing theory using observed economic and financial variables can be divided into three main steps: identifying the observed variables; generating the innovation terms of observed variables; and estimating their prices of risk. The first and second steps were presented in the last chapter. The second step, which deals with generating the unexpected changes, was the subject of the analysis in Chapter 4, where we presented two techniques for generating innovations from the observed variables. The first technique is used by Clare and Thomas (1994) and Clare, Priestley and Thomas (1999) and is based on using residuals from restricted autoregressive models as innovation terms. The second technique is proposed by Chen, Roll and Ross (1986) and is applied by Costa, Gardini and Paruolo (1999) and is based on using the residuals from the vector autoregressive (VAR) model as innovation terms. Based on the general and statistical properties of the two types of residuals that are generated by the two techniques, in the last chapter we concluded that the residuals that are generated from restricted autoregressive models have an advantage over those that are generated by vector autoregressive models. The objective of this chapter is to determine the economic and financial variables that command a risk premium in determining excess returns of listed shares in our sample of five countries, which is the third step in testing the APT model using the non-linear least square method and the reduced rank regression method of estimation.

The rest of this chapter will be organised in the following sections. In the next section, we will show how the return generating process equation and the expected return equation of the APT model can be derived as one single equation. The empirical results of applying the APT model using the least square method of estimation will be presented in section 9.3 for the UK, Norway, Mexico, Venezuela and Oman. In section 9.4, the APT model is derived in reduced rank form. The empirical results of testing the reduced rank APT model using excess returns of eight randomly selected sectors as dependent variables and the seven innovation terms of the seven observed variables in the UK stock market will be presented in section 9.5. Finally, in section 9.6, a summary of the chapter will be presented.

9.2 Using Non-Linear Least Square Method

Estimating risk premiums of observed economic and financial variables is introduced by Chen, Roll and Ross (1986), who apply the two-step cross sectional regression procedure which was introduced by Fama and MacBeth (1993). In the first step, the ordinary least square (OLS) method of regression is used to estimate the coefficients or factor loadings of the observed variables in each equation. The number of equations is equal to the number of listed shares. For example, if there are 60 listed shares, we need to run the OLS regression 60 times. All equations have the same observed factors and a constant term as independent variables and the excess return of each listed company as the dependent variable. Then in the second step, the estimated factor loadings are used as independent variables in cross-sectional regressions to estimate the risk premium of the observed variables. This method of testing the APT became a common approach used by a number of researchers such as Beenstock and Chan (1988), Hamao (1988) and Clare and Thomas (1994). But Shanken (1992) points out that the two-step method suffers from an error-in-variables (EIV) problem, which, if not corrected, would lead to incorrect inferences regarding which factors command a risk premium in asset returns. To remove the EIV problem, some researchers suggested forming portfolios of listed shares in the first step and using the factor loadings of these portfolios in the second step, in cross-sectional regressions. But Clare and Thomas (1994) point out that the prices of risk for the observed factors changes depending on the method by which portfolios are formed. In other words, the portfolios that are formed on the basis of share betas would have different prices of risk from portfolios that are formed on the basis of listed shares size, that is, market capitalization.

An alternative method of estimating the risk premiums of the observed economic and financial variables to the two-step procedure was first introduced by McElroy, Burmeister and Wall (1985), who showed that the APT can be expressed in a system of non-linear seemingly unrelated equations (NLSURE) in which the factor loadings and the prices of risk are estimated simultaneously in one step. There are three main advantages of this one-step method over the traditional two-step. Firstly, the EIV problem is totally eliminated. Secondly, it is possible to use individual asset returns rather than forming portfolios of assets when estimating the risk premiums. Finally, the APT cross equation restrictions of having the same prices of risk for the observed factors can be easily tested. To show how the APT can be expressed in a system of non-linear equations, we will look at the return generating process of the linear system as shown in equation (9.1):

$$R(t)_i = E[r(t)_i] + \sum_{j=1}^{k} b_{ij} F(t)_i + \varepsilon(t)_i \ ,$$

$$t = 1,\ldots, T \; i = 1,\ldots, N \; j = 1, 2,\ldots, k \qquad (9.1)$$

where:

R_i is the returns on asset i;
$E(r_i)$ is the expected returns on asset i;
F_j is the value of the jth factor that influence returns on asset i;
b_{ij} is the sensitivity of asset i to factor j;
ε_i is the usual random error term.

The expected returns $E[r(t)_i]$ on asset i is defined in the APT framework by equation (9.2):

$$E[r(t)_i] = \lambda(t)_0 + \sum_{j=1}^{k} b_{ij} \lambda(t)_j \qquad (9.2)$$

where:

λ_0 is the risk-free rates of returns;
λ_j is the risk premium associated with F_j.

The APT model has two parts; the return generating process in equation (9.1) and the expected return of asset prices in equation (9.2). By substituting the expected return of listed shares in equation (9.2) in the return generating process in equation (9.1), we get a single equation APT model, as in equation (9.3), expressed below:

$$R(t)_i = \lambda(t)_0 + \sum_{j=1}^{k} b_{ij} \lambda(t)_j + \sum_{j=1}^{k} b_{ij} F(t)_j + \mu(t)_i . \qquad (9.3)$$

Furthermore, equation (9.3) can be written in terms of excess return which is defined by $R(t)_i - \lambda(t)_0$, as in equation (9.4):

$$\rho(t)_i = \sum_{j=1}^{k} b_{ij}\lambda(t)_j + \sum_{j=1}^{k} b_{ij}F(t)_j + \mu(t)_i \tag{9.4}$$

where $\rho(t)_i$ is the excess return on asset i.

To test the cross-equation restrictions of having the same risk premiums for all assets in the context of the APT, we define a constant $\alpha(t)_i = \sum_{j=1}^{k} b_{ij}\lambda(t)_j$ in equation (9.4) which represents the non-linear restriction, as in equation (9.5) given below:

$$\rho(t)_i = \alpha(t)_i + \sum_{j=1}^{k} b_{ij}F(t)_j + \mu(t)_i. \tag{9.5}$$

The above one-step method of NLSURE is further developed by Burmeister and McElroy (1988) who treat the market portfolio as an endogenous variable and introduce a non-linear three stage least square (NL3SLS)[1] technique in testing the APT using observed variables. The authors point out that the NL3SLS technique would perform better than the NLSURE in empirical testing of the APT when using a system of non-linear simultaneous equations, as in equation (9.5). The NL3SLS method of estimation is valid when the inequality condition NT > K (N + 1) is satisfied in order to ensure that there are more equations than unknowns in the system, where N is the number of equations in the system, T is the number of observations for each asset and K is the number of observed factors.

By factoring out the coefficient matrix of parameter b_{ij} from the first and second terms in equation (9.4), we get (9.6) which is non-linear in variables and can be solved by using the three stage least square method:

$$\rho(t)_i = \sum_{j=1}^{k} b_{ij}[\lambda(t)_j + F(t)_j] + \mu(t)_i. \tag{9.6}$$

The rationale for using a system of simultaneous equations in testing the APT is that the residual terms of different assets are not assumed to be strictly independent, that is, the covariance matrix of the residual terms is not diagonal. This implies that the APT follows an approximate factor structure when using the NL3SLS technique, which makes an explicit use of the estimated covariance matrix of the residual terms in the system of equations.

The one-step approach of measuring the prices of risk using the NL3SLS technique requires a set of instrumental variables[2] for the independent factors because the residual terms of the observed variables are more likely to have a significant correlation with the residual terms of the dependent variables due to the simultaneity between the equations in the system. These instrumental variables should be highly correlated with the observed variables and are uncorrelated with the residual terms of the dependent variables.[3] There should be at least as many instrumental variables as there are independent variables. While there are methods to make an optimal choice of instrumental variables in empirical applications, it has been common practice in identifying instrumental variables to use a different order of the independent variables, such as their square values. In the context of the APT applications, researchers like Priestley (1996) and Clare et al. (1999) have used the current and squared values of the exogenous variables and the fitted squared values from the regression of the excess returns from the market index on the exogenous variables as instrumental variables in NL3SLS applications. But Gallant (1987) points out that a major drawback to this technique is that the estimated parameters are not invariant to the choice of instrumental variables. This means that a different choice of instrumental variables would lead to different estimates of the parameters, even though the observed factors and the method of estimation are the same.

The significant issue to point out in the empirical applications of the APT model, using the NL3SLS method, is that while McElroy, Burmeister and Wall (1985), McElroy and Burmeister (1988) and Burmeister and McElroy (1988) have all stressed that the coefficient matrix of regression, b_{ij}, should be of full rank, none of the articles which are stated above have formally tested the rank order of the coefficient matrix. Instead, all assumed that the matrix has a full rank.

9.3 Empirical Results of Using the Non-Linear Least Square Method

When Priestley (1996) estimates the single equation APT model, in equation (9.6), using the non-linear three stage least square method, he uses 69 listed companies and the FT all share price index in the UK market (a total of 70 equations). Also, Clare, Priestley and Thomas (1999) use the three stage least square method to estimate the risk premium for 56 portfolios in which each has 15 listed shares in the United Kingdom stock market. The non-linear three stage least square method of estimation is appropriate to solve a system of equations simultaneously. Since we are interested in solving a single non-linear equation in which the excess return on the general stock market price index in each of the five countries is a function of a set of innovation terms from observed economic and financial variables – specific to each country – in order to determine which of the observed variables command risk premium, we will be using a non-linear least square method of estimation to test the APT model.

The rest of this section is organised in the following subsections. Subsection 9.3.1 presents the restricted autoregressive models for the seven observed variables in the United Kingdom and tests their structural stability. Then the non-linear single equation APT model will be tested to determine which of the seven observed variables command a risk premium. The same procedure will be followed for Norway in subsection 9.3.2, Mexico in subsection 9.3.3 and Venezuela in subsection 9.3.4. Since we have already presented the restricted autoregressive models for the five variables in Oman in Chapter 4, subsection 9.3.5 will use the innovation terms from the last chapter to test the APT model. This will be followed by presenting an overview of the local stock market development in Oman.

9.3.1 The United Kingdom

We have identified seven observed variables for the United Kingdom stock market in Chapter 3. These variables are: the term structure of interest rates; oil prices; the S&P composite price index; the money supply (M4); commercial banks' lending to the private sector; the retail price index; and the industrial production index. Also, the order of integration for these observed variables has been determined in Chapter 3. The first six observed variables have first order of integration, that is I (1), but the seventh observed variable has zero order of integration, that is I (0). Furthermore, in Chapter 4, we have concluded that generating innovation terms from observed variables using single equation autoregressive models are more appropriate than using vector autoregressive models. As a result, we will use the stationary form of the observed variables in unrestricted autoregressive models to generate the innovation terms for the seven variables in the United Kingdom stock market. Table 9.1 presents the restricted autoregressive models for the seven observed variables in the period from January 1992 to December 1999.

The restricted autoregressive model for the first difference of the term structure of interest rate variables has two statistically significant lags – the third and the fifth, as indicated by their t-statistics. The zero restrictions on the coefficients of deleted variables are valid because the estimated chi-square (χ^2) statistic of the likelihood ratio test, in column four of Table 9.1, is less than its critical value [χ^2 (10) = 18.31] at the 5 per cent level of significance. This means that the restricted autoregressive model for the first difference of

Table 9.1 Test of linear restrictions and serial correlation of residuals from restricted autoregressive models for the UK

Variables	Restricted autoregressive model	F test	χ^2 test
Term structure of interest rate	$\Delta T_t = -0.90E{-3} + 0.26\ \Delta T_{t-3} - 0.20\ \Delta T_{t-5}$ (0.02) (2.46) (–1.90)	1.06	13.05
Oil price	$\Delta O_t = 0.002 + 0.24\ \Delta O_{t-6}$ (0.26) (2.14)	1.55	19.12
S&P composite price index	First difference	0.98	9.63
Money supply	First difference	0.61	9.25
Commercial bank lending to the private sector	$\Delta L_t = 0.004 + 0.28\ \Delta L_{t-4}$ (3.99) (2.48)	1.18	16.05
Retail price index	$\Delta P_t = 0.65E{-3} + 0.91\ \Delta P_{t-12}$ (2.40) (12.06)	0.93	6.10
Industrial production	$D_t = 0.002 - 0.30\ D_{t-1}$ (2.94) (–3.04)	0.56	5.26

Note: The figures in parenthesis are t-statistics.

the term structure of interest rate is correctly specified. Also, the residuals from the restricted autoregressive model are serially uncorrelated because the estimated value of the F version of the Lagrange multiplier test, in column three, is less than its critical value, which is F (12, 95) equal to 1.92, at the 5 per cent level of significance.

We have already demonstrated in the previous chapter, in the case of Oman, the validity of zero restrictions and the serially uncorrelated residuals for the first differences of the oil prices variable. For the first difference of the S&P composite price index variable, none of the 12 lags in the unrestricted autoregressive model is significant. The zero restrictions on the coefficient of 12 lags is valid, as indicated by the estimated value of chi-square, and the first difference of the S&P composite price index is serially uncorrelated, as indicated by the estimated F statistic, in Table 9.1. The same results can be found for the first differences of the money supply, commercial banks' lending to the private sector and retail price index variables. This applies equally to the level of the industrial production index variable. Figure 9.1 shows the residuals of the seven observed variables that are generated from the restricted autoregressive models.

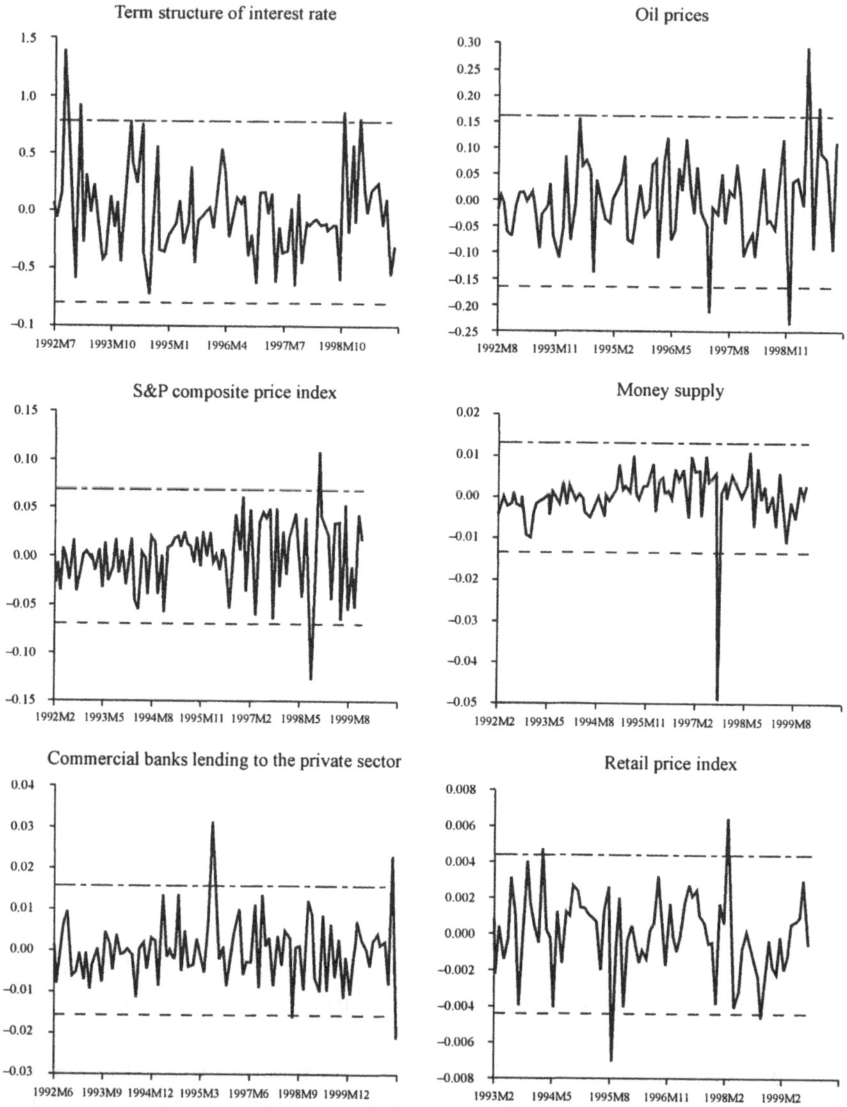

Figure 9.1 Residuals generated by restricted autoregressive models for the UK

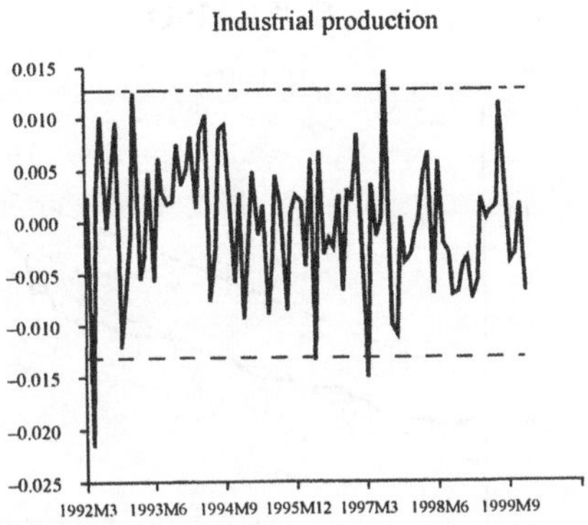

Figure 9.1 (cont'd)

The cumulative sum and the cumulative sum of squares tests of structural stability provide evidence of the parameter stability of restricted autoregressive models (see Table 9.1).

Figure 9.2 shows the cumulative sum (CUSUM) test on the left and the cumulative sum of squares (CUSUMSQ) test on the right. Recall that the two displayed straight lines in each graph represent the 5 per cent level of significance.

The cumulative sum and the cumulative sum of squares test for the seven observed variables are generally within the 5 per cent level of significance

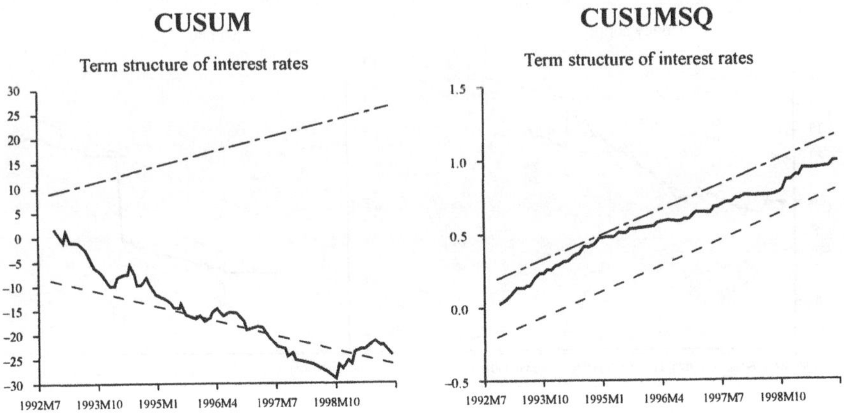

Figure 9.2 **Plot of cumulative sum and cumulative sum of squares of the recursive residuals for the UK**

Figure 9.2 (cont'd)

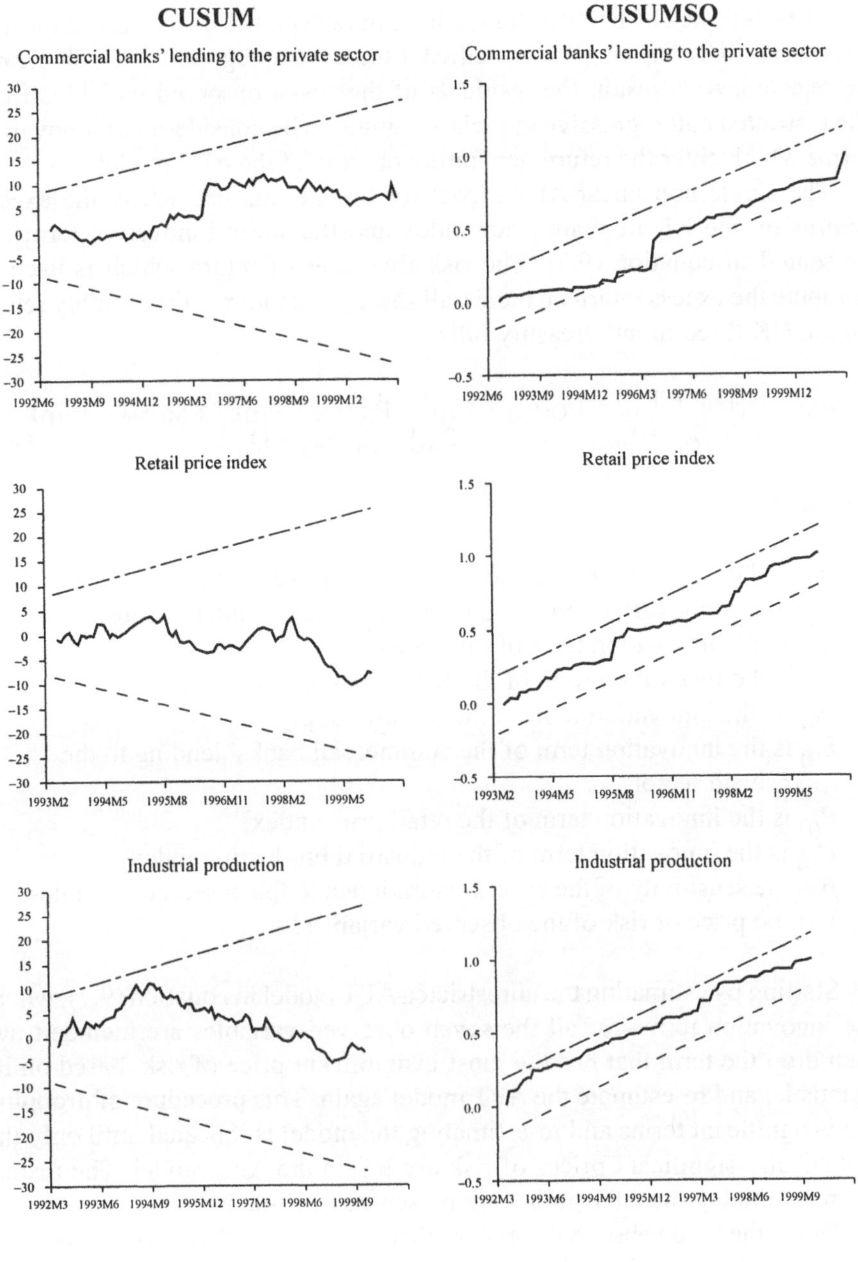

Figure 9.2 (cont'd)

which is indicated by the two straight lines in each plot. This means that the null hypothesis of having correctly specified restricted autoregressive models cannot be rejected. As a result, the residuals of the seven observed variables from the restricted autoregressive models are going to be considered as innovation terms which enter the return generating process of the APT model.

The single non-linear APT model for the UK market, where the excess returns on the FT all share price index and the seven innovation terms, is presented in equation (9.7). The risk-free rates of return which is used to compute the excess return on the FT all share price index is the monthly return on the UK three-month treasury bills:

$$\begin{aligned}\rho_{(t)} = {} & \beta_T[\lambda_T + T_{(t)}] + \beta_O[\lambda_O + O_{(t)}] + \beta_S[\lambda_S + S_{(t)}] + \beta_M[\lambda_M + M_{(t)}] \\ & + \beta_L[\lambda_L + L_{(t)}] + \beta_P[\lambda_P + P_{(t)}] + \beta_D[\lambda_D + D_{(t)}] \qquad (9.7)\end{aligned}$$

where:

$\rho_{(t)}$ is the excess return on the FT all share price index;
$T_{(t)}$ is the innovation term of the term structure of interest rates;
$O_{(t)}$ is the innovation term of oil prices;
$S_{(t)}$ is the innovation term of the S&P composite price index;
$M_{(t)}$ is the innovation term of the money supply;
$L_{(t)}$ is the innovation term of the commercial banks' lending to the private sector;
$P_{(t)}$ is the innovation term of the retail price index;
$D_{(t)}$ is the innovation term of the industrial production index;
β is the sensitivity of the excess return index to the observed variables;
λ is the price of risk of the observed variables.

Starting by estimating the unrestricted APT model in equation (9.7), where the innovation terms for all the seven observed variables are included, we then drop the term that has the most insignificant price of risk, based on its t-statistic, and re-estimate the APT model again. This procedure of dropping the insignificant terms and re-estimating the model is repeated until only the statistically significant prices of risk are left in the APT model. The results from estimating the APT model are presented in Table 9.2.

Out of the seven observed variables that are considered as a potential source of systematic risk in the UK stock market, only two are statistically significant in commanding risk premiums in the period from February 1993 to December 1999. These variables are the S&P composite price index and the industrial

Table 9.2 Estimate for prices of risk in the UK stock market

Factors	Values	T-statistic	Significance
λ_S	0.93	9.30	0.00
λ_D	1.02	2.19	0.03

where:

λ_S is the price of risk for the S&P composite price index.
λ_D is the price of risk for the industrial production index.

production index. The positive price of risk for the US S&P composite price index variable indicates that there is a very high direct relationship between the UK and the US stock markets. The movement of share prices in the US stock market exerts a strong influence on share prices in the UK stock market. For example, if there is a significant drop in the prices of listed shares in the US stock market due to a negative sentiment about the economic outlook for the US economy and at the same time the fundamental factors (which are expected to be significant in determining share prices in the UK stock market) are sound justifying stability in the prices of listed shares, it is more likely that the net effect would be a proportionate decline in the UK stock prices due to there being a significant positive price of risk for the S&P composite price index factor.

Furthermore, the results in Table 9.2 show that the industrial production variable has a positive price of risk, which is consistent with the results from earlier articles that investigated the UK stock market. When taking into consideration that this variable has a positive price of risk in the US (see Chen et al. (1986)), but not found to be significantly priced in the Clare and Thomas (1994) and Clare, Priestley and Thomas (1999) articles in the period from January 1983 to December 1990, and has a significant positive price of risk in the Priestley (1996) article in the period from December 1999 to August 1993, our findings in this case are consistent with previous findings in the UK and US markets.

9.3.2 Norway

The term structure of interest rates, oil prices, the FT/S&P world stock market price index, the money supply, the commercial banks' lending to the private sector, the consumer price index and the Norwegian Kroner per US dollar exchange rate are the seven variables that have been identified as potential sources of systematic risk for the Norwegian stock market in Chapter 3, along with their order of integration.

We have already presented the restricted autoregressive model for the oil price variables in the previous subsection. The following set of variables has first-order of integration; term structure of interest rates; commercial banks' lending to the private sector; and the exchange rate. But the second set: the FT/S&P price index; the money supply; and the consumer price index has zero order of integration. This means that the first differences of the observed variables in the first set enter the unrestricted autoregressive models whereas the second set enter in levels. Table 9.3 presents the restricted autoregressive models for the other six observed variables in Norway.

Table 9.3 Test of linear restrictions and serial correlation of residuals from restricted autoregressive models for Norway

Variables	Models	F test	χ^2 test
Term structure of interest rates	First difference	1.29	18.59
FT/S&P world Stock Market price index	$F_t = 0.04 + 0.99\ F_{t-1}$ (0.50)(61.66)	1.13	14.19
Money supply	$M_t = 0.9 + 0.6M_{t-1} + 0.3\ M_{t-2} + 0.4M_{t-6} - 0.4M_{t-9}$ (2.6) (6.6) (2.4) (3.3) (–4.0)	1.59	11.98
Commercial banks' lending to the private sector	First difference	1.24	18.69
Consumer price index	$P_t = -0.02 + 0.86\ P_{t-1} + 0.15\ P_{t-6}$ (–0.64)(15.55) (2.69)	1.62	14.13
Exchange rates	First difference	0.90	9.85

Note: The figures in parenthesis are t-statistics.

None of the 12 lags in the first differences of the term structure of interest rate variable is significantly different from zero. The estimated chi-square statistic, in the fourth column of Table 9.3, is less than its critical value, which is χ^2 (12) equals 21.02 at the 5 per cent level of significance. This means that the zero restrictions on the coefficient of the deleted variables are valid. Also, the residuals from the restricted autoregressive model of the first difference of the term structure variable are serially uncorrelated because the estimated value of F-statistic is less than its critical value, which is F (12, 58) equals 1.92, at the 5 per cent level. The same conclusions for the other five variables can be found based on the estimated chi-square and the F tests. Figure 9.3 shows residuals from the six restricted autoregressive models and Figure 9.4 shows the CUSUM and CUSUMSQ tests of structure stability.

So far in this subsection, we have presented the seven restricted autoregressive models and tested whether they are correctly specified using the likelihood ratios and the cumulative sum and cumulative sum of squares tests. Based on these tests, it is possible to conclude that the restricted autoregressive models, which are presented in Table 9.3, are generally valid and their residuals are serially uncorrelated. Therefore, these residuals will enter the single equation APT model as innovation terms. The non-linear APT model for Norway, where the excess return on the Oslo bourse total stock market price index is a function of the seven innovation terms, is presented in equation (9.8) below:

$$\begin{aligned}\rho_{(t)} = {} & \beta_T[\lambda_T + T_{(t)}] + \beta_O[\lambda_O + O_{(t)}] + \beta_F[\lambda_F + F_{(t)}] + \beta_M[\lambda_M + M_{(t)}] \\ & + \beta_L[\lambda_L + P_{(t)}] + \beta_P[\lambda_P + P_{(t)}] + \beta_E[\lambda_E + E_{(t)}]\end{aligned} \quad (9.8)$$

where:

$\rho_{(t)}$ is the excess return on the total stock market price index;
$T_{(t)}$ is the innovation term of the term structure of interest rate;
$O_{(t)}$ is the innovation term of the oil prices;
$F_{(t)}$ is the innovation term of the FT/S&P world stock market price index;
$M_{(t)}$ is the innovation term of the money supply;
$L_{(t)}$ is the innovation term of the commercial banks' lending to the private sector;
$P_{(t)}$ is the innovation term of the consumer price index;
$E_{(t)}$ is the innovation term of the exchange rate;
β is the sensitivity of the excess return index to the observed variables;
λ is the price of risk of the observed variables.

Similar to the United Kingdom results, there are two observed variables that command risk premium in the Norwegian stock market during the period from February 1993 to December 1999. These variables are the term structure of interest rates and the FT/S&P world stock markets price index. The other five observed variables are statistically insignificant in determining the excess

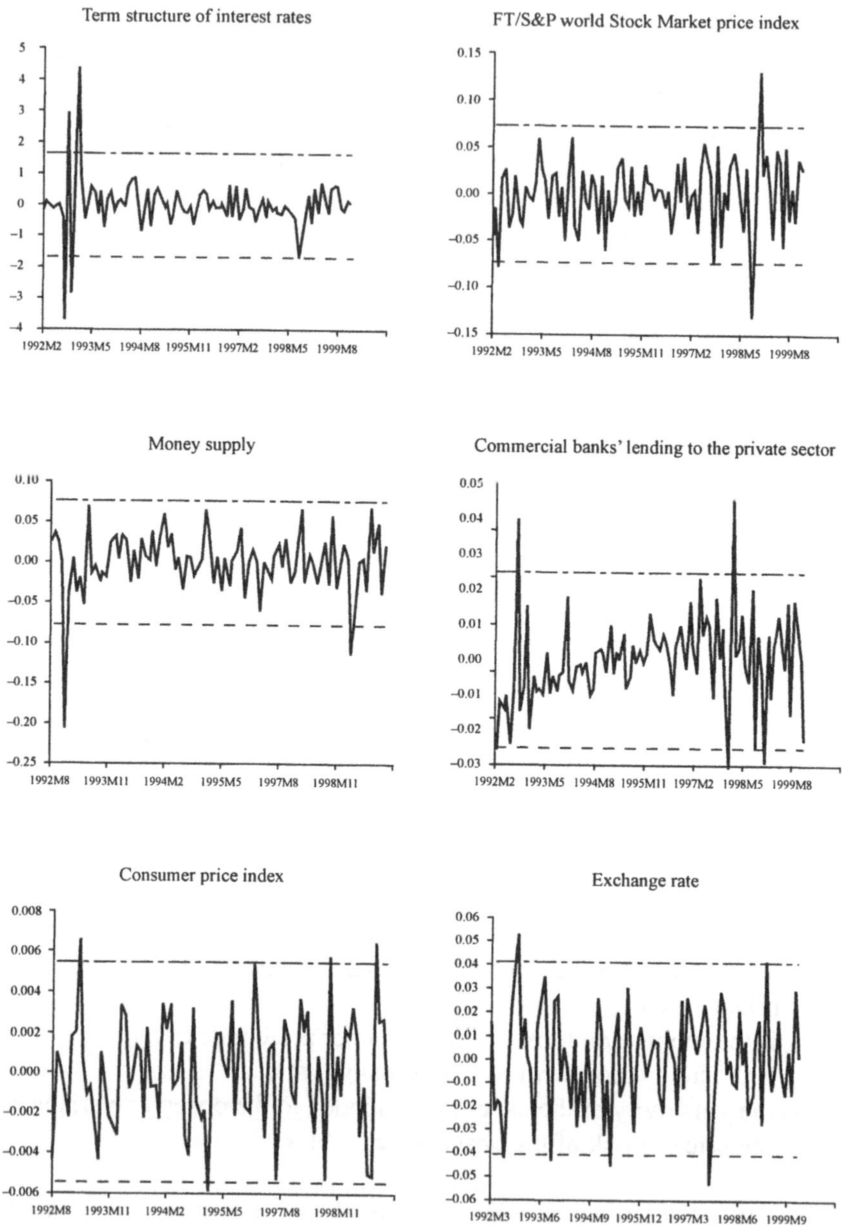

Figure 9.3 Residuals generated by restricted autoregressive models for Norway

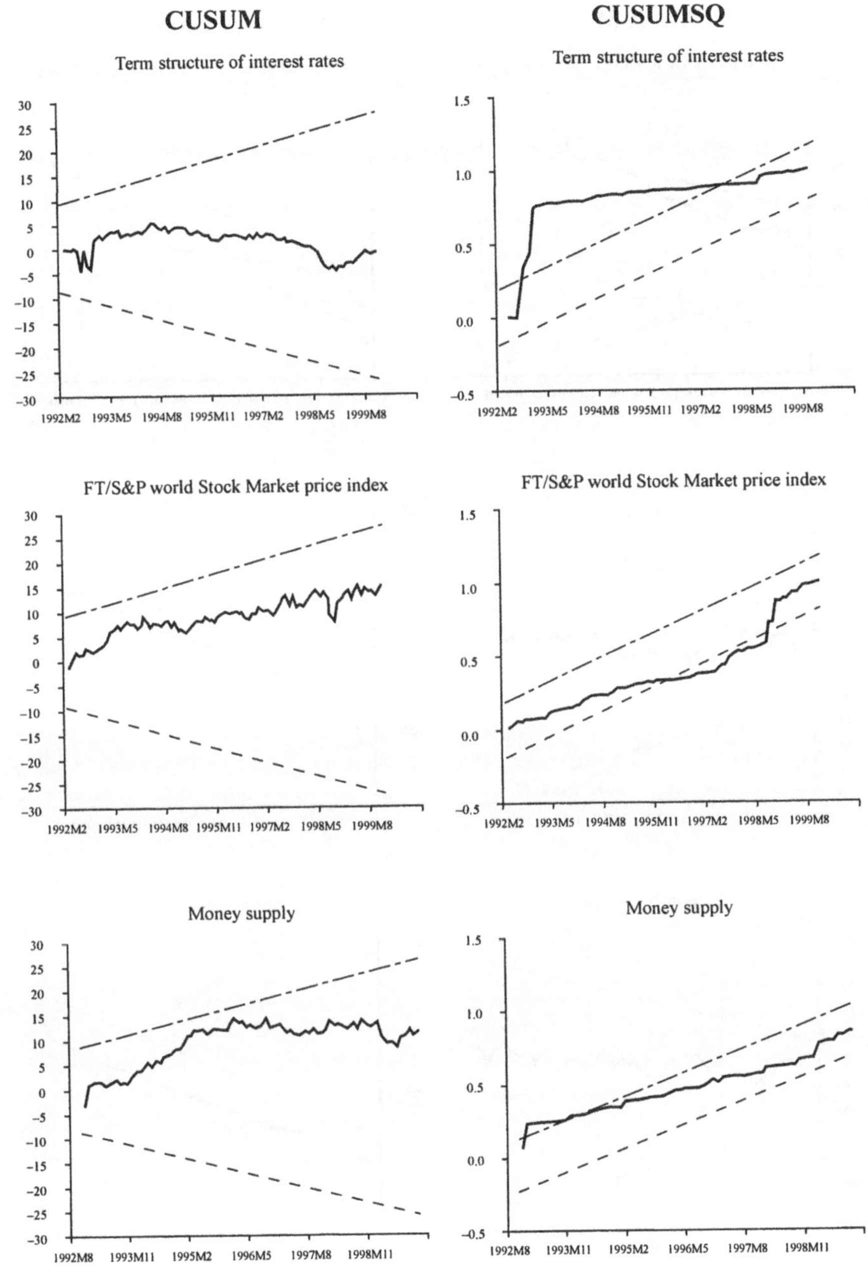

Figure 9.4 Plot of cumulative sum and cumulative sum of squares of the recursive residuals for Norway

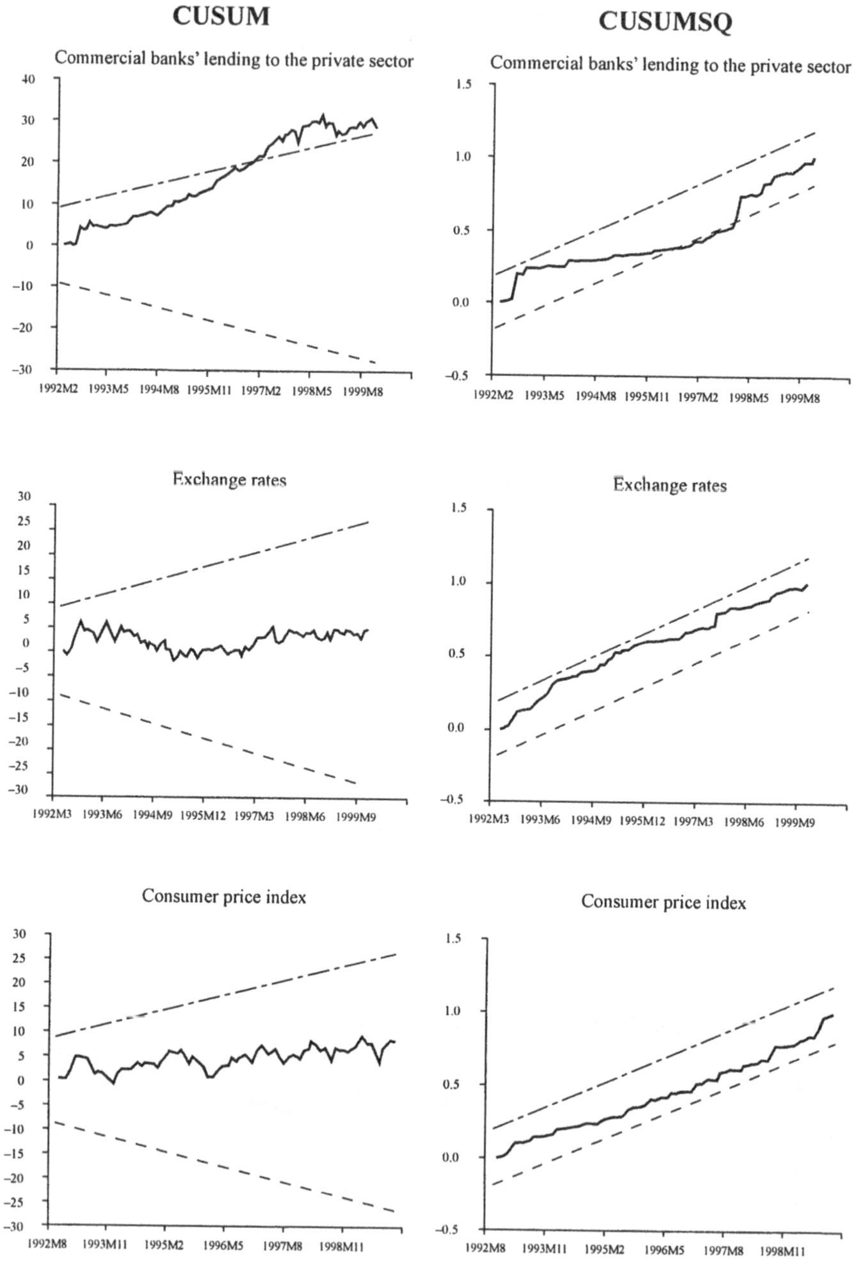

Figure 9.4 (cont'd)

return on the total stock market price index. The results from the restricted APT model, in equation (9.8), are presented in Table 9.4.

Table 9.4 Estimate for prices of risk in Norway's stock market

	Coefficients	T-statistic	Significance
λ_T	0.02	3.42	0.00
λ_F	1.09	9.62	0.00

where:
λ_T is the price of risk for the term structure of interest rate
λ_F is the price of risk for the FT/S&P world stock market price index.

The term structure of interest rates is significantly priced in the Oslo bourse and it has a positive sign. Likewise, the FT/S&P world stock market price index variable has a very high and positive price of risk.

9.3.3 Mexico

The Mexican stock market, which is known also as the Bolsa, was open to foreign investors in 1989. The Bolsa price index has been very volatile during the period of analysis. For example, the Bolsa increased in real terms by 34.4 per cent in 1999, dropped by 45 per cent in 1998, and by the middle of 1999 had increased by 45 per cent in local currency (according to the Economist Intelligence Unit, 2000).

In previous chapters we have identified seven observed variables as potential risk factors in the Mexican stock market. These variables are the money market rate of interest; oil prices; the FT/S&P world stock market price index; the money supply; the Mexican Pesos per US dollar exchange rate; the consumer price index; and the commercial banks' lending to the private sector.

Since the restricted autoregressive models for oil prices and the FT/S&P world stock market price index have been presented in the previous two subsections, the other five restricted autoregressive models are presented in Table 9.5.

The above five observed variables have first order of integration, that is I (1), which means that their first differences enter the restricted autoregressive models. The estimated chi-square tests of zero restrictions, in the fourth column

Table 9.5 Test of linear restrictions and serial correlation of residuals from restricted autoregressive models for Mexico

Variables	Models	F test	χ^2 test
Interest rate	$\Delta I_t = -0.002 + 0.28\ \Delta I_{t-1} + 0.31\ \Delta I_{t-8}$ (−0.14) (2.81) (3.16)	0.92	13.99
Money supply	First difference	0.28	3.49
Exchange rate	First difference	1.29	14.13
Consumer price index	$\Delta P_t = 0.003 + 0.90\ \Delta P_{t-1} - 0.16\ \Delta P_{t-4}$ (3.21) (13.92) (−2.44)	1.94	14.25
Commercial banks lending to the private sector	$\Delta L_t = 0.01 + 0.38\ \Delta L_{t-11}$ (1.19) (2.92)	1.44	14.49

Note: The figures in parenthesis are t-statistics.

of Table 9.5, are less than their critical values at the 5 per cent level. Hence, they are correctly specified. Likewise, the estimated values of F-statistics are less than their critical values, which means that the residuals from the above five restricted autoregressive models are serially uncorrelated. The residuals of the five observed variables are shown in Figure 9.5.

The null hypothesis of having correctly specified restricted autoregressive models, in Table 9.5, can be further tested using the cumulative sum and the cumulative sum of square tests that are shown in Figure 9.6.

The single equation non-linear APT model for Mexico is presented in equation (9.9) below:

$$\rho_{(t)} = \beta_I[\lambda_I + I_{(t)}] + \beta_O[\lambda_O + O_{(t)}] + \beta_F[\lambda_F + F_{(t)}] + \beta_M[\lambda_M + M_{(t)}] + \beta_E[\lambda_E + E_{(t)}] + \beta_P[\lambda_P + P_{(t)}] + \beta_L[\lambda_L + L_{(t)}] \quad (9.9)$$

where:

$\rho_{(t)}$ is the excess return of the total stock market price index;
$I_{(t)}$ is the innovation term of the money market rate of interest;
$O_{(t)}$ is the innovation term of the oil price;
$F_{(t)}$ is the innovation term of the FT/S&P world stock market price index;
$M_{(t)}$ is the innovation term of the money supply;
$E_{(t)}$ is the innovation term of the exchange rate;
$P_{(t)}$ is the innovation term of the consumer price index;

$L_{(t)}$ is the innovation term of the commercial banks' lending to the private sector;
β is the sensitivity of the excess return index to the observed variables;
λ is the price of risk of the observed variables.

The risk-free rate of return for Mexico is the rate of return on Mexican Treasury bills, which is used to calculate the monthly excess returns on the Mexican Bolsa stock market price index. Starting with the APT model, in equation (9.9), which includes seven innovation terms and eliminates those that are insignificantly priced, we have found that three out of the seven observed variables are significantly priced. These are the interest rates, the FT/S&P world stock market price index and the money supply variables. The

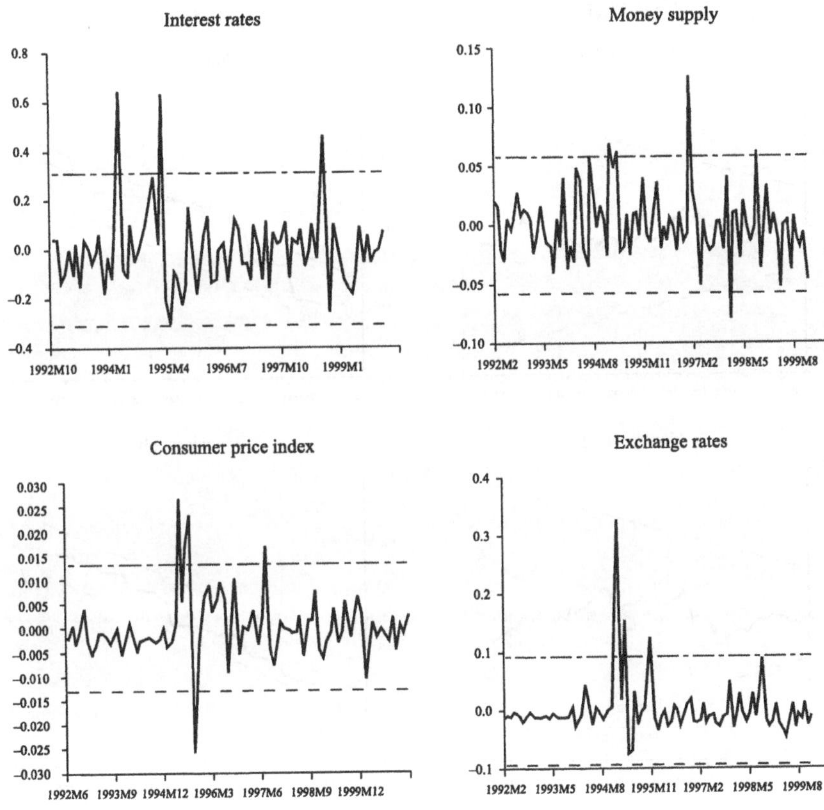

Figure 9.5 Residuals from restricted autoregressive models for Mexico

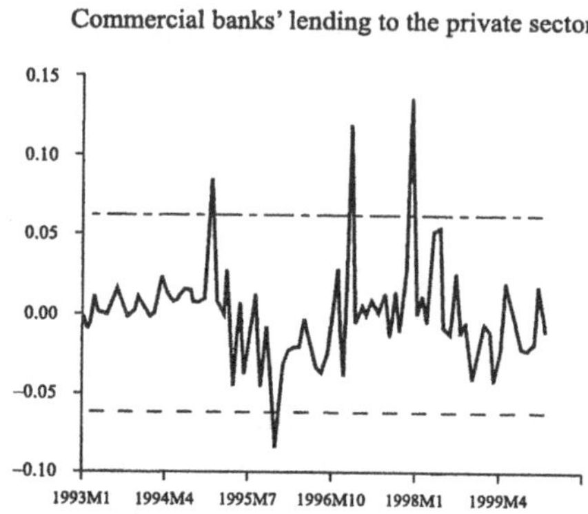

Figure 9.5 (cont'd)

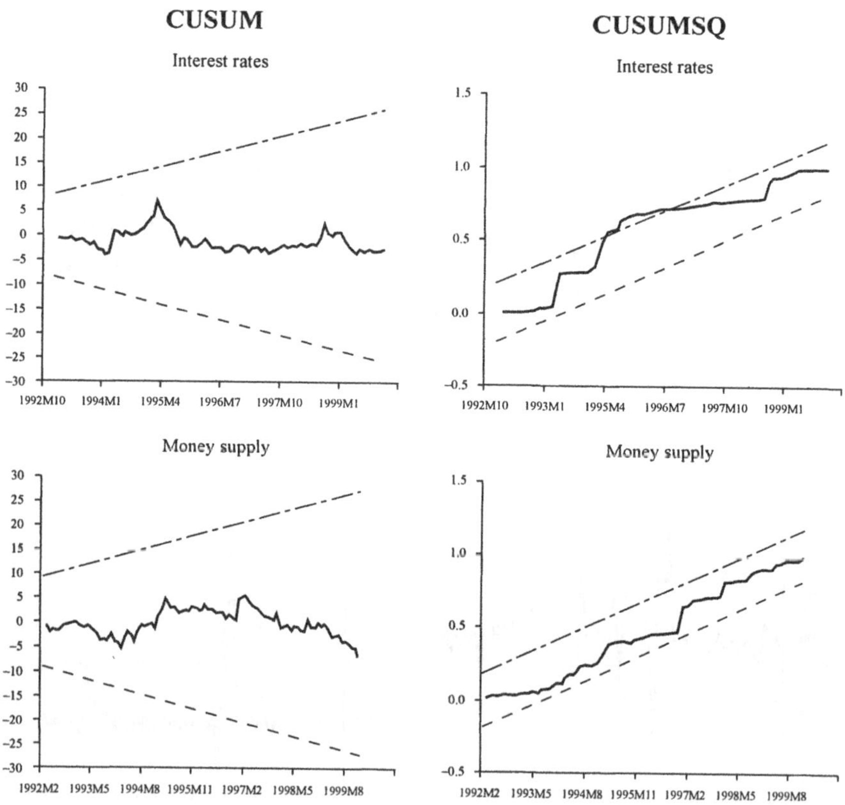

Figure 9.6 Plot of cumulative sum and cumulative sum of squares of the recursive residuals for Mexico

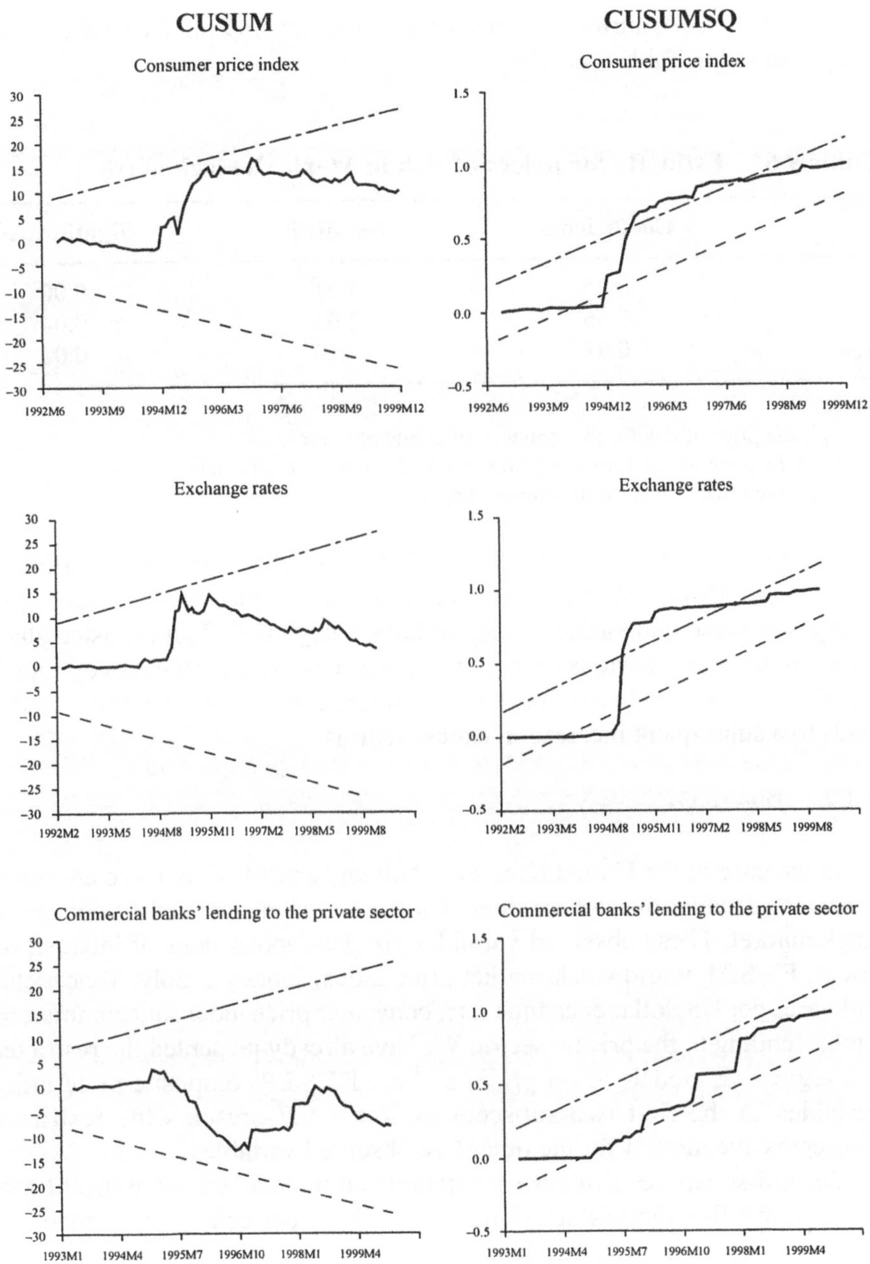

Figure 9.6 (cont'd)

results for Mexico, during the period from February 1993 to December 1999, are presented in Table 9.6 below.

Table 9.6 Estimate for prices of risk in Mexico's stock market

	Coefficients	T-statistic	Significance
λ_I	–0.25	–4.51	0.00
λ_F	–0.56	–2.05	0.04
λ_M	0.91	4.19	0.00

where:
- λ_I is the price of risk for the money market rate of interest;
- λ_F is the price of risk for the FT/S&P world stock market price index;
- λ_M is the price of risk for the money supply.

The interest rate and FT/S&P world stock market price index variables are significantly priced and have negative signs. This implies that unexpected changes in these two variables tend to have a negative effect on listed share prices in the Mexican stock market. But the price of risk for the money supply variable is positive which implies that an unexpected increase in this variable leads to a subsequent increase in excess returns.

9.3.4 Venezuela

As in the case of the United Kingdom, Norway and Mexico, there are seven observed variables that are considered potential risk factors in the Venezuelan stock market. These observed variables are the deposit rates of interest, oil prices, FT/S&P world stock market price index, money supply, Venezuelan Bolivares per US dollar exchange rate, consumer price index and commercial banks' lending to the private sector. We have already presented the restricted autoregressive models of oil prices and the FT/S&P composite price index variables in the first two subsections. Table 9.7 presents the restricted autoregressive models for the other five observed variables.

The chi-square tests of zero restrictions on the deleted insignificant lags in the above five models are significant at the 5 per cent level. Hence, the restricted autoregressive models are all correctly specified. Furthermore, residuals for the above models are all serially uncorrelated as shown by the F-tests in Table 9.7. The residuals of the five restricted autoregressive models are shown in Figure 9.7 below.

Table 9.7 Test of linear restrictions and serial correlation of residuals from restricted autoregressive models for Venezuela

Variables	Models	F test	χ^2 test
Interest rate	First difference	1.25	13.99
Money supply	First difference	0.86	19.68
Exchange rate	$\Delta E_t = 0.02 + 0.36\ \Delta_{t-1}$ (2.46) (3.68)	1.96	19.52
Consumer price index	$\Delta P_t = 0.01 + 0.81\ \Delta P_{t-1}$ (2.90)(13.01)	1.13	11.89
Commercial banks lending to the private sector	$\Delta L_t = 0.02 + 0.36\ \Delta L_{t-2}$ (3.00) (3.64)	1.58	18.04

Note: The figures in parenthesis are t-statistics.

The cumulative sum and the cumulative sum of squares tests of parameter stability for the five restricted autoregressive models, in Table 9.8, are shown in Figure 9.8.

The non-linear APT model, which has seven innovation terms of the observed variables for Venezuela, is presented in equation (9.10):

$$\rho_{(t)} = \beta_I[\lambda_I + I_{(t)}] + \beta_O[\lambda_O + O_{(t)}] + \beta_F[\lambda_F + F_{(t)}] + \beta_M[\lambda_M + M_{(t)}] + \beta_E[\lambda_E + E_{(t)}] + \beta_P[\lambda_P + P_{(t)}] + \beta_L[\lambda_L + L_{(t)}] \tag{9.10}$$

where:

$\rho_{(t)}$ is the excess return of the total stock market price index;
$I_{(t)}$ is the innovation term of the lending rate of interest;
$O_{(t)}$ is the innovation term of the oil price;
$F_{(t)}$ is the innovation term of the FT/S&P world stock market price index;
$M_{(t)}$ is the innovation term of the money supply;
$E_{(t)}$ is the innovation term of the exchange rate;
$P_{(t)}$ is the innovation term of the consumer price index;
$L_{(t)}$ is the innovation term of commercial banks' lending to the private sector;
β is the sensitivity of the excess return index to the observed variables;
λ is the price of risk of the observed variables.

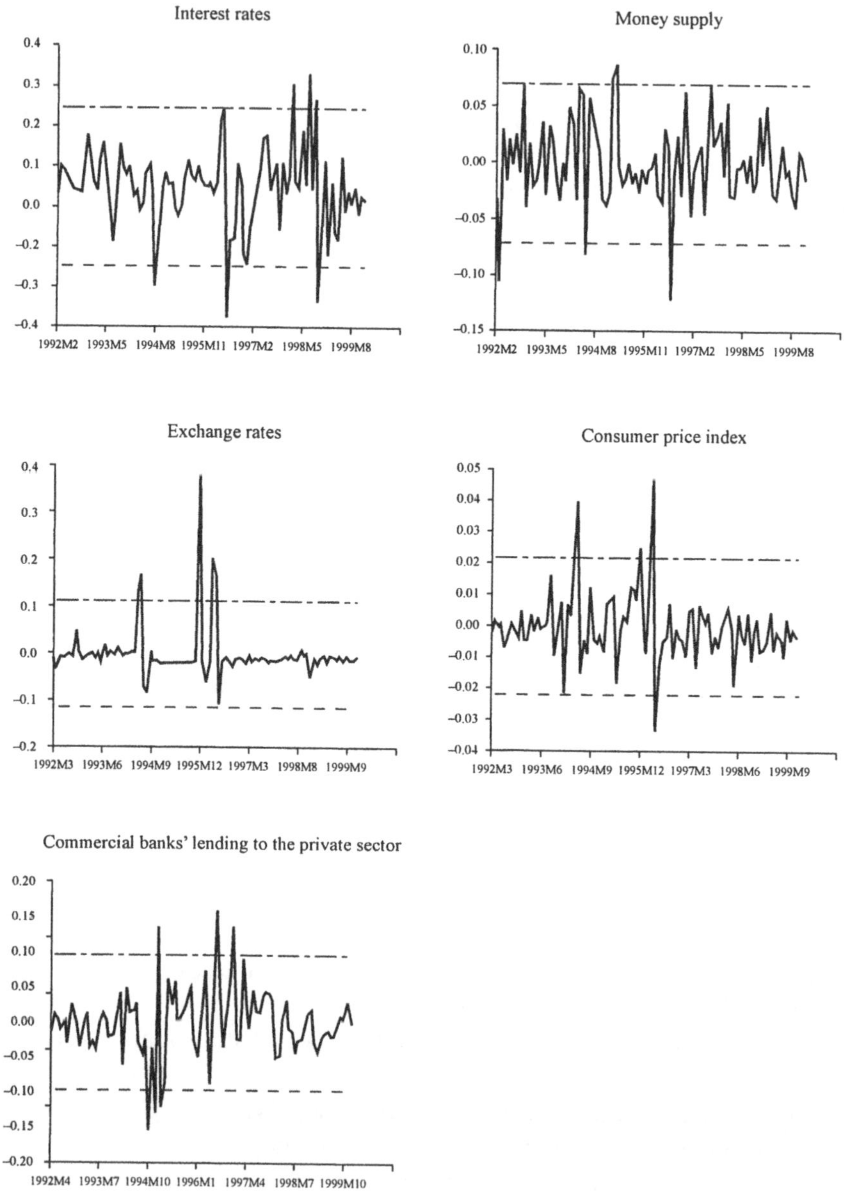

Figure 9.7 Residuals generated by restricted autoregressive models for Venezuela

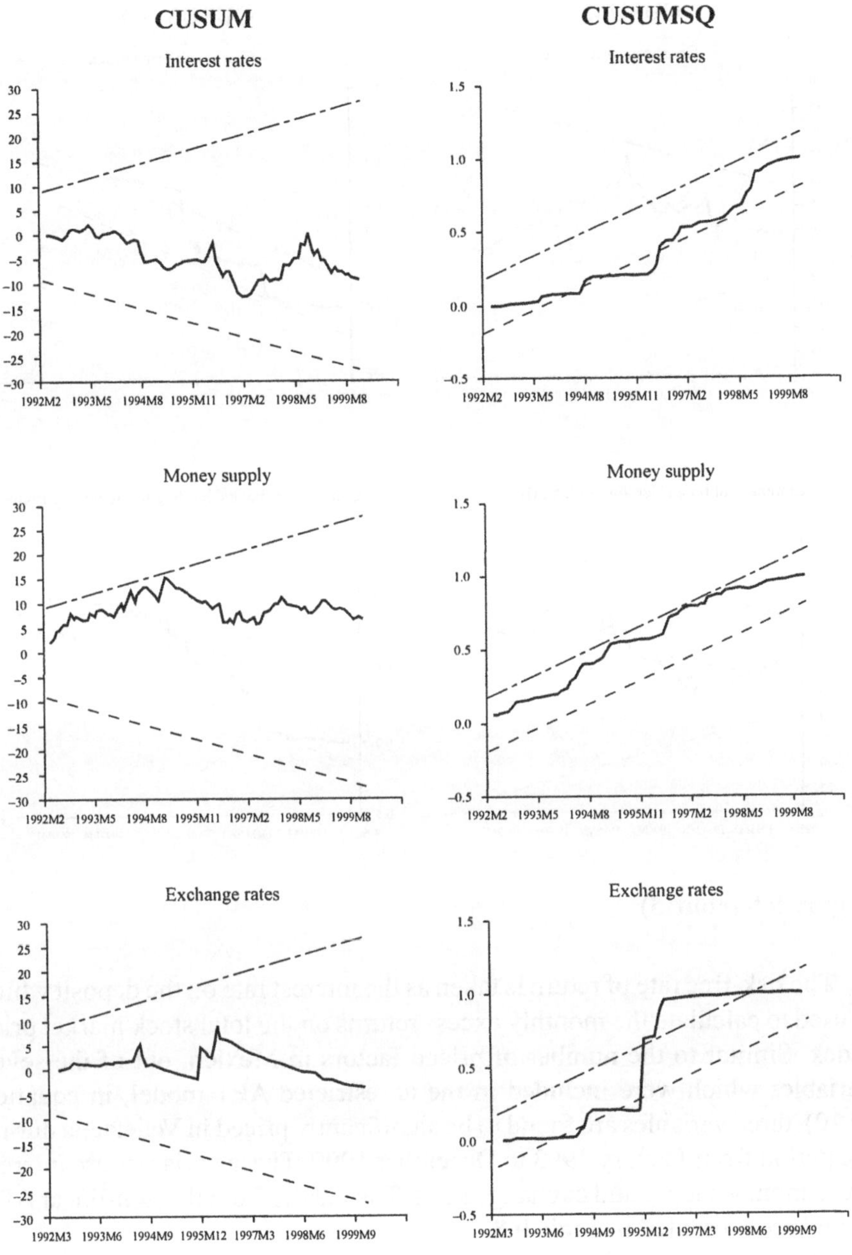

Figure 9.8 Plot of cumulative sum and cumulative sum of squares of the recursive residuals for Venezuela

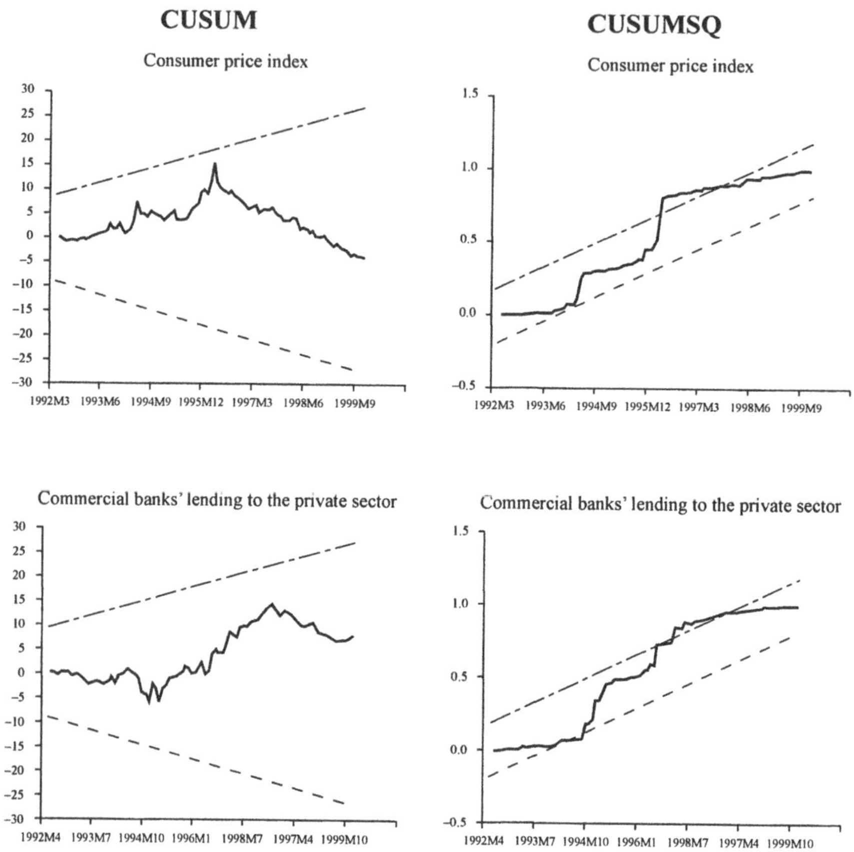

Figure 9.8 (cont'd)

The risk-free rate of return is taken as the interest rate on the deposit which is used to calculate the monthly excess returns on the total stock market price index. Similar to the number of priced factors in Mexico, out of the seven variables which were included in the unrestricted APT model, in equation (9.10), three variables are found to be significantly priced in Venezuela during the period from January 1993 to December 1999. These variables are interest rates, money supply and exchange rates. The results from the non-linear APT model are presented in Table 9.8.

While the price of risk for the interest rates variable is negative, the prices of risk for the money supply and the exchange rate variables are positive. The signs of the prices of risk for the interest rates and the money supply in

Table 9.8 Estimate for prices of risk in Venezuela's stock market

	Coefficients	T-statistic	Significance
λ_I	–0.34	–2.58	0.01
λ_M	0.58	2.26	0.03
λ_E	0.89	2.05	0.04

where:
λ_I is the price of risk for the money market rates of interest;
λ_M is the price of risk for the money supply;
λ_E is the price of risk for the Venezuelan Bolivares per US dollar exchange rate.

Venezuela are consistent with our findings in Mexico. But we expected the sign of the price of risk for the exchange rate to be negative rather than positive because unexpected changes in the exchange rates are expected to lead to a fall in listed share prices in Venezuela.

So far, the oil price variable has not been found to be statistically significant for any of the four countries, namely the United Kingdom, Norway, Mexico and Venezuela, during the period of analysis. The next subsection will cover the application of the APT model to Oman.

9.3.5 Oman

The five potential systematic observed variables for the stock market in Oman are interest rate on the Eurodollar, oil prices, FT/S&P world stock market price index, money supply and commercial banks' lending to the private sector. They have been identified in Chapter 3 and all have first-order of integration. We have also presented in Chapter 4 the restricted autoregressive models for these observed variables, used to generate the innovation terms that enter the APT model. The unrestricted APT model for Oman includes innovation terms of the five observed variables which are likely to be a potential source of systematic risk in the local stock market. This is presented in equation (9.11) below:

$$\rho_{(t)} = \beta_I[\lambda_I + I_{(t)}] + \beta_O[\lambda_O + O_{(t)}] + \beta_F[\lambda_F + F_{(t)}] + \beta_M[\lambda_M + M_{(t)}] + \beta_L[\lambda_L + L_{(t)}] \quad (9.11)$$

where:

$\rho_{(t)}$ is the excess return of the general market price index;

$I_{(t)}$ is the innovation term of the interest rates;
$O_{(t)}$ is the innovation term of the oil price;
$F_{(t)}$ is the innovation term of the FT/S&P world stock market price index;
$M_{(t)}$ is the innovation term of the money supply;
$L_{(t)}$ is the innovation term of the commercial bank lending to the private sector;
β is the sensitivity of the excess return index to the observed variables;
λ is the price of risk of the observed variables.

The risk-free rates of returns are based on the three-month US Treasury bills which are used to calculate the monthly excess return on the general price index of the local stock market. The final result from the APT model is presented in Table 9.9, where only the oil price variable is significantly priced during the period from January 1993 to December 1999.

Table 9.9 Estimate for prices of risk in Oman's stock market

	Coefficients	T-statistic	Significance
λ_O	0.14	1.80	0.08

where:
λ_O is the price of risk for the oil price variable.

The oil price variable has a positive price of risk, which implies that unexpected changes in this variable tend to have a positive effect on the excess return in Oman.

To summarize our results in this part, for the UK stock market, out of the seven observed variables that are considered as the potential sources of systematic risk in the unrestricted APT model, only two are found to have statistically significant prices of risk. They are the S&P composite price index and the industrial production index. Norway, like the United Kingdom, has seven variables in the unrestricted APT model and two are found to be significantly priced. These two priced variables for Norway are the term structure of interest rates and the FT/S&P world stock market price index.

The unrestricted APT model for Mexico and Venezuela both have seven variables and three are found to be significantly priced in each country. The three risk factors for Mexico are the lending rate, the FT/S&P world stock market price index and the money supply variables. Whereas for Venezuela, the interest rate, the money supply and the Venezuelan Bolivar per dollar exchange rate variables are systematically priced. Hence, the interest rate and the money supply are the two variables that are commonly priced in the two oil producing Latin American countries. Oman is the only country of the five net oil-exporting countries that has an oil prices variable which is significantly priced. There are five observed variables that are included in the unrestricted APT model for Oman and only one commands a risk premium.

We would like to point out that testing the APT using observed variables is a joint test of the theory and the relevancy of the observed variables. We have demonstrated that the APT is testable in all five countries. Furthermore, in the five net oil-exporting countries, the oil prices variable is only relevant in the case of Oman which has the highest dependency on oil earnings. With regards to the issue of the increasing trend of stock markets integration in the world and its impact on asset returns with respect to the five countries, it is possible to state that this global risk factor plays an important role in determining the excess returns of the three largest economies, which are the UK, Norway and Mexico. Even though the FT/S&P world stock market price index factor is statistically significant in Norway and Mexico, its price of risk is not the same in the two countries. Furthermore, our empirical results from applying the APT model in the five net oil-exporting countries indicate that local factors do not drive out international factors. This finding is opposite to that stated in Ferson and Harvey (1998) but this can be attributed to the differences in the methodology of analysis. The authors used the mean-variance method whereas we used the non-linear least squares method.

Since the FT/S&P world stock market price index variable is irrelevant in determining the excess returns in Venezuela and Oman, we can conclude that these two stock markets are less integrated with the world financial market.

9.4 Using Reduced Rank Regression Method

In section 9.2, we showed that the two equations of the APT model – namely, the return generating process equation and the expected return equation – can be combined in one equation, as expressed in equation (9.12) below:

$$\rho(t)_i = \sum_{j=1}^{k} b_{ij} \, [\lambda(t)_j + F(t)_j] + \mu(t)_i \qquad (9.12)$$

where:

$\rho(t)_i$ is the excess return on asset i;
$F(t)_j$ is the jth factor that influences the return on asset i;
$\lambda(t)_j$ is the risk premium associated with $F_{(t)j}$;
β_{ij} is the sensitivity of asset i to factor j;
$\mu(t)_i$ is the random error term.

The above single equation APT model is non-linear in the term $[\lambda(t)_j + F(t)_j]$ and because of this non-linearity we used the non-linear least square method of estimation in applying the APT model in equation (9.12). To transform this non-linear term, we start by dividing it into two parts $[(\lambda(t)_j, I_k), (\gamma(t), F(t)_j)]$, where I_k is the identity matrix and $\gamma(t)$ is a column of ones. Then defining a new matrix $A_{ij} \equiv \beta_{ij}(\lambda_j, I_k)$ and defining a new term $Z(t)_j \equiv [\gamma(t), F(t)_j]$, and substituting them in equation (9.12), results in equation (9.13), which represents the single equation APT model in a matrix form. This APT model is linear in the variable:

$$\rho(t)_i = \sum_{j=1}^{k} A_{ij} Z(t)_j + \mu(t)_i. \tag{9.13}$$

Thus, the non-linear term in equation (9.12) has been transformed into a linear term, $Z(t)_j$, and a restricted reduced rank matrix of regression coefficients, A_{ij}, as in equation (9.13) which represents the APT model. equation (9.13) linearly relates the excess return of listed share prices, $\rho(t)_i$, to a set of unexpected changes of observed financial and economic variables, $Z(t)_j$, which are represented by the residuals from the restricted autoregressive models in the previous chapter. Traditionally, when applying the APT model in equation (9.13), researchers have assumed that the coefficient matrix, A_{ij}, is of full rank and regress all the variables in the term, $Z(t)_j$, using the OLS method. While including all the observed variables in a regression will normally lead to having high correlation of the regression, Zhou (1995) argued that:

> in data modelling, the greater the number of regressors, the better the model fits the data, but the worse the sampling behaviour of the parameters. So, for a given level of goodness of fit, we would like the number of explaining variables to be at a minimum and the rank test determines this minimum number. (p. 96)

The rank test of the coefficient matrix, A_{ij}, is helpful in determining how many of the observed variables are significant in explaining the variation in the excess return of listed share prices. There are three outcomes that the rank test can have. Firstly, if the rank test of the coefficient matrix of regression reveals that all the seven observed variables are significant in explaining the variation of the excess return of listed share prices, then it is possible to conclude that A_{ij} has a full rank. Secondly, if the rank test reveals that none of the observed variables are significant, then A_{ij} has a zero rank. Finally, if the number of observed variables is significantly less than the total number of regressors and more than zero, then the rank of the coefficient matrix is a reduced one. The first and second outcomes of the rank test are not of interest to us, but the third one is. The method of testing the rank of the coefficient matrix of regression is presented in the next section.

We are interested in measuring the linear relationship, if any, between two sets of variables – the excess return of listed shares set, $\rho(t)_i$, and the unexpected change of the observed variables set, $Z(t)_j$. Therefore, we would only focus on the analysis of the covariance matrix, Σ, of the two sets of variables. If all the variables in one set are correlated to the variables in the other set, then it is possible to partition the covariance matrix Σ, into four submatrices, as shown below in equation (9.14):

$$\Sigma = \begin{bmatrix} \Sigma_{zz} & \Sigma_{z\rho} \\ \Sigma_{\rho z} & \Sigma_{\rho\rho} \end{bmatrix}. \tag{9.14}$$

The Σ_{zz} submatrix represents the covariance between the variables in the first set, $Z(t)_j$, and the $\Sigma_{\rho\rho}$ submatrix represents the covariance between the variables in the second set, $\rho(t)_i$. The submatrix $\Sigma_{z\rho}$ is equal to the inverse of the $\Sigma_{\rho z}$ submatrix, represents the covariance between the variables in the $Z(t)_j$ set and the variables in the $\rho(t)_i$ set. In this case, $\Sigma_{z\rho}$ has a full rank, since we assumed that all the variables in one set are correlated to the variables in the other set. But, it is possible to have a zero rank in the submatrix, $\Sigma_{z\rho}$, in which case there is no correlation between the variables in the first and the second sets. The implication of having a full rank or a zero rank covariance matrix between the variables in the two sets is straightforward in the sense that when the rank is full, then it is possible to apply the OLS method of regression, and when the rank is zero then there is no point in carrying out regression analysis because the two sets are not linearly related. But, when the rank test reveals that the covariance submatrix, $\Sigma_{z\rho}$, is less than full and greater than zero, then the main implication for our analysis is that it is not appropriate to include all the independent variables in the regression analysis. Therefore, determining the rank of the coefficient matrix would reveal the minimum number of independent variables that are necessary to explain the variation in the dependent variables, as has been pointed out above by Zhou

(1995). So, the next step is to determine how to test the rank of the covariant submatrix, $\Sigma_{z\rho}$.

Anderson (1951) suggests using canonical analysis to test the rank of the covariant submatrix, $\Sigma_{z\rho}$, in order to determine how many of the independent variables in one set, $Z(t)_j$, are significant in explaining the variation in the dependent variables in the other set, $\rho(t)_i$. In other words, testing the rank of the coefficient matrix of the regression can be done by using canonical analysis.

Canonical analysis is a general multivariate statistical technique that simultaneously measures the relationship between one set of independent variables and another set of dependent variables. It can be viewed as a natural extension of the multiple regression analysis that measures the relationship between one dependent variable and a set of independent variables. Unlike factor analysis, which is concerned with determining a small number of common factors from a large set of variables, canonical analysis measures the inter-relationship between two different sets of variables (that is, a set of dependent variables and a set of independent variables).

There are two principal assumptions in canonical analysis – linearity and normality of the underlying variables. Unless the underlying variables are linear, canonical analysis would not show any significant correlations between the different sets of variables. While the normality of the underlying variables is not strictly required in canonical analysis, nevertheless, it is important to have multivariate residuals that are normally distributed, as is argued by Hair, Anderson, Tatham and Black (1998), Johnson and Wichern (1992) and Anderson (1984).

The objective of canonical analysis is to identify and measure the strength of the inter-relationships between two sets of variables that are assumed to be linearly correlated.

The strength of the inter-relationships is known as the canonical correlation which is based on using the canonical variates. The canonical variates are linearly related to each set of the variables in the following way. Let C be the canonical variate of the term $\rho(t)_i$ and D be the canonical variate of the term $Z(t)_j$, then define the two canonical variates as a linear function of the two observed terms, as shown below in equation (9.15):

$$C = \theta' \rho(t)_i \qquad \text{and} \qquad D = \gamma Z(t)_j.$$

The canonical variates, C and D, can be further subdivided into the following canonical variates which correspond to each variable in a set, as shown below:

$$C = \begin{bmatrix} C_1 \\ C_2 \\ : \\ : \\ C_i \end{bmatrix} \quad \text{and} \quad D = \begin{bmatrix} D_1 \\ C_2 \\ : \\ : \\ D_j \end{bmatrix} \simeq \tag{9.15}$$

The variances (Var), covariance (Cov) and correlation (Corr) of the canonical variates are presented in the following equations:

$$\text{Var (C)} = \theta' \,\text{Cov}(\rho(t))\, \theta = \theta'\Sigma_{\rho\rho}\theta; \tag{9.16}$$

$$\text{Var (D)} = \gamma'\text{Cov}(Z(t))\, \gamma = \gamma'\Sigma_{zz}\,\gamma; \tag{9.17}$$

$$\text{Cov (C,D)} = \theta' \,\text{Cov}(\rho(t), Z(t))\, \gamma = \theta'\Sigma_{\rho Z}\,\gamma. \tag{9.18}$$

Having defined the canonical variates, their variances, covariances and correlation for each set of variables, the next step is to determine the number of canonical functions that maximize the relationship between the canonical variates. These canonical functions are independent of each other and the maximum number of canonical functions is equal to the number of variables in the smallest set of variables. For example, if there are five independent variables in one set and three dependent variables in the other set, the maximum number of canonical functions is equal to three which is the number of variables in the smallest set.

Therefore, letting the term λ represent the canonical functions between the two canonical variates, C and D as in equation (9.15), the number of canonical functions between the two canonical variates is equal to the number of roots in the covariance matrix Σ in (9.14) that are different from zero, which can be found by solving the eigenvalue problem in equation (9.19) as below:

$$\left|\lambda\sum\rho\rho - \sum\rho z \sum\nolimits_{zz}^{-1} \sum zp\right| = 0. \tag{9.19}$$

The order of the characteristic roots is $\lambda_1 > \lambda_2 > \ldots\ldots. > \lambda_r$, equal to the square roots of the canonical functions. The first canonical function λ_1 represents the maximum linear combination between the two canonical variates. The second canonical function λ_2 represents the maximum linear combination between the canonical variates that are not correlated to the first canonical function, that is, λ_1 is orthogonal to λ_2. The procedure of finding more canonical functions is continued until the last λ_r is found. This means that the canonical functions are independent of each other, hence implying a diagonal matrix, which is shown below:

$$\lambda = \begin{bmatrix} \lambda_1 & 0 & .. & .. & 0 \\ 0 & \lambda_2 & .. & .. & 0 \\ \vdots & \vdots & & & \vdots \\ \vdots & \vdots & & & \vdots \\ 0 & 0 & .. & .. & \lambda_r \end{bmatrix}.$$

To solve the problem in equation (9.19) above for λ, Anderson (1951) proposed using the maximum likelihood method of estimation and the likelihood ratio to test the null hypothesis. The maximum likelihood method of estimation[4] is equal to the OLS method when analyzing linear regression for large samples. In this case, both estimators are unbiased and consistent. But when analyzing small samples of data, as in our case, the maximum likelihood estimator is biased downward, which means that it underestimates the true variance but it is more efficient than the OLS estimator. Assuming that Σ_{ZZ} and $\Sigma_{\rho\rho}$ are non-singular matrices, Izenman (1995) argued that if the regression coefficient matrix, A_{ij}, has a rank equal to r which is less than full rank where $1 \leq r < j$, then there exist two matrixes – namely α β such that $A_{ij} = \alpha_{ir}\ \beta_{rj}$. The maximum likelihood estimator iterates between α_{ir} and β_{rj} until an estimated value of A_{ij} finally converges. The null hypothesis for testing whether any of the characteristic roots are equal to zero can be carried on by using the likelihood ratio statistic that has chi-square distribution and degrees of freedom equal to the number of restrictions, as explained by Anderson (1984).

The likelihood ratio statistic, which was proposed by Anderson (1951) to test the restriction on the coefficient matrix of parameters, is asymptotically efficient and has been developed further by Izenman (1995) and Tso (1981), among others. There are three common statistical tests of significance for the multivariate canonical correlations, which are the Wilks' lambda, Pillai's trace and Hotelling's trace. All these three tests of significance are based on the likelihood ratio.

When r is equal to zero, this indicates that there is no correlation between the excess return term and the innovations term and the coefficient matrix is equal to zero. Also, when rank r is equal to the number of regressors, then the coefficient matrix has full rank and the OLS method is an efficient method of estimation. On the other hand, if the rank, r, is greater than zero and less than the number of regressors, i.e. $0 < r < j$, then the coefficient matrix has a reduced rank which Izenman (1995) defines as, 'the maximal amount of reduction in dimensionality of the data that is possible without destroying the informational content' (p. 249). The empirical results of the reduced rank regression method will be presented in the next section.

9.5 Empirical Results of Using the Reduced Rank Regression Method

The APT model in equation (9.13) shows that the excess returns of listed share prices in the set $\rho(t)_i$ are conditional on a set of factors in $Z(t)_j$ which represents the unexpected changes of economic and financial variables. In this section, we are going to apply the reduced rank regression method of testing the APT model in the United Kingdom stock market. We have selected a random sample of eight sectors and used their excess returns in the $\rho(t)_i$ set and the seven innovation terms of observed variables which were estimated in Chapter 7, in the $Z(t)_j$ set, as shown below:

$$\rho(t)_i = \begin{bmatrix} \Delta B_t \\ \Delta C_t \\ \Delta D_t \\ \Delta I_t \\ \Delta M_t \\ \Delta R_t \\ \Delta E_t \\ \Delta P_t \end{bmatrix} \quad \text{and} \quad Z(t)_j = \begin{bmatrix} TS_t \\ SP_t \\ OP_t \\ MS_t \\ LP_t \\ PC_t \\ IP_t \end{bmatrix}$$

where the excess return variables in the $\rho(t)_i$ set are the price indices of the following sectors: banks (Δ_t), construction and building materials (ΔC_t), distributors (ΔD_t), insurance (ΔI_t), media and photography (ΔM_t), general retailers (ΔR_t), real estate (ΔE_t), and personal care and household products (ΔP_t). The unexpected changes of the observed variables in equation (9.13) are represented by the residuals from the restricted autoregressive models. The innovation terms in the $Z(t)_j$ set are the following observed variables: term structure of interest rate (TS_t), S&P composite price index (SP_t), oil prices (OP_t), money supply (MS_t), commercial banks' lending to the private sector (LP_t), retail price index (RI_t), and industrial production index (ID_t). These residuals or innovations of the seven observed variables, which enter the Z(t) set in equation (9.13), are stationary and serially uncorrelated, that is, they are all I(0) variables. The excess returns of the eight sectors price indexes are shown in Figure 9.9 below.

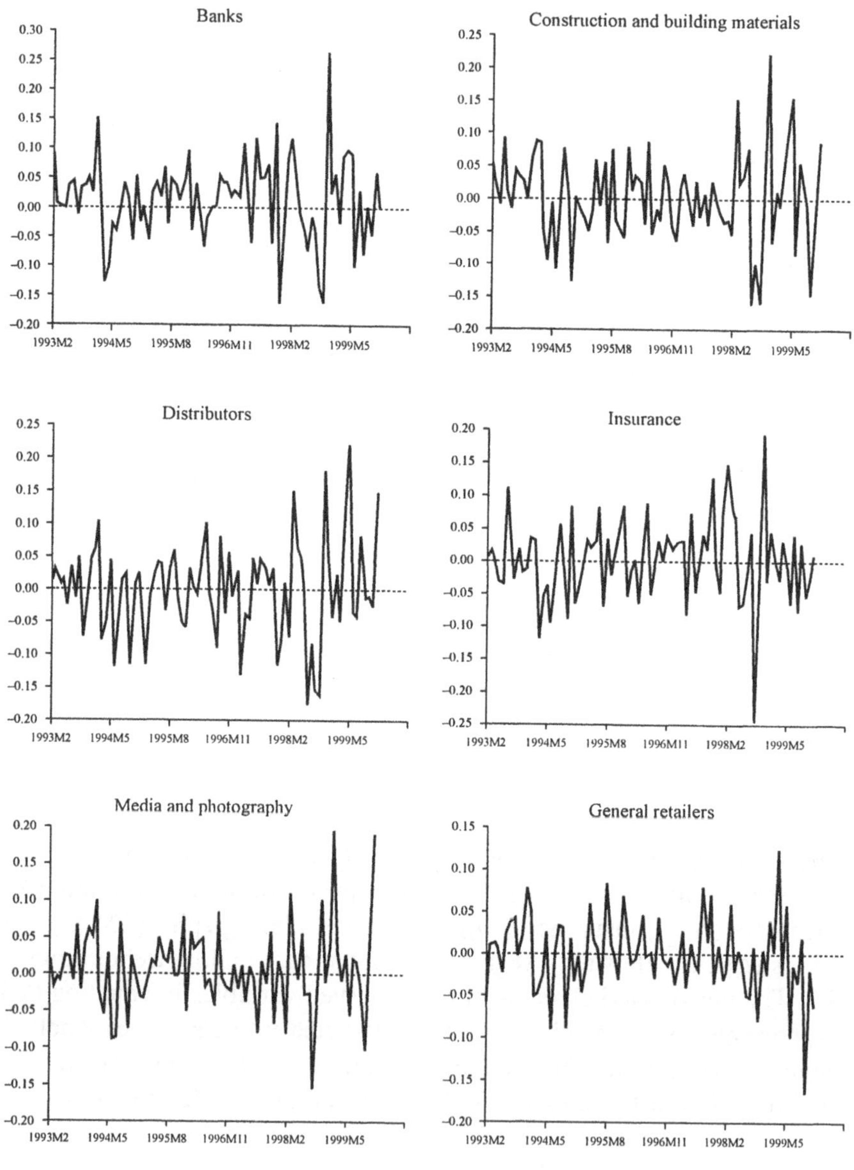

Figure 9.9 Excess returns of eight sector indices in the UK stock market

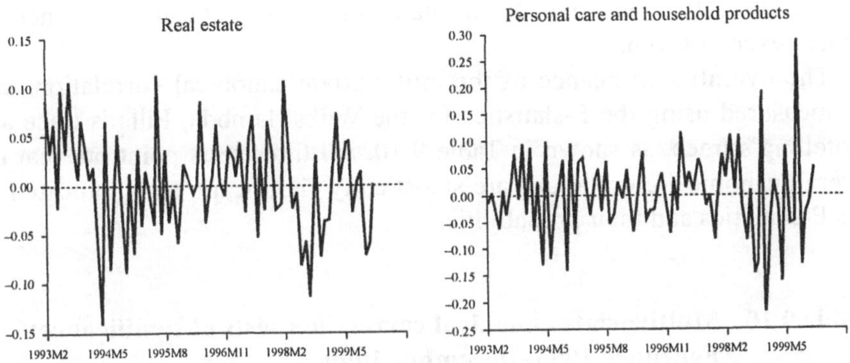

Figure 9.9 (cont'd)

The excess returns on the eight sector indexes, which are shown in Figure 9.9, are all stationary around their zero mean, and that means they all have zero order of integration, that is they are I(0). Hence, both the dependent variables set and the independent variables set are of the same order of integration.

The canonical analysis will be used in determining the rank of the coefficient matrix of regression for the APT model in equation (9.13). The procedure for using the canonical analysis to test the rank of the coefficient matrix starts by firstly defining canonical variates in each of the two sets. The canonical variates are linearly correlated to each of the original variables in each set. There are eight canonical variates in the first set of excess return variables and seven canonical variates in the second set of the innovation terms. The second step is to determine the number of canonical functions, which are defined as the maximum correlation between a pair of canonical variates, one from the dependent variables set and the other one from the independent variables set. The first canonical function explains the maximum inter-relationship between a pair of canonical variates and the second function explains the maximum inter-relationship between another pair of canonical variates that is not captured by the first canonical function. Each one of the canonical functions is independent from the other functions, that is, they are orthogonal. In the third step the canonical correlations, which measure the strength of the canonical variates, will be tested using the Wilks' lambda.

There are eight excess return variables available in the first set, which represents the dependent variables, and there are seven innovation terms of the observed economic and financial variables in the second set of variables, which represents the independent variables. Since the number of variables in the smallest set is equal to seven, the maximum number of canonical functions cannot exceed seven.

The overall significance of the multivariate canonical correlations can be measured using the F-statistics for the Wilks' lambda, Pillai's trace and Hotelling's trace, as shown in Table 9.10. All three tests point out that the overall canonical correlations are statistically significant, as is indicated by the F-statistics and their probabilities.

Table 9.10 Multivariate canonical correlation tests of significance: February 1993–December 1999

Tests	Values	F-statistic	Probability
Wilks' lambda	1.13	1.99	0.00
Pillai's trace	1.88	2.22	0.00
Hotelling's trace	0.24	2.02	0.00

This means that there is at least one significant canonical correlation that exists between the dependent variables set and the independent variables set. In order to determine how many significant canonical correlations there are between the dependent and the independent sets, we need to examine the eigenvalues and the canonical correlations values that are presented in Table 9.11. The first root has an eigenvalue of about one and accounts for 54 per cent of the total eigenvalues. It has a canonical correlation of 91 per cent, which means that the first canonical function accounts for 91 percent of the variation between the canonical variates of the dependent variables and the independent variables. The second root has an eigenvalue of 0.59 and accounts for 30 per cent of the total eigenvalues. The canonical correlation for the second root explains 60 per cent of the variation between the canonical variates of the dependent and the independent sets.

The third root accounts for less than 20 per cent of the total eigenvalues and 39 per cent of the canonical correlation. The remaining roots, from 4 to 9, have a total contribution to the eigenvalues of less than the contribution of the third root, and their canonical correlations are relatively low when compared to the first and the second roots. The results of the eigenvalues and the canonical correlations indicate the presence of two significant canonical correlations between the variates of the dependent and the independent variables. To confirm this finding, we conduct a dimension reduction analysis

Table 9.11 Eigenvalues and canonical correlations in the UK stock market: February 1993–December 1999

Roots	Eigenvalues	Percent	Canonical correlations
1	1.02	54.15	0.91
2	0.59	30.22	0.60
3	0.16	8.34	0.39
4	0.06	3.43	0.25
5	0.04	2.25	0.20
6	0.03	1.34	0.16
9	0.01	0.28	0.09

using Wilks' lamda. The object of this analysis is to determine the exact number of significant canonical correlations, which will determine the rank of the coefficient matrix in equation (9.11). The results of the dimension reduction analysis are presented in Table 9.12.

Table 9.12 Dimension reduction test in the UK stock market: February 1993–December 1999

Roots	Wilks' lambda	F-statistic	Probability
1 to 9	0.24	2.02	0.00
2 to 9	0.48	1.31	0.10
3 to 9	0.96	0.68	0.90
4 to 9	0.88	0.49	0.99
5 to 9	0.93	0.44	0.95
6 to 9	0.99	0.39	0.90
9 to 9	0.99	0.19	0.83

The Wilks' lambda statistic indicates that the first and the second roots are significant as evidenced by the F-statistics, in the third column of Table 9.12, and their probability in the fourth column. This means that the rank of the coefficient matrix is equal to two. As a result, there are two factors that are significant in determining the excess returns of the share prices in the UK stock market, and that is consistent with the findings in the previous chapter where two of the observed variables were found to be significantly priced.

At this stage it is not clear which of the seven innovation terms command risk premium and whether the same observed variables are consistently priced for each of the eight sectors' excess returns. Also, the correlations between the dependent set and the independent set and the seven canonical variates are not indicated so far. The contribution of the underlying variables in the dependent and independent sets to the seven canonical variates can be measured by their correlations, which are known, also, as canonical loadings. The linear correlations between the excess returns of the eight sectors in the London Stock Exchange and the seven canonical variates are presented in Table 9.13.

Table 9.13 Correlations between excess returns variables and canonical variates in the UK stock market: February 1993–December 1999

	Canonical variates						
Sectors	First	Second	Third	Fourth	Fifth	Sixth	Seventh
ΔB_t	–0.94	0.04	0.04	–0.01	0.20	–0.23	–0.10
ΔC_t	–0.50	0.49	–0.33	–0.19	0.49	0.02	0.12
ΔD_t	–0.43	0.44	–0.59	–0.26	–0.06	–0.16	–0.35
ΔI_t	–0.84	–0.08	–0.36	0.05	0.02	0.30	0.12
ΔM_t	–0.59	0.33	–0.19	0.13	–0.18	0.08	0.09
ΔR_t	–0.25	–0.22	–0.39	0.40	0.55	–0.18	–0.16
ΔE_t	–0.25	–0.12	–0.49	0.01	0.12	–0.56	0.60
ΔP_t	–0.39	–0.36	–0.25	–0.66	0.10	0.03	–0.04

where

ΔBt is the excess returns on the banks sector price index;
ΔCt is the excess returns on the construction and building materials sector price index;
ΔDt is the excess returns on the distributors sector price index;
ΔIt is the excess returns on the insurance sector price index;
ΔMt is the excess returns on the media and photography sector price index;
ΔRt is the excess returns on the general retailers sector price index;
ΔEt is the excess returns on the real estate sector price index;
ΔPt is the excess returns on the personal care and household products sector price index.

The correlations between the first canonical variate and the excess returns of the eight sectors price indexes, in the second column of Table 9.13, appear to be higher than the correlations between the other six canonical variates and the dependent variables. About 34 per cent of the variation in the dependent variables is explained by the first canonical variate, and the third canonical variate explains 13 per cent of the variation in the dependent variables. The second, fourth, fifth, sixth and seventh canonical variates each explain less than 10 per cent of the variation in the dependent variables. The estimated correlations between the seven canonical variates and the seven innovation terms are presented in Table 9.14.

Table 9.14 Correlations between the innovation terms and the canonical variates in the UK stock market: February 1993–December 1999

	Canonical variates						
Sectors	**First**	**Second**	**Third**	**Fourth**	**Fifth**	**Sixth**	**Seventh**
TS_t	0.11	0.40	0.66	–0.39	0.19	0.35	0.30
SP_t	–0.95	0.14	–0.03	0.13	–0.13	–0.19	0.10
OP_t	0.19	0.46	–0.24	–0.05	0.29	–0.61	0.49
MS_t	–0.25	–0.16	0.41	–0.29	–0.15	–0.69	–0.39
LP_t	–0.32	–0.59	0.19	–0.00	0.68	–0.29	–0.01
RI_t	–0.08	–0.39	–0.41	–0.99	–0.24	0.13	0.10
IP_t	–0.11	0.32	–0.32	–0.48	0.51	0.06	–0.53

where:

TS_t is the innovations of the term structure of interest rate;
SP_t is the innovations of the S&P composite price index;
OP_t is the innovations of the oil prices;
MS_t is the innovations of the money supply;
LP_t is the innovations of the commercial banks' lending to the private sector;
RI_t is the innovations of the retail price index;
IP_t is the innovations of the industrial production index.

The variances of the seven innovation terms are explained by 8 per cent of the variation in the first canonical variate, as shown in the second column in Table 9.14, while the second canonical variate explains 5 per cent of the variation in the innovation terms. Clearly, the correlations between the innovation terms and the canonical variates in this case are much lower than the correlations between the excess returns variables and the canonical variates in Table 9.13. These results indicate that the first, second and third canonical variates have high correlations with both dependent and independent variables. The main problem with using the canonical loadings as an indication of the canonical relationships is that they are very unstable, as has been pointed out by Hair et al. (1998). These loadings have a strong tendency to change from one sample size to another and from one period of analysis to the next. They are sample-specific criteria, which means that they are unstable in different sample sizes or for different periods of analysis.

Having determined the rank of the coefficient matrix for the system of eight equations to be equal to two, which is consistent with the findings from using the non-linear least square method for the UK stock market, in chapter five, during the period from February 1992 to December 1999, the next step of estimating the risk premiums associated with the observed variables is straight forward using the ordinary least square method of regression. The results for the eight excess returns sectors' price indexes are shown in Table 9.15.

The variation in the excess returns of the banks' sector price index, in the first APT model, is 42 per cent explained by the variation in the innovation terms of the S&P composite price index and the commercial banks' lending to the private sector variables. The risk premium associated with the S&P composite price index variable is highly significant but the risk premium associated with the commercial banks' lending to the private sector variable is only significant at the 10 per cent level. Similarly, the previous two observed variables command risk premiums in determining the sixth APT model for the excess returns of the general retailers sector price index. But, the risk premium associated with the S&P composite price index is much weaker in the sixth model in comparison to the first model, as is indicated by the t-statistics in Table 6.6. Both constant terms in the first and sixth models are insignificant. The F-statistics, in the fourth column, for the two APT models show an overall level of significance.

The excess returns on the construction and building materials sector and the distributors' sectors' price indexes have the same priced observed variables. These are the S&P composite price index and the industrial production index. Both have highly significant risk premiums. The constant terms in these two models are statistically insignificant.

There are two similar and significantly priced variables that determine the excess returns on the insurance sector price index and the personal care and household products sector price index. These risk factors are associated with the S&P composite price index variable and the retail price index variable. While the price of risk for the S&P composite price index is highly significant in the fourth APT model, the price of risk associated with the retail price index is only significant at the 10 per cent level. Furthermore, the constant term is significantly priced at the 7 per cent level. But in the eighth model, the constant term is insignificant and the risk premium associated with the retail price index is highly significant at the 1 per cent level. The two innovation terms in the fourth model explains 33 per cent of the variation in

Table 9.15 Estimating the risk premiums of the observed variables in the UK stock market: February 1993–December 1999

Sector	Model	R-square	F-statistic
1 ΔB_t	$-0.00 + 1.16\ SP_t + 1.23\ LP_t$ (–0.29) (9.35) (1.69)	0.42	29.00
2 ΔC_t	$-0.01 + 0.91\ SP_t + 2.82\ IP_t$ (–1.33) (3.99) (2.52)	0.20	10.12
3 ΔD_t	$-0.01 + 0.68\ SP_t + 2.98\ IP_t$ (–1.38) (3.39) (2.28)	0.19	8.09
4 ΔI_t	$-0.01 + 0.99\ SP_t + 4.34\ RI_t$ (–1.85) (6.20) (1.65)	0.33	20.02
5 ΔM_t	$-0.00 + 0.66\ SP_t$ (–0.20) (4.29)	0.18	18.26
6 ΔR_t	$-0.01 + 0.25\ SP_t + 1.03\ LP_t$ (–1.11) (1.88) (1.69)	0.09	3.98
9 ΔE_t	$-0.14 + 0.25\ SP_t$ (–0.02) (1.64)	0.03	2.69*
8 ΔP_t	$-0.01 + 0.46\ SP_t + 9.68\ RI_t$ (–0.81) (2.06) (2.62)	0.12	5.24

Notes

1 The figures in parenthesis are the t-statistics.
2 * = the F(1, 81) is significant at the 10 per cent level of significance.

where:

ΔB_t is the excess returns on the banks sector price index;
ΔCt is the excess returns on the construction and building materials sector price index;
ΔDt is the excess returns on the distributors sector price index;
ΔIt is the excess returns on the insurance sector price index;
ΔMt is the excess returns on the media and photography sector price index;
ΔRt is the excess returns on the general retailers sector price index;
ΔEt is the excess returns on the real estate sector price index;
ΔPt is the excess returns on the personal care and household products sector price index.

the excess returns of the insurance sector, in comparison to only 12 per cent in the eighth model.

The excess returns on the media and photography sector price index (the fifth model), and the real estate sector price index (the seventh model), have only one significantly priced risk premium which is associated with the S&P composite price index. The price of risk in the seventh model is only significant at the 10 per cent level, but in the fifth model it is highly significant, as indicated by the t-tests. Both the constant terms in these two models are insignificant. The innovation terms of the S&P composite index, in the seventh model, explains only three percent of the variation in the excess returns of the real estate sector price index, and that is the lowest power of explanation among the eight models. Finally, all the priced observed variables in Table 9.15 have positive signs.

9.6 Concluding Remarks

This chapter starts by showing how the return generating process equation and the expected return equation which make up the APT equilibrium model can be derived into one single non-linear equation. This single non-linear equation is then tested by using the non-linear least square method of estimation to determine which observed variables for the UK, Norwegian, Mexican, Venezuelan and Omani stock markets command a risk premium.

Next we have used the reduced rank regression method of estimation technique in combining the two different approaches in testing the APT model. The first approach is based on using factor analysis to determine the number of latent factors that are significant in measuring the risk premiums, however, the main drawback of this approach is that it is not possible to associate any economic meaning to the priced factors. The second approach is based on using observed economic and financial variables to determine the risk premiums associated with the priced variables. Neither the two-step approach nor the non-linear least square techniques, which are common in testing the APT model, are appropriate to offer any insight into determining the number of latent factors that are significantly priced when using the observed variables. However, the reduced rank regression method, which uses observed variables, can determine the number of latent factors by knowing the rank of the coefficient matrix of regression. The rank indicates the number of latent factors that are expected to be priced in the APT model.

From the empirical results, we have determined the rank of the coefficient matrix to be equal to two. That is, there are two latent factors that are significant in determining the excess returns in the UK stock market. One consistent latent factor is significantly correlated to the innovation term of the S&P composite price index in all the eight sectors that are tested. But the second latent factor is either insignificantly correlated to the innovation terms of the other six observed variables, as in the case of the media and photography sector and the real estate sector, or it is not the same innovation term. For example, the second latent factor is correlated to the innovation term of the commercial banks' lending to the private sector in estimating the excess returns of the banks sector and the excess returns of the general retailers' sector. In the case of determining the excess returns of the construction and building materials and the distributors' sectors, the second latent factor is significantly correlated to the innovation term of the industrial production variable. Furthermore, the second latent factor is correlated to the innovation term of the retail price index variable in determining the excess returns of the insurance and the personal care and household products sectors.

The empirical results from testing the APT model in the UK Stock Market in the last chapter using observed variables, demonstrate that the innovation terms from the S&P composite price index and the industrial production index variables are statistically significant in determining the excess returns of the FT all share price index. The fact that the eight sectors' excess returns are influenced by different observed variables when compared with the excess returns on the FT all share price index is an expected outcome. This is because the individual sector is normally more sensitive to particularly observed variables, which are more likely to be different from those that tend to influence the general market index.

Notes

1 The three-stage least square technique, which is used in estimating a system of simultaneous equations, is an extension of the two-stage least square and the least squares methods of estimating regressions for single equations. It is known as full information technique because it estimates the whole system of equations in one step using all information available on each of the equations in the system.

2 The concept of the instrumental variables technique is based on a two step procedure. In the first step, an instrument, z, which is highly correlated with independent variable, x, and uncorrelated with the residual term of the dependent variable, y, is identified. Then use the OLS method to regress the independent variable, x, on the instrument, z. The fitted value of x is known as the instrumental variable. In the second step, the dependent variable, y, is regressed on the instrumental variable x.

3 Pindyck and Rubinfeld (1991) point out that the OLS estimation method is a special case of the instrumental variables technique because the independent variables are perfectly correlated with themselves and uncorrelated with the error term of the dependent variable.

4 The likelihood function of a simple linear regression: $y_i = a + bx_i + e_i$ is shown in equation (F1) below:

$$L = (2\pi\sigma^2)^{-\frac{n}{2}} \exp\left[-\frac{1}{2\sigma^2}\sum_{i=1}^{n}(y_i - a - bx_i)^2\right]. \tag{F1}$$

The log likelihood function can be obtained by taking the natural logarithm of equation (F1):

$$LnL = -\left(\frac{n}{2}\right)\ln 2\pi - \left(\frac{n}{2}\right)\ln\sigma^2 - \frac{1}{2\sigma^2}\sum_{i=1}^{n}(y_i - a - bx_i)^2. \tag{F2}$$

The maximum likelihood estimator of the two coefficients, a and b, and the variance σ^2 can be found by partially differentiating the log likelihood function with respect to the three parameters and setting it equal to zero. The two estimated coefficients, a and b, from using the maximum likelihood function are the same as those obtained by using the OLS estimator. But the estimated variance would differ in the two methods.

Bibliography

Abrahamson, I.G. (1964), 'Orthant Probabilities for the Quadrivariate *Normal* Distribution', *Annals of Mathematical Statistics*, 35, pp. 1685–703.

Akaike, H. (1969), 'Fitting Autoregressive Models for Prediction', *Annals of the Institute of Statistical Mathematics*, 21, pp. 243–47.

Akaike, H. (1973), 'Information Theory and an Extension of the Maximum Likelihood Principle', in B.N. Petrove and F. Caski (eds), *Second International Symposium on Information Theory*, Akademiai Kiado, Budapest, pp. 267–81.

Akaike, H. (1974), 'A New Look at the Statistical Model Identification', *IEEE: Transactions on Automatic Control*, 19, pp. 716–23.

Akaike, H. (1981), 'Likelihood of a Model and Information Criteria', *Journal of Econometrics*, 16, pp. 3–14.

Ali, M. (2002), *Historical Ex-post and Ex-ante Forecasts for Three Kinds of Pulse in Bagladesh: Masu, Gram and Khesuri*, unpublished PhD thesis, Jahangir Nagar University, Bangladesh.

Ali, M., Hossain, M.Z. and Bhatti, M. I. (2004), 'An Econometric Analysis of Some Major Manufacturing Industries: A Case Study of Bangladesh', *Managerial Auditing*, 19 (6), pp. 790–96.

Al-Shanfari, H. (2001), *Testing the Arbitrage Pricing Theory in the Global Context*, unpublished PhD thesis, University of Strathclyde, Scotland.

Al-Shanfari, H., Hossain, M.Z., and Bhatti, M.I. (2004), 'Model Selection in the Context of Arbitrage Pricing Theory Model,' *Journal of Applied Statistical Sciences*, 3(1), pp. 33–52.

Amemiya, T. (1971), 'The Estimation of Variances in a Variance-components Model', *International Economic Review*, 12, pp. 1–13.

Amemiya, T. (1972), *Lecture Notes on Econometrics*, Department of Economics, Stanford University.

Amemiya, T. (1980), 'Selection of Regressors', *International Economic Review*, 21, pp. 331–54.

Amemiya, T. (1985), *Advanced Econometrics*, Harvard University Press, Cambridge, MA.

Anderson, T.W. (1984), *An Introduction to Multivariate Statistical Analysis*, 2nd edn, Wiley, New York.

Andrews, D.F. (1971), 'A Note on the Selection of Data Transformation', *Biometrika*, 58, pp. 249–54.

Aneuryn-Evans, G. and Deaton, A. (1980), 'Testing Linear Versus Logarithmic Regression Models', *Review of Economic Studies*, 47, pp. 275–91.

Ansley, C.F. (1979), 'An Algorithm for the Exact Likelihood of a Mixed Autoregressive-moving Average Process', *Biometrika*, 66, pp. 59–65.

Ara, I. (1995), *Marginal Likelihood-based Tests of Regression Disturbances*, unpublished PhD thesis, Monash University, Melbourne, Australia.

Ara, I. and King, M.L. (1993), *Marginal Likelihood-based Tests of Regression Disturbances*, paper presented at the 1993 meeting of the Australasian meeting of the Econometrics Society, University of Sydney, Sydney, Australia.

Atkinson, A.C. (1973), 'Testing Transformations to Normality', *Journal of the Royal Statistical Society, Series B*, 35, pp. 473–9.

Atkinson, A.C. and Lawrance, A.J. (1989), 'A Comparison of Asymptotic Equivalent Test Statistics for Regression Transformation', *Biometrika*, 76, pp. 223–9.

Atukorala, R. (1999), *The Use of an Information Criterion for Assessing Asymptotic Approximations in Econometrics*, unpublished PhD thesis, Monash University, Melbourne, Australia.

Bai, J., Jakeman, A.J. and McAleer, M. (1990), *Discrimination Procedures for Fitting Nested and Non-nested Distributions to Environmental Quality Data*, Working Paper in Economics and Econometrics No. 200, Australian National University.

Bairam, E. (1992), 'A New Test for Heteroscedasticity and its Application', *Statistica*, 2, pp. 232–9.

Balestra, P. and Nerlove, M. (1966), 'Pooling Cross-section and Time Series Data in the Estimation of a Dynamic Model The Demand for Natural Gas', *Econometrica*, 34, pp. 585–612.

Baltagi, B.H. (1981), 'Pooling: An Experimental Study of Alternative Testing and Estimation Procedures in a Two-Way Error Component Model', *Journal of Econometrics*, 17, pp. 21–49.

Baltagi, B.H. (1996), *Econometrics Analysis of Panel Data*, John Wiley and Sons, New York, New York.

Baltagi, B.H. and Li, Q. (1991), 'A Joint Test for Serial Correlation and Random Individual Effects', *Statistics and Probability Letters*, 11, pp. 277–80.

Baltagi, B.H. and Raj, B. (1992), 'A Survey of Recent Theoretical Developments in the Econometrics of Panel Data', *Empirical Economics*, 17, pp. 85–109.

Baltagi, B.H., Chang, Y.J. and Li, Q. (1992), 'Monte Carlo Results on Several New and Existing Tests for the Error Component Model', *Journal of Econometrics*, 54, pp. 95–120.

Barlow, R.E., Bartholomew, D.J., Bremner, J.M. and Brunk, H.D. (1972), *Statistical Inference under Order Restrictions: The Theory and Application of Isotonic Regression*, John Wiley and Sons, New York.

Barnes, P. (1986), 'Thin Trading and Stock Market Efficiency: The Case of the Kuala Lumpur Stock Exchange', *Journal of Business Finance and Accounting*, 13 (4), pp. 609–17.

Bartholomew, D.J. (1959a), 'A Test of Homogeneity for Ordered Alternative', *Biometrika*, 46, pp. 36–48.

Bartholomew, D.J. (1959b), 'A Test of Homogeneity of Means under Restricted Alternatives', *Journal of the Royal Statistical Society*, B, 23, pp. 239–72.

Beach, C.M. and MacKinnon, J.G. (1978), 'A Maximum Likelihood Procedure for Regression with Autocorrelated Errors', *Econometrica*, 46, pp. 51–8.

Beenstock, M. and Chan, K. (1988), 'Economic Forces in the London Stock Market', *Oxford Bulletin of Economic and Statistics*, 50, pp. 27–39.

Begum, N. (2003), 'A New Class of Hypothesis Tests which Maximize Average Power', unpublished PhD thesis, Monash University, Melbourne, Australia.

Beran, R. (1987), 'Prepivoting to Reduce Level Error of confidence sets', *Biometrika*, 74, 457–468.

Bergstrom, A.R. (1993), 'What is Econometrics?', in P.C.B. Phillips (ed), *Models, Methods and Applications of Econometrics*, Basil Blackwell, Cambridge, MA, pp. 9–11.

Bhansali, R.J. and Downham, D.Y. (1977), 'Some Properties of the Order of an Autoregressive Model Selected by a Generalization of Akaike's FPE Criterion', *Biometrika*, 64, pp. 547–51.

Bhatti, M.I. (1991), 'Optimal Testing for Block Effects in Regression Models', *The Third Pacific Area Statistical Conference Pre-Prints*, The Pacific Statistical Institute, Tokyo, Japan, pp. 401–4.

Bhatti, M.I. (1992), 'Optimal Testing for Serial Correlation in Large Number of Small Samples', *Biometrical Journal*, 34, pp. 57–67.

Bhatti, M.I. (1993), 'Efficient Estimation of Random Coefficient Models Based on Survey Data', *Journal of Quantitative Economics*, 9 (1), pp. 99–110.

Bhatti, M.I. (1995), 'On Testing for Equality of Equicorrelation in Random Coefficient Models', *Biometrical Journal*, 37 (4), pp. 383–91.

Bhatti, M. I. (1995a), *Testing Regression Models Based on Sample Survey Data*, Avebury, Aldershot.

Bhatti, M.I. (2000), 'On Optimal Testing for the Equality of Equicorrelation: An Example of Loss in Power', *Statistical Papers*, 41, pp. 345–52.

Bhatti, M.I. (2001), 'On the Distribution of Bayesian Invariant Test for Structural Change', in V.M. Ahsanullah (ed.), *Applied Statistical Science*, Nova Science Publisher, New York, pp. 237–44.

Bhatti, M.I. (2001a), 'Environmetric Analysis in Complex Surveys', *Complexity*, 6, pp. 41–55.

Bhatti, M.I. (2004), 'On Cluster Effects in Mining Complex Econometric Data', in H. Bozdogan (ed.), *Statistical Data Mining and Knowledge Discovery*, Chapman and Hall/CRC Press, USA, pp. 387–99.

Bhatti, M.I. and Barry, A. (1997), 'A Note on Testing Spatially Autocorrelated Linear Regression Models', *Journal of Applied Statistic Sciences*, 5 (2/3), pp. 173–9.

Bhatti, M.I. and Khan, I.H. (2000), 'Complex versus Simple Models: An Example of Estimation using Bangladeshi Agricultural Data', *Journal of Statistics and Management System*, 3 (3), pp. 295–304.

Bhatti, M.I. and King, M.L. (1990), 'A Beta-optimal Test for Equicorrelation Coefficients', *Australian Journal of Statistics*, 32, pp. 87–97.

Bhatti, M.I. and Wang, J. (1998), 'Power Comparison of Some Tests for Testing Change-point', *Statistica*, LVIII, (2), pp. 127–37.

Bhatti, M.I. and Wang, J. (2000), 'On Testing for a Change-point in Variance of Normal Distribution', *Biometrical Journal*, Vol. 42 (8), pp. 1021–32.

Bhatti, M.I. and Wang, J. (2005 forthcoming), 'Tests and Confidence Intervals for Change-point in Scale of Two-parametric Exponential Distributions', *Journal of Applied Statistical Sciences*, 14 (1).

Bickel, P.J. and Doksum, K.A. (1981), 'An Analysis of Transformations Revisited', *Journal of the American Statistical Association*, 76, pp. 296–311.

Bickel, P.J. and Freedman, D.A. (1983), 'Bootstrapping Regression Models with Many Parameters', in P.J. Bickel, K.A. Doksum and J.C. Hodges (eds), *A Festschrift for Erich L. Lehmann*, Wadsworth, Belmont, pp. 24–48.

Bickel, P.J. and Freedman, D.A. (1981), 'Some Asymptotic Theory for the Bootstrap', *Annals of Statistics*, 9, pp. 1196–217.

Billah, M.B. and King, M.L. (2000), 'Time Series Model Selection and Forecasting via Optimal Penalty Estimation', *Pakistan Journal of Statistics*, 16, pp. 126–45.

Bodie, Z., Kane, A. and Marcus, A. (1996), *Investments*, 3rd edn, Irwin, Sydney.

Bohrer, R. and Chow, W. (1978), 'Weights for One-sided Multivariate Inference', *Applied Statistics*, 27, pp. 100–104.

Bose, G.K. (2002), *An Optimal Approach into Constructing a Penalty Function in Small Samples*, unpublished PhD thesis, Monash University, Melbourne, Australia.

Bowley, A.L. (1906), 'Address to the Economic Science and Statistics Section of the British Association for the Advancement of Science', *Journal of the Royal Statistical Society*, 69, pp. 548–57.

Box, G.E.P. and Cox, D.R. (1964), 'An Analysis of Transformations', *Journal of the Royal Statistical Society*, B, 26, pp. 211–52.

Boylan, T.A., Cuddy, M.P. and O'Muircheartaigh, I. (1980), 'The Functional Form of the Aggregate Import Demand Equation', *Journal of International Economics*, 10 (56), pp. 561–6.

Breiman, L. (1992), 'A Little Bootstrap and Other Methods for Dimensionality Selection: X-fixed Prediction Error', *Journal of the American Statistical Association*, 87, pp. 738–54.

Breiman, L. and Freedman, D. (1983), 'How Many Variables Should be Entered in a Regression Equation?', *Journal of the American Statistical Association*, 78, pp. 131–6.

Breiman, L. and Spector, P. (1992), 'Submodel Selection and Evaluation in Regression: The X-random Case', *International Statistical Review*, 60, pp. 291–319.

Breusch, T.S. (1980), 'Useful Invariance Results for Generalized Regression Models', *Journal of Econometrics*, 13, pp. 327–40.

Breusch, T.S. and Pagan, A.R. (1980), 'The Lagrange Multiplier Test and its Applications to Model Specification in Econometrics', *Review of Economic Studies*, 47, pp. 239–53.

Brooks, R. (1993), 'Alternate Point Optimal Tests for Regression Coefficient Stability', *Journal of Econometrics,* 57, pp. 356–76.

Brooks, R. and King, M.L. (1994), 'Hypothesis Testing of Varying Coefficient Regression Models: Procedures and Applications', *Pakistan Journal of Statistics*, 10, pp. 301–57.

Burmeister, E. and McElroy, M. (1988), 'Joint Estimation of Factor Sensitivities and Risk Premia for the Arbitrage Pricing Theory', *Journal of Finance*, 43, 3, pp. 721–36.

Buse, A. (1980), *Tests for Additive Heteroscedasticit: Some Preliminary Results*, paper presented to the Fourth World Congress of the Econometric Society, Aix-en-Provence.

Butler, K. and Malaikah, S. (1992), 'Efficiency and Inefficiency in Thinly Traded Stock Markets – Kuwait and Saudi Arabia', *Journal of Banking and Finance*, 16, 1, 197–210.

Campbell, C. (1977), 'Properties of Ordinary and Weighted Least Squares Estimates of Regression Coefficients for Two-Stage Samples', in *Proceedings of the Social Statistics Section*, American Statistical Association, pp. 800–805.

Carroll, R.J. (1980), 'A Robust Method for Testing Transformation to Achieve Approximate Normality', *Journal of the Royal Statistical Society*, B, 42, pp. 71–8.

Chacko, V.J. (1963), 'Testing Homogeneity against Ordered Alternatives', *Annals of Mathematical Statistics*, 34, pp. 945–56.

Chamberlain, G. and Rothschild, M. (1983), 'Arbitrage, Factor Structure, and Mean-Variance Analysis on Large Asset Markets', *Econometrica*, 51, 5, pp. 1281–304.

Chang, H.S. (1980), 'Functional Form and the Demand for Meat in the United States: A Reply', *Review of Economics and Statistics*, 62, pp. 148–50.

Chaturvedi, A. and Bhatti, M.I. (1998), 'On the Double K-class Estimators in Linear Regression', *Journal of Quantitative Economics*, 14 (1), pp. 57–62.

Chaturvedi, A., Kumar, K.and Bhatti, M.I. (2000), 'Bayesian Analysis of Disturbances Variance in the Linear Regression Model under Asymmetric Loss Functions', *Applied Mathematics and Computations*, 114 (2/3), pp. 149–53.

Chen, N., Roll, R. and Ross, S. (1986), 'Economic Forces and the Stock Market', *Journal of Business*, 59 (3), pp. 383–403.

Chen, S. (1988), *Some Empirical Tests in the Arbitrage Pricing Theory: Macro-variables vs Derived Factors*, unpublished PhD thesis.

Childs, D.R. (1967), 'Reduction of the Multivariate Normal Integral to Characteristic Form', *Biometrika*, 54, pp. 293–300.

Christensen, R. (1984), 'A Note on Ordinary Least Squares Methods for Two-Stage Sampling', *Journal of the American Statistical Association*, 79, pp. 720–21.

Christensen, R. (1986), 'Methods for the Analysis of Cluster Sampling Models', *Technical Report*, No. 7, Department of Mathematical Sciences, Montana State University, pp. 22–86.

Christensen, R. (1987a), 'The Analysis of Two-stage Sampling Data by Ordinary Least Squares', *Journal of the American Statistical Association*, 82, pp. 492–8.

Christensen, R. (1987b), *Plane Answers to Complex Questions: The Theory of Linear Models*, Springer-Verlag, New York.

Clare, A., Priestley, R. and Thomas, S. (1997a), 'Stock Return Predictability or Mismeasured Risk?', *Applied Financial Economics*, 7 (6), pp. 679–88.

Clare, A., Priestley, R. and Thomas, S. (1997b), 'The Robustness of the APT to Alternative Estimators', *Journal of Business Finance and Accounting*, 24 (5), pp. 645–55.

Clare, A. and Thomas, S. (1994), 'Macroeconomic Factors, the APT and the UK Stockmarket', *Journal of Business Finance and Accounting*, 21 (3), pp. 309–30.

Clayton, M.K., Geisser, S. and Jennings, D.E. (1986), 'A Comparison of Several Model Selection Procedures', in P. Goel and A. Zellner (eds), *Bayesian Inference and Decision Techniques*, Elsevier Science Publisher, New York, pp. 425–39.

Cochran, W.G. (1942), 'Sampling Theory When the Sampling Units are of Unequal Sizes', *Journal of the American Statistical Association*, 37, pp. 199–212.

Cochran, W.G. (1946), 'Relative Accuracy of Systematic and Stratified Random Samples for a Certain Class of Population', *Annals of Mathematical Statistics*, 17, pp. 164–77.

Cochran, W.G. (1953), *Sampling Techniques* 1st edn (2nd edn 1963), John Wiley, New York.

Collins, S. (1991), 'Prediction Techniques for Box-Cox Regression Models', *Journal of Business and Economic Statistics*, 9, pp. 267–77.

Connor, G. (1984), 'A Unified Beta Pricing Theory', *Journal of Economic Theory*, pp. 13–31.

Connor, G. and Korajczyk, R.A. (1993), 'A Test for the Number of Factors in an Approximate Factor Model', *Journal of Finance*, 48 (September), pp. 1263–91.

Costa, M., Gardini, A. and Paruolo, P. (1997), 'A Reduced Rank Regression Approach to Tests of Asset Pricing', *Oxford Bulletin of Economics and Statistics*, 59, pp. 163–81.

Cox, D.R. (1961), 'Tests of Separate Families of Hypotheses', *Proceedings of the Fourth Berkeley Symposium on Mathematical Statistics and Probability, I*, University of California Press, Berkeley, pp. 105–23.

Cox, D.R. (1962), 'Further Results on Tests of Separate Families of Hypotheses', *Journal of the Royal Statistical Society*, B, 24, pp. 405–24.

Cox, D.R. and Hinkley, D.V. (1974), *Theoretical Statistics*, Chapman and Hall, London.

Cox, D.R. and Solomon, P.J. (1986), 'Analysis of Variability with Large Numbers of Small Samples', *Biometrika*, 73, pp. 543–54.

Cox, D.R. and Solomon, P.J. (1988), 'On Testing for Serial Correlation in Large Numbers of Small Samples', *Biometrika*, 75, pp. 145–8.

Cressie, N. and Lahiri, S.N. (1993), 'The Asymptotic Distribution of REML Estimators', *Journal of Multivariate Analysis*, 45, pp. 217–33.

Crowder, M.J. (1985), 'A Distributional Model for Repeated Failure Time Measurements', *Journal of the Royal Statistical Society*, B, 47, pp. 447–52.

Davidson, R. and MacKinnon, J.G. (1993), *Estimation and Inference in Econometrics*, Oxford University Press, Oxford.

Davies, R.B. (1969), 'Beta-optimal Tests and an Application to the Summary Evaluation of Experiments', *Journal of the Royal Statistical Society*, B, 31, pp. 524–38.

Davies, R.B. (1980), 'Algorithm AS155. The Distribution of a Linear Combination of χ^2 Random Variables', *Applied Statistics*, 29, pp. 323–33.

Davies, R.B. and Harte, D.S. (1987), 'Tests for Hurst Effect', *Biometrika*, 74, pp. 95–101.

Deaton, A. and Irish, M. (1983), *Block Effects in Regression Analysis Using Survey Data*, unpublished manuscript.

Deming, W.E. (1950), *Some Theory of Sampling*, Wiley, New York.

Dhrymes, P., Friend, I. and Gultekin, M. (1984), 'A Critical Re-examination of the Empirical Evidence on the Arbitrage Pricing Theory', *Journal of Finance*, 39, 2, pp. 323–46.

Dickens, W.T. (1990), 'Error Components in Grouped Data: Is it ever Worth Weighting?' *The Review of Economics and Statistics*, 72, pp. 328–33.

Dickey, D. and Fuller, W. (1979), 'Distribution of the Estimators for Autoregressive Time Series with a Unit Root', *Journal of the American Statistical Association*, 74, pp. 427–31.

Dickinson, J. and Muragu, K. (1994), 'Market Efficiency in Developing Countries – A Case-Study of the Nairobi Stock Exchange', *Journal of Business Finance and Accounting*, 21, 1, pp. 133–50.

Diebold, F.X. and Chen, C. (1996), 'Testing Structural Stability with Endogenous Breakpoint: A Size Comparison of Analytic and Bootstrap Procedures', *Journal of Econometrics*, 70, pp. 221–41.

Doan, T. (1996), *RATS Users' Manual*, Version 4, Estima. Evanston, IL.

Dorfman, A.H. (1993), 'A Comparison of Design-Based and Model-Based Estimators of the Finite Population Distribution Function', *Australian Journal of Statistics*, 35 (1), pp. 29–41.

Economist Intelligence Unit (2000), *Country Profile: Mexico*, London.

Efron, B. (1975), 'Defining the Curvature of a Statistical Problem (with Applications to Second Order Efficiency)', *Annals of Statistics*, 3, pp. 1189–242.

Efron, B. (1979), 'Bootstrap Methods: Another Look at the Jackknife', *Annals of Statistics*, 7, pp. 1–26.

Efron, B. (1982), *The Jackknife, the Bootstrap and Other Resampling Plans*, Monograph No. 38, Society for Industrial and Applied Mathematics (SLAM), NSF–CBMS, Philadelphia.

Efron, B. (1983), 'Estimating the Error Rate of a Prediction Rule: Improvement on Cross-validation', *Journal of the American Statistical Association*, 78, pp. 316–31.

Efron, B. (1986), 'How Biased is the Apparent Error Rate of a Prediction Rule?', *Journal of the American Statistical Association*, 81, pp. 461–70.

Efron, B. (1987), 'Better Bootstrap Confidence Intervals' (with discussion), *Journal of the American Statistical Association*, 82, pp. 171–200.

Efron, B. (1992), 'Jackknife-after-bootstrap Standard Error and Influence Functions' (with discussion), *Journal of the Royal Statistical Society*, B, 54, pp. 83–127.

Efron, B. and Gong, G. (1983), 'A Leisurely Look at the Bootstrap, the Jackknife and Cross-validation', *The American Statistician*, 37, pp. 36–48.

Efron, B. and Tibshirani, R. (1986), 'Bootstrap Methods of Standard Error, Confidence Intervals, and Other Measures of Statistical Accuracy', *Statistical Science*, 1, pp. 54–77.

Efron, B. and Tibshirani, R. (1993), *An Introduction to the Bootstrap*, Chapman and Hall, New York.

El-Erian, M. and Kumar, M. (1995), 'Emerging Equity Markets in Middle Eastern Countries', IMF Staff Papers, 42, 2, International Monetary Fund, pp. 313–43.

Elton, E. and Gruber, M. (1995), *Modern Portfolio Theory and Investment Analysis*, 5th edn, John Wiley & Sons, New York.

Engle, R. and Granger, C. (1991), *Long-run Economic Relationships: Reading in Cointegration*, Oxford University Press.

Engle, R.F., Hendry, D.F. and Trumble, D. (1985), 'Small Sample Properties of ARCH Estimators and Tests', *Canadian Journal of Economics*, 18, pp. 66–93.

Evans, M.A. and King, M.L. (1985), 'A Point Optimal Test for Heteroscedastic Disturbances', *Journal of Econometrics*, 27, pp. 163–78.

Fama, E. (1970), 'Efficient Capital Markets: A Review of Theory and Empirical Work', *Journal of Finance*, 25 (2), pp. 385–417.

Fama, E. (1991),'Efficient Capital Markets: II', *Journal of Finance*, 46, 5, pp. 1575–617.

Fama, E. and MacBeth, J. (1973), 'Risk Return and Equilibrium: Empirical Tests', *Journal of Political Economy*, 38, pp. 607–36.

Farebrother, R.W. (1980), 'Algorithm AS153: Pan's Procedure for the Tail Probabilities of the Durbin-Watson Statistic', *Applied Statistics*, 29, pp. 224–227 and 30, p. 189.

Ferguson, T.S. (1967), *Mathematical Statistics A Decision Theoretic Approach*, Academic Press, New York.

Ferson, W. and Harvey, C. (1998), 'Fundamental Determinants of National Equity Market Returns; A Perspective on Conditional Asset Pricing', *Journal of Banking and Finance*, 21, pp. 1625–65.

Fisher, N.I. and Hall, P. (1990), 'On Bootstrap Hypothesis Testing', *Australian Journal of Statistics*, 32, pp. 177–90.

Fisher, R.A. (1925), 'Theory of Statistical Estimation', *Proceedings of the Cambridge Philosophical Society*, 122, pp. 700–25.

Fogler, H. (1982), 'Common Sense on CAPM, APT and Correlated Residuals', *Journal of Portfolio Management*, pp. 20–28.

Fomby, T.B., Hill. R.C. and Johnson, S.R. (1984), *Advanced Econometric Methods*, Springer-Verlag, New York.

Forbes, C.S., King, M.L. and Morgan, A. (1995), *Small Sample Variable Selection Procedures*, unpublished manuscript, Monash University.

Fox, K.J. (1995), *Model Selection Criteria: A Reference Source*, unpublished manuscript, University of New South Wales.

Freedman, D.A. (1981), 'Bootstrapping Regression Models', *Annals of Statistics*, 9, pp. 1218–28.

Fuller, W.A. (1975), 'Regression Analysis for Sample Surveys', *Shankhya*, C, 37, pp. 117–32.

Fuller, W.A. and Battese, G.E. (1973), 'Transformations for Estimation of Linear Models with Nested Error Structures', *Journal of the American Statistical Association*, 68, pp. 626–32.

Fuller, W.A. and Battese, G.E. (1974), 'Estimation of Linear Models with Cross-Error Structure', *Journal of Econometrics*, 2, pp. 67–78.

Fuller, W.A., Kennedy, W., Schnell, D., Sullivan, G. and Park, H.J. (1986), *PC CARP Ames*, Iowa State University Laboratory.

Gallant, A.R. (1989), *Nonlinear Statistical Models*, Wiley, New York.

Gauss Documentation Version (1996), *Gauss Constrained Optimization: Application Module*, Aptech Systems, Inc. Washington.

Gaver, K.M. and Geisel, M.S. (1974), 'Discriminating among Alternative Models: Bayesian and Non-Bayesian Methods', in Paul Zarembka (ed.), *Frontiers of Econometrics*, Academic Press, New York, pp. 49–77.

Geisser, S. (1963), 'Multivariate Analysis of Variance for a Special Covariance Case', *Journal of the American Statistical Association*, 58, pp. 660–69.

Godambe, V.P. (1966), 'A New Approach to Sampling from Finite Populations', *Journal of the Royal Statistical Society*, B, 28, pp. 310–28.

Godfrey, L.G. (1988), *Misspecification Tests in Econometrics: The Lagrange Multiplier Principle and Other Approaches*, Cambridge University Press, Cambridge.

Godfrey, L.G. and Wickens, M.R. (1981), 'Testing Linear and Log-linear Regressions for Functional Forms', *Review of Economic Studies*, 48, pp. 487–96.

Goldfeld, S.M. and Quandt, R.E. (1965), 'Some Tests of Heteroscedasticity', *Journal of the American Statistical Association*, 60, pp. 539–47.

Gourieroux, C., Holly, A. and Monfort, A. (1980), *Kuhn-Tucker, Likelihood Ratio and Wald Tests for Non-linear Models with Inequality Constraints on the Parameters*, Discussion Paper No. 770, Harvard Institute of Economic Research, Harvard University.

Gourieroux, C., Holly, A. and Monfort, A. (1982), 'Likelihood Ratio Test, Wald Test and Kuhn-Tucker Test in Linear Models with Inequality Constraints on the Regression Parameters', *Econometrica*, 50, pp. 63–80.

Granger, C.J.W., King, M.L. and White, H. (1995), 'Comments on Testing Economic Theories and the Use of Model Selection Criteria', *Journal of Econometrics*, 67, pp. 173–87.

Grassa, A.A. (1989), *Econometric Model Selection: A New Approach*, Kluwer Academic Press, Boston.

Graybill, F.A. (1969), *Introduction to Matrices with Applications in Statistics*, Wadsworthy, Belmont, CA.

Greene, W.H. (1993), *Econometric Analysis*, Prentice Hall, New Jersey.

Greenwald, B.C. (1983), 'A General Analysis of the Bias in the Estimated Standard Errors of Least Squares Coefficients', *Journal of Econometrics*, 22, pp. 323–38.

Grose, S.D. (1998), *Marginal Likelihood Methods in Econometrics*, unpublished PhD thesis, Monash University, Melbourne, Australia.

Grose, S.D. and King, M.L. (1994), *The Use of Information Criteria for Model Selection between Models with Equal Numbers of Parameters*, paper presented at the 1994 Australiasian Meeting of the Econometric Society, Armidale.

Gujarati, D. (1992), *Essentials of Econometrics*, McGraw-Hill, New York.

Gupta, S.S. (1963), 'Probability Integrals of Multivariate Normal and Multivariate t', *Annals of Mathematical Statistics*, 34, pp. 792–838.

Hair, J., Anderson, R., Tatham, R. and Black, W. (1998), *Multivariate Data Analysis*, 5th edn, Prentice Hall, New Jersey.

Hall, P. (1986), 'On the Bootstrap and Confidence Intervals', *Annals of Statistics*, 14, pp. 1431–52.

Hall, P. (1986a), 'On the Number of Bootstrap Simulations Required to Construct a Confidence Interval', *Annals of Statistics*, 14, pp. 1453–62.

Hall, P. (1988), 'Theoretical Comparison of Bootstrap Confidence Interval' (with discussion), *Annals of Statistics*, 16, pp. 927–85.

Hall, P. (1988a), 'On Symmetric Bootstrap Confidence Intervals', *Journal of the Royal Statistical Society*, B, 50, pp. 35–45.

Hall, P. (1992), *The Bootstrap and the Edgeworth Expansion*, Springer-Verlag, New York.

Hall, P. and Wilson, S.R. (1991), 'Two Guidelines for Bootstrap Hypothesis Testing', *Biometrics*, 47, pp. 757–62.

Halperin, M. (1951), 'Normal Regression Theory in the Presence of Intra-Class Correlation', *The Annals of Mathematical Statistics*, 22, pp. 573–80.

Hamao, Y. (1988), 'An Empirical Examination of the Arbitrage Pricing Theory: Using Japanese Data', *Japan and the World Economy*, 1, pp. 45–61.

Hannan, E.J. (1981), 'Estimating the Dimensions of a Linear System', *Journal of Multivariate Analysis*, 11, pp. 211–21.

Hannan, E.J. and Quinn, B.G. (1979), 'The Determination of the Order of an Autoregression', *Journal of the Royal Statistical Society*, B, 41, pp. 190–95.

Hansen, M.H. and Hurwitz, W.N. (1949), 'On the Determination of the Optimum Probabilities in Sampling', *Annals of Mathematical Statistics*, 20, pp. 426–32.

Hansen, M.H., Hurwitz, W.N. and Madow, W.G. (1953), *Sampling Survey Methods and Theory*, Vols I and II, John Wiley, New York.

Harrington, D. (1987), *Modern Portfolio Theory, The Capital Asset Pricing Model and Arbitrage Pricing Theory: A User's Guide*, 2nd edn, Prentice Hall, New Jersey.

Harris, R. (1995), *Using Co-integration Analysis in Econometric Modelling*, Prentice Hall, New Jersey.

Harrison, M.J. (1980), 'The Small Sample Performance of the Szroeter Bounds Tests for Heteroscedasticity and a Simple Test for Use When Szroeter's Test is Inconclusive', *Oxford Bulletin of Economic and Statistics*, 42, pp. 235–50.

Harrison, M.J. and McCabe, B.P.M. (1979), 'A New Test for Heteroscedasticity Based on Ordinary Least Squares Residuals', *Journal of the American Statistical Association*, 74, pp. 494–9.

Hartley, H.O. and Rao, J.N.K. (1968), 'A New Estimation Theory for Sample Survey', *Biometrika*, 55, pp. 547–57.

Hartley, H.O. and Rao, J.N.K. (1969), 'A New Estimation Theory for Sample Survey II', in N.L. Johnson and H. Smith (eds), *New Developments in Survey Sampling*, Wiley Interscience, New York, pp. 147–69.

Harvey, A.C. and Phillips, G.D.A. (1974), 'A Comparison of the Power of Some Tests for Heteroscedasticity in the General Linear Model', *Journal of Econometrics*, 2, pp. 307–16.

Hausman, J.A. (1978), 'Specification Tests in Econometrics', *Econometrica*, 46, pp. 1251–71.

Heckman, J. and Polachek, S. (1974), 'Empirical Evidence of the Functional Form of the Earning–Schooling Relationship', *Journal of the American Statistical Association*, 69, pp. 350–54.

Hidiroglou, M.A., Fuller, W.A. and Hickman, R.D. (1980), *SUPER CARP*, 6th edn, Ames Iowa State University, Statistical Laboratory.

Hillier, G.H. (1987), 'Classes of Similar Regions and Their Power Properties for Some Econometric Testing Problems', *Econometric Theory*, 3, pp. 1–44.

Hinkley, D.V. (1988), 'More on Score Tests for Transformation in Regression', *Biometrika*, 75, pp. 366–9.

Hinkley, D.V. (1989), 'Bootstrap Significance Test', in *Proceedings of the 47th session of the International Statistical Institute*, 3, Paris, pp. 65–74.

Hocking, R.R. (1976), 'The Analysis and Selection of Variables in Linear Regression', *Biometrika*, 32, pp. 1–49.

Holmes, J.M. and Hutton, P.A. (1989), 'Optimal Model Selection when the True Relationship is Weak and Occurs with a Delay', *Economics Letters*, 30, pp. 333–9.

Holt, D. and Scott, A.J. (1981), 'Regression Analysis Using Survey Data', *The Statistician*, 30, pp. 169–78.

Holt, D., Smith, T.M.F. and Winter, P.D. (1980), 'Regression Analysis of Data from Complex Surveys', *Journal of Royal Statistical Society*, A, 143, pp. 474–87.

Holt, M.M. (1977), *SURREGR: Standard Errors of Regression Coefficients From Sample Survey Data*, Research Triangle Park Research Triangle Institute.

Honda, Y. (1985), 'Testing the Error Components with Non-normal Disturbances', *Review of Economic Studies*, 52, pp. 681–90.

Honda, Y. (1989), 'On the Optimality of Some Tests of the Error Covariance Matrix in the Linear Regression Model', *Journal of the Royal Statistical Society*, Series B, 51, pp. 71–9.

Honda, Y. (1991) 'A Standardized Test for the Error Components Model with the Two-way Layout', *Economic Letters*, 37, pp. 125–8.

Hoque, A. (1988), 'Farm Size and Economic-Allocative Efficieny in Bangladesh Agriculture', *Applied Economics*, 20, pp. 1353–68.

Hoque, A. (1991), 'An Application and Test for a Random Coefficient Model in Bangladesh Agriculture', *Journal of Applied Econometrics*, 6, pp. 77–90.

Hossain, M. (1990), 'Natural Calamities, Instability in Production and Food Policy in Bangladesh', *The Bangladesh Development Studies*, XVIII (4), pp. 33–54.

Hossain, M.Z. (2002), 'Modified Akaike information criterion (MAIC) for Statistical Model Selection', *Pakistan Journal of Statistics*, 18 (3), pp. 383–93.

Hossain, M.Z. and Bhatti, M.I. (2003), 'Recent Development in Econometrics Analysis of Model Selection', *Managerial Finance*, 29 (7), pp. 92–113.

Hossain, M.Z. and King, M.L. (1996), 'New Information Criterion-based Model Selection Procedures', in L.Nailon (ed.), *Proceedings of Second Annual Doctoral Research Conference*, Faculty of Business and Economics, Monash University, pp. 56–64.

Hossain, M.Z. and King, M.L. (1997), 'New Information Criteria for Model Selection', in P. Bardsley and V.L. Martin (eds), *Proceedings of the Econometric Society Australasian Meeting*, 2, University of Melbourne, pp. 585–612.

Hossain, M.Z. and King, M.L. (2000), 'Model Selection Using AIC in the Context of Inequality Restrictions on Key Parameters', *Journal of Applied Statistical Science*, 12 (4), pp. 305–20.

Hossain, M.Z. and King, M.L. (2000a), 'The Effect of Nuisance Parameter on the Probability of Correct Selection in Model Specification', *Pakistan Journal of Statistics*, 16 (2), pp. 181–94.

Hsiao, C. (1986), *Analysis of Panel Data*, Cambridge University Press, Cambridge.

Hughes, A.W. (1997), *Improved Model Selection Based on AIC-type Criteria*, unpublished PhD dissertation, Monash University.

Hughes, A.W. and King, M.L. (2003), 'Model Selection Using AIC in the Presence of One-sided Information', *Journal of Statistical Planning and Inference*, 115, pp. 397–411.

Hughes, A.W., King, M.L. and Kwek, K.T. (2004), 'Selecting the Order of an ARCH Model', *Economic Letters*, 83, pp. 269–75.

Hurvich, C.M. and Tsai, C.-L. (1989), 'Regression and Time Series Model Selection in Small Samples', *Biometrika*, 76, pp. 297–307.

Hurvich, C.M. and Tsai, C.-L. (1990), 'The Impact of Model Selection on Inference in Linear Regression', *The American Statistician*, 44, pp. 214–17.

Hurvich, C.M. and Tsai, C.-L. (1991), 'Bias of the Corrected AIC Criterion for Underfitted Regression and Time Series Models', *Biometrika*, 78, pp. 499–509.

Hurvich, C.M. and Tsai, C.-L. (1993), 'A Corrected Akaike Information Criterion for Vector Autoregressive Model Selection', *Journal of Time Series Analysis*, 14, pp. 271–79.

Hwang, H.S. (1981), 'Demand for Money: Tests of Functional Forms and Stability', *Applied Economics*, 13, pp. 235–44.

Ibrahim, J.G. and Laud, P.W. (1994), 'A Predictive Approach to the Analysis of Designed Experiments', *Journal of the American Statistical Association*, 89, pp. 309–19.

Imhof, P.J. (1961), 'Computing the Distribution of Quadratic Forms in Normal Variables', *Biometrika*, 48, pp. 419–26.

IMSL Math/Library (1989), *User's Manual*, Softcover Edition 1.1, Houston ISML Inc., USA.

Isaacson, S.L. (1951), 'On the Theory of Unbiased Tests of Simple Statistical Hypotheses Specifying the Values of Two or More Parameters', *Annals of Mathematical Statistics*, 22, pp. 217–34.

Ishiguro, M. and Sakamoto, Y. (1991), *WIC: An Estimator-free Information Criterion*, Research Memorandum, The Institute of Statistical Mathematics, Tokyo.

Ishiguro, M., Sakamoto, Y. and Kitagawa, G. (1994), *Bootstrapping Log Likelihood and EIC, and Extension of AIC*, Research Memorandum, The Institute of Statistical Mathematics, Tokyo.

Izenman, A. (1975), 'Reduced-rank Regression for the Multivariate Linear Model,' *Journal of Multivariate Analysis*, 5, pp. 248–64.

Jayaraman, J., Saber, H. and Bhatti, M.I. (2004), 'Towards Optimal Testing of a Hypothesis Based on Dynamic Technology Transfer Model', *Applied Mathematics and Computation*, 147 (2/3), pp. 115–29.

Jeong, J. and Maddala, G.S. (1993), 'A Perspective on Application of Bootstrap Method in Econometrics', in G.S. Maddala, C.S. Rao and H.D. Vinod (eds), *Handbook of Statistics II*, Elsevier Science Publishers, New York, pp. 573–610.

Johansen, S. (1988), 'Statistical Analysis of Cointegration Vectors', *Journal of Economic Dynamics and Control*, 12, pp. 231–54.

John, J.A. and Draper, N.R. (1980), 'An Alternative Family of Transformations', *Applied Statistics*, 29, pp. 190–97.

Johnson, R. and Wichern, D. (1992), *Applied Multivariate Statistical Analysis*, 3rd edn, Prentice Hall, New Jersey.

Judge, G.G., Griffiths, W.E., Hill, R.C., Lutkepoht, H. and Lee, T.C. (1985), *The Theory and Practice of Econometrics*, Wiley, New York.

Judge, G.G., Hill, R.C., Griffiths, W.E., Lutkepohl, H. and Lee, T.-C. (1985), *The Theory and Practice of Econometrics*, 2nd edn, John Wiley, New York.

Kau, J.B. and Lee, C.F. (1976), 'The Functional Form in Estimating the Density Gradient: An Empirical Investigation', *Journal of the American Statistical Association*, 71, pp. 326–7.

Kendall, M.G. and Buckland, W.R. (1960), *A Dictionary of Statistical Terms*, 4th edn, Logman Scientific and Technical Publication, England.

Kendall, M.G. and Stuart, A. (1973), *The Advanced Theory of Statistics*, 3rd edn, Charles Griffin, London.

Khan, A., Muttlak, H. and Bhatti, M.I. (1999), 'Adaptive Cluster Sampling for Characteristics other than total number of Elements', *Parisankhyan Samikkha: An International Journal of Statistics*, 6 (1/2), pp. 19–32.

Khan, M.S. and Ross. K.Z. (1977), 'The Functional Form of the Aggregate Import Demand Equation', *Journal of International Economics*, 7, pp. 149–60.

Khan, S. and Bhatti, M.I. (1998), 'Predictive Inference on Equicorrelated Linear Regression Models', *Applied Mathematics and Computations*, 9(2–3), pp. 205–17.

Kiaer, A.N. (1895), 'Observation et Experiences Concernant Des Denombrements Representatifs', discussion appears in Liv. 1, XC111–XCV11, *Bulletin of the International Statistical Institute*, 9, Liv. 2, pp. 176–83.

Kim, M. and Hill, R.C. (1993), 'The Box-Cox Transformation of Variables in Regression', *Empirical Economics*, 18, pp. 307–19.

King, M.L. (1980), 'Robust Tests for Spherical Symmetry and Their Application to Least Squares Regression', *Annals of Statistics*, 8, pp. 1265–71.

King, M.L. (1981), 'The Alternative Durbin-Watson Test: An Assessment of Durbin and Watson's Choice of Test Statistic', *Journal of Econometrics*, 17, pp. 51–66.

King, M.L. (1982), *A Locally Optimal Bounds Test for Autoregressive Disturbances*, paper presented at the European meeting of the Econometric Society, Dublin.

King, M.L. (1983), 'Testing for Moving Average Regression Disturbances', *Australian Journal of Statistics*, 25, pp. 23–34.

King, M.L. (1985a), 'A Point Optimal Test for Autoregressive Disturbances', *Journal of Econometrics*, 27, pp. 21–37.

King, M.L. (1985b), 'A Point Optimal Test for Moving Average Regression Disturbances', *Econometrics Theory*, 1, pp. 211–22.

King, M.L. (1986), 'Efficient Estimation and Testing of Regressions with a Serially Correlated Error Component', *Journal of Quantitative Economics*, 2, 231–47.

King, M.L. (1987a), 'Testing for Autocorrelation in Linear Regression Models: A Survey', in M.L. King and D.E.A. Giles (eds), *Specification Analysis in the Linear Regression Model*, Routledge and Kegan Paul, London, pp. 19–73.

King, M.L. (1987b), 'Towards a Theory of Point Optimal Testing', *Econometric Reviews*, 6, pp. 169–218.

King, M.L. (1989), 'Testing for Fourth-order Autocorrelation in Regression Disturbances when First-order Autocorrelation is Present', *Journal of Econometrics*, 41, pp. 284–301.

King, M.L., and Bose, G.K. (2003), 'Finding Optima Penalties for Model Selection in the Linear Regression Model', in D.E.A. Giles (ed.), *Computer-Aided Econometrics*, Marcel Dekker, New York, pp. 37–68.

King, M.L. and Evans, M.A. (1986), 'Testing for Block Effects in Regression Models Based on Survey Data', *Journal of the American Statistical Association*, 81 (395), pp. 677–9.

King, M.L. and Evans, M.A. (1988), 'Locally Optimal Properties of the Durbin-Watson Test', *Econometric Theory*, 4, pp. 509–16.

King, M.L. and Giles, D.E.A. (1984), 'Autocorrelation and Pre-Testing in the Linear Model Estimation, Testing and Prediction', *Journal of Econometrics*, 25, pp. 35–48.

King, M.L. and Hillier, G.H. (1985), 'Locally Best Invariant Tests of the Error Covariance Matrix of the Linear Regression Model', *Journal of the Royal Statistical Society*, B, 47, pp. 98–102, *Econometrics*, 25, pp. 35–48.

King, M.L. and Skeels, C.L. (1984), *Joint Testing for Serial Correlation and Heteroscedasticity in the Linear Regression Model*, paper presented at the Australasian Meeting of the Econometrics Society, Sydney.

King, M.L. and Wu, X.P. (1990), *Locally Optimal One-Sided Tests for Multiparameter Hypothesis*, paper presented at the Sixth World Congress of the Econometric Society, Barcelona, Spain.

King, M.L., Forbes, C.S. and Morgan, A. (1995), *Improved Small Sample Model Selection Procedures*, paper presented at the 1995 World Congress of the Econometric Society, Tokyo.

Kipnis, V. (1989), *Model Selection and Prediction Assessment in Regression Analysis*, Working Paper No. M8910, University of South California.

Kish, L. (1965), *Survey Sampling*, John Wiley, New York.

Kish, L. and Frankel, M.R. (1974), 'Inference from Complex Samples', *Journal of the Royal Statistical Society*, B, 36, pp. 1–37.

Kloek, T. (1981), 'OLS Estimation in a Model Where a Microvariable is Explained by Aggregates and Contemporaneous Disturbances are Equicorrelated', *Econometrica*, 49, pp. 205–7.

Kodde, D.A. and Palm, F.C. (1986), 'Wald Criteria for Jointly Testing Equality and Inequality Restrictions', *Econometrica*, 54, pp. 1243–8.

Koerts, J. and Abrahamse, A.P.J. (1969), *On the Theory and Application of the General Linear Model*, Rotterdam University Press, Rotterdam.

Konijn, H.S. (1962), 'Regression Analysis in Sample Surveys', *Journal of the American Statistical Association*, 57, pp. 590–606.

Körösi, G., Mátyás, L. and Székely, I. (1992), *Practical Econometrics*, Avebury, Aldershot.

Kott, P.S. (1991), 'A Model-Based Look at Linear Regression with Survey Data', *The American Statistician*, 45, 2, pp. 107–12.

Krämer, W. and Sonnberger, H. (1986), *The Linear Regression Model Under Test*, Physica-Verlag, Heidelberg.

Kudô, A. (1963), 'A Multivariate Analogue of the One-sided Test', *Biometrika*, 50, pp. 403–48.

Lawrance, A.J. (1987a), 'The Score Statistic for Regression Transformation', *Biometrika*, 74, pp. 275–9.

Lawrance, A.J. (1987b), 'A Note on the Variance of the Box-Cox Regression Transformation Estimate', *Applied Statistics*, 36, pp. 221–3.

Leamer, E.E. (1978), *Specification Searches*, Wiley, New York.

Lehmann, B.N. and Modest, D.M. (1988), 'The Empirical Foundations of the Arbitrage Pricing Theory', *Journal of Financial Economics*, 21 (September), pp. 213–254.

Lehmann, E.L. (1959), *Testing Statistical Hypothesis*, 1st edn (2nd edn 1986), John Wiley, New York.

Lehmann, E.L. (1983), *Theory of Point Estimation*, Wiley, New York.

Lehmann, E.L. and Stein, C. (1948), 'Most Powerful Tests of Composite Hypothesis, I. Normal Distributions', *Annals of Mathematical Statistics*, 19, pp. 495–515.

Lin, T.K.H and Huang, C.L. (1983), 'Use of Box-Cox Transformation Technique for Fitting Crop Yield Trends', *Agronomy Journal*, 75, pp. 310–14.

Linhart, H. and Zuchini, W. (1986), *Model Selection*, Wiley, New York.

Lintner, J. (1965), 'Valuation of Risk Assets and the Selection of Risky Investments in Stock Portfolios and Capital Budgets', *Review of Economics and Statistics*, 47, pp. 13–37.

Lutkepohl, H. (1991), *Introduction to Multiple Time Series Analysis*, Springer-Verlag, Germany.

MacKinnon, J.G. (1983), 'Model Specification Tests against Non-nested Alternatives' (with discussion and reply), *Economic Reviews*, 2, pp. 85–157.

Maddala, G.S. (1971), 'The Use of Variance Components Models in Pooling Cross Section and Time Series Data', *Econometrica*, 39, pp. 341–58.

Maddala, G.S. (1977), *Econometrics*, Kogakusta, McGraw-Hill, New York.

Maddala, G.S. (1992), *Introduction to Econometrics*, Macmillan, New York.

Madow, W.G. and Madow, L.H. (1944), 'On the Theory of Systematic Sampling', *Annals of Mathematical Statistics*, 20, pp. 333–54.

Magnus, J.R. (1978), 'Maximum Likelihood Estimation of the GLS Model with Unknown Parameters in the Disturbance Covariance Matrix', *Journal of Econometrics*, 7, pp. 281–312.

Mallows, C.L. (1964), *Choosing Variables in a Linear Regression: A Graphical Aid*, paper presented at the Central Regional Meeting of the Institute of Mathematical Statistics, Manhattan, KA.

Mallows, C.L. (1973), 'Some Comments on Cp', *Technometrics*, 15, pp. 661–76.

Mammen, E. (1991), *When Does Bootstrap Work: Asymptotic Results and Simulations*, Springer Lecture Notes in Statistics, 77, Springer, New York.

Manly, B.F. (1976), 'Exponential Data Transformation', *The Statistician*, 25, pp. 37–42.

Markowitz, H. (1952), 'Portfolio Selection', *Journal of Finance*, 7 (1), pp. 77–91.

Martin, R.S., Reinsch, C. and Wilkinson, J.H. (1968), 'Householder's Tridiagonalization of a Symmetric Matrix', *Numerische Mathematik* 11, pp. 181–95.

Mátyás, L. and Sevestre, P. (1992), *The Econometrics of Panel Data*, Kluwer Academic Publishers.

McAleer, M. (1987), 'Specification Tests for Separate Models: A Survey', in M.L. King and D.E.A. Giles (eds), *Specification Analysis in the Linear Model: Essays in Honour of Donald Cochrane*, Routledge and Kegan Paul, New York, pp. 146–96.

McElroy, M. and Burmeister, E. (1988), 'Arbitrage Pricing Theory as a Restricted Non-linear Multivariate Regression Model: ITNLSUR Estimates', *Journal of Business and Economic Statistics*, 6, pp. 29–42.

McElroy, M., Burmeister, E. and Wall, K. (1985), 'Two Estimators for the APT Model when Factors are Measured', *Economic Letters*, 35, pp. 271–5.

McFadden, J.A. (1960), 'Two Expansions for the Quadrivariate Normal Integrals', *Biometrika*, 47, pp. 325–33.

Mills, J.A. and Prasad, K. (1992), 'A Comparison of Model Selection Criteria', *Econometric Reviews*, 11, pp. 201–33.

Mills, T.C. (1978), 'The Functional Form of the UK Demand for Money', *Applied Statistics*, 27, pp. 52–7.

Mooney, C.Z. and Duval, R.D. (1993), *Bootstrapping: A Nonparametric Approach to Statistical Inference*, Sage, Newbury Park.

Moran, P.A.P. (1948). 'Rank Correlation and Product Moment Correlation', *Biometrika*, 35, pp. 203–6.

Morey, M.J. and Schenck, L.M. (1984), 'Small Sample Behaviour of Bootstrapped and Jackknifed Regression Estimators', *ASA Proceedings of Business, Economic and Statistics Section*, American Statistical Association, Washington, DC, pp. 437–42.

Moulton, B.R. (1986), 'Random Group Effects and the Precision of Regression Estimates', *Journal of Econometrics*, 32, pp. 385–97.

Moulton, B.R. (1990), 'An Illustration of a Pitfall in Estimating the Effects of Aggregate Variables on Micro Units', *The Review of Economics and Statistics*, 72, pp. 334–8.

Moulton, B.R. and Randolph, W.C. (1989), 'Alternative Tests of the Error Components Model', *Econometrica*, 57, pp. 685–93.

Nathan, G. and Holt, D. (1980), 'The Effect of Survey Design on Regression Analysis', *Journal of the Royal Statistical Society*, B., 42, pp. 377–86.

Nerlove, M. (1971), 'A Note on Error Components Models', *Econometrica*, 39, pp. 383–96.

Newey, W.K. (1985), 'Maximum Likelihood Specification Testing and Conditional Moment Tests', *Econometrica*, 53, pp. 1047–70.

Newman, P. (1977), 'Malaria and Mortality', *Journal of the American Statistical Association*, 72, pp. 257–63.

Neyman, J. (1934), 'On the Two Different Aspects of the Representative Method: The Method of Stratified Sampling and the Method of Purposive Selection', *Journal of the Royal Statistical Society*, 97, pp. 559–606.

Neyman, J. (1935), 'Sur la Vérification des Hypothéses Statistiques Composées', *Bulletin de la Société Mathematique de France*, 36, pp. 346–66.

Neyman, J. and Pearson, E.S. (1936), 'Contributions to the Theory of Testing Statistical Hypothesis. I. Unbiased Critical Regions of Type A and Type A1', *Statistical Research Memoirs*, 1, pp. 1–37.

Neyman, J. and Pearson, E.S. (1938), 'Contributions to the Theory of Testing Statistical Hypotheses II', *Statistical Research Memoirs*, 2, pp. 25–37.

Neyman, J. and Scott, E.L. (1967), 'On the Use of C(α), Optimal Tests of Composite Hypotheses', *Bulletin of the International Statistical Institute*, 41, pp. 477–97.

Nishii, R. (1988), 'Maximum Likelihood Principle and Model Selection When the True Model is Unspecified', *Journal of Multivariate Analysis*, 27, pp. 392–403.

Oberhofer, W. and Kmenta, J. (1974), 'A General Procedure for Obtaining Maximum Likelihood Estimates in Generalized Regression Models', *Econometrica*, 42, pp. 579–90.

Pagan, A.R. and Wickens, M.R. (1989), 'A Survey of Some Recent Econometric Methods', *Economic Journal*, 99, pp. 962–1025.

Palm, F.C. and Sneek, J.M. (1984), 'Significance Tests and Spurious Correlation in Regression Models with Autocorrelated Errors', *Statistische Hefte*, 25, pp. 87–105.

Pan, J.-J. (1964), 'Distributions of the Noncircular Serial Correlation Coefficients', *Shuxue Jinzhan*, 7, pp. 328–37.

Parikh, K.S. (2000), *India Development Report 2000*, Oxford University Press, New Delhi.

Parikh, K.S. and Radhakrishna, R. (2002), *India Development Report 2002*, Oxford Universit Press, New Delhi.

Perlman, M.D. (1969), 'One-sided Problems in Multivariate Analysis', *Annals of Mathematical Statistics*, 40, pp. 549–67.

Pfefferman, D. (1985), 'Regression Models for Grouped Population in Cross-Section Surveys', *International Statistical Review*, 53, pp. 37–59.

Pindyck, R. and Rubinfeld, D. (1991), *Econometric Models and Economic Forecasts*, 3rd edn, McGraw-Hill, New York.

Plackett, R.L. (1954), 'A Reduction Formula for Normal Multivariate Integrals', *Biometrika*, 41, pp. 351–60.

Pollak, R.A. and Wales, T.J. (1991), 'The Likelihood Dominance Criterion: A New Approach to Model Selection', *Journal of Econometrics*, 47, pp. 227–42.

Pötscher, B.M. (1991), 'Effects of Model Selection on Inference', *Econometric Theory*, 7, pp. 163–85.

Prakash, S. (1979), *Contributions to Bayesian Analysis in Heteroscedastic Models*, unpublished PhD thesis, University of New England, Armidale, NSW, Australia.

Priestley, R. (1996), 'The Arbitrage Pricing Theory, Macroeconomic and Financial Factors, and Expectations Generating Processes', *Journal of Banking and Finance*, 20, pp. 869–90.

Quinn, B.G. (1988), 'A Note on AIC Order Determination for Multivariate Autoregressions', *Journal of Time Series Analysis*, 9, pp. 241–5.

Rahman, M.S. and King, M.L. (1997), 'Probability of Correct Identification in Model Selection', in P. Bardsley and V. L. Martin (eds), *Proceedings of the Econometric Society Australisian Meeting, 2*, University of Melbourne, Australia, Melbourne, pp. 613–40.

Rahman, M.S. and King, M.L. (1999), 'Improved Model Selection Criterion', *Communication in Statistics: Simulation and Computation*, 28 (1), pp. 51–71.

Raj, B. (1989), *The Peril of Underestimation of Standard Errors in a Random-coefficients Model and the Bootstrap*, unpublished manuscript, invited chapter presented in the Department of Econometrics, Monash University.

Rao, C.R. (1962), 'Efficient Estimates and Optimum Inference Procedures in Large Samples', *Journal of the Royal Statistical Society*, B, 24, pp. 46–72.

Rao, C.R. (1963), 'Criteria of Estimation in Large Samples', *Sankhÿa*, 25, pp. 189–206.

Rao, C.R. (1973), *Linear Statistical Inference and Its Applications*, John Wiley, New York.

Rao, C.R., and Kleffe, J. (1980), 'Estimation of Variance Components', in P.R. Krishnakumar (ed.), *Handbook of Statistics*, 1, North Holland, Amsterdam, pp. 1–40.

Rao, J.N.K., Sutradhar, B,C. and Yue, K. (1991), *Generalised Least Squares F-test in Regression Analysis with Two-stage Cluster Samples*, Technical Report, Laboratory for Research in Statistics and Probability, Carleton University, Canada.

Rao, J.N.K., Sutradhar, B.C. and Yue, K. (1993), 'Generalised Least Square F-test in Regression Analysis with Two-stage Cluster Samples', *Journal of the American Statistical Association*, 88 (424), pp. 1388–91.

Raveh, A. (1985), 'A Note on Factor Analysis and Arbitrage Pricing Theory', *Journal of Banking and Finance*, 9, pp. 317–21.

Rissanen, J. (1986), 'Stochastic Complexity and Modelling', *Annals of Statistics*, 14, pp. 1080–100.

Rissanen, J. (1987), 'Stochastic Complexity and Modelling', *Journal of the Royal Statistical Society*, B, 49, pp. 223–39 and pp. 252–65, with discussions.

Rissanen, J. (1988), 'Stochastic Complexity and the MDL principle', *Econometric Reviews*, pp. 85–102.

Roll, R. and Ross, S. (1980), 'An Empirical Investigation of the Arbitrage Pricing Theory', *Journal of Finance*, 35, pp. 1073–104.

Ross, S. (1976), 'The Arbitrage Theory of Capital Asset Pricing', *Journal of Economic Theory*, 13, pp. 341–60.

Rothman, D. (1968), 'Letter to the Editor', *Technometrics*, 10, p. 432.

Royall, R.M. (1968), 'An Old Approach to Finite Population Sampling Theory', *Journal of the American Statistical Association*, 63, pp. 1269–79.

Royall, R.M. (1970), 'On Finite Population Sampling Theory under Certain Linear Regression Models', *Biometrika*, 57, pp. 377–87.

Royall, R.M. and Cumberland, W.G. (1981), 'An Empirical Study of the Ratio Estimator and Estimators of its Variance', *Journal of the American Statistical Association*, 76, pp. 66–87.

Sakamoto, Y., Ishiguro M. and Kitagawa G. (1986), *Akaike Information Criterion Statistics*, D. Reidel Publishing Company, Tokyo.

Sakia, R.M. (1992), 'The Box-Cox Transformation Technique: A Review', *The Statistician*, 41, pp. 169–78.

Sampson, A.R. (1976), 'Stepwise BAN Estimators for Exponential Families with Multivariate Normal Applications', *Journal of Multivariate Analysis*, 6, pp. 167–75.

Sampson, A.R. (1978), 'Simple BAN Estimators of Correlations for Certain Multivariate Normal Models with Known Variances', *Journal of the American Statistical Association*, 73, pp. 859–62.

Sargan, J.D. (1964), 'Wages and Prices in the United Kingdom', in P.E. Hart, G. Mills and J.K. Whitaker (eds), *Econometric Analysis for National Economic Planning*, Butterworths, London.

Särndal, C.E. (1978), 'Design-based and Model-based Inference in Survey Sampling', *Scandinavian Journal of Statistics*, 5, pp. 27–52.

Sawa, T. (1978), 'Information Criteria for Discriminating among Alternative Regression Models', *Econometrica*, 46, pp. 1273–91.

Schmidt, P. (1971), *Methods of Choosing among Alternative Models*, Econometrics Workshop Paper No. 7004, Michigan State University.

Schmidt, P. (1973), 'Calculating the Power of the Minimum Standard Error Choice Criterion', *International Economic Review*, 14, pp. 253–5.

Schmidt, P. (1975), 'Choosing among Alternative Linear Regression Models: A Correction and Some Further Results', *Atlantic Economic Journal*, 3, pp. 61–3.

Schneider, H. (1986), *Truncated and Censored Samples from Normal Populations*, Mercel Decker, New York.

Schwarz, G. (1978), 'Estimating the Dimension of a Model', *Annals of Statistics*, 6, pp. 461–4.

Scott, A.J. and Holt D. (1982), 'The Effect of Two-stage Sampling on Ordinary Least Squares Methods', *Journal of the American Statistical Association*, 77, pp. 848–54.

Scott, A.J. and Smith, T.M.F. (1969), 'Estimation in Multistage Surveys', *Journal of the American Statistical Association*, 64, pp. 830–40.

Searle, S.R. (1971), *Linear Models*, John Wiley, New York.

Searle, S.R. and Henderson, H.V. (1979), 'Dispersion Matrices for Variance Components Models', *Journal of the American Statistical Association*, 74, pp. 465–70.

Selliah, J.B. (1964), *Estimation and Testing Problems in a Wishart Distribution*, Technical Report No. 10, Stanford University.

SenGupta, A. (1981), *Tests for Standardized Generalized Variances of Multivariate Normal Populations of Possibly Different Dimensions*, Technical Report No. 50, Department of Statistics, Stanford University.

SenGupta, A. (1983), 'Generalized Canonical Variables', in N.L. Johnson and S. Kotz (eds), *Encyclopaedia of Statistical Sciences*, 3, Wiley, New York, pp. 326–30.

SenGupta, A. (1987), 'On Tests for Equicorrelation Coefficient of a Standard Symmetric Multivariate Normal Distribution', *Australian Journal of Statistics*, 29, pp. 49–59.

SenGupta, A. (1988), 'On Loss of Power under Additional Information – An Example', *Scandanavian Journal of Statistics*, 15, pp. 25–31.

SenGupta, A. and Vermeire, L. (1986), 'Locally Optimal Tests for Multiparameter Hypotheses', *Journal of the American Statistical Association*, 81, pp. 819–25.

Shah, C. (1994), *Forecast Model Selection for Time Series using Statistical Discriminant Analysis*, unpublished PhD thesis, Monash University, Melbourne, Australia.

Shanken, J. (1992), 'The Current State of the Arbitrage Pricing Theory', *Journal of Finance*, 47, 4, pp. 1569–74.

Shao, J. (1988), 'On Resampling Methods for Variance and Bias Estimation in Linear Models', *Annals of Statistics*, 16, pp. 986–8.

Shao, J. (1993), 'Linear Model Selection by Cross-validation', *Journal of the American Statistical Association*, 88, pp. 486–94.

Shao, J. (1996), 'Bootstrap Model Selection', *Journal of the American Statistical Association*, 91, pp. 655–65.

Shibata, R. (1976), 'Selection of the Order of an Autoregressive Model by Akaike's Information Criterion', *Biometrika*, 63, pp. 117–26.

Shiller, R. (1981), 'Do Stock Prices Move Too Much to be Justified by Subsequent Changes in Dividends', *American Economic Review*, 71, 3, pp. 421–36.

Shively, T.S. (1988), 'An Exact Test for Stochastic Coefficient in a Time Series Regression Model', *Journal of Time Series Analysis*, 9, pp. 81–8.

Shively, T.S., Ansley, C.F. and Kohn, R. (1990), 'Fast Evaluation of the Distribution of the Durbin-Watson and Other Invariant Test Statistics in Time Series Regression', *Journal of the American Statistical Association*, 85, pp. 676–85.

Shorack, G.R. (1982), 'Bootstrapping Robust Regression', *Communication in Statistics – Theory and Methodology*, 11, pp. 961–72.

Shukla, R. and Trzcinka, C. (1990), 'Sequential Tests of the Arbitrage Pricing Theory: A Comparison of Principal Components and Maximum Likelihood Factors', *Journal of Finance*, 45, pp. 1541–64.

Silvapulle, P. (1991), *Point-optimal Tests for Non-nested Time Series Models and Illustrations*, unpublished PhD thesis, Monash University, Clayton.

Silvapulle, P. and King, M.L. (1991), 'Testing Moving Average Against Autoregressive Disturbances in the Linear Regression Model', *Journal of Business and Economic Statistics*, 9, pp. 329–35.

Sims, C. (1980), 'Macroeconomics and Reality', *Econometrica*, 48, pp. 1–48.

Sin, C.-Y. and H. White (1992), *Information Criteria for Selecting Parameter Models: A Misspecification Analysis*, Working Paper, Department of Economics, University of California, San Diego.

Sirivastava, M.S. (1965), 'Some Tests for the Intra-class Correlation Model', *Annals of Mathematical Statistics*, 36, pp. 1802–6.

Spitzer, J.J. (1976), 'The Demand for Money, the Liquidity Trap and Functional Forms', *The International Economics Review*, 17, pp. 220–27.

Spitzer, J.J. (1978), 'A Monte Carlo Investigation of the Box-Cox Transformation in Small Samples', *Journal of the American Statistical Association*, 73, pp. 488–94.

Spitzer, J.J. (1982). 'A Premier of Box-Cox Transformation', *Review of Economics and Statistics*, 64, pp. 307–13.

Spitzer, J.J. (1982a), 'A Fast and Efficient Algorithm for the Estimation of Parameters in Models with the Box and Cox Transformation', *Journal of the American Statistical Association*, 77, pp. 760–66.

Stine, R.A. (1985), 'Bootstrap Prediction Intervals for Regression', *Journal of the American Statistical Association*, 80, pp. 1026–31.

Stine, R.A. (1990), 'An Introduction to Bootstrap Methods: Examples and Ideas', in J. Fox and J.S. Long (eds), *Modern Methods of Data Analysis*, Sage, Newbury Park, pp. 325–73.

Sukhatme, P.V. (1954), *Sampling Theory of Surveys, with Applications*, Ames, State College Press, Iowa.

Swamy, P.A.V.B. (1970), 'Efficient Inference in Random Coefficient Regression Models', *Econometrica*, 38, pp. 311–23.

Swamy, P.A.V.B. and Arora, S.S. (1972), 'The Exact Finite Sample Properties of the Estimators of Coefficients in the Error Components Regression Models', *Econometrica*, 40, pp. 253–60.

Swanepoel, J.W.H. (1990), 'A Review of Bootstrap Methods', *South African Journal of Statistics*, 24, pp. 1–34.

Sweeting, T.J. (1980), 'Uniform Asymptotic Normality of the Maximum Likelihood Estimator', *Annals of Statistics*, 8, pp. 1375–81.

Tauchen, G. (1985), 'Diagnostic Testing and Evaluation of Maximum Likelihood Models', *Journal of Econometrics*, 30, pp. 415–43.

Theil, H. (1961), *Economic Forecasts and Policy*, 2nd edn, North-Holland, Amsterdam.

Theil, H. (1971), *Principles of Econometrics*, Wiley, New York.

Thompson, M.L. (1978), 'Selection of Variables in Multiple Regression', *International Statistical Review*, 46, pp. 1–19 and pp. 129–46.

Tong, H. (1975), 'Autoregressive Model Fitting with Noisy Data by Akaike's Information Criterion', *IEEE Transactions on Information Theory*, 21, pp. 476–80.

Trzcinka, C. (1986), 'On the Number of Factors the Arbitrage Pricing Model', *Journal of Finance*, 41, pp. 347–68.

Tso, K.K.-S. (1981), 'Reduced-rank Regression and Canonical Analysis', *Journal of the Royal Statistical Society B*, 43, pp. 183–9.

Tukey, J.W. (1957), 'The Comparative Anatomy of Transformation', *Annals of Mathematical Statistics*, 28, pp. 602–32.

Ullah, A. and Breunig, R. (1998), 'Econometric Analysis in Complex Surveys', in D. Giles and A. Ullah (eds), *Handbook of Applied Economic Statistics*, Marcel Dekkar, pp. 325–54.

Vinod, H.D. (1995), 'Double Bootstrap for Shrinkage Estimators', *Journal of Econometrics*, 68, pp. 287–302.

Vipul and Gianchandani, K. (1997), 'A Test of Arbitrage Pricing Theory in Indian Capital Market', *Finance India*, 11, 2, pp. 353–62.

Votaw, D.F. (1948), 'Testing Compound Symmetry in a Normal Multivariate Distribution', *Annals of Mathematical Statistics*, 19, pp. 447–73.

Wallace, T.D. and Hussain, A. (1969), 'The Use of Error Components Models in Combining Cross Section with Time Series Data', *Econometrica*, 37, pp. 55–72.

Walsh, J.E. (1947), 'Concerning the Effect of Intra-Class Correlation on Certain Significance Tests', *Annals of Mathematical Statistics*, 18, pp. 88–96.

Wang, S. (1987), 'Improved Approximation Diagnostics', *Communication in Statistics – Theory and Methodology*, 16, pp. 1797–819.

White, H. (1982a), 'Maximum Likelihood Estimation of Misspecified Models', *Econometrica*, 50, pp. 1–25.

White, H. (1982b), 'Model Specification', *Journal of Econometrics*, 20, pp. 1–157.

White, H. (1983), 'Non-nested Models', *Journal of Econometrics*, 21, pp. 1–160.

White, H. (1990), 'A Consistent Model Selection Procedure Based on M-testing', in C.W.J. Granger (ed.), *Modelling Economic Series: Reading in Econometric Methodology*, Oxford University Press, Oxford.

White, K.J. (1972), 'Estimation of the Liquidity Trap with a Generalized Functional Form', *Econometrica*, 40, pp. 193–9.

Wilks, S.S. (1946), 'Sample Criteria for Testing Equality of Means, Equality of Variances, and Equality of Covariances in a Normal Multivariate Distribution', *Annals of Mathematical Statistics*, 17, pp. 257–81.

Williams, E.J. and Yip, P. (1989), 'Conditional Inference About an Equicorrelation Coefficient', *Australian Journal of Statistics*, 31, pp. 138–42.

Williams, P. and Sams, D. (1981), *Household Headship in Australia: Further Developments to the IMPACT Projects's Econometric Model of Household Headship*, IMPACT Project Research Centre Working Paper BP–26, University of Melbourne.

Wolak, F.A. (1987), 'An Exact Test for Multiple Inequality Constraints in the Linear Regression Model', *Journal of the American Statistical Association*, 82, pp. 782–93.

Wu, C.F.J. (1986), 'Jackknife, Bootstrap and Other Resampling Methods in Regression Analysis' (with discussion), *Annals of Statistics*, 14, pp. 1261–350.

Wu, C.F.J., Holt, D. and Holmes, D.J. (1988), 'The Effect of Two-stage Sampling on the F-statistics', *Journal of the American Statistical Association*, 83, pp. 150–59.

Wu, P.X. (1991), *One-sided and Partially One-sided Multiparameter Hypothesis Testing in Econometrics*, unpublished PhD thesis, Monash University, Clayton.

Wu, P.X. and Bhatti, M.I. (1994), 'Testing for Block Effects and Misspecification in Regression Models based on Survey Data', *Journal of Statistical Computation and Simulation*, 50 (1–2), pp. 75–90.

Wu, P.X. and King, M.L. (1994), 'One-sided Hypothesis Testing: A Survey', *Pakistan Journal of Statistics*, 10, pp. 261–300.

Yates, F. (1949), *Sampling Methods for Census and Surveys*, 1st edn (2nd edn 1953; 3rd edn 1969), Griffin, London.

Young, G.A. (194), 'Bootstrap: More Than a Stab in the Dark?' (with discussion), *Statistical Science*, 9, pp. 382–415.

Zarembka, P. (1968), 'Functional Form in the Demand for Money', *Journal of the American Statistical Association*, 63, pp. 502–11.

Zarembka, P. (1974), *Frontiers in Econometrics*, Academy Press, New York.

Zhang, P. (1992), 'On the Distributional Properties of Model Selection Criteria', *Journal of the American Statistical Association*, 87, pp. 732–7.

Zhou, G. (1995), 'Small Sample Rank Tests with Application to Asset Pricing', *Journal of Empirical Finance*, 2, pp. 71–93.

Zhu, L.X., Fang, K.T. and Bhatti, M.I. (1997), 'On Estimated Projection Pursuit Type Cramer-von-mises Statistics', *Journal of Multivariate Analysis*, 63 (1), pp. 1–15.

Index

For Product Safety Concerns and Information please contact our EU representative GPSR@taylorandfrancis.com Taylor & Francis Verlag GmbH, Kaufingerstraße 24, 80331 München, Germany